IMAGE MAKERS

IMAGE

MAKERS

Advertising, Public Relations, and the Ethos of Advocacy

Robert Jackall and Janice M. Hirota

THE UNIVERSITY OF CHICAGO PRESS · CHICAGO AND LONDON

ROBERT JACKALL is Class of 1956 Professor of Sociology & Social Thought at Williams College. His books include *Wild Cowboys: Urban Marauders & the Forces of Order* (1997), *Propaganda* (1995), and *Moral Mazes: The World of Corporate Managers* (1988).

JANICE M. HIROTA is an anthropologist who has done extensive fieldwork in urban America. In addition to her work with ad makers, she has studied community activists, social service providers, and poor and homeless populations in New York and other U.S. cities.

The University of Chicago Press, Chicago 60637
The University of Chicago Press, Ltd., London
© 2000 by Robert Jackall and Janice M. Hirota
All rights reserved. Published 2000
Printed in the United States of America

09 08 07 06 05 04 03 02 01 00   1 2 3 4 5
ISBN: 0-226-38916-2 (cloth)
Library of Congress Cataloging-in-Publication Data
Jackall, Robert.
     Image makers : advertising, public relations, and the
  ethos of advocacy / Robert Jackall and Janice M. Hirota.
       p. cm.
     Includes bibliographical references and index.
     ISBN: 0-226-38916-2 (alk. paper)
     1. Advertising—United States.   2. Public relations—
  United States.   I. Hirota, Janice M.   II. Title.
  HF5813.U6J33 2000
     659'.0973—dc21   99-050270
∞ The paper used in this publication meets the minimum requirements of the American National Standard for Information Sciences—Permanence of Paper for Printed Library Materials, ANSI Z39.48–1992.

For Yuriko

CONTENTS

ILLUSTRATIONS

Following Page 63

Alonzo Earl Foringer, *The Greatest Mother in the World* (1918). Poster. 27.5″ × 20.5″. Courtesy of the American Red Cross Museum and the Williams College Museum of Art, anonymous gift, 39.1.148.

Charles Buckles Falls, *Teufel Hunden* [Devil Dogs] (c. 1918). Courtesy of the Chapin Library of Rare Books, Williams College.

C. R. Macauley, *Bird of Evil* (1917). From the Macauley cartoon series "America's Spirit in the War," distributed by the Butterfield Syndicate.

C. R. Macauley, *The Trail of the Beast* (1917). From the Macauley cartoon series "America's Spirit in the War," distributed by Butterfield Syndicate.

War Advertising Council, *A Slip of the Lip Will Sink a Ship* (1943). Courtesy of the Advertising Council.

Ohrbach's, *I Found Out about Joan* (1958). Courtesy of Orchid Properties, Inc., formerly Ohrbach's, Inc., and DDB Worldwide, Inc.

El Al Israel Airlines, *No Goose, No Gander* (c. 1960). Courtesy of El Al Israel Airlines and DDB Worldwide, Inc.

Arnold's Products, Inc., *You Don't Have to Be Jewish to Love Levy's Real Jewish Rye* (1970). Courtesy of Arnold's Products, Inc., and DDB Worldwide, Inc. Levy's is a registered trademark of Arnold's Products, Inc.

Alka Seltzer, *Mama Mia, 'Atsa Spicy Meatball* (1970). Courtesy of Bayer Corporation and DDB Worldwide, Inc.

ACKNOWLEDGMENTS

This book has been a long time in the making and owes a great deal to many institutions and people. Grants from the Interpretive Research Division of the National Endowment for the Humanities, supplemented by support from Herbert A. Allen, the late Richard C. Gallop, and Francis T. Vincent, and from the Wenner-Gren Foundation for Anthropological Research, made possible the archival research and fieldwork that ground the book. The Willmott Family Third Century Professorship at Williams College provided resources to extend the inquiry in unanticipated directions. The Oakley Center for the Humanities and Social Sciences at Williams College sponsored a faculty seminar that was invaluable in working out ideas for the book. We wish to thank Mark C. Taylor, then director of the Center, and the Williams faculty participants in the seminar, with special appreciation to Thomas Kohut, Clara Park, and James Wood for their insights into our field material. Students in various classes at Williams College contributed excellent critiques of many ideas in progress; Eric Cohen and Jennifer Dolloff gave close readings of an early version of the manuscript. Williams College provided research monies to help ready the manuscript for publication. The audio-visual staff at Williams College provided us with excellent technical assistance. The library staffs at Williams College, the National Archives, the Center for Advertising History at the Archives Center of the Smithsonian Institution, the DDB Worldwide Information Center, and the Public Relations Society of America, as well as staff members at the Advertising Council, the Society of Illustrators, the Museum of Broadcasting, and the American Association of Advertising Agencies, were very helpful to us. At appropriate points in the endnotes, we thank specific individuals for particular contributions to our work. But we single out here Peter Giordano, Walter Komorowski, and Christine Ménard of Sawyer Library at Williams College, whose regular expert assistance aided us immeasurably.

We are indebted to several people whose permissions and assistance made possible the gallery of illustrations. We thank Steven Shulman of the American Red Cross and Diane Agee and Stefanie Spray Jandl of the Williams College Museum of Art; Robert Volz and Wayne Hammond of the Chapin Library of Rare Books at Williams College; William Tedeschi of American Retail Group; Laurie Samet and Sheryl Stein of El Al Israel Airlines; Marge Post of Bayer Corporation; Linda Scipione of Volkswagen and Adam Karp of Arnold Communications; John Wolfe and Rachel Sheriff of the American Association of Advertising Agencies; and Paula Veale of the Advertising Council. We owe special thanks to Cristina Capello of the Advertising Council and Shannon McDonough of DDB Worldwide for their generous help in providing us with hard-to-find images, to Bruce Wheat of Williams College for his assistance in reproducing them, and to Robert Devens of the University of Chicago Press for coordinating the production of the gallery.

We are especially grateful to the hundreds of men and women in advertising and public relations who have shared their experiences with us over the years. David Altheide, John Budd, Richard Q. Ford, Wendy Griswold, Guy Oakes, and Arthur J. Vidich provided us with extremely helpful comments on an early version of the manuscript. Duffy Graham exceeded all calls of friendship by critically commenting on the manuscript in different stages of its progress. We owe special thanks to Douglas Mitchell, our editor at the University of Chicago Press, who grasped the project immediately and who shepherded it to publication; to Maia Rigas, whose manuscript editing greatly improved the book; and to Michael Brehm for his fine work on the design. Finally, we wish to thank Donna Chenail, Margaret Weyers, Shirley Bushika, and Rebecca Brassard of Williams College for their patient and careful work on the project over the years.

Yuriko Hirota Jackall's own intellectual passions sparked many lines of inquiry in our work. She later read the manuscript with her usual critical acumen. We are delighted to dedicate this book to her.

FUN-HOUSE MIRRORS

On a typical morning in New York City, a businesswoman getting ready for work hears the radio blaring "sound bites" of several speeches framing important economic issues uttered by high corporate or governmental officials. With his morning coffee, a corporate lawyer reads a ghosted opinion piece in the *New York Times* bylined by a United States senator, urging public support for U.S. foreign policy in the Middle East. A full-time parent on the Upper East Side, after getting her children off to school, channel surfs through talk shows, a presidential press conference, and interviews with engagingly attractive, though relentless, men and women pitching books, political ideologies, or social causes, all schooled in self-presentation by media consultants. A designer taking his midtown walk after lunch, pauses at a newsstand. As he flips through a fashionable magazine, he reads about a newly rich matron from Brooklyn who is eager to mingle in Manhattan's high social circles and whose "deep interest in art," verified by a fictitious degree in art history from a liberal arts college, has been so artfully crafted by her public relations adviser that she has begun to believe it herself. A work-at-home computer consultant in Staten Island receives solicitations in her mail or e-mail from some of the thousands of organizations of every political and social stripe that routinely manufacture official or counterofficial versions of reality suiting their purposes or, in cruising the World Wide Web, she encounters advertisements for every product and experience imaginable, both in screenwide banners and increasingly in elaborate videos with sound. A tourist shepherds his

1

family into the New York Stock Exchange Visitors' Center, or any number of other corporate headquarters in the city, to see elaborate, sanitized versions of institutional history. A Barnard College student visits a Barnes & Noble bookstore where she browses through a few of the dozens of authorized biographies of famous, would-be famous, or infamous figures. A young financial analyst ends his grueling fourteen-hour Monday carousing with his buddies at his favorite watering hole, glancing up at the big-screen TV to catch a make-believe, virtual-reality blimp with a banner advertisement hovering above the gridiron. A construction worker in Queens settles down on the couch with his teen-age daughter after dinner and longingly peruses a glossy admissions brochure from an Ivy League college, produced by a public relations firm, that carefully portrays the institution as a diverse, congenial setting dedicated to the pursuit of a healthy mind in a healthy body.

Every day, throughout the southland, across the Great Plains and over the Rockies, into the dust bowls, through California's artificially lush farmlands, and up into the rugged Northwest, men and women see on television scores of mininarratives, often complete with wholly constructed pitchmen ranging from dogs in trench coats and animated green giants to flesh-and-blood, characteristically energetic spokes-people, dramatizing products, individuals, or causes of every sort, from beer to haute cuisine, from toy trucks to custom-made automobiles, from legal eagles to presidential candidates, from AIDS prevention messages to recruitment appeals for the priesthood, from pro-choice to right-to-life campaigns. They hear, on television or radio, the catchy tunes, up-beat jingles, easily memorable slogans, and diversely applicable tag lines that enter, for a time, the popular vocabulary ("You make America work and this Bud's for you," "Where's the beef?" "When you care enough to send the very best," "Reach out and touch someone," "Just say no," or "Just do it!"). In perusing any of hundreds of magazines, newspapers, or journals of opinion, they encounter highly stylized but compelling images of everyday life and of how life might be lived.

At virtually every turn, Americans encounter, in both print and broadcast form, the incessant drumbeat of media events pounding out moralistic claims about what is wrong with the world or how the world ought to be—from interviews with priests who pour blood over nuclear weapons, to press conferences with black activists condemning all of white society for the racist actions of a few, to radio broadcasts with right-wing militia members barricading themselves against a perceived behemoth government, to endless television shows with lawyers—as adroit in self-promotion as they are in casuistry—arguing vehemently for pet causes or wronged clients, to a walking interview with a film goddess ready to throw her Venus-like body into the machinery of science that uses dogs for medical research, to news reports of a demonstration by lesbians demanding that their sapphic predilections be lauded in school textbooks, to a front-page photo of the U.S. House majority leader surrounded by a pick-up crew of children—reputedly the targets of tobacco advertising—feeding the media with news about congressional debates on the evil weed, to speeches by a president promising to build a bridge to the twenty-first century.

In short, men and women, as well as youth and children in the United States, find themselves daily in a carnival-like world at once strange, boisterous, and familiar, besieged by symbols and images advocating action or at least tacit assent on issues both trivial and crucial: here a plea to buy Pepsi instead of Coke; there an argument on how to allocate limited economic and social resources; here a grand public drama, public affairs as soap opera writ large complete with heroes, villains, goats, fools, celebration, blame, retribution, humiliation, and reconciliation; here a city official issuing dire warnings unless a municipal bond is passed; everywhere voices clamoring with opinions about matters as diverse as leadership, accomplishment, race, ethnicity, fame, justice, and sexuality. The public faces of people, products, and organizations appear now this way, now that, transformed images in curved mirrors. Meager achievements loom large, slender talent assumes girth, limited ability appears gigantic, discernible reality gets stretched into elongated forms. Bogeymen leap out of dark corners scaring the wits out of huddled patrons while heroes stride forward to slay demons. Everywhere there are invitations to prove one's worth, by ringing the gong with a sledgehammer or shooting ducks in the gallery. Bells and whistles punctuate blaring brassy music and, from the midway, one hears the clamor of barkers selling glimpses of bearded ladies and exotic dancers, indeed everything under the sun, itinerant fortune tellers whispering promises of self-knowledge, and the occasional tub-thumping preacher condemning the sinfulness around him and bellowing promises of salvation. But the carnival also has a déjà vu feel. Gags scare the bejesus out of newcomers, but provoke guffaws among the regulars; goblins have Christian names; images startle but do not surprise. Amidst the thrills of the fun house and the clang of the midway, one hears archetypal stories with comforting moral fables, old scripts spliced together, hackneyed phrases, sentimental appeals, set vocabularies, and, everywhere, the flamboyant self-posturing intrinsic to successful huckstering.

〜〜〜〜 The men and women who help create such a world are interpretive experts, image makers who are virtuosi in the arts of creating and interpreting symbols. Interpretive expertise is as old as humankind; ancient philosophers, augurs and prophets, sixteenth-century moral casuists, witch doctors and sorcerers in primitive societies, priests, ministers, rabbis, and assorted bureaucratic spin doctors in modern society, and even contemporary poststructuralist literary and cultural critics are only a few examples of highly specialized practitioners whose stock-in-trade is the creation, manipulation, and discernment of images and symbols. In all societies, at all times and places, men and women symbolize their experiences, often in ways that seem astonishing to other peoples or even to their own progeny. Interpretive experts, sometimes brilliant, often bogus, called by divine inspiration or driven by crass ambition, rooted in local communities, in service to royal courts, sequestered in remote monasteries, or wandering in urban milieux, emerge to cater to that basic human impulse.

Modern societies provide especially fruitful ground for interpretive experts. Typically, modern societies are largely devoid of overarching systems of meaning. Their social organization depends on large variegated bureaucracies, on highly rationalized markets governed largely by price, and on systems of social control based on rationalized procedures, all knit together by overlapping personal networks rooted principally in occupational communities. Modern societies place premiums on developing and sharing highly specialized expertise, on participation in webs of exchange, and on external conformity to common rules. With the exception of authoritarian states that are able to extract at least external adherence to political or religious ideological frameworks, modern societies require for their functioning few, if any, common beliefs from their members, leaving individuals free to invent or accept whatever images of the world they wish. The belief systems that do emerge and that matter the most tend to be highly localized, rooted in specialized contexts such as occupational worlds, and quickened by personal relationships that crisscross the great bureaucratic warps of modern societies. People live in meaningful worlds, but these are most often worlds apart.

At the same time, science, one of modernity's central institutions, continually overturns accepted definitions of reality, including those established by science itself, making the world simultaneously more intelligible but also more problematic and provisional. Moreover, the technology born of scientific knowledge, although it has provided inestimable benefits, has also unleashed untold destruction on the world. In the modern era, rationalized genocide and ecocide become actualities in a century of total wars, particularly when science, the epitome of Western rationality, places itself at the service of modern economies and states, both of which regularly become hostages to irrational forces. And scientists themselves, in fierce competition for primacy of discovery, continually create new images of the world through relentless advocacy of their own visions of what the world is or might become.

Experts with symbols leap into this cultural and experiential fray. The enormous personal freedom that modern institutions provide individuals in exchange for external conformity creates bottomless demand for ever-new images of the world even as science's continual destruction of the past and generation of future promises make modern culture boundlessly dynamic and creative.

〰〰〰〰 The modern epoch has produced a new type of interpretive expert, the image maker skilled in the creation and propagation of symbols to persuade mass audiences to some action or belief. Mass audiences are the vast, usually anonymous categories of unconnected men and women identified by interpretive experts themselves as linked together through some commonality of behavior or orientation. The quintessential experts with mass symbols, that is, symbols directed toward masses, are advertising and public relations practitioners. These experts are image makers and wordsmiths par excellence, commercial advocates dedicated to fashioning both vocabularies of sentiment, motive, and image and frameworks for perceiving social reality.

Both occupations are more firmly linked to the central institutions and processes of our social order than any other occupations that specialize in producing symbols and are formally dedicated to advocacy. Ad makers serve the mass consumer economy, and public relations practitioners are the principal occupational interlocutors between bureaucratized worlds apart whose denizens must communicate to function and survive. The ascendancy of these experts coincides with the astonishing growth in reach and scope of the media of mass communications, a phenomenon essentially of the twentieth century. Indeed, the media provide the technological basis of the apparatus of advocacy, the sprawling institutional framework of opinion formation and claim making within which experts with mass symbols exercise their legerdemain, whether acting as agents for large commercial bureaucracies, democratic or totalitarian states or state agencies, churches, educational or charitable organizations, wealthy individuals, or causes. Each of the major media—newspapers, mass market printed publications, film, radio, and television—has its own distinctive character, but each shares with the others a certain logic that shapes the work of experts with mass symbols.

Mass media reach large numbers of people from different social strata, with different experiences, and with different aspirations and worldviews; even relatively homogeneous audiences in the new segmented markets serviced by specialized media consist of strangers one to another, abstract categories rather than social groups. But commercial media, especially television—the pacesetter for all other media since its widespread commercial application in the late 1940s—survive precisely by maintaining and extending their audiences, by finding the lowest common denominator that links socially segmented masses. The logic of the mass media requires arcane knowledge to be simplified and the messy ambiguity of human experience to be constructed into clear narratives, into little stories, focused preferably on some individual who can be celebrated or demonized, with whom mass audiences can identify or despise, or distilled into visual images whose inviting ambiguity allows multiple and varying emotional responses. Experts with mass symbols, advertising and public relations practitioners foremost among them, are the cultural workers who construct such stories and images, acting as mediators between segments of our society and the mass media, the core of the apparatus of advocacy.

But the craft of these image makers and the consciousness their craft breeds have migrated far beyond the seedbed milieux of advertising and public relations to characterize advocates in every corner of our society. The more rapacious the appetite of the media for stories, the greater is the demand for men and women who can tailor the complexities of our social order to fit the media's exigencies while making their stories resonate with mass audiences. The more mighty the apparatus of advocacy, the more inviting it is for any group strong and wily enough to try to commandeer it and bend it to its own uses.

Thus interpretive experts of every sort, some as commercial professionals, some called to advocacy as a vocation, together create representations of complex, substantive realities, verbal and visual images that they hope will resonate with broader audiences. Usually these images accurately reflect some aspects of the world, but they are inevitably partial. They refract, distort, or even invert reality, often in fun-house-mirror fashion, sometimes in complex, subtle, and unexpected ways. Representations of reality proliferate at rapid rates. They begin to overlay one another, providing objects, persons, and institutions with many faces, fleeting chimeras that one sees but has little chance of grasping. In some cases, such images conceal the world and human experience entirely. Once fashioned, images assume a life and reality of their own. Once internalized, in an increasingly specialized society, they often become the only realities that matter.

〰〰〰〰 This book analyzes the making and workings of the apparatus and ethos of advocacy. In particular, it examines the work and habits of mind of advertising and public relations practitioners, the prototypical image makers of our era. It chronicles the modern rationalization of these occupations through the stories of two organizations, the Committee on Public Information and the Advertising Council, each born in times of world war. Each brought advertising and public relations under one roof for a common purpose, the former briefly, the latter for more than half of the twentieth century. The book also tells the story of a third organization, Doyle Dane Bernbach, the fabled advertising agency that pioneered the use of highly self-conscious, playful, and ironic images in order to penetrate a public consciousness surfeited with and increasingly skeptical of wartime and commercial propaganda. It explores the migration of the tools-in-trade of mass persuasion, the habits of mind that the regular use of those tools fosters, and the adoption of both by advocates of every political stripe and social station. Last, the book ponders some of the quandaries generated for our ways of knowing and judging by the endlessly shifting patterns of conflicting representations and claims that the apparatus and ethos of advocacy make possible and, indeed, inevitable.

THE APPARATUS OF ADVOCACY

1

ADVERTISING THE
GREAT WAR

Advertising and public relations both have ancient roots. Dating back to antiquity, merchants, tradesmen, and artisans have always found ingenious ways to proclaim the availability and virtues of their products and crafts, from public criers pitching wares, to signboards with symbols conventionally associated with certain goods or services, to handwritten and later printed handbills, to tradesmen's cards, to the public display of the implements of one's trade.[1] Although mass advertising became possible with the invention of printing, it was not until the mid-nineteenth century that the occupation began to assume its modern form with the appearance of the advertising agent who, acting as a broker, brought businesses seeking to advertise their wares together with newspapers wishing to sell space or with lithographers, printers, and engravers who could design and produce colorful posters.[2] Later, agencies provided a further service to their customers by having professionals produce advertising copy, sometimes accompanied by illustrations. Market exigencies and opportunities have probably always framed and paced the development of advertising.

What we know today as public relations historically depended on rulers' and officials' perceptions of the importance of public opinion to protect or extend their legitimacy.[3] Rulers have always relied on trusted counselors to help them justify their actions. They have also always sought to firm up their legitimacy by presenting idealized portraits of themselves on coins, statues, and monuments, often appearing as gods, or by staging grandiose ceremonies, the very solemnity of which inspires reverence for authority.[4] The dignified occupation of public relations counselor—personified at the turn of the twentieth century by Ivy Lee, adviser to magnates and rulers alike—had more dubious proximate ancestors, namely, press agents who specialized in ballyhoo and publicity stunts. Press agentry itself seems to have descended directly from the circus barker.[5]

But the rationalization of advertising and public relations in the twentieth century was largely a product of war. The exigencies of the two world wars and the long-term ideological struggle known as the cold war brought members of both occupations into periods of sustained cooperation with officials from various governmental bureaucracies. Throughout the century, state propaganda machines were crucial in bringing the art of propaganda to its zenith. From the Great War through the cold war, all major world powers competed, most of all, for the allegiance and goodwill of their own civilian populations since the military-industrial apparatus that produced ships, weaponry, and bombs could not have functioned without civilian support. All major powers have also advertised themselves to international audiences, competing for the international respect that alone ensures safety in a realpolitik world.

This periodic but intense institutional coupling coincided with the maturation of the technological groundwork of the apparatus of advocacy. Already well-advanced mass media such as print media flourished with the widening distribution networks that war provided. Other media were invented. The First World War—the Great War, the "war to end all wars,"—hastened the development of telephone and wire services and of the radio for military purposes, although commercial radio only got its start in 1922.[6] The film industry, in its infancy at the beginning of the Great War, heralded the orgy of visual images yet to come, not only in film but also in television. Television was introduced to the American public at the 1939 New York World's Fair, but it went fully commercial only after the Second World War, the beneficiary of technological improvements hastened by war. By 1960, television had penetrated 90 percent of the nation's households. Over the course of a troubled and troubling century, the techniques of image making grew in scope, range, and organizational complexity. And war brought interpretive experts together in overlapping networks and circles as they shaped the contemporary apparatus of advocacy and became big-time advocates not only in business, but in every institutional sector of American society.

〰〰〰 Within a week of the Congressional declaration of war on Germany on 6 April 1917 President Woodrow Wilson established the Committee on Public Information (CPI) by executive fiat.* Two years later, the organization was swept out of existence by an act of Congress on 30 June 1919; most of its main work had ceased with the armistice of 11 November 1918. During its brief existence, the CPI brought together under one organizational roof the leading journalists, publicists, and advertising men, along with novelists, academic intellectuals, moral crusaders, and muckrakers of every sort from across the land. A whole generation of experts with symbols—opinion shapers, interpretive geniuses, and storytellers, image makers all—honed their already sharp skills to sell America's Crusade to the American public and the idea of America to the world as a beacon of righteousness and hope. The history of this short-lived organization, in the infancy of mass communications, reveals the essential problems faced by men and women in organizations dedicated to mass persuasion, the techniques they characteristically adopt to solve those problems, and the habits of mind that such work typically generates.

Wilson appointed George Creel chairman of the CPI. Creel was a former muckraking journalist from Kansas City by way of Denver and New York City's Greenwich Village. At various times during his tumultuous career, he crusaded against governmental and police corruption, prostitution and other vices, and John D. Rockefeller's private industrial army, while he fought for child-labor laws, women's rights, and electoral reform. Creel was also a longtime booster of Wilson and had worked assiduously for the president's reelection in 1916, organizing, among other things, a "blue ribbon" committee of publicists and writers to produce pamphlets on the president's behalf. In fact, as the entrance of the United States into the European war seemed inevitable in the spring of 1917, Creel himself had urged Wilson to create a government agency to coordinate "[n]ot propaganda as the Germans defined it, but propaganda in the true sense of the word, meaning the 'propagation of faith,'"[7] reflecting somewhat arcane knowledge gained, perhaps, from his Roman Catholic father and certainly reflecting the moralistic urges of many public figures of the day.

Creel held that such an agency was imperative both to ensure news-

---

*An early version of this chapter was published by the authors as "America's First Propaganda Ministry: The Committee on Public Information During the Great War," in *Propaganda,* edited by Robert Jackall (New York: New York University Press, 1995), 137–173. Republished here by permission of New York University Press.

papers' voluntary self-censorship on military matters and especially to develop and sell the powerful motivating ideas that alone could galvanize support for the war effort within a society splintered into warring factions by years of ambivalent neutrality.[8] Even more to the point, such an effort had to contend with incipient social splits of various sorts. The United States of 1917 evinced many of the social characteristics also typical of the brawling, raucous social order of the late twentieth century: a "melting pot" of ethnic, racial, and language groups that never coalesced; a large foreign-born population that neither read nor spoke English and a large sector of illiterate or semiliterate native-born citizens; a battlefield of class conflicts, some naked, some mediated by bureaucratic structures, all largely obscured by intense status scrambling within classes; an urbanizing social order clinging to rural myths; and a hodgepodge of clanging political and cultural ideologies.

Both in order to "[h]old fast the inner lines" on the domestic front and to "[c]arry the gospel of Americanism to every corner of the globe," all in a fight for the mind of mankind, Creel created a vast, sprawling organization marked by on-the-spot innovations and frequent reorganizations.[9] At various times, the CPI had more than twenty divisions and bureaus; there were also commissioners' offices in nine foreign lands. The CPI directly engaged the full-time services of hundreds of professionals and support staff members, some as salaried employees, a great many as unpaid volunteers; it coordinated the part-time volunteer efforts of many thousands of other professional men and women.[10] The focus here is only on those CPI divisions most directly concerned with shaping public opinion in the United States through image making and symbol manipulation.

As a newspaperman, Creel's instinct was to commandeer the written word. He established the News Division that for the duration of the war produced a daily newspaper, the *Official Bulletin,* with a circulation of 100,000. The News Division also put out regular bulletins, the forerunner of today's news handouts, sometimes complete with editorials for distribution to the nation's newspapers. Later, the CPI's Division of Civic and Educational Cooperation, headed by University of Minnesota history professor Guy Stanton Ford, engaged scholars at all of the nation's leading universities to produce over one hundred publications. These included ten publications for the Red, White and Blue Series with titles like *Conquest and Kultur* and *How the War Came to America.*[11] This division also produced seven Loyalty Leaflets written in the simplest fashion to reach the least literate citizens with titles like *Friendly Words to the Foreign Born* and *The Prussian System.*[12] The division published twenty-one booklets in the War Information Series. Two of the most important of these were *Why America Fights Germany,* which contained a widely quoted terrifying scenario of the depredations that Americans could expect if the Germans invaded the United States, and *The Study of the Great War,* which was used in classrooms across the country.[13] Millions of copies of these publications, many of them little more than dignified broadsides, were distributed worldwide. Many were translated into several languages.

A bottleneck in this massive printing of pamphlets cranked out under Ford's leadership led Creel, at the suggestion of Edward Sisson, to recruit Carl Byoir as a troubleshooter. Byoir had worked for Sisson when the latter was the editor of *Cosmopolitan Magazine.* Byoir hailed from Iowa. At the age of twenty-eight, he already had sales, advertising, publishing, and newspaper reporting and editing experience, as well as a Columbia University law degree. Byoir had also purchased U.S. rights to the materials and practices of the famed Italian educator Dr. Maria Montessori, and he successfully introduced her system of kindergarten education to the United States. When Byoir solved the printing logjam by bypassing the Government Printing Office and making a series of ingenious arrangements with printers in New York City whom he knew from his stint in the magazine world, Creel asked him to stay on as associate chairman of the Executive Division. Byoir became Creel's right-hand man, in charge of the CPI's vast administrative correspondence and intermittently the head of several CPI divisions.[14]

Creel's considerable experience had already taught him, however, that vast segments of the public formed their images of the world neither from news nor from pamphlets with scholarly trappings, but rather from stories with a human-interest angle. The Division of Syndicated Features captured the services of some of the most important novelists, short-story writers, and essayists of the day to produce a steady stream of feature stories and articles for the nation's press. Some of the most notable figures in this work were Samuel Hopkins Adams, Booth Tarkington, Mary Roberts Rinehart, Walter Lippmann, and Harvey O'Higgins, who also served for a time as an associate chairman of the CPI. Although some intellectuals protested vigorously against the Great War, they had little impact on national debate.[15] One of the CPI's great triumphs was the extent to which it succeeded in enlisting image makers and wordsmiths of every sort to frame the war as a crusade for democratic ideals and traditions threatened by autocracy, parameters that made dissent seem foolish at best.

The short-lived Division of Women's War Work complemented and extended all of these efforts by telling the story of what women were doing to win the war and by comforting women whose husbands or sons were "over there." Clara Sears Taylor, a newspaper reporter from Denver, was originally attached to the News Division but then convinced Creel to form a separate division. She drew around her a committed staff of fourteen women.[16] During the nine months of the division's existence, these women placed more than 2,300 stories about women's war work in more than 19,400 newspapers as well as publications aimed at women. They indexed more than 10,000 cards detailing women's organizations and individual women throughout the country whose war efforts were newsworthy. They furnished newspapers with more than 290 photographs of women engaged in war work; they spoke at girls' schools and women's colleges across the land and wrote widely distributed brochures about students' patriotic activities. They wrote more than 50,000 letters to women who had written some government official in agitation or anger about the war's disruption of their lives and relationships and enlisted many of those women in war work. And they went into the settlement houses, the churches, and other organizations in which women played a major role to give inspirational speeches and to enlist those organizations' support for their own work. Congress ended the division's work abruptly in June 1918 by declaring it redundant to the Women's Committee of the Council for National Defense.

Still, the written word had its limits in a nation with large numbers of semiliterate or illiterate residents.[17] Only personal persuasive fervor could gain recruits for a moral crusade filled with great visions. Creel gave Chicagoan Donald Ryerson official CPI sanction to go national with a fledging organization called the Four Minute Men, already speaking in Chicago's movie houses on war topics. Under the later leadership of William McCormick Blair, the Four Minute Men grew into an army of 75,000 men and women who gave 755,190 pointed, orchestrated speeches in movie houses in 5,200 communities nationwide on topics like "Why We Are Fighting," "Unmasking German Propaganda," "Where Did You Get Your Facts?" and, of course, on all the Liberty Loan campaigns that financed the war with titles like "To Help the Boys Over There."[18] The Four Minute Men were, in effect, a national broadcasting outfit years before commercial radio became available, at least for those social groups that regularly flocked to the movie houses.[19] The Speaking Division was headed by Arthur E. Bestor, president of the Chautauqua Institution, a remarkable cultural institution that placed great emphasis on public lectures.[20] The division complemented the

Four Minute Men and later became a bureau of that division. The Speaking Division is said to have had 10,000 index cards with names of speakers for various purposes and a separate file of 300 crackerjack speakers for particularly important occasions. The division arranged individual lectures and indeed whole speaking tours for thousands of speakers, men and women, American and allied, military and civilian, who crisscrossed every nook of the country to give rousing talks, very often to packed lecture halls for whole evenings. Creel jokes that many leather-lunged stalwarts of this division were known as the "Four Hour Men."

The CPI made its greatest, and perhaps its most lasting, impact with its use of visual images of the war to concretize the conflict for civilians. Some of these were presented in straightforward exhibitions. For instance, the CPI provided war exhibits to a number of state fairs in the spring of 1918, followed by a war exposition in Chicago complete with war paraphernalia of every sort, including huge guns and remnants of U-boats and German planes. The exposition featured army bands and soldiers, a Red Cross contingent, bayonet practice, airplane demonstrations, boxing matches, German war trophies, a network of trenches, and gun exhibits, and concluded with a mock battle that stirred great crowd enthusiasm. The exposition then traveled to more than twenty cities.

Different divisions of the CPI, working individually or collaboratively, manufactured outright the most important images of the war. The earliest visual images of the war were produced by the Division of Pictorial Publicity, headed by Charles Dana Gibson, the president of the Society of Illustrators and the creator of the famous "Gibson Girls." Creel notes in his autobiography that Gibson had wandered into Creel's makeshift office during the first week of the war with a poster that he wanted to contribute to the cause and left with a mandate to organize the artists of the United States behind the war effort.[21] James Montgomery Flagg, Herbert Paus, N. C. Wyeth, Howard Chandler Christy, Henry Reuterdahl, Joseph Pennell, Charles Buckles Falls, and Edmond Tarbell were only among the most well known of the scores of artists that flocked to Gibson's call and produced the hundreds of riveting visual images of bayoneted soldiers marching or going "over the top," of submarine victims, of defenseless mothers with clinging children about to be attacked, of coyly seductive Christy girls appealing to men to prove their manhood by joining the service, or of the "Spirit of America" as a reembodied Joan of Arc.[22] The clients for the work included the American Red Cross, the American Library Association, the

Signal Corps, the YMCA and YWCA, the U.S. Boys Working Reserve, the National Committee of Patriotic Societies, and the CPI's Division of Films.[23]

The Bureau of Cartoons sometimes borrowed material directly from the Division of Pictorial Publicity but usually generated its own widely accessible images on virtually every aspect of the war. The bureau issued a weekly *Bulletin for Cartoonists* that coordinated the work of the nation's cartoonists. Each bulletin encouraged the production of cartoons around a number of specified themes, often complete with captions to unify a particular campaign, while leaving the pictorial details to the creativity of cartoonists themselves. Among many other suggestions, the bureau encouraged cartoonists to do the following: to urge "manly" boys to work on farms during summers (bulletin no. 1); to urge farmers to feed garbage to hogs "to give the hog a chance to do its bit" (bulletin no. 2); to urge women to take over the jobs of men gone to war since "she also fights who helps a fighter fight" (bulletin no. 3); to urge the public to save coal by personally supervising the care of furnaces and to limit the consumption of sugar to three pounds per person per month (bulletin no. 4); to urge women to become army or navy nurses and to encourage people to send the boys in training camps Smileage Books ("Send him a smile") admitting them to Liberty Theaters (bulletin no. 5); and to point out to industrial workers the disastrous results of striking during wartime (bulletin no. 6). The bureau also prompted the following: to arouse the public to "kick" German property interests out of the United States (bulletin no. 7); to sound the call to women to join the "army of food producers" by picking fruits and berries and to tell the public to beware of German lies (bulletin no. 8); to stimulate greater patriotism by depicting what Americans are doing "over there" as contrasted with "over here" and to oppose the lynching of Negroes and attacks on those suspected of being enemy sympathizers (bulletin no. 9); to tell industrial workers of all sorts to stick to their jobs because of the high costs of labor turnover (bulletin no. 10); to undercut German propaganda at home by supporting the "Where did you get your facts?" campaign; to encourage the public to salvage pencils, old kid gloves, and tin foil, and to call American soldiers "Yanks" instead of "Sammies," a term the soldiers despised (bulletin no. 11); and to warn the public of the dangers of overconfidence "even though the boys over there seem to have the Huns on the run" (bulletin no. 12). The bureau also asked cartoonists: to stress the importance of making English the universal spoken language in the United States as a means of "patriotizing" foreign-born citizens (bulletin no. 13); to help legitimate as a war-related necessity the national prohibition of the making or selling of intoxicating beverages (bulletin no. 14); to spur the public to greater efforts by pointing out France's enormous sacrifices in blood and treasure (bulletin no. 15); to create public censure of soldiers who are AWOL by encouraging fathers, and especially mothers, wives, and sweethearts, to send their soldiers back to duty with a smile and to urge resistance to premature "peace propaganda" "until the last vestige of Germany's crime is atoned for" so "that these dead [an estimated 8 million soldiers in combat, 2 million more to disease and malnutrition, and 6.5 million civilians] shall not have died in vain" (bulletin no. 19); to keep alive "the tradition of the American mother" by helping the United War Work campaign organizations that are "mothering our boys" (bulletin no. 20); and, after the 11 November 1918 armistice, to remind the public that the war's end will not bring the boys home until the rebuilding of France and Belgium is well begun (bulletin no. 23).[24]

Some cartoons were syndicated and sent around the country and world. Perhaps the best known were the scathing cartoons of C. R. Macauley, distributed by the Butterfield Syndicate in New York. Macauley specialized in caricatures of "soap box traitors," that is, anyone who criticized any aspects of war policies ("Theirs but to reason why; theirs not to do or die!") and especially in portraits of the bestial "Hun," usually depicted as a bellowing, fang-toothed, waxed-mustachioed gorilla wearing a *pickelhaube,* the infamous Prussian spiked helmet, leaving a trail of ravished young maidens named "Law of God and Man," "Right," "Justice," "Humanity," "Hope," "Faith," "Charity," and "Decency."[25]

The cover of one of the last bulletins (no. 25) reflects the estimate that the Bureau of Cartoons had of its own work in comparison with that of other divisions.[26] The cover's cartoon pictures a balance held by a right-hand fist with "Public Opinion" written across the knuckles. On one side, high in the air, is the side of the scale with parchment, quill, and inkpot, stacks of papers marked "Speeches," and heavy tomes labeled "Pamphlets" and "Editorials." On the other, tilting the scale sharply downward with its weight and importance, is a single sheet of paper labeled "Cartoons." However self-congratulatory, the judgment expressed in the cartoon seems accurate. Harking back to the Elizabethan era of chapbooks and broadsides, mass cartoons in the Great War reduced infinitely complicated matters to single specific images, complete with pointed slogans. They became harbingers of the simplifying interpretive expertise necessary for communicating with mass audiences.[27]

The same kind of immediate, graphic appeal came out of the Division of Films, which produced, promoted, approved, or distributed a flood of films on all aspects of the war.[28] The CPI produced a number of documentaries on the actual machinery of war, like *Torpedo Boat Destroyers, Making of Big Guns, The Bath of Bullets,* and *The Storm of Steel.* Others recounted the social dimensions of army life, like *In a Southern Camp* and *Army and Navy Sports.* Still others focused on particular occupational groups essential to the war effort, such as engineers, lumberjacks, and shipbuilders. This division also produced a handful of feature films, including *America's Answer, Under Four Flags, Our Colored Fighters,* and, the most famous, *Pershing's Crusaders.* The handout advertising the showing of *Pershing's Crusaders* in Chicago's Orchestra Hall suggests the tone of most of the film propaganda of the period:

> This first official American War Film shows the grim earnestness of the United States Government in its war activities and its determination to stamp out Kaiserism. Our boys in Khaki are pictured in the very front firing lines. You see Americans taking over the fighting trenches. You see Secretary of War Baker and General Pershing inspecting our preparations in France. You see the first German prisoners captured by our brave boys,—two dozen disheartened, defeated Boches. The last half of the picture is entirely devoted to what our boys are accomplishing 'over there.'
>
> You also see what Uncle Sam's countless civilian army is doing 'over here.' Miles of cantonments grow over-night. You see the raw recruit become the hardened fighter. Fleets of aeroplanes darken the skies. Massive ships of steel, concrete and wood speed down the ways. Mighty guns and projectiles are made before your very eyes. Millions of uniforms are turned out with magic-like rapidity. You realize that every American is doing his best to help win this war. Our great Navy, our huge and growing Army, and all our immense resources of field and mine and forest are in this struggle to the successful end. It is a picture that every soldier's mother, wife, or sweetheart will want to see. YOU MAY SEE YOUR BOY OVER THERE.[29]

The Division of Films also subcontracted the production of several one-reelers, for which it provided the scenarios and all necessary authorization and assistance, including film shorts on women in war work, on the merchant marine, and on American Indians in the armed forces. Through an export licensing agreement, the division also forced all producers of commercial entertainment films destined for release abroad to require their foreign exhibitors to show CPI propaganda films as the price of seeing Charlie Chaplin and other American film heroes. The export agreement also enabled the CPI to prohibit the export of gangster films, which key members of the committee felt portrayed American society in an unfavorable light. Finally, the Division of Film sanctioned the production of many entertainment films that were actually thinly disguised propaganda, such as *Mutt and Jeff at the Front*, *To Hell with the Kaiser*, and the remarkable *The Kaiser, The Beast of Berlin*, a film boosted by several national patriotic societies apparently because of the exuberant animosities that it stirred. American film stars, notably Theda Bara, Douglas Fairbanks, and Mary Pickford among many others, worked tirelessly in the war effort, particularly in selling Liberty bonds, thus forging an early link between celebrity and national power.

The CPI's Division of Advertising connected the power of visual images with sharply pointed interpretive texts. Advertisers and advertising men were involved in war-related work almost from the beginning of U.S. involvement in the conflict. Right after the United States entered the Great War and the First Liberty Loan drive was started, a group of advertising men went to Washington, D.C., to suggest that the government advertise the campaign by purchasing space in various printed media. The notion was rejected, of course, because the swell of patriotic sentiment at the war's outset demanded voluntary contributions in every area. One member of the group, William Rankin, head of a leading advertising agency in Chicago, developed a plan whereby individual advertisers purchased advertising space and donated it to the government. Following Rankin's lead, many publications donated space outright for war advertising and, by the war's end, eight hundred publishers of big-city newspapers, farm town papers, college papers, trade publications, magazines, and corporate internal newsletters, among others, had donated space for war-related advertising.

The situation seems to have been chaotic for most of 1917 with, on one hand, offers of donated space pouring in from all over the country as well as from different organizations of advertising groups, and, on the other, government agencies of every sort approaching the CPI with campaigns that they wanted advertised. Finally, after the November receipt of a formal offer of assistance from William H. Johns, the president of both the George Batten Advertising Agency and the American Association of Advertising Agencies (AAAA) representing one hundred fifteen firms, Creel met with representatives of the New York advertising community and established the Division of Advertising in December 1917, with its formal launching on 20 January 1918. As a first order of business, Creel appointed William Johns the chairman of the new division. He told Johns that the new division was to be "a clearing house for all advertising aid offered to the Government." While Creel was to identify the needs of the government, Johns was to ascertain "what the advertising interests of the country can offer for the fulfillment of these needs." Johns was to make a list of organizations representing advertising interests of the country and "to proceed at once to invite all of the organizations of national advertising, not now represented, to organize themselves on a basis of self-organization for war work in order that they may offer their services to this new National Board."[30] Creel also appointed Carl Byoir liaison with the new division with power to act on Creel's behalf, a task that Byoir fulfilled with great relish, not only because he considered himself an advertising man,[31] but because it brought him into association with the most prominent and powerful advertising men of the time. In addition to Johns, the rest of the board of directors was a Who's Who of the advertising world. It included William D'Arcy, president of the Associated Advertising Clubs of the World representing one hundred eighty advertising clubs; Herbert S. Houston, former president of the same organization; O. C. Harn, chairman of the National Commission of the same organization; L. B. Jones, president of the Association of National Advertisers; and Jesse H. Neal, secretary of Associated Business Papers, representing five hundred trade publications. Thomas Cusack of Chicago, the acknowledged king of outdoor advertising, was later added to the board of directors. The division was housed in the Metropolitan Tower in New York City at Madison Square, immediately adjacent to, and essentially a part of, the offices of the AAAA.[32]

The Division of Advertising worked on several major campaigns during its brief history. The Fourth Liberty Loan drive featured, for general audiences, Public Opinion as a young woman in a toga, feared by all, who judges not on the basis of declarations of allegiance with "uncovered head and solemn mien," but by the material aid given to the fighting men. For college audiences, the drive pictured an image of the kaiser in cap and mortarboard looming over a college campus that resembled Belgium's University of Louvain being stormed by military troops; the caption reminds viewers that "in the vicious guttural language of Kultur the degree A.B. means Bachelor of Atrocities." The War Savings Stamps drive urged the public to turn away from self-indulgence, which contrasts so sharply with the self-sacrifice of soldiers in arms, and to "save the thoughtless dollars" and buy Savings Stamps. One of the most famous campaigns personified the Red Cross as the "Greatest Mother in the World," a mature woman in flowing robes complete with the Red Cross nurse's cap clasping a battered doughboy on a stretcher to her breast with pietà-like sorrow. The "Spies and

Lies" campaign urged the public to help suppress groundless rumors and gossip and to report anyone spreading pessimistic stories. The Selective Service campaign displayed advertisements about draft registration in thousands of public buildings, streetcars, subways, railway stations, banks, YMCA branches, and other locales. The "Kill Every Rat" campaign for the department of agriculture urged the extinction of grain-eating vermin. The "Smileage" campaign aimed to provide free entertainment for the boys in training camps. Several campaigns advertised the YMCA, which provided comfort and rest for soldiers coming "Out of the Mouth of Hell." A series of campaigns pressed parents and sweethearts to "be game" and write only cheerful letters to the boys at the front, remembering that "He Will Come Back a Better Man." Finally, one campaign pleaded with the public to write to the CPI for its war publications to help thwart "The Hohenzollern Dream," that is, a huge bayoneted German soldier with a *pickelhaube* stomping over Manhattan's skyscrapers.[33]

The Division of Advertising was a crossroads for everyone who worked in advertising during the Great War, knitting together widely scattered and decentralized groups and individual practitioners into an occupational community. It worked with war advertising committees in more than eighty clubs across the country affiliated with the Associated Advertising Clubs of the World. It worked with the war service committees of two dozen national associations; it employed the services of thirty-nine advertising agencies, fifty-one artists, and thirty printing houses. It coordinated the contributions of more than one hundred thirty advertisers and of hundreds of general semimonthly, monthly, and weekly magazines, farm papers, and technical and trade publications.

The division's work made other occupational communities take notice of advertising. In the judgment of its chairman, William H. Johns, the division had succeeded in "educating official Washington to the use and value of advertising and of the skillful direction of it."[34] Right after the war, the Department of Labor asked for and received the AAAA's assistance in helping to minimize labor unrest by persuading advertisers to insert prepared messages in advertising copy. The AAAA received similar requests, such as one from the United States Shipping Board regarding the future of the merchant marine. In July 1919, after the United States War Department became a national advertiser with an appropriation of $185,000 for recruitment advertising, the AAAA Executive Board authorized a committee of its own members to present to the secretary of the navy the idea of forming a composite advertising agency to respond to the government's advertising needs. The request was approved, and the resulting Advertising Agencies Corporation worked with the army and navy in recruiting and in the disposal of surplus stores until the organization was disbanded in March 1928.[35] In this sense, modern public service advertising began with the Great War.[36]

〰〰〰 In the process of all this work, the men and women of the CPI developed *ex germine* the entire vast apparatus of advocacy, of public opinion formation and claim making that are now taken for granted. They also internalized occupational worldviews typical of image-making experts with mass symbols dedicated to persuasion. The organization is a paradigmatic model for all subsequent propaganda bureaucracies.

First, the concentration-fastening event of the Great War, coupled with the CPI's monopoly over the flow of war information and the policy of "voluntary censorship" by newspapers, accelerated a movement toward "placing news," the permeation of the news media with official viewpoints of one sort or another. This practice was initiated earlier in the century on a much smaller scale by the public relations counsels of magnates and corporations in trouble.[37] Essentially, the war reported in American newspapers was the war that the CPI wanted the American public to see, a moral struggle against cruel tyranny, barbarity, and imperialist expansion with no hint of commercial motivation.[38] After the war, large organizations and individuals of every sort became skilled at placing their own news, that is, issuing their own propaganda. In a speech given in 1935, Carl Byoir suggested the extent of this practice:

> You can pick up your morning paper, pick up the papers that most pride themselves on being the finest sources of news and if you read them with the practiced eye of the publicist or propagandist, you will find that perhaps 60 per cent of all the news of that paper, outside of the results of ball games, sporting events and financial items, is propaganda.[39]

Today, public relations practitioners privately estimate the amount of placed news to be 80 percent of all that is printed or appears in the electronic media. Even allowing for professional exaggeration, a great deal of what the public reads, sees, or hears is material that promotes some vested viewpoint.

Second, years before the availability of radio, the CPI developed prototypical centralized and standardized techniques of mass communication. These involved a coordinated promulgation of themes, usually complete with technical advice on how to execute them but with considerable allowance for local innovative variation and initiative. For instance, one Katherine Ridgeway of Brookline, Massachusetts, wrote the committee that "I am going to speak to more than one hundred thousand people within the next 10 weeks on Chautauqua work in the east New England states and New York. I fill the entire evening in interpreting stories, plays, and poems and shall devote 30 minutes or more to the vital issues of the war. Now may I ask you to give me the outline of the most needful things to tell these people. . . ."[40] The Speaking Division typically provided such people with a copy of its regular bulletin with its "Hints for Speakers: The Issues of the War at a Glance," which encapsulated the salient issues, complete with rhetorical flourishes that the Chautauqua speakers could use as they wished.[41] Again, in January 1918, the United States Shipping Board desperately needed more workers in the shipyards. The Four Minute Men undertook a campaign to recruit skilled workers in all relevant trades to the yards and to alert the public to the importance of shipbuilding. The campaign was deemed so important that the director, William McCormick Blair, took the unusual step of presenting in the bulletin the full text of a very long speech entitled "The Man of the Hour—The Shipbuilder," complete with a detailed outline abstracting all the major themes, with asterisks referring back to boldfaced material in the text for easy reference for speakers preparing their own speeches.[42]

This was only an elaborate version of the kind of systematizing work that always characterized the bulletins of the Four Minute Men. The bulletin normally provided the subject for any given week's speeches, complete with a list of "important points for all speakers." The latter usually included the admonition to "drive home one thought"; some "points for every speech"; and "answers to objectors." For instance, for the campaign on the Third Liberty Loan drive, speakers were urged to stress to their movie-house audiences that "fighters despise a slacker." "How the red-blooded American soldier abhors a slacker! The *traitor* he hates! The *coward* he pities! But the *slacker* who deliberately puts the burden on his brother? No words can express the contempt!" The same bulletin also contained suggestions for openings ("I want to ask you a question, a question personal to me and not to you: If I know a young man who has given up home, friends, life plans, and a salary of $1,000 a year, given up his all to go to that hell of shot and poisonous gases on a $30 a month job, if that young man is willing to fight my battles for me, how many bonds must I buy to keep my self-respect?") as well as suggestions for outlines for whole speeches.[43] Bulletins also sometimes provided whole paragraphs that speakers could incorporate into their talks and often two "typical illustrative speeches." But, though provided with uniform material that they could cobble together, speakers were always encouraged to prepare their own speeches and to say what was on their minds about a topic.

Similarly, the weekly *Bulletin for Cartoonists* provided a steady stream of "cartoon tips" for cartoonists around the country to encourage a certain timely uniformity in selecting war themes to treat. For example, a special edition of the bulletin suggested that cartoonists develop their work around the following ideas for the 6 April 1918 "Win-the-War Day": "A patriot is as a patriot does," "Do more than your 'bit,' do your best," and "By buying bonds, help halt the Hun."[44] Cartoonists were encouraged to send the bureau any cartoons that utilized the ideas of the bulletin. The best of these were then circulated to gain a wider, perhaps national audience.

The CPI's strategy of providing strong centralized guidance in the shaping of public opinion generated emulators. For instance, the National Committee of Patriotic Societies, only one of the innumerable private patriotic organizations spawned by the war, put out a detailed magazine-sized booklet entitled *How to Put in Patriotic Posters the Stuff That Makes People STOP—LOOK—ACT!*[45] Intended as a guide to competitors in the ship poster competition of the United States Shipping Board, the publication details the steps one must undertake to analyze the composition of one's audience and underscores the crucial importance of emotional rather than intellectual appeals, the necessity of stark simplicity rather than fine detail in design, the fundamental power of visual images conveying action rather than rest, and the desirability of bold colors rather than subtle hues. The Division of Advertising adopted a similar course for organizing all of the advertising it generated. Government officials who wanted advertising for some campaign approached the division and worked out with its leaders a detailed statement of purpose and strategy. With such frameworks in hand, the division delegated the work to volunteer advertising agencies and to members of the Division of Pictorial Publicity, who then returned the finished work for review by a committee composed of division leaders and government officials. The advertisements were then published as circulars or displayed in newspaper or magazine space paid for by contributions from various business and community groups.

By the end of the war, CPI leaders, with almost all of the sprawling organization's divisions in place and operating at full tilt, saw the possibilities of even greater coordination, as illustrated by the proposed campaign to raise money for the war work of the Young Men's Christian Association. The plan reads:

> It is proposed that the Committee on Public Information offer the services of its various divisions in the form of an organized and definite plan of campaign each cooperating with the other, and in turn cooperating with the principal unit—the Y.M.C.A. organization. The work the Committee is thus called upon to do is no more than it perhaps would do under any circumstance, but instead of each division working independently and at different times, the service of the entire committee is put into one definite message and so told or merchandized to the American Public through the channel of a campaign plan put out over the name of the Y.M.C.A.

The plan goes on to argue that there is "only one story to be told and one way to tell it." To this end, the Division of Advertising was to prepare a series of advertisements for publication in a whole range of journals, from farming magazines to women's journals, educational publications, and local newspapers. The Division of Pictorial Publicity was also asked to develop a series of posters, coordinated with the illustrations used in the advertising campaign. The Division of Films was to work up a newsreel-length film showing the YMCA's work in France. The Four Minute Men were to speak in fifty-three hundred communities telling their audience the same story as that appearing in the advertising, the posters, and "linking very closely with the message carried in the films." The Speaking Division was to send nationally prominent speakers to all states to reinforce the work of the Four Minute Men. The Division of Pictures was to secure a complete series of original pictures of YMCA men in service in the war zone and syndicate them throughout the country. The Division of Syndicated Features was to develop a series of feature articles that combined pictures and written messages "into one dominating feature story." The Division of News was to place hundreds of genuinely newsworthy items about the YMCA in newspapers everywhere. The Foreign Section was to help the YMCA prepare its message for the thirty-four different nationalities with which it was in regular contact. And the vast distribution network of the CPI was to deliver all the printed literature effectively and promptly.

In short, the idea was, in the words of the proposal, to "marshal all these working forces into a dominating and working machine."[46] Segments of this plan were already in place from earlier CPI work on behalf of the YMCA, but the armistice obviated any point of fully implementing it. Still, the proposal suggests early perceptions of the possibilities of using the apparatus of advocacy to saturate public opinion on a particular issue. An almost identical plan of wholly coordinated communications activity was also in the works to "encourage and stimulate labor production in industries engaged in war work."[47]

Third, this mass communications apparatus depended for its real effectiveness on the thorough mobilization of crucial targeted publics, today, of course, commonplace wisdom in the field of public relations. In brief, the problem is always this: How does one market a message to a society thoroughly segmented by class, education, religion, ethnicity, and generational differences? Ad makers have always tried to embed multiple appeals in advertisements to reach out to different groups. For instance, organizers of the First Liberty Loan drive designed the copy to appeal to "the wealthy through patriotism and the fact that the bonds are nontaxable. . . . to the middle classes . . . through patriotism and the fact that to purchase a bond will be the beginning of a beneficial habit of thrift. . . . to the poorer classes the absolute safety of the investment . . . [and] to the foreign born . . . that here is an opportunity for them to prove . . . their loyalty."[48] But advertising is always a scattershot blast into the wind when contrasted with the careful rifle aim of public relations. To mobilize publics, as Carl Byoir explained in 1935, one has to take several steps: first, set up an actual or fictive organization adorned with the names of respected people that "establish in themselves the soundness of the movement and the integrity of its purpose." Second, "enlist those organizations already in existence which can be of assistance in carrying out [a] plan," taking care to identify the real policymakers of these organizations rather than the titular heads, and third, "[a]fter you have national organization . . . go after local organization, by states, by cities and towns. Last, "put behind your local leader the local representatives of all the national forces which you have previously enlisted. Then . . . drive for the result [one] is after."[49]

Working men comprised one of the most important publics during the Great War. Industrial working conditions were abysmal, unions were organized only with the greatest of difficulty; and, from the perspective of employers, relatively high wages in the shipbuilding and munitions industries were causing disruptive labor mobility. Among the many efforts that the CPI adopted to address the "labor question," two in particular illustrate the effective use of local organizations. First, after briefly coordinating labor activities through its own Division of Industrial Relations, the CPI set up and bankrolled the American Alliance for Labor and Democracy with offices on Chambers Street in New York City. The legendary Samuel Gompers, then the president of the

American Federation of Labor, was named president of the alliance, with several populists and former socialists appointed to its executive committee. According to one of its own publications, in just half a year the alliance formed 150 branches throughout the country; distributed 1,198,000 pamphlets nationwide; held a National Labor Loyalty Week; conducted 200 public mass meetings; placed 10,000 columns of publicity; and mailed a weekly news service to 600 newspapers.[50] Among the alliance's publications were pamphlets by the dean of labor historians, John R. Commons, including "German Socialists and the War" and "Why Workingmen Support the War." The latter was an exhortation to all workers, but particularly to socialists, to back the war because "[n]ever before was a war carried on by workingmen. Never before, in war or in peace, was the voice of labor in government so powerful as it is now in America."[51] A falsehood so obvious, of course, may have had self-reassurance or the calming of middle-class anxieties as its primary goals. At the same time, employers of every sort were writing the CPI suggesting ways of stimulating patriotism among workers. These included ideas to distribute motivational posters for bulletin boards in the shipyards or to point out to workers the many ways they could help the fighting boys, from buying bonds to knitting sweaters.[52]

The CPI approached employers in an exactly parallel manner. In the spring of 1918, one Clarence Howard, president of Commonwealth Steel Company in St. Louis, sent a letter to his employees stressing teamwork and emphasizing how important domestic production was to the war effort. The letter attracted Byoir's attention, and the two subsequently met in Washington. With Byoir's help and encouragement, Howard sent out scores of another letter to heads of companies engaged in government work across the country soliciting opinions about a centralized plan to educate workers by establishing a regular educational service at every plant: "The plan would go out to every plant including patriotic posters, patriotic booklets or pay roll inserts signed by the U.S. Government. *There would be an official button sanctioned by the War and Navy Departments and a Service Flag for the home, to stimulate the pride of the worker and his family in the work he is doing toward winning the war."* The plan also involved motion pictures about the war to bring the struggle home to workers and to show them quality work being done by other workers at home and abroad. Howard stressed that he aimed at cooperation between capital and labor and wanted "[h]umanics as well as mechanics." Enthusiastic letters promptly poured back to him, many with additional suggestions. All replies were, of course, forwarded to Byoir, who likely had a large hand in the entire scheme, including the drafting of the second letter.[53] As James Mock and Cedric Larson point out in their fine treatment of the CPI's dealings with the labor question, CPI leaders maintained a remarkably balanced position in industrial disputes. In particular, they often pointed out to business interests the unseemliness of calling for sacrifice by workers without reciprocal concessions on profits, and they eschewed ideological positions of either the right or the left and kept their eyes on the goal of maintaining civilian morale.[54]

The CPI made similarly skillful use of organizational fronts as well as already existing institutional machinery and leadership in dealing with other important publics, notably foreign-born Americans, through the various "loyalty leagues."[55] Perhaps the CPI's most famous use of the front was Byoir's invention of the "League of Oppressed Nations," an organization that coordinated all the ethnic loyalty groups. On 4 July 1918, Byoir arranged for a pilgrimage by leaders of thirty-three of these groups to Mount Vernon, Virginia, where President Wilson addressed them. On the same day, in eight hundred U.S. cities, ethnic groups of all sorts staged loyalty demonstrations. Byoir also arranged an early-fall fête for Thomas G. Masaryk, then president of the Czechoslovak National Council. The Carnegie Hall event was entitled "The Will of the Peoples of Austria Hungary: Victory Meeting for the Oppressed Nationalities of Central Europe" and was sponsored by an honorary committee of New York luminaries to help strengthen Masaryk's claim of leadership of free Czechoslovakia. In October, with CPI assistance, Masaryk promulgated the Czech Declaration of Independence at Independence Hall in Philadelphia.[56]

Fourth, by inventively exploiting the possibilities of every available medium, the CPI tried to give a pointed direction and a common vocabulary—slogans, rallying cries, pictorial symbols, as well as the requisite loathsome images of the enemy—to the frenzy of patriotic fervor that swept the nation during the war to end all wars. One can glimpse the range and depth of this fervor by looking at only a few of the suggestions that poured into CPI headquarters at 10 Jackson Place in Washington or were referred there by government officials. There were innumerable ideas for propaganda themes and strategies, some of which were adopted outright or in altered form, although most were politely declined. For instance, a letter to Creel warning of the dangers of gossip and rumormongering and suggesting an advertising campaign cautioning the public "to keep their mouths shut" led to the famous "Spies and Lies," the "Gossip That Costs Human Lives!" and the "Have

You Met this Kaiserite?" campaigns run by the Division of Advertising.[57] One letter suggested that "in order to more perfectly stimulate the home spirit for victory, you ask all Americans to sign all their business and personal correspondence with the phrase 'yours for victory and liberty.'"[58] Another envisioned CPI support for a national movement to encourage Americans "in every hall where people meet" to "sing the [National] Anthem Every Day."[59] A Mississippian suggested that the CPI sanction the formation of a nationwide "How Do You Know It Club," whose members would be "furnished with a button asking this question and whenever anyone makes a remark about the army, navy, or government, it will be the duty of said member to flash this button and ask how do they know it to be true."[60] Ideas for anti-German propaganda abounded. One proposed CPI sanction for "The Society of the Lusitania" with the insignia of a "coat of arms of the Imperial German Empire with a clot of blood across with the slogan 'the blot that won't come off'"; society members would "boycott everything German, [and] have nothing to do with anything German, goods, language, music or sentiments."[61] Similar letters suggested that German be suppressed in all schools, in addition to shutting down all German newspapers[62] and that the CPI give more extensive publicity to German atrocities to convince American farmers about the dangers of the war.[63] To ensure mass support for the war, one letter suggested that local councils of defense present every man with a pledge card to "protect [the soldier's] home from the enemy within." One either signed or went on record as having refused.[64]

In addition to proposed action, the CPI also heard about actions already taken by different groups or individuals in a spirit of patriotism, such as the "On Your Guard" poster and card campaign by the Worchester [Massachusetts] Chamber of Commerce urging the suppression of any remarks that might "give aid or comfort to our enemies," or the speech "Over Here" given to any audience that Earl Derr Biggers could find. The speech described a scene in which young Jimmy Gerson, about to go off to war, explains to his old German grandfather how the war has saved America from becoming a "nation of softies."[65] And the CPI was also sometimes asked to act as a moral arbiter of patriotism to prevent the misconstruction of wholly well-meaning actions, such as when the Basking Ridge Fire Company, no. 1, wrote to the CPI as a federal authority, asking whether the CPI thought the fire company's annual fund-raising carnival displayed an "unpatriotic spirit." Byoir responded, "I do not see how anyone could construe as unpatriotic an event designed to support the fire company," adding that the organization might wish to incorporate "some purely patriotic features" in its affair.[66]

In short, any notion that the CPI manufactured out of whole cloth the stridently moralistic, deeply resentful, xenophobic, highly emotional wash of public sentiments about the Great War that engulfed the entire nation gains little support from a close reading of the CPI files. A significant portion of the U.S. citizenry has always listened closely to nativist, primitive appeals, and the Great War helped foster chauvinistic groups like the National Security League and the American Defense Society. Moreover, for two years before the CPI's origin, in a concerted effort to get the United States involved in the war, British propagandists had pounded the American public with largely fabricated images of the rape of "little Belgium," the outraging of nuns, and the massacre of women and children.[67] If anything, as Byoir noted later, the real issue was discarding the "tens of thousands of impractical suggestions and unworkable plans with which every war-time organization is promptly flooded . . . the great danger [of which] is that they do not all, by any means, come from the cracked-pots and half-wits of the nation but most of the worst of them come from people whose very eminence and success in other fields make their theories dangerous because they catch you off-guard."[68]

Given such public sentiment, the task of the CPI was not to create opinion about the war but to mold it. Seen from this perspective, of course, the very name of the committee was disingenuous, a front for its principal mission, although the name seems to have confused some people. For instance, a W. Ray Lewis wrote to the CPI offering a chart of nations at war that he thought might be useful in the committee's educational work. Byoir responded: "This generally informative matter is not part of our task. As I conceive it, we are here to interpret, as far as we are able, to the people of America the high ideals for which America fights, the justice of our cause, and the autocratic aims of our enemies."[69] He wrote somewhat more pointedly to Bruce Bliven of *Printer's Ink:* "[I]n a sense the whole work of the Committee is in the last analysis simply a tremendous world advertising job."[70] Advertising and public relations both take the dough of existing sentiment—the world as it is—and knead it into forms that lead people to think and especially to act in certain ways. In this sense, the CPI was America's first propaganda ministry, a term that all the leaders of the organization used without embarrassment or hesitation.

Fifth, the CPI was a modern workplace, filled with men and women of great talent and sizable egos, and, like all bureaucracies, a cockpit of personal ambition and competition. Genuinely felt patriotic sentiments fueled the organization's fantastic range of activities, but as happens in any large organization, the CPI's leaders were also besieged with requests for patronage and favors of all sorts, from letters of recommendation to secure admission to an officers' training program to requests to sanction an application for a post as a noncommissioned regimental sergeant major.[71] Moreover, hundreds of people sought a post with the CPI itself, often men deferred from the draft like William Magill who wrote, "I chafe that at fifty I am a mere spectator where I should be an active participant, partaking of the dangers of the conflict" or from applicants who felt "[I]t is every man's duty to do everything in his power to help win the war."[72] Even when such men were willing to work for nothing, there were so many applicants that names were simply kept on file. Those who asked for remuneration were usually told that nothing was or would be available, although there were some important exceptions.[73] At the higher levels of the organization, the scramble for prestige typical of all bureaucracies with the upward-looking stance they inevitably engender was particularly intense. The prestige of doing war-related work and, most especially, the social access to important peers that such work afforded were, after all, the principal rewards that the CPI offered businessmen, most of whom worked for the CPI while still engaged in their own affairs.

The struggle for ascendancy in the Division of Advertising between the New York and the Chicago practitioners suggests the kinds of tensions at issue. The tight circle of New York advertising men grouped around the newly formed American Association of Advertising Agencies. The AAAA dominated the Division of Advertising from its informal start in December 1917 when Creel gave the nod to this organization over several others that had offered help. All of the original appointees to the board of the Division of Advertising were part of that inner circle, including William D'Arcy, who, though he hailed from St. Louis, was considered an "Eastern man." Nonetheless, D'Arcy pushed for the appointment of Thomas Cusack of Chicago, whose outdoor advertising firm was the largest in the country. The Chicago admen resented the New York crowd's influence; D'Arcy saw Cusack's appointment as one way to mollify that anger. Cusack wrote to Creel on 1 December 1917 formally offering his services. But Creel delayed in making a formal appointment. There was opposition to Cusack's appointment from industrial plant owners, and this reason was eventually cited for the delay.

However, correspondence between William Rankin of Chicago and Byoir suggests that matters were more complicated. Byoir greatly admired Rankin's energetic work on the First Liberty Loan drive, and the two regularly corresponded, exchanged humorous notes, and frequently met up either in New York or Chicago. Rankin's letters burn with the Chicago man's resentment of New York dominance in the CPI, and it is abundantly clear that Rankin expected a place on the board of directors of the Division of Advertising, although he also desired an even bigger job, indeed an entire division of which he would be chairman.[74]

In the meantime, Cusack engineered a barrage of wires and letters to Washington from third parties on his own behalf, indicating that he would accept the appointment to the board when it was offered, although other evidence suggests that his friends were warning him away from the position. Creel was under pressure on a number of fronts: the New York men wanted to maintain their dominance; Chicago wanted in; both Cusack and Rankin wanted the Chicago slot and, in fact, Rankin, who was personally backed by Creel's right-hand man, wanted more than one spot for the west. Creel told Byoir to meet with Cusack and straighten things out. There was a comical missed meeting in New York between Byoir and Cusack, followed by indignant wires and letters from Cusack to Creel. In the end, Creel gave the nod to Cusack to represent Chicago. Rankin was never appointed to the board or to the big job with the CPI that he desired.[75] All large organizations breed these sorts of struggles for prestige. The ferocity of the struggles is a shorthand indicator of the influence that men and women in a particular occupational community attach to the social networks, circles, cliques, and personal associations of their world in making and breaking reputations and careers. Those who already were and especially those who wanted to be big-time advocates saw the CPI and the Great War as the chance of a lifetime.

Finally, the CPI helped shape among emerging experts with symbols notions of malleable publics and the power of mass persuasion, now characteristic habits of mind of image makers of every sort. A profound disillusionment followed the Great War among former soldiers, intellectuals and artists, the general public in all belligerent countries, and even among some former propagandists.[76] When the full extent of the war's human carnage became evident and the enormous social dislocation that it created in Europe began to produce the early harbingers of political fanaticism, some of the leading participants in the CPI wondered about the mass irrationalities that they had helped fan, such as the cartoonlike stereotypes of bestial, bloodthirsty Germans, the unbridled moral fervor sanctified by images of the cross and motherhood, and the suspicions about the loyalties of dissenters of any sort.[77] President Wilson himself, according to George Creel, was especially afraid of the disillusionment that would follow the inevitable dashing of expectations about the United States as the world's savior, an expectation created to a great extent by CPI propaganda.[78] But, instead of producing searching questions about the implications of the techniques of mass image making and persuasion, such reflections typically took a practical turn. Struck by the gullibility of the public, experts with mass symbols wondered whether propaganda might work as well in peacetime as it had during the Great War.[79]

2 PUBLIC RELATIONS FOR ADVERTISING

The years between the Great War and the Second World War brought mixed blessings to mass image makers. Both advertising and public relations flourished during the Roaring Twenties as businesses shaped new markets and tried to expand old ones. The new medium of radio, half-understood Freudian notions about the efficacy of nonrational appeals, and pseudoscientific techniques borrowed from the new social science disciplines came into use. Consumer demand seemed insatiable. Even the stock market crash of 1929 and the onset of the Great Depression presented great opportunities for public relations to flourish. As the economic crisis worsened, the public began to listen more attentively to the appeals of labor unions. Leftist political radicalism gained ground with the young, and the bureaucratic apparatus of the New Deal burgeoned, led by a president who was himself a master propagandist. Business countered with a massive public relations campaign to herald the virtues of the capitalist system, with leading businesses in every industry hiring their own in-house staffs of practitioners. In the process, the field of public relations developed many of its now stock-in-trade devices, including multimedia saturation techniques and internal communications programs designed to turn workers into ambassadors of good will for companies.

But the Great Depression had a different effect on advertising, always the more flamboyant of the image-making occupations. Advertising revenues fell precipitously as some businesses failed and others moved to lower-cost communications programs, including public relations. More significantly, by devastating the material aspirations of millions of people, the Great Depression undercut the legitimacy of the whole U.S. business system, which then, as now, depended on the promise of ever-rising prosperity. As the clarion of business, advertising came under vituperative attack. Industry executives began to talk about a public relations effort to advertise advertising.

〰〰〰 The Advertising Council, the organization still at the heart of much contemporary public service advertising, was born out of the coincidence of advertising executives' worries about the attacks on both advertising and business itself and the opportunities for honorable self-promotion through public service suddenly presented by the Second World War.[1] Right up to the eve of the war, the attacks on business in general and advertising in particular mounted in volume and stridency[2] and began to be translated into proposed regulation of aspects of advertising.[3] Key figures from the American Association of Advertising Agencies (AAAA) and the Association of National Advertisers sought to bring about a coalition of advertisers, advertising agencies, and media owners to launch a counterattack and, to that end, arranged for a national conference to be held at Hot Springs, Virginia, in mid-November 1941.

The closing, and most important, speech at the conference was given by James Webb Young, a former professor at the University of Chicago and vice president of J. Walter Thompson, then and now a giant advertising firm, and a former president of the AAAA.[4] In his talk, Young surveyed the main bases of anti-business and anti-advertising sentiment. He noted that some antagonism to advertising is social and cultural. He recounted two personal experiences with academic snobbery toward advertising,[5] attributing the condescension they revealed to residual nineteenth-century English prejudices that viewed trade as unfit for gentlemen. He allowed little hope that a campaign for advertising could change such sentiments among opinion leaders, rooted, as they were, in a "repugnance for some of the manifestations of advertising— for its banality, its bad taste, its moronic appeals, and its clamor. We just ain't refined enough."[6] But Young went on to stress that the real danger to advertising was the political ascendancy of "idealists and humanitarians" trying to be "practical" and who were intent on overhauling or replacing altogether the free enterprise system on which advertising depended. He expressed skepticism that a campaign to sell advertising to the public could be efficacious: "Advertising is a force like electricity, which can be judged only in its applications." Moreover, in some of these applications, advertising's only true defense is an indictment of the public; advertising is the way it is "because the public is that way." Finally, "everybody believes in advertising—even the critic of it—when he is on the sending end. But nobody believes in advertising—not even the producer of it—when he is on the receiving end."[7]

What, then, must be done? Young exhorted his colleagues to address the "distaste with which too many people view advertising" by suggesting that admen be "a little less brutal in the newspapers [and] a little less silly in the magazines." At the same time, he noted that admen could take an important public relations tip from John D. Rockefeller, who escaped the charge of being a robber baron only when he became a philanthropist. Young understood advertising as the premier means for reaching a mass audience: "Advertising is the most modern, streamlined, high-speed means of communication plus persuasion yet invented by man." This mix of "communication plus persuasion," Young argued, "has potentialities for use far beyond its present levels."

> [Advertising] ought to be used extensively by governments, as it is in England today. It ought to be used by political parties, not just in elections, but continuously. It ought to be used by labor unions, by farm organizations, by the National Association of Manufacturers, by the great philanthropic foundations, by churches and by universities. It ought to be used for open propaganda in international relations, to create understanding and reduce friction. It ought to be used to wipe out such diseases of ignorance as child-bed fever. It ought to do the nutritional job this country needs to have done. It ought to be the servant of music, of art, of literature, and of all the forces of righteousness, even more than it is.

Young wondered when fighting over "just the existing business" would end. When would admen begin to "sell [advertising] into these new levels of usefulness, this larger stature?" He predicted that when this happens, "the critics of advertising will all be on the sending end too—and they will all be on our side."[8]

As to the more dangerous group of reformers bent on dismantling the free enterprise system, Young argued that the advertising community had to kindle "a new faith in the possibilities of the dynamic economy; to make that faith so strong that business will be ready to back it with the necessary capital investments, in spite of political deterrents to such investments."[9] "What will it profit us," he asked, paraphrasing the famous question asked by Ignatius of Loyola, "to win the battle of advertising and lose the war of business?" He concluded:

Let us light again the torch of business expansion which advertising used to carry. . . . But let us do more. Let us ask ourselves whether we, as an industry, do not have a great contribution to make in this effort to regain for business and [*sic*] leadership of our economy. We have within our hands the greatest aggregate means of mass education and persuasion the world has ever seen, namely, the channels of advertising communication. We are the masters of the techniques of using these channels. We have power. Why do we not use it?

Young had a clear idea of how advertising, this "torch of business," should be used: not just to " 'sell' advertising" or to "print frothy essays on the American way of life," but also to sell the idea of business to the public.

Use it to talk about what old Sam Adams said every man was interested in—his girl and his dinner. [Then] [u]se it to show him how we all make our living. Use it to put him on his guard against the false labels. Use it for real consumer education. Use it to give the whole of business a new faith in our destiny—a faith that will start flowing again all the little waters of enterprise. Use it to create an atmosphere in which business can hope and plan and dream again. Use it to confound the critics of advertising with the greatest demonstration of its power they have ever seen.[10]

The Hot Springs meeting ended with several resolutions affirming Young's analysis. Specifically, the assembled executives agreed that "advertising is an important part of American business—that attacks on advertising are attacks on business. [Therefore] the best defense consists of (a) better taste in copy and commercial, (b) dissemination of facts on the function and effects of advertising, [and] (c) re-teaching a belief in a dynamic economy." They also agreed to use "the skills and facilities of advertising for information and persuasion in other than commercial ventures, and specifically in the public interest."[11] Work toward all of these goals became a central tenet of the organization that emerged from the Virginia meeting, although its leaders have generally preferred the identity of advocate for public causes. The name, Advertising Council, seems to have been first used at a follow-up meeting in late November in New York even as disagreements continued about the proper shape of an organization to link advertisers, advertising agencies, and the media.

One month following the Hot Springs conference, Paul West, president of the Association of National Advertisers and one of the prime movers of the conference, was on his way to Washington to get a first-hand feel for the ominous drift of world events when Japan attacked

Pearl Harbor. Two days later, West had in hand priority requests from Donald M. Nelson, executive director of the United States Supply, Priorities and Allocation Board and director of priorities for the Office of Production Management, the over-all defense agency that, in January 1941, replaced the ineffective National Defense Advisory Board. Nelson asked for a meeting to establish a working relationship between the government and "the Advertising Council." At that meeting a week later, Nelson specified the areas of conservation, health and welfare, civilian defense, and increased production as being among the most vital national concerns of the moment.[12] Almost entirely by accident, as the council's longtime stalwart Harold B. Thomas recounts, the original purpose of a council "to counter the attacks on business and advertising had . . . given way to putting the skills and facilities of advertising at the service of our country at war."[13] On 10 January 1942, Chester J. LaRoche, chairman of Young & Rubicam and the just-named chairman of the Advertising Council, sent a memorandum to the new members of the fledgling organization acknowledging the group's sharp change of direction while stressing the need to subordinate all other objectives to that of winning the war.[14] A series of meetings with government officials followed, establishing liaisons between the emerging council, the Information Division of the Office for Emergency Management, the Office of War Information, and the Office of Facts and Figures headed by the poet Archibald MacLeish, who also chaired the important War Information Board.[15]

The wide range of projects for which the help of the advertising industry was solicited in these meetings suggests the staggering task involved in converting an entire industrial economy to a war footing within a democratic political framework where the principal tool of policy must be persuasion. In the early days of 1942 alone, the Advertising Council was asked to think about ways to prevent the hoarding of goods, particularly of rubber, wool, and sugar; to develop ideas for the "Share the Meat" rationing plan; to map out rationales for conservation programs of every sort as well as campaigns to salvage rubber and fats; to work out appeals to the industrial worker, the "soldier in overalls," the key to successful modern warfare; to help sell defense bonds and stamps; to help write and clarify government propaganda in foreign languages; and to help create the images of the enemy necessary to provide men under arms with a "fight-to-win" morale and civilians with the will to work and to sacrifice.[16] Such responsibilities encouraged the organization's leaders to adjust the public rationale for the council's origins. By the spring of 1942, the rationale had become, "In the grave task of converting our nation from peacetime habits and customs to a war basis with the utmost speed . . . the Advertising Council has been organized at the specific request of our government."[17]

Indeed, the Advertising Council closely followed the government's lead in developing advertising related to the war. The procedures for initiating a campaign were straightforward. Typically, when a government bureau targeted an issue for advertising, it went to the Office of War Information (OWI). The OWI, together with the originating bureau, gathered the requisite information and then went to the Advertising Council. Once the council decided to undertake the project, it assembled a "task force" from its list of 450 volunteer advertising agencies, which then planned the campaign from start to finish. The completed advertising was then placed throughout the country with magazines and newspapers that donated time and space for war messages.[18]

Selling the idea of advertising with broader social purposes to fellow businessmen was not always easy. Indeed, many businesses saw the war mainly as a hook to sell more products, such as the bread maker who told America to slice her way to victory with his bread, the cigarette maker who had the general staff measuring his cigarettes in the war room, or the cast-iron pipe manufacturer who had a soldier tell his girl not to worry since he was as tough as cast iron.[19] The executives on the Advertising Council saw themselves as engaged in "missionary" work in industry to legitimate the diversion of corporate resources to help the government make its war advertising campaigns successful.[20] Essentially, the Advertising Council had to encourage wide business participation while recognizing the financial exigencies that are the lot of businessmen everywhere.

Moreover, the council could not in any way impugn the patriotism of businessmen reluctant to participate by insisting on notions like duty. It stressed, therefore, that "advertising which helps the war also helps your product, your company and your stockholders."[21] The council suggested four techniques for wartime advertising. The first was the "All-Out" campaign, in which "the advertiser definitely subordinates his product, devotes the lion's share of the space to aiding the chosen war theme. This is the purest form of selflessness—and the best public relations." For example, Wamsutta Mills of Massachusetts ran an advertisement encouraging women to join the Women's Army Corps (WAC), hoping—in passing—that the company would have enough of its supercale sheets for all of Uncle Sam's nieces when they returned home. The second technique was the "Double-Barrelled" campaign that, recognizing the crucial importance of timeliness in advertising, used war themes to sell products. Thus, "dog food is hitched to V-mail, coffee to Womanpower, cosmetics to WAC recruitment." DuPont, for instance, ran an advertisement urging housewives to help the war effort by not throwing out food, while pointing out the virtues of DuPont cellophane in saving leftovers. This method of "hitchhiking" onto powerful social trends and ideas (also called "borrowed interest") is a commonplace advertising strategy. The third was the "Sneak Punch" approach, which had advertisers slipping war messages into regular product ads. Maxwell House coffee, for instance, frequently featured Rosie the Riveter, the iconic female war worker, enjoying a cup during her time on the swing shift. Finally, the "Plug with a Slug" approach had advertisers print war-related messages in the corners of their regular advertisements, such as Kraft pushing victory gardens at the bottom of a salad dressing spot.[22] In short, the essential task for Advertising Council staff was to establish in advertisers' minds the broad-minded notion that advertising for the public interest was the most effective kind of self-advertisement, a theme to which the council has returned repeatedly in the postwar years.[23] There were occasional retreats to more parochial stances even among the council's executives. When the U.S. Army and Selective Service took the hard-nosed position that unless 55 percent of an advertisement was clearly war-related, then the whole ad was not "war advertising," council members feared that advertising itself might be put on the list of "deferrable" activities. They studied the possibility of radio programs dramatizing advertising as an institution that carried war information and enabled the public "to do its patriotic duty,"[24] but no action on this issue seems to have been taken.

The council itself hitchhiked onto the powerful wave of sentiments generated by modern warfare. The Second World War enabled the council to touch on virtually every aspect of life in the United States. There were recruitment campaigns for the armed services, for specialized jobs in the services like amphibious units, aviation, and air gunners, for the merchant marine, for the WACs and the WAVES (Women Accepted for Volunteer Emergency Service, a branch of the navy), for army, navy, and civilian nurses ("We feel awfully good about Mary's joining the Cadet Nurse Corps"), and for women to take defense industry or other important civilian jobs ("My husband's in the Army. I'm in a shipyard. . . . We're in the war together," and "Will it take a bomb to break up that afternoon bridge game? Get out and drive a truck, load a freight car, work in a day nursery, operate an elevator"). The council also helped recruit millions of men and women as blood donors, nurses' aides, auxiliary police and firefighters, ration-board workers, and for other civilian war-related jobs. At the end of the war, the council's recruitment work extended even to trying to gather sixteen hundred large dogs for scout duty in the South Pacific.[25] Together with waste fighting and forest-fire prevention campaigns, there were conservation campaigns for food, fuel, rubber, tin cans, fats, cutting tools, rope, paper, as well as transportation conservation campaigns that urged citizens not to travel and collection drives for used clothing. There were campaigns to explain price administration and to discourage loose spending ("How to prevent inflation in one easy lesson. *Put that money back in your pocket"*). There were food rationing and nutrition campaigns. There were campaigns urging the planting of victory gardens and the virtues of home canning, efforts that were at least partially responsible for the 18 million victory gardens planted in the United States in 1944 alone, producing an estimated 3.5 billion quarts of home-preserved foods.[26] There were campaigns exhorting homeowners to create spaces in their houses for war workers. There were campaigns to cut work absenteeism, reduce labor turnover and improve labor utilization, and increase industrial plant safety. There were campaigns lauding farmers, the U.S. Army Medical Department, the U.S. Army Conservation Program, and the Red Cross. There were campaigns to send Christmas packages overseas, to use lightweight V-mail in overseas mail ("Can you pass a mailbox with a clear conscience?"), and to halt the rise of venereal disease, which it was said, had reached epidemic proportions. There was a whole series of campaigns selling war bonds to finance the war, with millions of individual ads and donations of space and time running to $400 million. The massive mobilization of patriotism also produced campaigns that appealed to raw, primitive emotions, such as the advertisement picturing a Nazi official leering at a lineup of three young girls ("[A] Gauleiter with an eye for beauty may decide she is a perfect specimen for one of their experimental camps. A high honor for your daughter"), or the picture of a hangman's noose against the backdrop of five people hanged ("Try this for size. . . . Designed for conquered people").[27]

Perhaps in recognition of their organization's total interconnectedness with the war effort, not only for its work but for its legitimacy, the council's leaders voted to change the organization's name to the War Advertising Council on 14 May 1943.[28] By the end of the war, the council claimed that it had helped coordinate contributions by U.S. businesses of more than one billion dollars worth of advertising space, time, and service in support of various home front campaigns.[29] Moreover, the council's insistent focus on the sacrifices the war required prompted other advertisers to reverse their own traditional appeals. Many campaigns urged people to buy less, to conserve more, to make things last longer, to avoid heavy use of public utilities, and even to share their goods with their neighbors. The watchword became "Use it up, wear it out, make it do or do without," a slogan later officially adopted by the government for its own thrift campaigns.

As the end of the war came into view, however, council leaders, who operated the council as an exclusive club,[30] began to consider the organization's role in postwar America and the obstacles to such an organizational transition. On 24 July 1944, in the wake of the aborted 20 July attempt on Hitler's life that precipitated widespread speculation about Germany's imminent collapse, T. S. Repplier, the executive director of the council, wrote a memorandum to Chairman Harold B. Thomas urging an immediate exploration of the postwar role of the council. Repplier also argued that the council should adopt some "war campaigns which have a 'feel' of the future" in order to thwart wholesale defections among advertisers from the concept of war-related advertising in what were thought to be the waning days of conflict.[31] Repplier's memorandum launched a lengthy series of discussions at council meetings for the rest of the war about the council's future.[32]

By May 1945, council leaders began to get specific about postwar plans for their organization. They wished to carve out areas of public service "in which advertising could help solve national problems." Uppermost in the minds of some leaders, like Chester LaRoche, were potential threats to "the stability of the private enterprise system" from ideological battles prompted by unemployment or other socioeconomic disruptions. LaRoche and others saw the council's future role as one of public enlightenment about the virtues of the American economic system.[33] But James W. Young, the newly elected chairman, broadened the focus of discussion. Young conceded that the public in a market system needs information about the "free exchange of goods," but, he pointed out, it also needs information on issues such as public health and the conservation of the environment. Young suggested that the council's engagement with such issues should be legitimated by a public mandate of some sort, such as a congressional law or a decisive stamp of approval from a representative committee of well-respected citizens.[34]

Within a few weeks, Young and other council leaders had developed a whole program to sell the postwar council to a variety of publics, including the always troublesome business community itself.[35] Later,

Young took pains to articulate the kind of rationales for public service work requisite in the business world. He argued against the misconception that the council was engaged in a great humanitarian project. Instead, Young asserted, the council had "discovered and demonstrated a technique of advertising which increases the effectiveness and power of advertising." The council could inestimably aid the advertiser who not only wanted to sell goods but desired to enhance his corporate reputation in the public eye.[36] Young stressed that the council had no intention of pressuring advertisers and their advertising agencies into "a Boy Scout program of doing a good deed daily." Still, he argued that public service advertising was the best possible public relations for business.[37]

With other publics, council leaders put forward a more expansive view of the organization's new work. In a major pamphlet issued after the war's end, council leaders pointed to the role of mass persuasion in maintaining a democracy in the midst of stringent exigencies.

> In a war for survival, all bets are off. Action—swift, decisive action—is all that counts. A warring nation *must* remedy its shortages. It *must* get the scrap, the fats, the paper, the money, the factory manpower it needs—or its army and navy have little to fight with. It must man its merchant ships, change the people's habits, increase its food supply—*or lose the war.* Government cannot do these things. Only the people can. And the people must either be compelled or persuaded—*there is no other way.* During the entire war, for the most part, they were persuaded. There were no compulsory savings. No national service act, no labor draft. . . . The Country, the people, did the job the democratic way, and just one thing made it possible . . . . This nation used every known channel to carry to the people the news of what needed to be done—to explain, persuade and inspire. *The people did the rest.* Thus, our great wartime information mechanism enabled this nation to fight through our first global war—with a minimum of compulsion. In a period when the trend toward centralized controls might well have become an irresistible force, this was a service of lasting significance to every business and every citizen.

Then, council leaders argued, as in war, so in peace—

> [T]he battle for the preservation of American democracy did not end on the last day of the war. One crisis ended. Another began. In peace, as in war, the informed and intelligent cooperation of the people is the priceless ingredient of a working democracy.[38]

In modern warfare, foreign battlefield triumphs depend on domestic morale, the willingness of civilians to make sacrifices, and the ability of leaders to provide people with reasons to continuing sacrificing. In peacetime, domestic tranquility and prosperity depend on persuading rather than coercing the citizenry to accept the basic parameters of social life. The pamphlet goes on to delineate the types of projects council leaders thought the postwar council should undertake. These include campaigns to combat tuberculosis through X-ray examinations and diabetes through urinalysis; campaigns to encourage wide employment and foster foreign trade; to fight for control of forest fires; to stimulate desire for home ownership; to guard against precipitous cashing of war bonds; to continue the fight against inflation; to stimulate international cooperation; to assist returning veterans; to help proven national organizations such as the Red Cross raise money; and to assist the government in its short-term or emergency management problems.

The council completed its transition to its postwar identity when its leaders changed its name back to The Advertising Council, Inc., the name the organization retains today.[39] Even before the transition was official, proposed campaigns began pouring in from a variety of potential clients. These included the army, the Girl Scouts, the Marine Corps, the National Safety Council, the Famine Emergency Committee, the Salvation Army, the Infantile Paralysis Association, the Cooperative for American Remittances to Europe (CARE), the National Society for Crippled Children, and the National Conference of Christians and Jews. Requests came from organizations of every stripe addressing the panoply of human ills and social issues endemic to an industrial social order, from tuberculosis control to accident prevention, from blood drives to advocacy for atomic energy, from group prejudice control to raising the prestige of the army and of the nation's teachers.[40] With a renewed sense of the organization's mission, namely that "[t]he best public relations advertising is public service advertising,"[41] the council set out to establish itself as "the clarion of the nation."

〰〰〰 The Advertising Council's postwar history illustrates many of the dynamics and vicissitudes of advocacy organizations in a society roiling with advocacy. At least in its early years, the council was an anomaly in the business world, its own principal constituency. Council leaders identified themselves with the national interest, that is, the interests of business and government working together. This view, symbolized by the council's wartime, hand-in-glove cooperation with the government, prompted deep suspicion from many in business, especially proprietors of small and medium-sized enterprises but also rank-and-file managers in the growing big corporations, who had loathed and feared President Franklin Roosevelt and his New Deal. Many believed deeply in the ideology fashioned by the National Association of Manufacturers (NAM) in the 1930s to counter Roosevelt's successful pillorying of business.[42] The NAM's creed emphasized the centrality of business and the unabashed assertion of the profit motive in U.S. civilization. Those in business who adhered to this creed, a group that included many admen, saw the Advertising Council's relationship with the government as flirtation with a dangerous enemy.

But Advertising Council leaders eschewed such a monolithic view of Washington. Along with other forward-looking businessmen and women, they recognized that, for better or worse, the bureaucratization of the society was already a fait accompli, even though they cast the council and the advertising industry as combating that trend.[43] They saw clearly that bureaucracy fragments rather than unifies the governmental apparatus, splintering official viewpoints and creating exploitable opportunities instead of binding constraints.[44] They felt that a governmental imprimatur of any sort lends legitimacy to business undertakings because people, with whatever warrant, assumed government's disinterested concern for the common good. Council leaders recognized that the price of our economic system's energetic and creative productiveness is destruction and wastefulness, not only of resources but of human lives. In the aftermath of the Great Depression, the choice facing business was stark: either tackle the human problems wrought by the machine age or face centralized governmental solutions to them, with the concomitant loss of liberties for individuals and businesses. Among other endeavors, the council held a conference entitled "The Human Problems of Our Changing Industrial Society: To What Extent Should They Concern Business?" cosponsored by the business schools at Columbia and Harvard universities. Council leaders saw the following problems as basic: worries about security of income and retirement pensions; health concerns; adequate housing; parental responsibilities, including those related to schools; and satisfaction for workers, both on and off the job.[45] To broaden its base, the council put together in 1946 a Public Advisory Committee, later called the Public Policy Committee, composed of distinguished intellectuals and men and women of affairs, to review its proposed campaigns in terms of both their overall purposes and particular themes. At various times the committee included E. Franklin Frazier, the renowned sociologist; Herbert H. Lehman, later United States senator; Ralph Bunche of the United Nations; Evans Clark, executive director of the Twentieth Century Fund; Helen Hall of the Henry Street Settlement; Eugene Meyer, chairman of the *Washington Post;* the theologian Reinhold Niebuhr;

James B. Conant, president of Harvard University; and George Gallup and Elmo Roper, two of the pioneers of public opinion polling.[46] Although the committee served principally to legitimate the council to a range of publics, the advice of its members often saved the council from the parochialism that afflicts many business organizations. In short, working with stalwarts from civic and intellectual spheres, the council's leaders framed a certain vision of America's future, one in which they saw the council as a force to push the business community to link its self-interest with the interest of the commonweal.

Such a notion of common interest and fate was, and indeed is, singular in a centrifugal social order based on extreme individualism. By harnessing advertising to public service, council leaders became early practitioners and partners in the crisis management that is the central goal of the bureaucratized U.S. welfare state. But selling such a strategy to many of their business associates, schooled in ideologies of laissez-faire, social Darwinism, and dog-eat-dog competitiveness, was hard flogging indeed, and the council has always been vulnerable to attacks from businessmen of the old school. Although council leaders developed effective techniques of "converting" many in business to their mission,[47] they typically had little choice when pitching for business support, but to cloak social concern, whether strategic or heartfelt, as self-interest, even as they strove in the broader public arena to be emissaries of an enlightened capitalism.

With such a mission in mind, and always with a wary eye to its right, the leaders of the council chose to address for the most part relatively settled, mainstream, noncontroversial issues, a policy that, with important exceptions, has continued to the present day. What reasonable person can quarrel with the desirability of recruiting student nurses (1946–55), of increasing the prestige of the army (1946–50), of fostering golden rule religious values (1949–84), of preventing home fires (1950–52, 1955–56), or of thwarting man-made forest fires (1943–present)? Who can dispute calls to control tuberculosis (1946–49), to support community chests (1948–55) or the Red Cross (1955–present), to register and vote (1956–60, 1964), to cooperate with the Bureau of the Census (periodic), to stamp out paralytic polio (1957–58, 1960), to support the idea of the United Nations (1957–1976), to keep America beautiful (1960–65, 69), to halt drug abuse (1969–72, 1985–present), to curb drunk driving (1982–84), or to support the United Negro College Fund (1971–present)?

But, like all groups striving to reach mass audiences, advocacy organizations inevitably move with the emotional and political currents, frameworks, and vocabularies of their times. In the postwar years, indeed well into the 1960s, several council campaigns mirrored the cold war, a period of economic turmoil, cultural and political anxiety, indeed sometimes hysteria, accusation and blame, and jingoistic rhetoric. Particularly after the 1949 discovery that the Soviet Union had developed the atom bomb, cold war anxieties framed and enveloped most political discussions in the United States and decisively stamped the council's work. For instance, in 1947, along with the attorney general of the United States and the American Heritage Foundation, the council launched its "American Heritage" campaign. Its purpose was to increase citizens' awareness and exercise of their individual rights, liberties, and duties lest external or internal enemies steal them away (even as the Supreme Court, extending a series of decisions begun in the First World War, maintained limits on the right to free speech, particularly political speech[48]). The campaign also aimed to augment pride in past accomplishments of the United States and enthusiasm for the country's future in order to foster an internationalist stance toward world problems. A streamlined "Freedom Train" carried several key historical documents to 328 cities to spark patriotic interest. Among these documents were a thirteenth-century manuscript of the Magna Carta, a letter by Christopher Columbus on the discovery of America, Thomas Jefferson's rough draft of the Declaration of Independence, George Washington's personal copy of the U.S. constitution, and Abraham Lincoln's draft of the Emancipation Proclamation. The council produced booklets and brochures either for free distribution on the train or to promote its journey.[49] The purpose of the campaign was to "strengthen the nation against the poisonous flood of Communist propaganda from within and without."[50] Among several other intellectuals involved in the Freedom Train campaign, sometime Yale University European history professor Frank Monaghan, who had been the official historian for the 1939 New York World's Fair, played an especially important part as organizer. Monaghan later wrote the official book of the campaign, *Heritage of Freedom*, which explained the significance of the historical documents.[51]

Perhaps an even more striking example of the pervasiveness of cold war thinking was the council's five-year campaign (1952–57) for the Ground Observer Corps, a civilian volunteer operation run by the U.S. Air Force and the Federal Civil Defense Administration from 1949 to 1959 to spot low-flying Soviet bombers that might launch a sneak nuclear attack on the United States. The corps recreated a similar wartime organization formed in the immediate aftermath of the attack on Pearl

Harbor. The air force and civil defense officials aimed at recruiting a corps of five hundred thousand volunteers to spend two hours a week as spotters at 19,400 observation posts in thirty-six states all across the country. Neither these goals of recruitment nor those of establishing "skywatch" posts to observe certain designated zones thought most likely to be used by Soviet bombers were, it seems, ever fully attained, but the nation's actual defense suffered little for the shortfall.[52] Volunteer spotters flooded reporting centers with sightings of planes that turned out to be civilian and commercial transport.[53] Late in 1953, Major General Walter E. Todd, the commander of the Western Air Defense Force, said that the Ground Observer Corps was "useless in peacetime . . . [because of] the deluge of reports of what was obviously friendly air traffic."[54] Although many of its moving spirits and key figures were completely convinced of the imminent danger to the United States from Soviet bombers, the actual function of the corps, and its purpose in some military quarters, was to overcome "public apathy" and mobilize public opinion around the idea of civil defense in order to sustain the enormous military expenditures of the cold war.[55] In particular, the corps helped the newly established U.S. Air Force, made a separate branch of the service only in 1947, sell itself and its mission to the public.[56] In the process, the Advertising Council campaigns relied on strong anti-Soviet themes, as well as scare tactics, including the production of a broadcast called "Bomb Target, U.S.A.," narrated by Arthur Godfrey, who was thought by many contemporaries to be the most trustworthy man in the United States. The campaign's slogan was "Wake Up, Sign Up, Look Up."[57] The council also benefited unexpectedly from this campaign. Its key liaison with the air force was Lieutenant Colonel Robert Keim, then acting as the service's public relations officer. In 1967, Keim became the council's second president.[58]

Cold war thinking, along with its ideological conflicts, also permeated the first and second "American Economic System" campaigns. As originally conceived by a joint committee of the American Association of Advertising Councils and the Association of National Advertisers right at the end of the war, the first campaign aimed at improving public understanding of the U.S. economic system, with a special emphasis on the importance of worker productivity. When reviewed in early 1947 by the Advertising Council's newly formed Public Policy Committee, several committee members objected that the economic philosophy of the proposed campaign was too "laissez-faire" and "right wing Republican," stressing production rather than distribution,[59] an opinion shared by officials of the American Heritage Foundation, which had been expected to bankroll the campaign. Despite dissent from the council's advisors and the initial ambiguity of sponsorship, the McCann-Erickson advertising agency pressed ahead and produced a booklet for the Advertising Council called *The Miracle of America,* which, accompanied by the usual deluge of publicity through planted newspaper articles, billboards, radio and matchbook-cover advertisements, and comic-book blurbs and cartoons, celebrated the virtues of free enterprise.[60] Early on, the campaign was directed toward mobilizing public support for the "American Way of Life" against a possible renewal of New Deal regulatory policies; this phase of the campaign suggests council leaders' attentiveness to the anxiety of its core business constituency, apprehension spurred momentarily by President Truman's surprise victory in the 1948 election. But, as things turned out, Truman's Fair Deal was not the New Deal and, despite considerable labor unrest, the economy did not go into a tailspin after the war. Media interest in the campaign flagged. Moreover, most shipments of *The Miracle of America* were not to individuals, but in bulk to companies presumably for distribution to their employees. Then, the cold war, already well underway, accelerated late in 1948. The campaign became increasingly anti-Communist in tone, particularly after the start of the Korean War in June 1950. Along with the classic wartime arguments for increased productivity in order to fill both military and domestic needs without inflation ("It's Time We Got *Working* Mad"), the council ran advertisements with the themes "This Is the Iron Curtain" and "Ivan Is Watching You," emphasizing that "Stalin and His Gang Respect Just One Thing—Strength."[61] Eventually, the first American Economic System campaign ran aground in 1952 after sharp critiques of its somewhat stridently self-celebratory character, principally from forces to the left of the council.[62]

But, if Scylla loomed on the council's left, Charybdis waited on the right. On 23 and 24 March 1949, Lewis Haney, a professor of economics at New York University and a syndicated columnist, wrote two articles that appeared in the *New York Journal-American* and other Hearst newspapers across the country. Haney charged the Advertising Council's Public Policy Committee with insinuating communistic thinking into the American Economic System campaign, damning among other things the absence from the campaign of explicit references to ethics and religion. Committee members had, as noted earlier, objected to the conservative thrust of the campaign. Haney's articles singled out the chairman of the Public Policy Committee, Evans Clark of the Twentieth Century Fund and later of the *New York Times,* for special abuse because

of some of Clark's past work experiences in the aftermath of the First
World War, which Haney construed as sympathetic to communism.
Haney also had harsh words for *The Miracle of America*, sentiments
echoed in the editorial pages of the *New York Journal-American*, which
called the publication "a misleading leftist booklet."[63] Through Hector
Perrier of the council staff, Charles Mortimer, the chairman of the
council, and Theodore Repplier, its president, were able to discuss the
situation with William Randolph Hearst, Jr., the publisher of the Hearst
newspapers. At the meeting, Mortimer presented Hearst with a letter summarizing the issues that the Advertising Council wished Hearst
to consider, stressing, in particular, the purely advisory character of
the Public Policy Committee. In closing, Mortimer noted the irony of
Haney's attacks:

> The American Economic System campaign was approved by the Coun-
> cil primarily because we believed it would be a powerful factor to com-
> bat communism. We find it somewhat ironical, therefore, that anyone
> on the *Journal-American* should consider the Council associated with
> dangerous left-wing propaganda.[64]

Hearst decided to block a proposed third article by Haney, although the
council had not urged that course of action. *Advertising Age*, which had
been planning a feature on the controversy, dropped its story, and the
matter ended. Somewhat abjectly, however, Evans Clark ended up
defending entirely proper aspects of his past to Charles Mortimer for
any embarrassment the scurrilous newspaper articles might have oc-
casioned council members. Clark wrote in part that

> I have had a growing realization of how references to my youthful ac-
> tivities have been embarrassing—at least to some of you. . . . Thirty
> years ago, I served a few months with the so-called 'Soviet Bureau' in
> New York—a mission sent over by the new government shortly after
> the revolution to promote Russian-American trade. The Bureau had
> nothing to do with political propaganda. Its functions and mine were
> limited to dealing with the steady flow of American businessmen who
> were trying to arrange business contracts with the new Russian gov-
> ernment. . . . I was not then, nor was I before, nor have I been since,
> associated, directly or indirectly, with the communist party. [And] I
> have never been associated with any organization controlled or influ-
> enced by communists.[65]

The ideological currents of the cold war drove even crafts that tried to
stay in the midstream into the shoals.[66]

The second American Economic System campaign emerged in the
midst of the similarly sharp ideological currents of the 1950s. Because

of a perceived threat to America's existence and way of life, indicated by the difficulties in recruiting for the Ground Observer Corps, organizing for civil defense, securing donations of blood, confusion about the Korean War, and the demand for tax reductions that might imperil the nation's military defense, the council began planning in July 1953 for an "Age of Peril" public information program, consisting of five broadcasts by prominent public figures. The program aimed at convincing the public that they faced a "tough, capable and fanatic foe," that the cold war was the "new normalcy," and that only through "endurance" and appropriate civil defense measures could the nation avoid a new world war.[67] Several months later, in early 1954, the council launched the "Future of America" campaign, as it was initially called, emphasizing that "Great Changes Are Bringing Great Opportunities."[68] Then, at the end of 1954, the council's president, Theodore Repplier, long an advocate for business participation in the U.S. international propaganda war, went on a six-month international tour funded by the Eisenhower Foundation.[69] When he returned, he urged both his own organization and other private concerns to become actively involved in overseas propaganda to combat the communist threat.[70] What was needed was a "crusade," something that might stimulate moral "fervor" to combat the "moralistic and idealistic" appeal of communism.[71] In this view, propaganda was simply advocacy writ large. The Advertising Council affirmed its president's view by appointing an Ad Hoc Committee on Propaganda Policy.[72]

The notion of "People's Capitalism," a domestic propaganda effort that paralleled overseas efforts, came from such waters. Originally conceived by Stuart Peabody, the sometime chairman of the Advertising Council's board of directors, People's Capitalism was defined as "a third way of life, differing from communism, and from capitalism as it is thought of in a large part of the world." The United States Information Service (later Agency) solicited the council's help to erect a huge exhibit at Union Station, Washington, D.C., consisting of a house from 1775, complete with a nail-making machine from Republic Steel, a modern ranch house donated by United States Steel Corporation, and exhibits showing social and economic changes in the intervening one hundred eighty years on color transparencies donated by Eastman Kodak. Council leaders actively propagated the notion and the ideology of People's Capitalism. They planted editorials in a number of newspapers, including the *New York Times* through its director Evans Clark; they placed articles and advertisements about the wonders of People's Capitalism in various journals; and they worked hard to produce a television spectacular on the subject, although there is no record of this program's screening. Because they feared a "Made in Madison Avenue" label, council leaders set up a series of round tables at Yale University and enlisted respected intellectuals to write articles in order to give the idea an authoritative and respectable stamp.[73] Evans Clark approached August Heckscher, his successor as head of the Twentieth Century Fund, and persuaded him to bankroll the whole affair. Council leaders secured the commitment of a major publishing house to publish suitable manuscripts that might result from the round tables. They published thousands of digest reports of the first round table and, with a covering letter on Yale University letterhead from Dean Emeritus Edmund Sinnott of the Graduate School, distributed them to libraries, college presidents, heads of social science departments, and deans of liberal arts colleges. Council leaders also widely distributed the digest to the press, various opinion leaders, top officials of public relations firms, business and labor leaders, and the entire membership of the American Economic Association. The United States Information Service distributed several thousand copies of the digest overseas. Finally, council leaders promoted the idea through the endless round of luncheon speeches that mark American civic life and arranged for polls to measure the penetration of the idea into public consciousness, statistics that, of course, became the fuel for the manufacture of still more stories.[74]

Other council campaigns of the time mirrored the self-castigation, often transvalued into rousing exhortation, that is now a prominent feature of much new-middle-class moralism and the advocacy fueled by it. The interminable deadlock of the cold war bred widespread ambiguity and confusion, fertile ground for corrosive self-doubt. The nation itself seemed to drift, rudderless, tossed back and forth by the irreconcilable conflicts endemic to a brawling society, but with no clear direction. The lack of clarity of national purpose created special problems for propagandists. As Theodore Repplier ruefully noted at the end of the 1950s, "the lot of the democratic propagandist is not a happy one." He has "180 million clients breathing down his neck," and can never hope to satisfy even half of them. In particular, the fragmentation and rivalry of government agencies undercut the possibility of thematic unity for one's propaganda. Even an idea like "People's Capitalism [which] alarmed the communists wherever it was used" was promulgated inconsistently or not at all. One obvious solution to increase the effectiveness of American propaganda effort would be to hire an advertising man, a professional who grasps the importance of simplified and coordinated communication. But, Repplier adds that, given "the public image of the advertising man . . . this would be most unwise."[75] The best that one can do is to continue the twilight struggle of persuading those in business that their own self-interests depend on working on behalf of the national weal.[76]

Despite the economic prosperity of the mid-1950s, a time of low inflation and low interest rates, Repplier's unquiet end-of-the-decade mood was widely shared by men and women of affairs, including some of his associates in council circles. To many, the United States seemed peculiarly vulnerable in the face of growing communist might and presumed discipline. In fall 1957, the Soviet Union had shattered the myth of American technological supremacy with its launching of *Sputnik I*, the first manned space satellite, alarming educators and policy-makers alike about presumed deficiencies in American science education programs. The sharp, although brief, recession of 1957 was a reminder of the cyclical nature of prosperity in a capitalist system, even though, by decade's end, the U.S. economy was poised for still greater growth. Moreover, the nation's intractable racial problems embarrassed the United States before the world and provoked growing domestic tensions.

In such a murky era, what does an advocacy organization that sees itself as the conscience of the nation advocate? Does it stick to talking about economic fundamentals, such as the growing national debt, rising taxes, inflation, and agricultural surpluses? Or does it address the presumed lag in scientific education and the dire economic and military implications of scientific illiteracy? Does it enter international political waters to address "missile gaps" or the political turmoil of precariously positioned client states? In February 1960, Repplier argued to his board that, despite the importance of these issues, the council should address the nation's root problem, namely, "a series of American attitudes, the attitudes of a people who have had it too good, too long." Citing Allen Drury, John Steinbeck, and the *Saturday Evening Post*, who variously had condemned shoddy workmanship, the chase for the fast buck, cheating on tests, and rigged quiz shows as evidence of everyday American immorality, Repplier decried America's "current softness and ethical shabbiness," traits especially alarming because the nation was "competing against a pioneering, intelligent, hard-working, and dedicated people." He warned that the 1960s would be "a testing time for America." He urged the Advertising Council to seek funds that would permit it to initiate campaigns on its own since "there is building up in America a restlessness with present standards which could be

harnessed and utilized . . . [since] a good many people are getting fed
up with dishonesty and phoniness and with extreme success
worship . . . weary of status symbols and . . . cynical about cynicism." [77]
Two months later, Repplier proposed a campaign on "American Attitudes." After reviewing earlier council discussions of campaigns on
"excellence," none of which ever materialized, he noted the enthusiastic press and industry reception to his February speech. Then, citing
a widely read *Look Magazine* article called "The Age of Payola," he went
on to attribute even more ills than he had in his earlier speech to America's quick-buck fixation, including mob-controlled gambling, municipal and police graft, income tax fraud, labor movement corruption, and
even the refusal of Mississippi grand juries to indict known murderers
of civil rights workers. He urged that the Advertising Council self-
sponsor a campaign in this area, launching its efforts with its tried and
true mechanism of garnering intellectuals for its round tables. [78]

The board split sharply over Repplier's recommendation. Some members, including the widely experienced industrialist Charles E. Wilson,
former president of General Electric, and Gibson McCabe, publisher of
Newsweek, strongly supported his proposal. Others, led by Leo Burnett,
head of one of the largest and most important advertising agencies,
expressed business's habitual unease about venturing onto always contested moral terrain. Still others wondered whether the campaign
would address the issue of "excellence" or that of "ethics." Others tried
to sidetrack the whole discussion by raising technical problems. But, in
the end, the board authorized Repplier to work out further details with
the council's Industries Advisory Committee. [79]

Because of the internal controversy, council leaders reframed the
campaign into one called "The Promise of America," inverting the appearance of Repplier's original idea while keeping its moralizing thrust.
The campaign had four parts: goals for citizens, confidence in a growing
America, knowledge of our enemy, and changes in our attitudes. [80]
Then, a year later, in response to the new rhetoric of sacrifice pro-
pounded by President Kennedy, the campaign was renamed "Challenge to Americans" and reframed once again in cold war terms. How
can the United States form ties with the "awakening peoples" in developing nations? How can the United States influence and benefit from
burgeoning geopolitical alliances around the world? What must America's educational system do to keep pace with ever-quickening scientific
discovery and technological innovation? How does the United States
confront the menace of communism while containing its own revolu-

tionary experiment in democracy? The widely distributed booklet announcing the campaign argues:

> We have never in our history faced this kind of world-wide struggle—a struggle in which the odds are, in many ways, against a democracy. This is obviously because decisions, instead of being made by twenty highly informed, ruthless communist chiefs, must be made by several hundred representatives of the people, backed by the force of public opinion. No measure opposed by public opinion, however vital, can be enacted. Never has there been so much for the citizen to know, to weigh and balance, to understand; never have the responsibilities of citizenship been so great; never has there been greater risk of wrong decisions, due to lack of information or lethargy. And never has there been more need for each American to do a little better in his own particular niche. If each of us can be a little more knowledgeable, a little more skillful, a little more dedicated, a little more useful as a citizen, the collective effort will be enormous.[81]

In this view, rooted in an eighteenth-century model of democratic politics in a republic, personal morality, defined broadly, assumes global import. The fate of American society's central institutions depends on the individual citizen's self-cultivation, careful sifting of information, and responsible exercise of his or her knowledge and abilities. In 1963, a year after the Challenge campaign was launched, Repplier, claiming that demand for the campaign booklet that "compresses the world struggle into 27 pages" was strong, explicated the reasoning behind the campaign:

> In the 'Challenge' campaign, we are, admittedly, shooting for the moon. We first try to convince our audience that they live in extraordinary times, deserving of extraordinary effort. And then we try to drop ideas into the American thought stream that we hope will flourish; ideas like: study science, learn a language, pursue excellence in whatever you do, watch your ethics, etc., all components which, taken together, make up the value standards or the 'quality' of an American citizen. This is . . . important. For short of a nuclear war, the quality of each side's citizens—their brains, depth of knowledge, excellence, ethics, industry, wisdom, resourcefulness and dedication—may well determine whether the Western world or the communist world eventually wins the cold war.[82]

Indeed, failure to reach for such quality might precipitate political disaster. The fervor and prophetic style of Repplier's remarks, both hallmarks of professional advocacy turned vocational, were his principal legacies to his beloved organization long after the cold war faded in importance. In his farewell report, while noting the nation's "massive and irresistible trend" toward more government bureaucracy, Repplier stressed once again the responsibility of "America's private forces for public good." He urged his colleagues to safeguard the "social invention" of the council, its "complex, painstakingly built system of public information," against bureaucratic encroachments by continuing "always [to] put the country's interests first."[83]

Robert Keim succeeded Repplier as president in 1966. Like his predecessor, he saw the council as the salvation of advertising against its critics.[84] But Keim was not the cold warrior that Repplier was; he turned the council's attention principally to America's domestic problems. Moreover, Keim felt that many of the council's traditionally tame campaigns, such as those on forest fires or traffic safety, while still important, no longer garnered the public attention essential to buttress an industry under constant attack. He felt that the Advertising Council needed, as James W. Young wrote to him, "more fire in the belly."

Advocacy organizations thrive on controversy. Indeed, Robert Keim often said: "Controversy has always been good for the Ad Council. It gives us life." Leaders in any organization can always best mobilize talent, commitment, and notice when they face crises, at least external ones, but controversy provides advocacy groups with special opportunities. Since they trade in moral exhortations, the stuff of persuasive appeals, controversy provides advocates with the arena for telling pronouncements, with the occasion to praise or condemn, and with themes to stir aspiration, longing, empathy, and pity, or indignation, anger, disgust, and rejection.

The social turmoil of American society that began to crest in the late 1960s and early 1970s gave the Advertising Council and its new president a battleground for moral combat on several fronts. In its 1967 report celebrating its twenty-fifth anniversary, the council positioned itself as the organization that addresses "democracy's unfinished business."[85] In conjunction with the Urban Coalition, the council launched its "Crisis in Our Cities" umbrella campaign, stressing that the real crisis was in the nation's spirit and that healing our racially torn cities depended on Americans joining coalitions to provide jobs to chronically unemployed people and educational opportunities to youth from low-income neighborhoods.[86] At the same time, the council "converted the Religion in American Life Campaign to take on the moral response to the urban racial crisis."[87] Council leaders also began to ponder the "student state of mind" and how to address student unrest on college campuses, as well as the growing problem of drug abuse. By 1971, the council had developed entirely independent campaigns to foster minority businesses, to encourage business alliances that create jobs for the unemployed, and to educate youth about the dangers of drugs. That same year marked the beginning of the Advertising Council's longtime advocacy for the United Negro College Fund.[88] The council's rhetoric, for both external and internal audiences, took on somewhat religious-like tones. Its watchwords became "volatility" and "relevancy." And "in a city that's threatening to come apart at the seams in a country whose many cities threaten to do the same," council leaders saw themselves as "roof raisers," lending a helping hand to neighbors in need.[89]

But by 1972, council leaders found themselves at a crossroads, uncertain about their organization's direction or identity. Keim's annual report to the board, entitled "Quo Vadis, Advertising Council?" self-consciously traces—with the same quasi religious overtones of the previous few years—the council's history as a "mirror image of the preoccupations and concerns of America and its people." In the same report, Keim stakes out yet another controversial area for council attention, namely, reform of the nation's prison system, which he argued, is "literally a vast assembly line producing criminals rather than correcting them."[90] Yet the year brought sustained debate within key council forums about the meaning of advocacy for the public interest in a society where advocacy groups had proliferated exponentially. Who, in fact, stands for the public good in a society clamoring with opposing claims? On what basis can the Advertising Council make its own claims? Has the council become too closely identified with the government in the public eye? How can the council maintain its independence from groups seeking its help, including the government, and still be "relevant" and "sensitive" in its choice of campaigns? How should the council address the growing reluctance of the media to support campaigns with "social relevancy?" How does the council clarify the difference between advocacy for action and action by policy-makers in order to avoid blame if the latter is inefficacious? After year-long wrangles, council leaders decided to "revitalize" the Public Policy Committee to include a greater range of perspectives of what, in fact, constitutes the public interest. At the same time, council leaders spent a great deal of time and money scrutinizing the council's self-presentation, particularly its name, logo, and motto, settling eventually on the abbreviated "Ad Council" to accompany all advertisements.[91]

But the leaders of advocacy organizations must always remember their primary constituencies. Even as the Ad Council became immersed

in the social controversies of the early 1970s, one of its longtime supporters, Howard J. Morgens of Procter & Gamble, pointedly reminded
the organization of the interests of the business community.[92] Morgens's powerful voice prompted council leaders to move to the forefront
of the council's agenda a new American Economic System (AES) campaign. Two cognate campaigns had already begun. One encouraged
increased productivity ("There's a New America in the Works" and
"America, It Only Works As Well As We Do").[93] The second, "Whip
Inflation Now" (WIN), conceived and implemented in a hurry at the
request of the new Ford White House, created an enormous imbro-
glio, with the council being accused by a member of Congress of pro-
pagandizing for business.[94] Neither the Congressman nor the chorus of condemning voices he orchestrated acknowledged the council's
recent engagement in the social issues of the day or its attempts to
encourage a greater sense of "social responsibility" in the business
community.

Stung by the Congressman's accusations and somewhat rueful about
the implacability of advocates to its left, whose good graces they
thought they had won, council leaders commissioned Compton Advertising to do extensive research for its new AES campaign with the help
of an initial seed grant from the United States Department of Commerce. The Compton researchers discovered that the public's "economic understanding . . . is incomplete and fragmentary," parochial
and based largely on personal experience, and tied principally to conceptions about "personal freedoms and opportunities for mobility." At
the same time, most Americans interviewed in the mid-1970s study
were unhappy with the state of the economy and looked to government intervention to provide economic solutions, alarming news to
the business community.[95] Given these findings, the Compton copywriters and art directors devised commercials that answered the question, "What's in it for me?" to take advantage of people's personal orientation to economic matters. The advertisements were also to pitch a
free booklet with further information. "Four highly talented writers
with differing economic backgrounds" separately worked on this booklet, grinding it through several drafts. Eventually, two versions were
completed, one with a "factual, academic approach favored by the
Department of Commerce," which was still the Ad Council's principal
sponsor, and the other a "simpler, easier to read treatment but [with]
points of view that might be challenged." Despite some worry that the
"business establishment [might] feel that [the council has] misrepre-

sented its [business's] case," council leaders opted for the booklet favored by the Department of Commerce in order to keep Commerce as its ally.[96] The council produced this booklet with the title "The American Economic System . . . and Your Part In It."

This time, controversy found the council. The AES campaign, launched on 21 April 1976, was disrupted by a counterconference held across the street by the People's Bicentennial Commission (PBC), later called the People's Business Commission, one of many groups that used the U.S. bicentennial's yearlong orgy of national self-celebration to present a leftist critique of America's whole social structure.[97] Two other groups, the Public Media Center and the Public Interest Economic Foundation, joined the PBC in its condemnation of the AES campaign. All three groups demanded equal access to free television time from the Federal Communications Commission under the "fairness doctrine." Allen Ferguson, the head of the Public Interest Economic Foundation, wrote to the Board of Economic Advisors blasting the AES booklet as "blatant propaganda . . . simply by virtue of its apparently purposeful ignoring of the fact that the market distributes income largely in accordance with the initial capital position of the participants." Ferguson wanted statements from members of the Board of Economic Advisors condemning the booklet.[98] The affair quickly gained momentum. The Public Media Center countered the Ad Council's AES booklet with a brochure entitled "If You Think the System's Working—Ask Someone Who Isn't." The major networks tentatively decided not to run the Ad Council's AES commercials. Then Congressman Rosenthal once again pounced on the council, citing top economists who decried the "emptiness" and the "Madison Avenue language" of the Ad Council publication, which "ignore[s] all of our society's economic problems."[99] Finally, the National Broadcasting Company rescinded its earlier tentative decision and ran the Ad Council's AES commercials. But other "public interest groups" filed a new round of petitions with the Federal Communications Commission trying to force television stations to limit their cooperation with national groups like the Ad Council and focus attention on local causes.

In his 1976 annual report to the board, entitled "The Year of the Locusts," a weary Keim discerned in the onslaught against the Ad Council a profound attack on business itself. He wondered, "Have we lost the power to defend ourselves?" Keim then changed the question to, "Have we lost the *will* to defend ourselves?"[100] Advocates typically become lightning rods for resentment against their clients. Advocacy organizations, such as the Advertising Council, that generally try to move their principal constituencies away from parochial interests, invite attack when they attend to those interests. Complexity of purpose is seen as weakness. And constant attacks sow self-doubt in any organization.

〰〰〰〰〰 In the last two decades of the twentieth century, through the organization's golden anniversary in 1992 under the presidency of Ruth A. Wooden, through her retirement in mid-1999 and the accession of Peggy Conlon as president, council leaders continued to cast the organization both as the "mirror that reflects the conscience of American business" and as the "town crier for a nation." [101] Through print, radio, and television and increasingly as one of the leading advertisers on the Internet, the council continues to address major issues in an increasingly contentious society, one facing disturbing, perhaps intractable, problems. [102] Among many other efforts during this period, council leaders have instituted campaigns against drunk driving ("Drinking and driving can kill a friendship"), drug abuse ("Just say no," "Cocaine: The big lie," and, complete with a picture of an egg frying, "This is your brain on drugs"), child abuse ("Words hit as hard as a fist"), illiteracy ("The only degree you need is a degree of caring"), on gender equity in education ("Expect the best from a girl. That's what you'll get"), on racial harmony in the wake of the 1992 riots in Los Angeles, and against environmental pollution ("People start pollution. People can stop it"). In the process of trying to "mak[e] a difference in the fabric of America," [103] the council's work, as well as the considerable amount of independent public service advertising it has inspired, undoubtedly benefits many organizations and many individual men, women, and children. [104]

At the same time, like the Committee on Public Information before it, the Advertising Council has played a decisive part in shaping the contemporary apparatus and ethos of advocacy. Both organizations helped weld business and government interests into a single interinstitutional complex through expertise with mass symbols. Both organizations brought talented men and women of affairs and well-placed intellectuals together into common milieux to debate and to confront vexing national problems, indeed at times burning causes. Both organizations provided the framework within which these key elites worked out most of the techniques and moral rationales for propaganda in a democratic society. Both organizations played a major role in civilizing the vocabularies of American business leaders, making unseemly their all-too-often naked, crass appeals to personal interest. And both organizations helped fill our public arena with highly emotional and moralistic appeals. Public service advertising, whether it advocates support for Liberty Bonds, victory gardens, the Red Cross, or the United Negro College Fund, implicitly divides the world into sheep and goats, into clusters of patriotic or compassionate souls, on one hand, and, on the other, clusters of unconcerned or selfish egoists unmindful of the sacrifice and plight of others. It triggers among those who choose to "do the right thing" self-images of moral superiority complete with self-congratulation, a desirable goal for all advertising and public relations. Advocates always promise some kind of salvation.

Alonzo Earl Foringer, *The Greatest Mother in the World* (1918). Poster. 27.5″ x 20.5″. A Great War *Pietà*. Courtesy of the American Red Cross Museum and the Williams College Museum of Art, anonymous gift, 39.1.148.

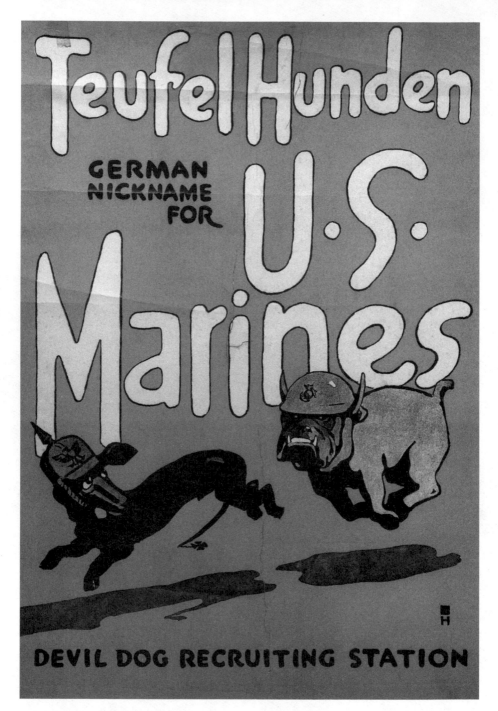

Charles Buckles Falls, *Teufel Hunden* [Devil Dogs] (c. 1918). Vigorous wartime recruiting. Courtesy of the Chapin Library of Rare Books, Williams College.

C. R. Macauley, *Bird of Evil* (1917). From the Macauley cartoon series "America's Spirit in the War," distributed by the Butterfield Syndicate.

C. R. Macauley, *The Trail of the Beast* (1917). Another image of "the enemy" from the series "America's Spirit in the War," distributed by the Butterfield Syndicate.

War Advertising Council, *A Slip of the Lip Will Sink a Ship* (1943). Creating homefront guardians. Courtesy of the Advertising Council.

The way she talks, you'd think she was in Who's Who. Well! I found out what's what with *her*. Her husband own a bank? Sweetie, not even a bank *account*. Why that palace of theirs has wall-to-wall *mortgages!* And that car? Darling, that's horsepower, *not* earning power. They won it in a fifty-cent raffle! Can you imagine? And those clothes! Of course she *does* dress divinely. But really...a mink stole, and Paris suits, and all those dresses...on *his* income? Well darling, I found out about that too. I just happened to be going her way and *I saw Joan come out of Ohrbach's!*

I found out about Joan

Ohrbach's

34ᵀᴴ ST. OPP. EMPIRE STATE BLDG. • NEWARK, MARKET & HALSEY • "A BUSINESS IN MILLIONS, A PROFIT IN PENNIES"

Ohrbach's, *I Found Out about Joan* (1958). Shaping personalities for clients. Courtesy of Orchid Properties, Inc., formerly Ohrbach's, Inc., and DDB Worldwide, Inc.

NO GOOSE

NO GANDER

No refueling stops at Goose Bay, Labrador or Gander, Newfoundland when you fly El Al jet-prop Britannia between New York and London or Paris. It's the only jet-powered airliner that makes it non-stop regularly across the Atlantic. Book El Al Britannia to London, Paris, Rome, Zurich, Athens, Tel Aviv. See your travel agent or **EL AL ISRAEL AIRLINES,** 610 Fifth Ave., New York 20, PLaza 1-7500.

El Al Israel Airlines, *No Goose, No Gander* (c. 1960). Witty integration of words and visuals at its sharpest. Courtesy of El Al Israel Airlines and DDB Worldwide, Inc.

Arnold's Products, Inc., *You Don't Have to Be Jewish to Love Levy's Real Jewish Rye* (1970).
A fond multicultural image. Courtesy of Arnold's Products, Inc., and DDB Worldwide, Inc.
Levy's is a registered trademark of Arnold's Products, Inc.

Alka Seltzer, *Mama Mia, 'Atsa Spicy Meatball* (1970). "Product as hero" to the rescue. Courtesy of Bayer Corporation and DDB Worldwide, Inc.

Or buy a Volkswagen.

Volkswagen makes the 3 highest mileage cars in America: the Rabbit Diesel 5-speed, Rabbit Diesel 4-speed and the Dasher Diesels. Rabbit Diesel 5-speed, est 41 mpg, 55 mpg est. hwy mileage. Rabbit Diesel 4-speed, est 40 mpg, 50 mpg est. hwy Dasher Diesels, est 36 mpg, 46 mpg est. hwy. (Compare these EPA est. to the est. mpg of other cars. Your mileage may vary with speed, weather and trip length. Hwy mileage will probably be less.)

Volkswagen, *Or Buy a Volkswagen* (1979). A simple image offers personal escape from economic crisis. Courtesy of Volkswagen of America, Arnold Communications, and DDB Worldwide, Inc.

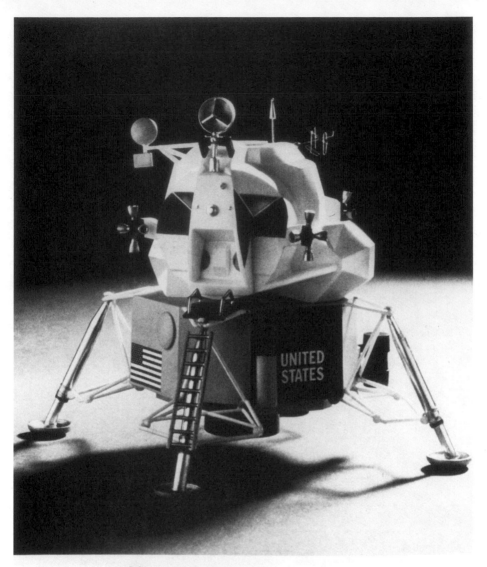

It's ugly, but it gets you there.

Volkswagen, *It's Ugly, but It Gets You There* (1969). Incisive metaphors subvert traditional car advertising. Courtesy of Volkswagen of America, Arnold Communications, and DDB Worldwide, Inc.

PEOPLE HAVE BEEN TRYING TO FIND THE BREASTS IN THESE ICE CUBES SINCE 1957.

The advertising industry is sometimes charged with sneaking seductive little pictures into ads.

Supposedly, these pictures can get you to buy a product without your even seeing them.

Consider the photograph above. According to some people, there's a pair of female breasts hidden in the patterns of light refracted by the ice cubes.

Well, if you really searched you probably *could* see the breasts. For that matter, you could also see Millard Fillmore, a stuffed pork chop and a 1946 Dodge.

The point is that so-called "subliminal advertising" simply doesn't exist. Overactive imaginations, however, most certainly do.

So if anyone claims to see breasts in that drink up there, they aren't in the ice cubes.

They're in the eye of the beholder.

ADVERTISING
ANOTHER WORD FOR FREEDOM OF CHOICE.
American Association of Advertising Agencies

American Association of Advertising Agencies, *Advertising: Another Word for Freedom of Choice* (1986). Advertising for advertising. Courtesy of the American Association of Advertising Agencies.

National Highway Traffic Safety Administration, *Crashing Glasses* (1990). Vintage symbolic inversion. Courtesy of the National Highway Traffic Safety Administration and the Advertising Council.

TAKE A BITE OUT OF CRIME®

National Crime Prevention Council, *McGruff the Crime Dog* (1980). A fictive spokesman who bespeaks credibility. Courtesy of the National Crime Prevention Council.

THE ETHOS OF
ADVOCACY

3 TURNING THE WORLD UPSIDE DOWN

One unintended consequence of the twentieth century's propaganda campaigns in wars hot and cold, as well as in peace, has been the emergence of wary, self-conscious publics, sated with images and increasingly suspicious of image makers. The 1930s attacks on advertising that prompted the formation of the Advertising Council accelerated once again right after the Second World War, followed soon after by attacks on public relations.[1] Criticisms of both fields have continued unabated ever since.[2] The main themes of the attacks are always the same: advertising channels people's desires into a docile acceptance of a spend-for-spending's sake mentality that fuels consumer demand, sometimes manipulating consciousness subliminally. Public relations hoodwinks people into action by mobilizing bandwagons of sentiment or into accepting the status quo by spinning so many plausible interpretations of any given situation that bewilderment produces inertia. By midcentury, image makers faced a new dilemma: How does one reach increasingly incredulous and numbed mass audiences? Does one rely on the traditional number crunching scientific research on consumer preferences and opinions mandated by champions of business rationality, complete with incessant repetition to drill brand names into audiences' memories? Or does one grapple directly with the public's skepticism, self-consciousness, and weariness of images and find new ways to frame mass appeals? The breakthrough came in advertising.

〜〜〜〜〜 Many occupational communities look back in charter-myth-like fashion to halcyon days when demigods brought fire to darkling jobs. Contemporary admen and women see the 1960s as the "creative revolution" in advertising, a period of unparalleled creativity for commercial art when copywriters and commercial artists kicked off the restraints of business rationality. Doyle Dane Bernbach (DDB)[3] advertising agency, established on 1 June 1949, invariably plays Prometheus in such stories. During the years it strode the earth, the agency set all standards for "creativity" in advertising. Most important, it recruited and nurtured scores of interpretive experts, becoming during its heyday a university of sorts for image-making experts with symbols, peopling agencies across the spectrum of advertising agencies with seasoned practitioners. The widely acknowledged creative genius of the agency and the informal leader of the creative revolution in the entire industry was William Bernbach. Bernbach and DDB decisively shaped the ethos of advocacy as we know it today.

Bill Bernbach became such a brilliant morning star of the advertising world that he was able, with the collaboration of other experts with symbols, to reconstruct an unpromising early biography into a foreshadowing of destiny. Bernbach graduated from New York University's School of Commerce, Accounts, and Finance in June 1933. He received a bachelor's degree in commercial science with a major in marketing.[4] In later years, he always claimed to have spent most of his college years focusing on English literature and writing, allowing his interviewers to credit him with a degree in those subjects. He also stressed his writing abilities, identifying himself closely with one of the central crafts in his field. Eventually, sheer journalistic repetition made his English degree official.[5] The discrepancy suggests a typical desire to legitimate one's good fortune and make one's success seem inevitable from the start. In fact, the early part of Bernbach's career seems to have been haphazard and to have been propelled as much by his special gifts of personality that attracted the attention of powerful figures as by his later-to-be-legendary creative talent.

The minor inconsistency also provides a clue to a larger pattern in Bernbach's construction of his biography for the press once he had become famous, reflecting his skill in inventing fictitious identities for products, one of the keys to his later great triumphs. It also provides a clue to the ethos of advertising. Right after graduating from college in the middle of the Great Depression, Bernbach went to work in the mail room at Schenley Distilling Corporation for sixteen dollars a week. According to his own story, dutifully reported in all subsequent press accounts about his origins, he wrote an advertisement for one of Schenley's products, American Cream whiskey, and submitted it to Schenley's advertising agency, Lord & Thomas. The agency published one of them without change in the *New York Times*. At the urging of Schenley's president's secretary, a woman who had befriended him, Bernbach went to Lord & Thomas to retrieve the longhand letter he had sent with the ad copy in order to prove his authorship. A secretary there noticed that he was carrying a book by Kahlil Gibran. She, too, was a devotee of the Syrian American romantic poet, and she retrieved Bernbach's letter from Lord & Thomas's files. As the story goes, this led to Bernbach's hasty promotion to Schenley's advertising department.

Such an heroic tale, embellished over the years, is probably apocryphal. Bernbach reports no specifics of the purported advertisement for American Cream whiskey in any extant version of the story, an uncharacteristic silence where his advertising triumphs are at issue. Bernbach may have worked in Schenley's advertising department, since he recounts in one interview the resentment of the department's head, a Mr. Greenlee, at having a college boy thrust upon him.[6] But the experience is never described in greater detail.

Bernbach, it seems, was rescued from Schenley in 1939 by Grover A. Whalen. Whalen, who styled himself "Mr. New York," was the former commissioner of the New York City Police Department and a widely experienced businessman. He was chairman of the board of Schenley during much of the 1930s and then left the corporation to assume fulltime duties as president of the New York World's Fair, which had been in the making since 1936 and opened formally on 30 April 1939.[7] Bernbach seems to have been a factotum for Whalen. Later, he described his perception of his relationship with Whalen:

> And he was a dear friend; he was grateful for whatever help I gave him; he was just wonderful to Evelyn [Bernbach, his wife] and me. I was a, you know, a green kid. And he took me on my first plane ride, down to Washington, to be with him, and taught me the ropes. We'd walk into the Carlton Hotel down there, and he'd give me $5 and say, 'Now, Bill, what you do is get quarters for these now, because we're going to need quarters for tips and so on.' And so I learned the ways. You know, I didn't have that kind of experience.
>
> So we grew very, very close, and until the day he died, I defended him in newspapers. . . . He never had a party or an affair without Evelyn or me, and we were just kids compared to them.
>
> That's why I was so loyal to him; he never forgot that I played a part in his affairs, a useful one.[8]

Whalen, however, does not mention Bernbach in his autobiography.

Bernbach's actual role at the fair is also murky. The "Voice of the Fair," and its chief publicist from 1936 to 1940, was Yale University European history professor Frank Monaghan, later a chief organizer of the "Freedom Train" campaign sponsored by the Advertising Council. Bernbach claimed that he got experience in ghostwriting occasionally when Monaghan was away and eventually ended up writing all of Grover Whalen's speeches, as well as speeches for prominent civic dignitaries visiting the fair. There is no sure way of assessing the accuracy of Bernbach's claims about the extent of his speech ghostwriting; ghosts are meant to be invisible. Bernbach also claimed to have coauthored a book on the history of fairs with Frank Monaghan. The two editions of Monaghan's pamphlet on the history of fairs do not mention, let alone credit, Bernbach. Moreover, the pamphlet was first published in 1938, presumably before Bernbach worked at the fair.[9]

The New York World's Fair closed in 1940. Whalen went on to work in the fashion industry as well as in civil defense during the Second World War. Monaghan, thoroughly weary of the fair, was offered a job by the advertising agency of Batten, Barton, Durstine and Osborn to be the historical consultant on the radio program *Cavalcade of America*, sponsored by DuPont.[10] Neither man took Bernbach with him. After a painful year of unemployment, unaccounted for in subsequent public interviews, Bernbach, now thirty years old, talked his way into a job at the newly formed (1941) Weintraub advertising agency. Bernbach's heroic version of the story in later years again highlights his writing ability. He claims that he went to see Bill Weintraub, who was "taken" with him. But Weintraub told Bernbach that he had other men applying for the copy job that Bernbach wanted. Bernbach said that he told Weintraub, "Well, I have no experience. . . . I don't know why I should have the job; I don't even know if I'm equipped," forgetting, it seems, the experience he claimed to have had working at Schenley's advertising department, ghostwriting scores of speeches during the fair, and coauthoring a book. But, according to Bernbach's narrative, Weintraub insisted that he write a letter anyway. He did write the letter, and Weintraub hired him over two men with big-agency experience.[11]

At Weintraub, Bernbach's self-creation and self-promotion received an enormous boost. He was lucky to meet Paul Rand, who had joined the agency as head of art direction. Rand was an important transmitter of European modernism to the United States, an admirer of Paul Klee, and a student of George Grosz. A leading pioneer of simple, straightforward, witty, and dynamic graphic art, Rand was thoroughly steeped in

Europe's already well-developed use of visual art for commercial purposes, an approach that relied on bold framing with color or white space. This contrasted sharply with American reliance on verbal images and the corresponding occupational dominance of copywriters over commercial artists. Bernbach claims to have worked closely with Rand on campaigns for, among other clients, Lee Hats and Dubonnet. Rand was such a notable graphic designer that, contrary to all practice before and since, he actually signed his advertisements; later he taught graphic design at Yale University and wrote several memoirs. Bernbach claims that he "helped Paul with some books he was writing," and Rand does briefly acknowledge Bernbach in the preface to his first book, although not in his subsequent works.[12] It was Rand who schooled Bernbach in the virtues of crisp visual images, in how to frame ideas as pictures. Moreover, it was Bernbach's own fruitful professional association with Rand that became the prototype of the workplace innovation later attributed to Bernbach, the pairing into teams of copywriters and commercial artists.

After a brief stint in the U.S. Army spent stateside during the Second World War and subsequent work at a small retail promotion outfit, Bernbach became a copywriter at Grey Advertising, then as now seen as an account-driven rather than a creative agency. The association seems to have embarrassed Bernbach in later years, probably because others saw Grey as stodgy, and he buried the connection whenever possible. But he did well at Grey, pitching and winning several major accounts. While there, he worked closely with commercial artist Bob Gage, producing several noted advertisements for Ohrbach's department store, an account that later launched his fame. Bernbach eventually rose to the position of vice president in charge of copy and art and came to know Ned Doyle, a vice president of business accounts. Bernbach and Doyle shared a disdain for the mannered courting of clients typical of all advertising agencies at the time. They also shared an appreciation for judging the merits of individual advertisements apart from the tangled, often incestuous, personal relationships between clients and agency staff. Doyle had worked at *Look* with Maxwell Dane, who had come to New York from Cincinnati years before to make a career in advertising but ended up doing mostly public relations work in various companies. Dane finally started his own small advertising agency in 1944.

Such personal ties are typical and crucial in an industry where associations forged through work histories coupled with compatible personal sensibilities have decisive organizational consequences. Indeed, in the U.S. business world such personal associations matter far more than personal genius. Here they led to the founding of DDB. Dane brought his core cluster of accounts with him, complemented by a few clients recruited by Doyle and Bernbach, along with the Ohrbach account. Bernbach also brought along his collaborator, Bob Gage, and Phyllis Robinson, a talented copywriter. Gage pioneered the use of first-rate New York photographers for print shoots, complete with their high-key lighting techniques that highlight one side of a subject while dramatically shadowing the other. Gage later used photographers to film commercials instead of relying on Hollywood cameramen. Together, Doyle and Dane adroitly managed the growing business fortunes of DDB until their retirements, Doyle in 1969 and Dane in 1971. It was, however, Bill Bernbach who received credit for creating DDB's distinctive organizational ethos.

〰〰〰 Historically, advertising agencies mirrored the bureaucratization of their industrial masters by segmenting and specializing the work tasks of account executives, research and marketing groups, media researchers and placement specialists, and "creative" personnel. Depending on the "mix" of accounts in an agency, different kinds of specialization gained ascendancy both between and within these main divisions. These included specialization of work groups by type of product, expertise with certain media, or experience in certain kinds of markets. Many of these differentiations remain in place today. "Creative" work was also largely segmented. Typically, copywriters received their "unique selling proposition," derived from "scientific research," directly from a board consisting of account executives, research staff members, and a liaison creative executive. Working within these pre-established frameworks, the writers produced the copy body and headlines for the advertisement and handed these over to the "bullpen" of commercial and graphic artists who tacked on the visuals for the ad.

In this system, account and research people invariably held the upper hand in an agency because they framed and paced the whole process of ad making. Moreover, they were able to claim both scientific legitimacy and the virtues of rational organization to worried clients who held the purse strings.

In a bold organizational stroke as creative head of the new agency, Bernbach fused copywriting and visual image making, requiring writers and selected artists to work together in teams of two during the entire idea gestation period. The bullpen remained the locus for the pasteup, engraving, and touch-up work that preceded printing and a training ground for young artists, and the everyday management of accounts remained in the hands of account executives in order to insulate creative teams from clients' incessant importuning. But Bernbach gave the creative teams firsthand access to whatever information they needed about a client or his products before they began fashioning images. Knowledge gained from research and marketing strategy were still crucial components of the advertising. But suddenly the "creatives"—copywriters and artists, the latter renamed "art directors"—had the upper hand in framing the direction and content of their work.[13] Further, art directors were now central, and very often lead, players in shaping advertising.

Within the framework of this workplace innovation, Bernbach stamped DDB's work with his own homespun philosophy of communications. His speeches are repetitive versions of the same basic ideas. Reporters who worked the advertising industry beat referred to all of his presentations as "The Speech," a cobbled-together mélange that belied its own call for "freshness," and one can readily discern the nub of his thinking as he articulated it publicly. Bernbach spoke in a world where the time-honored rules of advertising mandated the quantitative assessment of appeals to self-interest to sell products to consumers. It was assumed that consumers would logically and inevitably put their own selfish interests first if encouraged by the ceaseless hammering of slogans.[14] Bernbach sets the "dilemma of the communicator" in modern society more sharply and strikingly than anyone else of his time. He first poses the question:

> Our problem as communicators is: How do you satisfy all people? How do you reconcile the tremendous diversity of opinion in our world? How do you communicate with people whose environments conditioned them to believe, sometimes violently, in opposite philosophies?[15]

More specifically, he argues that there are two "walls" that the effective communicator has to penetrate. The first is the sheer din of troubling events in modern society.

> Why should anyone look at your ad? The reader doesn't buy his magazine or tune in his radio and TV to see and hear what you have to say. What brand of vanity or indifference leads an advertiser to believe that he can, so to speak, sit alongside world-shaking events like the Berlin crisis and the armaments race and even be noticed? Your reader is confronted daily with history-making news. His papers are full of sensationalism. The shocking news item is becoming a regular part of his news diet. With this deafening roar of frightening conflict beating

about his ears, how do we expect him to hear our advertising story? How are we going to pierce this wall around him—this wall of violence?[16]

The second wall is the little world each individual creates for himself. One of Bernbach's favorite stories was that of Hermie Stern (in some versions spelled Yermie), a "real gangster type," a boss excited by the marketing prospects of a new entertainment gadget. The morning that Hermie and his sales manager were to begin an important road trip to demonstrate the device, the sales manager failed to show at the appointed hour. Hermie grew more impatient with each passing minute. Finally, the sales manager telephoned. Hermie listened and then slammed the phone down, saying: "Son of a bitch. Everything happens to me. His father died." Bernbach goes on to say that

> In this true story of Hermie lies the beginning of all communication wisdom. Everyone feels that he is the center of the universe. He is the most important person in the world and nothing, but nothing, interests him as much as himself. You begin to communicate with him, you get his attention, when what you say has value for him. . . . Our own more sophisticated and civilized environments might have restrained us from his outburst. But deep down inside of us our little souls would gently nudge into our consciousness the same question in Hermie's mind: 'What the hell am I going to do now?'[17]

It is little wonder, in Bernbach's view, that 85 percent of all advertisements are ignored completely: they fail to penetrate people's little worlds and have little chance of being heard, let alone noticed.

How, then, does one reach individuals in a mass audience? Clearly, "facts are not enough." The real "giants" are poets, men who jump off the springboard of facts into the world of imagination ("Rules are what the artist breaks; the memorable never emerged from a formula"). Despite the claims of his many research-obsessed occupational colleagues, Bernbach never tired of arguing that science cannot help the mass communicator penetrate the walls surrounding men and women in modern society; science can only tell us how the world is, not how to change it. Neither are mere eye-catching gimmicks the full answer, although provoking attention underlies all communication: "The truth isn't the truth until people believe you; and they can't believe you if they don't know what you're saying; and they can't know what you're saying if they don't listen to you; and they won't listen to you if you're not interesting. And you won't be interesting unless you say things freshly, originally, imaginatively."[18] Audiences always notice the unusual, just as Bernbach's little son, watching his father shave, was entranced by the mend on his father's boxer shorts. "People remember the mend. The rough spot when everything else is smooth." Only the artistry of "pointed talent and intelligence," of "imaginative, original craftsmen" can get people to see a message and remember it. Only communications that exude "freshness" and "vitality" will penetrate consciousness at all.[19]

Moreover, only those messages that appeal to the "unchanging instincts and emotions of people" will move them to action. Bernbach argues that "[A]t the heart of an effective creative philosophy is the belief that nothing is so powerful as an insight into human nature, what compulsions drive a man, what instincts dominate his action, even though his language so often camouflages what really motivates him."[20] Overanalyzing a situation in a logical way sterilizes an idea: "*Logic* is not the answer. It is rather an insight into human nature. For if you know a man's compulsions, his basic instincts, his drives, you can touch him at the core of his being."[21] And what is this "human nature?" People's "basic, unchanging instincts" are their "obsessive drive to survive, to be admired, to succeed, to love, to take care of their own." "The fragile structure of logic fades and disappears against the emotional onslaught of a hushed tone, a dramatic pause, and the soaring excitement of a verbal crescendo," Bernbach explains. In this view, the wellsprings of human action are primal, if not primitive, often dark, and usually irrational; the notion that the crass positivism that often passes as science in advertising and marketing can tap those deep currents is fatuous. Only the magic of artistry can plumb such waters—"I can put down on a page a picture of a man crying, and it's just a picture of a man crying. Or I can put him down in such a way as to make you want to cry. The same research, virtually the same picture, but one will work and one won't work. The difference is artistry—the intangible thing that business distrusts."[22] Bernbach never tires of quoting towering scientists like Einstein or artists like Shakespeare, claiming that their greatest creative breakthroughs were "unforecastable," a quality of their creativity with which he deeply identifies. The main lesson he draws is the importance of intuition. He warns constantly about "intellectuality getting in the way," often telling a story about two carrier pigeons, one trained that flew in circles, and the other untrained that flew directly home.[23] By posing a clash between business rationality and creative artistry, Bernbach put a premium on doing work that turned the world of advertising upside down.

Such an emphasis on symbolic inversion became the hallmark of a great deal of DDB work during the 1950s and especially the 1960s, when unconventionality became conventional. For instance, DDB often ran advertisements that did not picture the product being hailed, although, in accordance with strict Bernbach admonitions, the concept of the advertisement emerged directly from the product. Thus, when the large fuel tanks of El Al Israel Airline's Bristol Britannia jet-prop airplanes allowed the airline to bypass refueling stops at Goose Bay, Labrador, or Gander, Newfoundland, where rival airlines had to stop, DDB ran an ad featuring a goose and a gander walking in opposite directions and the words "No Goose, No Gander." The same campaign had an advertisement of Noah standing on the bow of his ark watching the animals enter two-by-two. The tag line was: "We've been in the travel business a long time." Also, the agency at times cited a weakness or flaw in a product, something normally never done, as a way of dramatically pointing out compensating virtues. One need only recall the advertisement for Volkswagen, presenting not the dumpy Beetle, but the equally odd-looking lunar module on the moon's surface with the line: "It's ugly, but it gets you there." Or one might recall the famous Avis advertisements that not only admit the company's subordinate ranking to Hertz, but turn it into a strength: "Avis can't afford dirty ashtrays. . . . When you're not the biggest in rent a cars, you have to try harder." Similarly, DDB tread on taboo ground with its advertisement for El Al Israel Airlines when the company initiated jet-prop service that reduced flying time to Europe. The ad shows nothing but the Atlantic Ocean, normally a source of considerable anxiety for air travelers, but with a corner of the watery expanse torn off. The accompanying tag line read: "Starting Dec. 23 the Atlantic Ocean will be 20% smaller." Later, DDB made Heinz ketchup's slow-pouring thickness, an apparent disadvantage, into its greatest merit in comparison with other watery brands.

Instead of kindling brand loyalty, the classical approach to marketing, Bernbach and DDB stressed fashioning personalities for products so that customers could bond emotionally with them. DDB took Ohrbach's, a value-oriented rival of the more famous Macy's department store, and transformed it in the public eye into a mecca of low prices and high fashion by surrounding its name with superior graphic techniques and brittle humor that appealed to self-conscious consumers who appreciate irony. One ad depicts a man in a business suit carrying a woman under one arm, with the tag line, "Liberal trade-in: Bring in your wife and just a few dollars . . . we will give you a new woman." Another has a pretty, but exceedingly plump girl crammed into hot pants with the tag line, "It's in, but maybe you shouldn't be in it." There were also gossipy, clever ads, like that of a cat sporting a fashionable bonnet and cigarette-in-holder announcing, "I found out about Joan" (that is, saw her coming out of Ohrbach's). DDB also infused Utica Club, an unknown upstate New York beer with the aura of an old-time, handmade brew. Its mottos, "Our beer is 50 years behind the times (and we're proud of it)" and "I sometimes wonder if it pays to make beer this way," came complete with pictures of men with handlebar mustaches and bowler hats standing with nickel steins of beer and munching free lunches. One advertisement also had two old-fashioned beer steins, each with human features, facing each other while one was being filled with Utica Club. The motto was "Any mug can taste the difference." Later, DDB took Rheingold, an undistinguished but big-selling New York City beer, and through extremely popular Miss Rheingold contests featuring local beauties, as well as through pictures of people from ostensibly different ethnic groups drinking together, convinced many people that "We must be doing something right." The agency humanized a thoroughly mechanized and labor-exploitative industry by inventing "Juan Valdez" who picked coffee beans one at a time and "wash[ed] them in fresh mountain water" for the Federation of Coffee Growers of Colombia. To advertise Polaroid, the agency used celebrities as varied as Garry Moore, Steve Allen, Jack Paar, Johnny Carson, Candice Bergen, Louie Armstrong, Jane Fonda, Danny Kaye, and Sir Laurence Olivier. DDB also made Polaroid's instant pictures synonymous with remembrance, using intensely emotional scenarios such as the "Visit to Grandpa" that plays on the universal human desire to stop time in the shadow of death ("I used to think I could stop the earth, and hold time in my hands. But I watched it as it raced on by me, heading for tomorrow. So when this day is over, and the sun leaves the sky, let me see all the memories while they're clear in my eye. Let me reach out and touch all the faces and places that I love so much. Especially the people I love so much"). And DDB transformed Chivas Regal, a generic scotch, into an upscale whiskey ("Give dad an expensive belt," that is, of "the Chivas Regal of Scotches"). The extent to which a great many people still think of Alka Seltzer when they have eaten too much spicy food ("Mama mia, 'atsa spicy meatball"), or conjure up fond, multicultural images when they see Levy's "real" Jewish rye bread ("You don't have to be Jewish . . . ,") accompanied by images of an African American child or an American Indian enjoying a slice, or immediately think of the restless strength of a lion roaming Wall Street canyons when they see the name Dreyfus Fund is a measure of Bernbach's and DDB's success in making inanimate objects and impersonal organizations live and breathe.

Until the early 1970s, Bernbach personally approved every advertisement that DDB's creative teams produced, meeting informally with his art directors and copywriters in his office while answering scores, sometimes hundreds of phone calls a day. He seems to have been extraordinarily effective in this kind of intimate context, dispensing his wisdom and experience in a sometimes kindly, sometimes severe, always paternal manner. He set exacting criteria for work and rewarded those who met them with his approval. Indeed, he established an emotionally laden framework that made such approval contingent on creatives' internalization of his own standards. His possible disapproval of or disappointment in advertisements presented to him caused his creatives to objectify their work ruthlessly, anticipating what Bernbach might perceive as weaknesses.

Bernbach had a sure eye for great headlines, whatever their origin. For instance, when told by the chief of Olin Mathieson that he wished to shorten the company's name simply to Olin, Bernbach immediately said, "I've got the ad. 'Call me by my first name.'" Again, a copywriter assigned to the Chivas Regal account complained that Sam Bronfman, the CEO of Schenley, had changed Chivas Regal's bottle from dark green to clear in order to show off the liquor's pale amber color and catch the consumer wave toward "lite" alcoholic beverages: "What idiot changed the Chivas Regal bottle?" Bernbach countered, "That's the headline!"[24]

But Bernbach was uninterested in the actual working out of details.[25] He helped creatives frame an idea, exercising his adroit editorial skills to insist that everything be reduced to its simplest form before one added anything. After that, he became restless and impatient to move on to the next project. He wrote virtually no copy and left all details to his talented subordinates. He always claimed credit in public for his charges' finished work, as if he himself had actually executed the advertisements. But he did sell his creatives' ads to clients with passion and conviction. His creatives were delighted at his ability to sell their work. They were simultaneously pleased to have their work placed on "his" reel for showing at his public appearances and resentful that their anonymity fueled his glory. Many found such appropriation of credit disturbing,[26] especially as Bernbach reconstructed his own biography more vigorously as he grew older, altering not only minor details like the nature of his bachelor's degree but the meaning of his relationships with a wide variety of people. His stories about himself and the early days of DDB became weightier, and Bernbach himself emerged as a serious figure whose creative "genius" seemed foreordained.[27] In later tributes, several distinguished advertising practitioners referred publicly to Bernbach as their "father," perhaps the only term that adequately captures their profound affection for the man as well as their struggle against his domination of them.

The story of *Bill Bernbach's Book* sheds some light on the problem of image and substance in Bernbach's life and work. Several famous advertising figures of the day, including Bernbach's rivals David Ogilvy and Rosser Reeves, had written widely popular books on advertising that attracted business to their firms. Several publishers approached Bernbach, one of the first inductees into the Copywriters' Hall of Fame, to do a book on advertising. Eventually, in 1974, Bernbach accepted an advance and signed a contract with a major publisher. He told an interviewer that Brendan Gill had found his ideas for his book "very exciting" and that it was Gill's enthusiasm that had finally persuaded him to agree to write the book.[28] The book, eagerly awaited by friends, colleagues, and rivals on Madison Avenue,[29] dragged on for several years, though whenever Bernbach was asked about its progress he is said to have always responded with great enthusiasm that all was well. Those who knew how little copy Bernbach had actually written over the years had their doubts. Aphorisms and headlines, after all, are concepts, and not the hard work of actual writing. Others felt that Bernbach was faced with an impossible task. All the books on advertising, including those by Reeves and Ogilvy, focused on the rules for advertising, a tailor-made approach for the kind of book widely read in business circles; Bernbach's and DDB's whole approach consisted of inverting the rules.[30]

Bernbach had no book to write. He had only a few core ideas distilled into "The Speech," sayings that he honed over the years, and an admiration for great thinkers in whose number he counted himself. Still, he sustained the illusion of working on his book until he died, even writing a dedication that echoes the exhortation of James Webb Young that led to the founding of the Advertising Council:

> We in the communications field—in radio, in television, in magazines, in newspapers, in posters—have developed unprecedented skills in mass persuasion. You and I can no longer isolate our lives. It just won't work. What happens to society is going to affect us with ever-increasing rapidity. The world has progressed to the point where its most powerful force is public opinion. And I believe that in this new,

complex, dynamic world it is not the great book or the epic play, as once was the case, that will shape that opinion, but those who understand mass media and the techniques of mass persuasion. The metabolism of the world has changed. New vehicles must carry ideas to it. We must ally ourselves with great ideas and carry them to the public. We must practice our skills in behalf of society. We must not just believe in what we sell. We must sell what we believe in. And we must pour a vast energy into these causes.

After Bernbach died, Bob Levenson, his disciple, put out a glossy coffee-table volume, complete with Bernbach's dedication, well-known sayings, and DDB's best ads. The book is called *Bill Bernbach's Book*.[31] But Bernbach's failure to write his own book matters only because he insisted on presenting himself to others as a writer. Instead, he was a master of the memorable aphorism. Examples of his epigrammatic skill abound: "If your advertising goes unnoticed, everything else is academic," "It's not just what you say that stirs people. It's the way that you say it," "A great ad campaign will make a bad product fail faster. It will get more people to know it's bad," "The magic is in the product," "Our job is to bring the dead facts to life," "There are few things more destructive than an unsound idea persuasively expressed," and "In this very real world, good doesn't drive out evil. Evil doesn't drive out good. But the energetic displaces the passive."

This ability to clarify and distill the best of his occupational community's craft wisdom made Bernbach a symbol of intelligence and thoughtfulness in an occupation decried for the absence of such virtues. He was the adman's adman. Moreover, by almost any measure Bernbach was a great organizational leader of the creative end of the advertising business, at least until his last years. He instinctively recognized good ideas when he saw them and, unlike most people in most occupational worlds, he was never afraid of big ideas. He recognized, nurtured, honed, inspired, and rewarded people with talent. He had an extraordinarily sharp editorial eye, exceptionally high standards, and the personal charisma and sheer nerve to bind truly creative men and women together into working teams and, by the force of his personality, make them want to please him. In one of the later innumerable tributes to him, Levenson said, "What the man did was to invent the wheel of persuasion. He could explain us to ourselves."[32] His constantly asserted and jealously guarded reputation as a "great creative" was crucial to his most important role—that of great salesman who continually mustered the enthusiasm and conviction to sell his creatives' work to the firm's clients. If Bill Bernbach, great creative that he was assumed to be, had approved creative work, clients had every reason to believe that the advertising was on target. These remarkable gifts of pithy insight, personal leadership, and salesmanship, not his own writing abilities, were the keys to the enormous success that Bernbach and DDB achieved in the occupational world of advertising.

Indeed, DDB was called the "University of Bernbach" because it cultivated refined advertising skills and because it was so regularly raided for talent by other agencies. In a world where massive turnover is normal, a lot of creatives who left DDB eventually came back. A retrospective in 1982 named nearly one hundred agency employees who had returned to DDB after working in other agencies. DDB's longtime policy of redeploying rather than firing creative personnel when accounts "walked" undoubtedly drew many back, although that policy began to crumble under the economic vicissitudes of the middle and late 1970s. Most of the returnees, however, cited the collegial environment that Bernbach had created as their reason for returning. At least in its heyday, the agency refused to do speculative work, that is, organized intra-agency competition between creative teams. "Spec" work, also called "gangbangs" and "shoot-outs," produces ads that never run in order to win an account from a client, in effect a bet of hundreds of thousands of dollars with relatively short odds.[33] Nor did DDB do backup campaigns on a regular basis, feeling that these were a waste of time and talent; the point was to get it right the first time. Both practices set DDB apart from other agencies and made it a uniquely inviting workplace.

〰〰〰 The advertising industry's sense for the moment caused the "creative revolution," launched by Bernbach and DDB and disseminated by DDB emissaries, to spread rapidly. By the end of the 1960s, virtually all advertising agencies utilized the pairing of writers and art directors into creative teams instituted by Bernbach. The striking visuals of the best DDB ads, their often raucous humor, and especially their witty, self-conscious irony were appreciated by audiences across the land because the advertisements engaged people's intelligence, made them stop, look, and think, and often made them laugh at themselves. The advertisements were also widely appreciated by other creatives. First, they embodied a double consciousness about advertising valued by creatives, themselves a skeptical, ironic bunch. In an advertisement for itself, one DDB ad headlined a quote from its first client, N. M. Orhbach: "I got a great gimmick. Let's tell the truth." Second, stylish DDB ads adorned creatives' bulletin boards in agencies all across the country both as decoration and inspiration. And under pressure from clients who wanted the fame that DDB had given their rivals, the entire occupational community strove to emulate the "DDB look," sometimes with great success. Take as an example the riveting series of early commercials for Federal Express by Ally & Gargano, all with a theme still in use through the late 1990s. In one commercial, a bully boss pointedly reminds a timid executive that he is responsible for getting materials to a next-day meeting in a distant city, an assignment the now-cowering underling had completely forgotten. But FedEx's overnight delivery service saves the situation and the executive. In offering rescue from blame-time, and salvation from chumpdom and humiliation inflicted by overbearing superiors, the ads epitomize not only how advertising makes products into heroes but simultaneously caricatures the bureaucratic masters it serves.

As the creative revolution gained momentum, a clear split between traditional "account" agencies on the right of a continuum and new "creative" agencies on the left developed within the industry, even as all advertising workplaces were being reorganized to stimulate greater creativity. Ad makers' perception of different types of agencies is central to their occupational prestige system. From the days when Alfred D. Lasker, the renowned philanthropist and art collector, hired Claude Hopkins to do copywriting for the fabled Lord & Thomas agency,[34] advertising had always sold itself as a scientific enterprise wholly dedicated to selling clients' wares, a theme echoed repeatedly in the memoirs of several of the industry's leading practitioner-advocates.[35] Advertising's bread and butter has always been, and still remains, the lucrative accounts of firms like Procter & Gamble, General Foods, and Philip Morris that make highly standardized packaged products such as soaps, sodas, detergents, bleaches, cereals, flours, biscuits, and snacks. Packaged-goods work consists principally of inventing differences between very similar commodities, fashioning an individual identity for the product, and then stimulating brand loyalty. It relies on extensive marketing research, both to identify the target audience and, through surveys or focus groups, to elicit the key bases of consumer identification with one product rather than another, often articulated by consumers who recycle advertising slogans from previous campaigns. Some packaged-goods accounts, such as cigarette advertising (work that was prized until tobacco's legal travails in the 1990s), require technical virtuosity in symbolic inversion. But for the most part, such accounts depend on the hard sell, aggressively pushing products through repetitive and often loud advertisements. Moreover, most packaged-goods clients have large internal marketing divisions that map out strict guidelines for their advertising agencies, complete with monitoring of agency work. Agency account managers who supervise large packaged-goods accounts spend most of their time "servicing" clients, that is, interacting with their opposite numbers in the client's hierarchy, "holding the client's hand," and conveying clients' expectations to the agency's creative staff, who sometimes never even meet the clients. Few advertising agencies can survive without the cash flow that packaged-goods accounts provide. But the more packaged-goods accounts an agency has, the larger and more internally powerful are its account managers who, after all, keep clients happy by doing the hard people-work of the business. In an "account" agency, account managers frame creative work from its beginnings by enforcing the marketing parameters the client desires; they "throttle" work in its cradle if they feel it will not be to the client's liking; and they veto finished work even before it is presented to the client.

But, beginning with DDB, art directors and copywriters gained, and still hold, the upper hand in several agencies. "Creative" agencies, as they are called, are typically smaller, less hierarchical organizations than the giant agencies that depend principally on packaged goods. Creative agencies specialize in making famous previously unknown products or organizations, as DDB did with Sara Lee cakes ("Everybody doesn't like something; but nobody doesn't like Sara Lee"), or in refurbishing the reputations of industry laggards, as DDB did with Avis ("We try harder"), or in transforming commodities into specialty items, as Scali, McCabe & Sloves did in transforming an everyday commodity selling for nineteen cents a pound into Perdue "premium" chicken that now goes for sixfold that amount. In large part because of such highly visible successes, the notion of "creativity" acquired great caché in the advertising world, with the work emanating from creative agencies becoming the industry ideal. Year after year, for instance, creatives at DDB and at other agencies that emulated it garnered the top peer-judged prizes for art direction and copywriting in competitions, complete with annual extravaganzas run by industry and guild associations. In a relatively small occupational community where everyone watches everyone else, such awards translate almost immediately into greater salary, occupational mobility, and say-so. Moreover, top creatives promulgated and were often able to enforce a definition of workaday symbolic work on standardized products as "hack" work, even though most advertising legerdemain was exercised on just such products.

Within such a framework, "creativity" often became an end in itself with practitioners reaching for striking commercials to gain peer accolades, even if the advertisements were wholly unrelated to the products that they advertised or to the consumers who used those products. Bernbach preached on the subject ("Today everybody is talking 'Creativity,' and, frankly, that's got me worried. I fear lest we keep the good taste and lose the sell. I fear all the sins we may commit in the name of 'Creativity.' I fear that we may be entering an age of phonies"[36]). But even Bernbach himself, who insisted that all creative ideas emerge directly out of the product, sometimes got things entirely wrong, demonstrating just how chancy "creative" advertising can be. DDB once had the account of Seagram's Lord Calvert whiskey. Bernbach called the creatives working on the account into his office and showed them Lord Calvert's heavy, thick bottle displayed on a glass table. He told them: "That bottle says class. It's a classy product. Make some upscale ads to sell it." The creatives dutifully produced a series of preliminary advertisements featuring "Lord" Calvert, complete with burgundy velvet attire and sword. But a Seagram official got a peek at the preliminary work and cautioned the creatives that a remarkable percentage of Lord Calvert's sales were in deep rural Georgia. The creatives flew south to meet with heavy Lord Calvert drinkers. These men, all in blue jeans, work shirts, straw hats, and three-day beards, gave reasons different than were supposed for their brand loyalty. The heavy bottle, they explained, did not roll around their tractor or truck seats when they made cross-county runs and it was easy to distinguish from a milk bottle when, of a bleary morning, one had to chase the hair of the dog.[37] One regularly sees advertisements, such as many pure visual-image beauty-product commercials, that baffle even seasoned ad makers because they seem totally unconnected to any normal audience. One also sees advertisements that are totally unconnected to any product, such as the downright incomprehensible television commercials for the <www. cnet.com> on-line computer and technology Web site that have a young man inquiring about computer specifications from a lab instructor who offers him instead a pig pickled in formaldehyde, or from a physician who then proceeds with preparations for a rectal examination. Thus side by side with commercial work that many audiences find engaging, such as Alka Seltzer's "I can't believe I ate the whole thing" campaign, or El Al Israel Airlines's "My Son, the Pilot" ads, or Diet Coke's mid-1990s sexual role reversals that portray female office workers collectively lusting after a robust, bare-chested male construction worker, "creative" advertising often generates bizarre, obscure, or solipsistic images. Sometimes these are designed to draw attention principally to their makers within a tight-knit occupational community that values flamboyance for its own sake or for the pleasure of thumbing noses at clients while "communicating" with one's peers through arcane, self-referential symbols.

Despite charges and countercharges about the self-indulgence of pure "creativity," many agencies—in an industry remarkable for its adaptability—eschewed the raging ideological battles and absorbed the creative upheaval. Leo Burnett's Chicago-based agency not only serviced packaged-goods clients but produced creative work admired by the industry. Some large agencies, such as Ogilvy & Mather, famous for its ethos of account-person stewardship, set up, under the direction of Jock Elliot, in-house boutiques with a "creative" elan, even as other divisions of the agency continued to work on toothpaste and toilet bowl cleaners. Ogilvy & Mather celebrated its fiftieth anniversary in fall 1998, one index of its successful balancing act.[38] Such balance seems essential for the long-term survival of big firms in the advertising business. Still other advertising firms, fearing a mix of oil and water within one organizational structure, bought "creative" agencies outright and operated them as separate, wholly owned subsidiaries in order to "work both sides of the street" and position their agencies to pitch to all sorts of clients.

〰〰〰〰　The 1970s ravaged the advertising industry and signaled an end to the excesses of the creative revolution. The decade began in recession and ended with wildly high interest rates. Advertisers cut back sharply on expenditures and made new demands for more rational measures of advertising effectiveness. The retirements of Ned Doyle and Mac Dane marked the beginning of a long series of troubles even for fabled DDB, though DDB's travails were also typical of the industry.

Bernbach lacked Doyle's and Dane's adroit business acumen and led the agency into one financial mess after another, including a series of ill-advised corporate acquisitions paid for with agency profits from the fat years. Wall Street analysts did not look favorably on DDB, a public corporation since August 1964, dabbling in fly-by-night ventures. In addition to the agency's financial bleeding, its internal management slipped into a state of perpetual upheaval, bordering on chaos.[39] Bernbach refused to name his own successor as creative director, stirring up intense competition and ultimately factionalization among three strong-willed creative heads, Marvin Honig, Roy Grace, and Bob Levenson, each with his own band of loyalists and none known for excessive modesty. Further, Bernbach exacerbated the agency's organizational crisis by allowing Joe Daly, his right-hand man after the retirements of Doyle and Dane and later chairman of the board, to make a series of administrative appointments both to gain new business and to beef up account management, never the agency's strength.[40] But some of these appointees, like James Heekin from Ogilvy & Mather, found themselves pitted against Daly in bitter struggles for dominance and survival.[41] Another appointee, Paul Paulson from Compton, the home of "ring-around-the-collar" detergent ads, brought fresh MBAs into DDB armed with the latest managerial techniques. He so strengthened the agency's management structure that even well-managed agencies like Ogilvy & Mather began to raid DDB for talent. But the ascendancy of account managers under Paulson generated resentment among the creatives, long used to their dominant role in the agency, prompting, in some cases, a resurgence of creativity for its own sake. One famous creative, for instance, did a storyboard for American Tourister, the luggage company DDB had made famous by having a gorilla maul its bags, that pictured a gorilla wearing sneakers and velvet coming down a runway. Clients began to complain about the agency's arrogance and its creatives' scorn for standard marketing tools, such as surveys and focus groups, that most other agencies employed because clients found them comforting. Increasingly, DDB made clients feel uncomfortable, a fatal mistake in the world of business.

DDB's long winning streak with clients came to an abrupt halt. For years, Bernbach had had his pick of clients, all eager to be made famous by his wizardry. Now clients that the agency had served and served well creatively began to leave. From the agency's perspective, clients were enacting an ever-recurring, yet always troubling, final act between image makers and those whose public faces they have fashioned: clients come to believe the propaganda about themselves that image makers fashion and no longer wish to be reminded of the artifice that went into its making. Within a few years, DDB lost Uniroyal, for which the agency had created the "Rain Tire" campaign ("If it only saves your life once, it's a bargain"), Whirlpool ("At Whirlpool, you shape up or ship out"), Sara Lee, Lever Brothers ("Close-up is for close-ups"), as well as accounts from Werner-Lambert, Quaker Oats, and Cracker Jack, whose image and sales the agency's commercials had completely rejuvenated. Moreover, throughout the 1970s, American Airlines ("We're American Airlines . . . doing what we do best") continually threatened to take its huge account out of DDB. The agency's New Yorker–type cartoon advertisements that, among other things, spoofed businessmen's flirtations with stewardesses ("Any time you want to leave your wife is all right with us" and "People keep stealing our stewardesses," that is, "Within 2 years, most of our stewardesses will leave us for other men") were the premier ads for airlines at the time. Had DDB lost the American account, the agency might have collapsed. As it happened, Bernbach claimed that he resigned the account in 1981 in favor of Pan American World Airways. Such a triumphant denouement following several years of anxiety caps yet another heroic, but unlikely, Bernbach tale. In any event, Pan Am then "walked" only a couple of years later. In the midst of all of his troubles, Bernbach even flirted with selling his agency to Mary Wells Lawrence, a DDB alumna and the founder of Wells, Rich, Greene (later Wells BDDP), but Wells got cold feet and, in any event, the deal could not be financed.[42] The agency also pursued other merger talks, most notably with Foote, Cone & Belding, ironically an agency whose pedestrian approach to advertising was the antithesis of Bernbach's philosophy.[43] But this deal was also never consummated.

From another perspective, Bernbach and DDB were victims of their own success. Again, this business story is old and typical in the advertising industry. From a boutique agency with thirteen employees, serving principally upstart entrepreneurial companies that wanted offbeat advertising, the firm had grown into one of the nation's largest agencies (fifty-four offices in nineteen countries, thirty-four hundred employees) with international billings of more than 1 billion dollars a year. Big agencies need big clients, large established corporations with highly standardized products, the category that accounts for more than 50 percent of all corporate expenditures on advertising. But these kinds of clients, while in awe of DDB's reputation, increasingly found an agency where "the only good account person was a dead account person,"[44] an ethos uncongenial to their own needs for safe, predictable, research-based, well-managed, and especially, defensible advertising. Moreover, DDB's American, often ethnic, humor did not travel well and the firm never achieved international success comparable to its domestic triumphs.

The financial vicissitudes and loss of clients took their toll within the agency. For the first time in its history, DDB could no longer provide its staff with unfailing job security in a notoriously fear-driven business.[45] As a major shareholder in a firm whose stock fell from a high of $50 per share to $9 per share, as part of the general collapse of advertising agency stocks, Bernbach became consumed with the firm's market fortunes. At the same time his own health was failing, although the leukemia that eventually claimed him was a closely guarded secret.[46]

As Bernbach declined, animosities and rivalries increased among the agency's creative stars. Bernbach took less and less part in the agency's creative work and the quality of the firm's work slipped. Despite all of these upheavals, the agency still continued to garner an astonishing number of intra-industry awards for marketing effectiveness and creative excellence.[47]

Bernbach died on 2 October 1982. His death precipitated a tremendous outpouring of grief and praise throughout the advertising and general business communities. But almost immediately afterwards, DDB plunged into the serious battle for succession, and with it, for the agency's future identity. This battle was singular only in that it occurred in a revered organization with deep ties throughout the advertising industry, but in every other way, the struggle typified what occurs in all bureaucratic organizations when things fall apart. When organizations begin to come apart, one can see what held them together in the first place. Without Bernbach's symbolic paternal presence, DDB broke into open conflict, particularly in its creative division. By this point, Roy Grace and Bob Levenson were the main contenders for the throne, since Marvin Honig had already departed for another agency. Despite support from the Bernbach family for Levenson, Grace eventually got the nod from Barry Loughrane. Loughrane had become president in mid-1984, replacing Neil Austrian, a Bernbach-appointed, politically neutral, financial wizard who had led the agency out of the wilderness of the early 1970s. Eventually, Levenson resigned and took his "merry band" of creatives with him out of the agency to join Compton, recently acquired by Britain's Saatchi brothers. Grace became chairman and executive creative director of the agency, a position that he retained until January 1986, when he formed his own agency, Grace & Rothschild.

In the meantime, the agency's business faltered still further. More clients departed. Right after Bernbach's death, Procter & Gamble, always a lucrative if overbearing client, withdrew its accounts. El Al Israel Airlines and Polaroid left, both after thirty years, and Bankers Trust after seventeen years. Clients had gotten meaner as well, resentful of the big-buck bonanzas that many partners in advertising agencies gathered when they took their agencies public or sold them outright ("He's making money by selling my products and my reputation") and they increasingly demanded "spec" work for big accounts, always a way to garner top-flight free advice and ideas. DDB dropped its long-standing policy against spec work and engaged in a massive gangbang to win the Miller beer account. "Miller time" ads had been thoroughly bested by

Budweiser's "This Bud's for You" campaign. Although DDB was the odds-on favorite to win the prize going into the presentation and although it had spent enormous amounts of time preparing fifty-one campaigns, the three that the agency presented were very ordinary "Miller Men" campaigns, flattering celebrations of those who choose to drink the beer. The commercials drew no response from the panel of judges. DDB not only lost Miller's business, but it began to lose its reputation as an agency with a sure touch. Moreover, every time it lost business, the agency once known as a haven of security in a cutthroat world fired more people.[48]

Finally, on 28 April 1986, Doyle Dane Bernbach joined in a "big bang mega-merger" with Needham Harper of Chicago, another deeply troubled agency, and with BBDO, a soundly managed firm with deep pockets, under a parent company called Omnicom. The new agency, based in New York, took the name DDB Needham Worldwide, Inc. It was the largest agency group in the world for two weeks, until the Saatchi brothers purchased Ted Bates Worldwide and, in a sign of dog-eat-dog times in the advertising world, formed an even larger agency.

〰〰〰 For more than a dozen years, the only formal organizational traces of the once-fabled agency were its initials, overshadowed by the name of the firm that acquired it. But, on 1 June 1999, the fiftieth anniversary of the founding of Doyle Dane Bernbach, DDB Needham Worldwide changed its name to DDB Worldwide Communications Group. The name change came complete with a reissuing of the booklet of aphorisms *Bill Bernbach Said* and an acknowledgement from Keith Reinhard, chairman and chief executive officer of the corporation, that Bernbach and DDB had decisively shaped the contemporary world of image making. The agency's workplace innovations are thoroughly instituted in advertising agencies everywhere. The agency's legend lives on, particularly its reputation for symbolic inversion, a virtue that is now extolled in public relations as well as advertising. Freshness in professional advocacy means turning symbols upside down to encourage skeptical audiences to suspend disbelief long enough to entertain new frameworks, meanings, and associations for products, people, institutions, and causes. And such creativity with symbols has become a driving force in the proliferation of alternate ways of seeing the world.

4 ADVOCACY AS A PROFESSION

A close examination of the actual work of advertising and public relations practitioners illuminates the structure, exigencies, and accompanying social psychology of professional commercial advocacy. As it happens, the work of mass persuasion has a basic sameness to it in virtually all contexts. It is thoroughly bureaucratized; the struggle to achieve "creative" breakthroughs is always pitted against the forces of business rationality and concomitant standardization. It requires an incessant attentiveness to clients' desired constructions of the world. It is largely anonymous, except to peers. But, when it is successful, it produces images and symbols that resonate with the actual experiences, desires, or fantasies of unseen audiences and moves them to action.

〜〜〜〜 Advertising is the handmaiden of the mass consumer economy, itself a necessary consequence of the mid-nineteenth century breakthroughs in communications, transportation, technology, and workplace organization that led, first, to the possibility of mass distribution and, consequently, to the mass production system. Billions of dollars are spent on advertising in the United States each year. Many critics of advertising assail such huge expenditures as wasteful, an extravagance that inflates the costs of goods and services beyond measure. The advertising industry itself argues that without advertising to renew consumer demand the commercial stream would dry up. In this view, advertising provides requisite information to the sovereign consumer to make rational choices about economic alternatives. In private, advertising practitioners laugh at the desiccated rhetoric of their own spokespeople, as they do at the sometimes fantastic accusations of assorted critics about their calculated manipulativeness. They themselves are often unsure just how their legerdemain works. But they do know that through the wonderland of images, associations, and vignettes that they create, material objects and ideas alike become heroes of a sort, capable of delivering human beings from unwarranted fates or of leading them to promised rewards. Such elusive promises somehow kindle consumers' desires for this-worldly forms of salvation. They know that advertising provides the vocabularies of motive and sentiment that make consumption of all kinds of goods and services meaningful. Advertising has become synonymous with the market. No firm that hopes to capture large numbers of customers can do without it.

Copywriters and art directors in advertising agencies, called the "creatives" ever since Bill Bernbach's workplace innovation paired them into teams,* are the paradigmatic commercial advocates of our time. These interpretive experts shape the images and write the corresponding slogans for mass advertisements.

The advertising world is divided essentially into three parts: clients and, within the advertising agency, the account managers and the creatives.[1] The client is the "advertiser,"[2] that is, the group, person, or corporation that has a product, service, or idea to be sold or promoted. Clients buy advertising; agencies work for clients. The term "client" has many meanings. Men and women in advertising use it, for instance, to refer to the entire entity buying the advertising, such as Proctor & Gamble or General Motors. Or, client can refer to a particular product division of a large corporation, such as Taster's Choice coffee or Chevrolet. Even more specifically, client refers to the particular person with whom one interacts at the corporation, as when one says, "The client called." Moreover, while the term is usually employed in its singular form, its referent can be either singular or plural, as well as male or female. Thus, a client meeting might involve six corporate men and women who are, interchangeably, both collectively and individually referred to simply as "the client."

Among themselves, ad makers usually use this term as a means of reference even when clients' personal names are well known. The term

---

*Janice M. Hirota published portions of the following analysis of the work of advertising creatives as "Making Products Heroes: Work in Advertising Agencies," in *Propaganda,* edited by Robert Jackall (New York: New York University Press, 1995), 329–350. Those portions are republished here by permission of New York University Press.

focuses attention on the institutional relationship between the advertiser and the agency, and specifically the creatives. In particular, the term refers to the work relationship between occupational groups, a relationship seen by creatives to have structural similarities from person to person, product to product, corporation to corporation, and agency to agency. This focus on the work relationship helps reinforce in creatives the habit of mind that defines the client as client, regardless of the corporation or product at issue. In this sense, creatives see advertising in terms of servicing clients and not in terms of promoting any particular product, company, or brand name. Further, the term's anonymity cuts through the idiosyncrasies of a particular project and points to the critical factor for creatives: clients buy and therefore have ultimate decision-making power over the advertising that creatives fashion. The issue for creatives becomes how to maintain creative autonomy within a framework wholly dependent on others' wishes. Creatives' relationships with clients are thus always potentially antagonistic.

As a result, agencies generally have clients interact principally with the business side of an agency, that is, with the men and women in account management. The terms "account executives" or "account people" refer to everyone on the account side, a usage that suppresses the hierarchical rankings in account management departments. But the typical organizational ladder from the bottom up is trainee, account executive managing one account, account supervisor who manages several account executives, and then a general manager or vice president in charge of several supervisors.

Account executives act as the liaisons between agencies and clients. With clients, they determine the particular market to be addressed and work out the best advertising strategy and plan to capture that market. The advertising plan includes a description of previous campaign approaches, perceived differences between a client's product and rival brands, the desired marketing approach—usually based on market survey data—to find and exploit a particular market niche, a profile of the target audience, an outline of the product characteristics or image to be stressed, and the exact sorts of advertisements to be produced.[3] Account executives then explain both the target market and strategy to the creatives involved. Eventually, they help sell to the client the advertising produced by creatives.

Account executives have day-to-day contact with clients. They "coddle the client," "hold the client's hand," and, in general, do all that is necessary to keep the client happy. Most clients, buried in their own substantive expertise, have no understanding of how interpretive expertise works. As a result, clients often see advertising, along with public relations, as magic of a sort, an alchemy capable of transforming the deadening rounds of bureaucratic life and the prosaic products it produces into glittering, glamorous cultural images and symbols. Clients believe that striking advertising helps them in the market, and they know that dramatic public posturing bolsters their employees' identification with their organizations. Those who can claim credit for such advertising gain ground within their own occupational worlds.

Account executives also act as buffers between clients and creatives. They protect clients from "unpredictable" and "temperamental" creatives. They also protect creatives from importuning, meddling, and anxious clients, although the latter role is not generally appreciated by creatives. Indeed, though account executives see themselves as representatives of business rationality, creatives generally see those on the account side as clients' lackeys because of their constant attentiveness to clients. As it happens, the peculiar economic exigencies of advertising agencies help explain such attentiveness. Typically, a client assigns a piece of business exclusively to one agency, an assignment that may include all the advertising for a particular product, or the trade advertising for a product division, or, again, the corporate advertising for a company.[4] In this sense, an agency works for a client and the client commits itself for that piece of business to the agency. However, unless special arrangements are negotiated beforehand, clients do not pay agencies unless and until they buy particular advertisements, regardless of how many hours agency personnel spend on mandated projects. And, in late 1999, Procter & Gamble, along with other advertisers, instituted "performance-based compensation" that ties payment to agencies to the achievement of measurable sales or product-recognition goals. Of course, creatives and account executives continue to receive salaries whether the advertisements they make or broker are sold. But admen or women do not survive, let alone flourish, for very long at an advertising agency unless they work on ads that clients buy and that clients deem effective. Moreover, it is an axiom in advertising, as in public relations, that all clients, even well-served ones, eventually take their accounts elsewhere, wreaking organizational havoc at agencies as they leave. Account executives hold clients' hands not only to rekindle clients' hopes in the magic of images, but also to establish the face-to-face human contact that alone might ensure some advantage over competitors in difficult times.

The creative side of an agency usually has a flatter, less hierarchical organizational structure than the account side. Typically, the creative director oversees all the agency's creative work. Overall, an agency's creative director allocates clients and their projects to the creative group heads. These creative group heads, below the creative director in the agency's chain of command, are supervisors who manage a group of creatives.[5] The number of group heads varies from agency to agency, as does the size of their groups, even within agencies. Group size (from less than ten to over fifty) depends, among other factors, on the total size of the creative department, the size and number of clients at the agency, and the philosophy of the heads of an agency. Within a group, the lines of authority are also relatively flat, and in general, creative teams receive assignments from and take work to their group head.[6]

Within their groups, creatives almost always work in teams of two, with one art director and one copywriter paired for any given project. Some creative pairings are permanent partnerships, so strong on occasion that when one team member leaves an agency, the other leaves as well. But sometimes group heads shift creatives around according to the project, whether by whim or for administrative convenience. In such situations, since people work on more than one project at a time, creatives may have a number of different partners simultaneously.

The fusion of verbal and visual expertise, with copywriters and art directors on an equal footing, stands at the core of work with symbols in advertising and, more generally, of modern mass image making itself. Such work typically proceeds in stages. Initially, upon receipt of an assignment, partners "bounce ideas around" or "play ideas off" each other in a spontaneous, free-association way. Ideas, symbols, or phrases from one teammate trigger responses, ripostes, jokes, and amendments from the other in a quickly paced open-ended interchange. Sometimes the product, the client, the team's bosses, the entire agency, as well as celebrities and other public notables that might figure in future advertising for the product become objects of ridicule, caricature, or raucous and obscene satire. The established roles of art director and writer collapse, with the art director freely suggesting copy and the writer imagining sets, props, and other visual details. Sooner or later, one of the partners voices or sketches out an idea that "takes off," and the team subjects this to a more tempered, searching critique. If the idea survives, it is altered and refined until it becomes a "concept," that is, a guiding theme symbolically linking the product to the perceived needs or longings of the targeted market audience. At this point, the concept is presented to the group head and subjected to an elaborate approval process.

Creatives see their work partnerships as oases in the bureaucratic desert of the modern workplace. While others, including clients, agency account executives, and friends working in the mainstream corporate world, live by fixed procedures, creatives make and break rules at will. Whereas others constrain their behavior and wear public masks concealing emotions and intentions, creatives set their own schedules, dress as they wish, and express themselves openly and without fear, at least to their teammates, wearing their "creativity" as a badge. Because "creativity" is antithetical to the rationalizing thrust of the modern workplace, creatives must continually lay claim to their distinctive occupational identity, principally by appearing to be "creative."

Art directors and writers thus act in ways that enhance their social identities as people who are creative. Such self-presentation of creativity cannot, of course, be totally idiosyncratic, but must fit the prevailing social image of what it means to be a creative and of how creatives act. Thus, some creatives have "tantrums," that is, emotional outbursts, ranging from loud arguments to destructive behavior. Although the term tantrum suggests a contemptuous suspicion that a world based on self-control feels for irrational and childish behavior, such outbursts are not only generally tolerated but are, in fact, expected, since tantrums help assert and define the creative persona. Thus, to take only a few examples from fieldwork, an art director, in a fit of frustration over a client's demands, walks into the men's bathroom and sprays graffiti all over the walls, ceiling, and stalls with a can of red paint. Or a writer physically throws herself across a doorway to block an account executive from taking unfinished work to a client. Another, for a similar reason, challenges an account executive to a wrestling match that ends up on the floor. Another screams at her group head because other writers are getting all the plum assignments. An art director yells at a bewildered client. A writer stomps out of a meeting with clients, slamming the door as he leaves; and another dumps soup into a client's lap during lunch. If tantrums repeatedly obstruct work in an agency or permanently damage client relationships, whole careers can be jeopardized. Yet, the limits for such behavior are broadly set and only rarely result in firings or even reprimands. Instead, the very irrationality of extreme emotional displays becomes proof of creativity, in the sense of an unwillingness to subject oneself to the humdrum rationality of the business world. Most creatives do not have tantrums. But the reputation of those who do colors the occupational group of creatives as a whole.

Such lore circulates throughout the advertising work world. Each occupational group interprets such behavior differently. Because they hunger for the great burst of inspiration that might make them and their products famous, clients are likely to see tantrums as evidence of artistic genius. But account people see tantrums as the products of overly sensitive, unreliable, childish, and generally unpredictable natures that need to be tamed and controlled in order to accomplish the pragmatic tasks necessary to serve and retain clients. Yet even creatives who do not indulge in public emotional displays themselves or who sometimes label tantrum throwers as unprofessional subtly countenance such behavior by proffering exculpating accounts or by defining tantrums as expressions of free, open natures. Moreover, when tantrums are triggered by corporate attempts to tamper with creative work, they are always taken as evidence of the deep gulf between the standards of creative people and those of account people and clients.

Creatives also present public faces that set them apart from the standardized appearances characteristic of the business world. Account people wear the typical corporate uniforms—worsted wool suits, pima cotton button-down shirts, four-in-hand foulards or floppy polka-dot bow ties, wingtip shoes or sensible pumps, all in muted, conservative colors. By contrast, attire in creative departments runs the gamut from old sweaters and running shoes to bold-colored designer dresses and handmade boots. The dressed-down attire is said to help creatives work in a relaxed, unencumbered way, while the hip and stylish look is taken as evidence of creatives' obvious taste, flair, and general adventurousness.

Office decor can also proclaim creativity. Creatives' offices range from rarified to homey, from sleekly elegant to zany. One sees an extremely cluttered office with ceiling-high stacks of papers and a window shelf lined with pots of dead plants. Another office, a stark, nearly empty room with a bare desk and chair, features three gooseneck lamps in a row in the middle of the floor with heads turned up so the light reflects off the ceiling ("Creatives dislike direct fluorescent lighting," it is said). Neon signs emblazoning the occupant's name in lights decorate another office. A flamingo motif rules in one office, adorning coffee mug, lamps, statuettes, ashtrays, and framed prints; another office is similarly overrun with black Scottish terriers. Some are decorated with antique furnishings, others with starkly modern, polished glass-and-chrome pieces. Everywhere one sees idiosyncratic touches: shelves lined with plastic models of plates of food; a stuffed armadillo or mounted moose heads; a rubber chicken; props from past shoots such as a sign from a mock store named after the writer on the project;

a baseball autographed by the Boston Red Sox (a red flag in New York City); signs from restroom doors and street corners; rows of chopstick wrappers tacked on bulletin boards; license plates personalized with puns; and the usual array of snapshots of children, pets, families, and, of course, of creatives themselves especially when out on shoots in exotic locales. Some agencies design avant-garde architectural spaces for their creatives expressing ideologies of creativity, such as the policy at Chiat/Day (later Chiat/Day/Mojo, still later TBWA Chiat/Day) of "no walls, no doors, no 'offices'—to help foster a creative, nonbureaucratic working atmosphere."[7]

Such crafting of public behavior and appearance advertises one's unique qualities to others and helps carve out the freedom from bureaucratic constraints necessary for image making. Self-as-product entails a self-proclaiming stance whereby creatives fashion advertising contexts in which to dramatize their own personae, a paradigmatic instance of the self-referential quality of advertising work. Self-as-product means the use of dress, office décor, personal style, and interactional behavior to promote a creative persona. It also means self-as-hero of the stories that creatives promulgate and that make the round of agencies, stories that dramatize themselves as witty, adventurous, open men and women with glamorous, exciting lives.

In self-advertising, the two sides of a self-promotional stance—as both fabricator and product—come together in the most critical role for creatives' success: that of salesperson. Selling oneself and one's ideas entails many overlapping public faces. These include a knack for entertaining clients with clever casual conversation; a graceful acceptance of being the focus of attention; a talent for thinking on one's feet; a willingness to star at client presentations, throwing oneself with verve into proposed commercials and dramatizing children, animals, experts, housewives, talking fruit, and celebrities alike. It also requires a pose that allows creatives simultaneously to mystify the "creative leap," logically "talk the client through the creative process," and emphasize the essential difference between creatives and others. As successful salespeople, art directors and writers must project creative personae, but they must also know when and how to switch to more rational modes of discourse.

In all of this, "enthusiasm" and the ability to generate enthusiasm in different audiences is crucial. Enthusiasm is the social face of creatives' attitude toward themselves and their work. Enthusiasm means a generally up-beat energetic self-presentation, a can-do optimism, a great deal of self-confidence, and zeal about advertising in general and the immediate project in particular. Enthusiasm means generating and communicating excitement about one's self and one's ideas. Art directors and writers know the value of projecting enthusiasm since they often argue that unless one is enthusiastic about one's work—no matter what the product or who the client—no one else will be. Subordinates highly value supervisors who can spark this kind of excitement. Such bosses, after all, not only recharge creatives with the emotional energy critical to their work but help them develop the guises necessary to keep others off balance.

At the same time, art directors and writers generally take a cool, distanced stance toward the creative personae that they fashion, one tinged both with self-mockery and the kind of gleeful thrill that accompanies thumbing one's nose at established conventions. In private, they laugh uproariously at gawking prospective clients being given a tour of the creative warrens by account people who point out idiosyncratic office arrangements as evidence of the creativity that clients want in their advertisements. Or "Sam" and "Harry," a famous pair of creatives, make a presentation on "the creative process" as part of an in-house training session for new account people. The creatives begin their talk, when suddenly a professional striptease artist dances through the audience to loud, brassy music. With exaggerated bumps and grinds, she flings articles of clothing into the audience of predictably clean-cut, conservatively dressed young men and women. She leaves the stage dressed only in pasties and a G-string amidst uncertain laughter, while Sam and Harry start to run a film that reveals, they say, the "real creative process." The film stars Sam and Harry who walk toward the camera down a long empty corridor. The camera then follows them into a men's bathroom where they enter adjoining stalls. The camera focuses steadily on the closed stall doors, while the partners carry on a muffled conversation through the walls. A short time later, they emerge from the stalls and continue their indecipherable mumbling to each other as they wash their hands. The film concludes with Sam and Harry announcing that this is how they create award-winning advertising.

The performance warns future bureaucrats that all their efforts to rationalize creativity will come to naught. Moreover, it celebrates the distinctive stance of ironic skepticism that writers and art directors take toward everything, even toward their own craft. Such a stance has its practical uses; it permits creatives to manipulate freely the trappings of the creative image to dazzle, outwit, or befuddle audiences as the situation requires in order to sell their work to account people and clients alike. Such skepticism also breeds a habit of mind essential for image-making work itself, namely, a detachment that enables creatives to step back and observe dispassionately the foibles, mannerisms, public sentiments, and popular trends of social life for use in their advertisements.

⌇⌇⌇⌇⌇⌇ Bill Bernbach enjoined his colleagues: "To keep your ads fresh, you've got to keep yourself fresh. Live in the current idiom and you will create in it." Ironically, keeping oneself fresh demands subjecting oneself to unremitting discipline in order to master the familiarities of social life and continually see them anew. Cultivating the detachment of the social observer requires a high degree of self-rationalization, the systematic streamlining of self that is characteristic of all bureaucratic structures. Creatives' behavioral freedom in the workplace in comparison to, say, account executives or corporate clients, actually conceals this self-discipline at the core of their craft.

Creatives try to develop a methodical social attentiveness, one that continually forces them out of the rounds of their own milieux. Wherever possible, they eavesdrop on the conversations of people in different social classes both to get a sense of their concerns and especially to hear their use of language. They watch people closely, particularly in public places like airports and subways, to understand the subtle rules of crowd protocol or avoidance mannerisms. They go to trendy bars and museums with the explicit purpose of observing unusual behavior or dress, since they know that, in American society, today's idiosyncrasy is tomorrow's orthodoxy. Some adventurously plunge into wholly unfamiliar activities like hot-air ballooning precisely to meet new people with different viewpoints. In their attentiveness to social activity and especially in their willingness to enter new social worlds, creatives are commercial ethnographers of a sort whose subjects are the demeanor, the idioms, the interplay, and the foibles of others. Such detached social attentiveness underpins creative work in advertising, since one achieves resonance with mass audiences only by incorporating familiar and realistic elements into mass images. Whatever one's own viewpoints, one learns to discern the settled, taken-for-granted expectations of particular audiences, the commonplace cultural narratives that provide their frameworks of meaning. One does not incorporate into one's own work the experimentally esoteric, the alien or mysterious, or worst of all, the "offensive," until these have become familiar to the target audience.

Of course, ascertaining the familiar in a kaleidoscopic culture has become an increasingly difficult task. As a result, art directors and writers take popular cultural forms as the most reliable index of the currently familiar. They keep up therefore with all the swirling fads in American society, the shifting celebrity scenes, the just-opened films, plays, and musicals, the fashion changes, the museum shows, the latest best-selling books, the most current slang, and the ever-changing varieties of music. They watch television by the hour. They expect their colleagues to recognize and respond to their popular cultural allusions. Such knowledge of popular cultural lore becomes, in fact, a principal criterion for selecting new creative recruits. No one wants to work with a creative who, like account executives and clients, is slow on the uptake. The workplace thus becomes a forum for the systematic and ongoing assessment of taken-for-granted cultural lore, a locale that distills everyday knowledge into an occupational virtue. Creatives puzzle over the meanings of such lore to various audiences, appropriating insights for their own work. Perhaps most important, they keep alert to the quintessential popular cultural form, namely advertisements themselves. The occupational community of advertising creatives is small, numbering only a few thousand practitioners nationwide and a few hundred in New York City. Through clubs, associations, award competitions, local and national newsletters, trade newspapers, the advertising beat columns in the major dailies, and now the World Wide Web, they avidly watch the work of their peers both to gauge the shifting norms of their own world and to garner clues about how best to cast either central themes or detailed images to their audiences. Advertising, like all popular culture, thus has a highly self-referential quality, a circularity that makes déjà vu a normal and indeed expected part of everyday life and makes creatives continually look to each other for ideas, approval, and rewards.

Creatives also strive to make advertising as realistic as possible, even while they attend to the enormous premium on freshness in their world. Advertising plays back to audiences their already existing, enduring preoccupations, pointedly concretizing people's everyday concerns within a commercial context. To be effective, the presentation of familiar details of people's lives must look and sound as wholly plausible as possible, itself a task that requires close attention to extremely mundane aspects of situations, including common faux pas and mistakes. Some print advertisements, such as those for National Basketball Association properties selling basketball paraphernalia, contain scratched-out words or deliberate spelling mistakes to resonate with youngsters' disdain of "corporate sheen."[8] But advertising's focus on products always runs the risk of hitting strained false notes, however realistic the details. For instance, customers in most diners do not witness paper-towel absorption tests; shoppers rarely run into Mr. Whipple in supermarket aisles; roommates, husbands and wives, parents and children, coworkers, neighbors, lovers, and friends do not converse endlessly about toilet bowl cleaners or frozen dinners except at the risk of interpersonal mayhem or social isolation.

Creatives address the dilemma by endlessly searching for fresh ways to take the raw stuff of their culture and society and organize it into internally coherent messages, little stories in which "products are heroes," even as they provide a backdrop of convincing realism. In large and small agencies, those known for hard-sell advertising as well as those with more creative reputations, art directors and writers see themselves writing little stories, scenarios that cast products as heroes, protecting and rescuing men, women, and children from unwarranted fates, messy situations, tangled relationships, and even from dull careers and all-too-mundane lives. Thus Colt 45 malt liquor invariably snares luscious, long-maned women for Billy Dee Williams; Certs mints ignite close encounters of a romantic kind by destroying bad breath; Whisk detergent banishes "ring around the collar"; Volvo is a "civilized car for an uncivilized world"; AT&T not only rescues business deals but allows friends, lovers, and families to "reach out and touch" each other from afar; IBM personal computers turn small-business chaos into rationalized triumph; Windsong perfume keeps a woman on her lover's mind by tantalizing his nasal capillaries; Cascade saves social face by making unsightly spots on glassware disappear; Mr. Clean and Glade alike dispel musty household odors and the presumed shame they create; Volkswagen ownership endears a nephew to a rich uncle who rewards such thriftiness with a bequest of his entire fortune of 100 billion dollars; Federal Express's package-monitoring system enables a secretary to undercut a boss prone to humiliating his subordinates; 9 Lives cat food tempts even bossy, finicky cats into canine docility; Hefty bags hold and conceal all the debris from overstuffed lives; and the American Express card enables Jerry Seinfeld, after an inauspicious London comedy debut, to take a whirlwind tour of Great Britain to learn "the lingo" and return triumphantly to the same stage with wry punch lines.

Causes and organizations are also products to be cast as heroes. Causes promise uplifting moral sentiments and specific actions to alleviate the widespread but largely unfocused guilt and rage of the middle class in return for helping worthy victims, whether pregnant teenagers, earthquake survivors, elephants hunted for their tusks, or defenseless children. Organizations get cast as pillars of integrity in a corrupt world, or as inventive milieux defying stultifying bureaucratic standardization, or as beacons of harmonious multicultural diversity in a presumably race-torn society. Since heroes emerge with much greater clarity when set against sharp backdrops, forces opposing a hero are invariably presented in caricature.

Creatives dramatize and vitalize any product by highlighting and framing whatever seems to provide a salable edge. This means at times extending product traits to oversized proportions and endowing them with larger-than-life impact. The product packaged as hero performs extraordinary acts. One must therefore have a talent for exploiting equally product attributes or deficiencies. The point is always to find the right angle to applaud the product. Product attributes merely provide the necessary means, and not the cause, for advertising celebration. For example, creatives construct links that mesh a product trait with perceived needs or concerns of the buying public. Such construction elicits the interpretation of broad themes through the narrow focus of a product, sometimes entailing the use of "borrowed interest" to hook products onto larger fads or issues. Thus advertisements for caffeine-free soft drinks suddenly begin to tout this previously ignored feature when a general concern with preventive care helps make it a market asset. Or, again, advertising singles out wholly peripheral features of a product to help distinguish it from its competitors; the packaging of cigarettes or the literal weight of magazines supersede an emphasis on their actual value or utility. Indeed, advertising lauds anything thought to be "viable," that is, that can possibly be construed as unique, even a marginal or invented product feature such as the color of a pill ("It's orange!") or a standard product feature that no one else has claimed, such as a cigarette that trumpets "It's toasted!" about its tobacco.

Some genres of advertising, such as comedy, fantasy, parody, and what is called "new wave," are not meant to be literal reflections of everyday life. In this sense, they are less realistic than more straightforward advertisements such as those called "slice of life," typified by the cosmetician giving advice at the beauty shop, or advertisements that give direct comparisons of one product to another, or testimonials, or confessionals, or demonstrations complete with a presentation of a problem with its solution. However, even in less realistic advertisements, creatives present immediately recognizable aspects of contemporary life, though often in caricature or parody. Thus, Alaska Airlines, trying to gain a foothold in a fierce market, mocks airline food all too familiar to regular travelers ("banquet on a bun, pâté in a drum, plastic parsley, little chickens [accompanied by a picture of 125 chicks in a shoebox]") while claiming: "We spend a little more on our meals and you can taste the difference." And Pepsi Cola ("The Choice of a New Generation") parodies its arch rival by depicting an archaeological dig in a stereotypically constructed future space age in which a professor gives thoroughly wacky explanations of the uses of a baseball and electric guitar but is baffled and speechless when his students find an encrusted Coke bottle.

Even when advertisements do not directly present manifest social life, they reflect viewers' anxieties, daydreams, desires, senses of whimsy or nostalgia, and especially longings to be a certain kind of person. "Image advertising," for instance, fabricates user images, that is, images of the kind of person who uses a product. Of course, imagery forms a pivotal aspect of all of creatives' efforts. But campaigns for certain products, specifically cigarettes, liquor, cosmetics, and basketball shoes, consist almost entirely of imagery. Thus advertisements are peopled by Marlboro's macho loner, Chanel N° 5's sensualists, or basketball stars who can "sky." Others feature men who take Martell cognac "of course," or know that Hennessey is the "civilized way to call it a day," or count themselves among Cutty Sark's "leaders" who have "the right stuff." Others portray sleek yuppies finally out in the big world who realize that it is time to have a "real drink," namely Dewar's. Still other advertisements parade women who allow Vanderbilt perfume to "release the splendor" of themselves, or announce that they are, variously, Charlie, Scamp, or "Shalimar, all over," or have a place among Revlon's "most unforgettable women in the world." Thus, even the most fantastic advertisements present realistic, recognizable social types who invite others to join their company.

The stance of dispassionate observer that continually seeks to unpack the taken for granted and to discern precisely which details make for realism in given situations has consequences for a creative's own life. One stops interjecting one's personal views into conversations because this colors others' spontaneous expressions that might contain useful social clues; one suppresses one's urge to joke about everything because joking often subverts social reality instead of allowing one to absorb it. One develops a high degree of self-consciousness that others find discomforting but increasingly is central to one's self-image. One turns one's relentless eye in every direction, including toward one's own most intimate experiences and relationships. Thus, a writer in a nostalgic longing for his own father conceives an advertisement where a boy is brought by his father to Barney's for his first suit. Another creative presents his social rejection by classmates as the first act of a mini-drama of sweet revenge following the transformation of his lunchbox from an object of ridicule to one of envy with the inclusion of packaged cupcakes. Still another, in a commercial for dark glasses, recalls a blind date that blossomed into love at first sight. Personal experiences thus become rich bottomland for producing images and symbols with deep emotional resonance. All of one's life becomes material for one's work.

In short, with a kind of occupationally sanctioned affective promiscuity, creatives become willing to appropriate and alter material from any source and from any sphere of experience, whether public and secular, or private and sacred, and apply that material for whatever project and for whatever client is at hand. In the process, creatives' detachment continuously distances them from the experiences they seek or those they recall or imagine.

〰〰〰 The approval process in an agency brings together account executives, clients, and creatives in an organizational crucible out of which emerges the advertising presented to the public. As mentioned earlier, when an account comes into an agency, the client and the account people, typically in conjunction with the research wing, develop the advertising strategy. The agency creative director gives the account to the head of a creative group, who in turn assigns a team to the project. The size and prestige of the account, of course, directly influence the choice of creatives. One's past creative reputation is only one possible criterion in the assignment to choice jobs. Essentially, the creative director and the creative group head allocate choice jobs to their respective favorites of the moment. In this sense, the old adage still obtains: "You're only as good as your last ad."

Given the strategy, the chosen creative team of art director and writer work under a deadline to come up with the advertising concept. They develop four or five ideas that they like, complete with some specific suggestions for lines and visuals, and they present the ideas to their group head. The group head encourages them to work on some ideas and to drop others. Depending on the seniority of the creatives, fights often occur at this stage of the process when pet ideas get trashed. Inexperienced teams usually see the give-and-take with supervisors as part of their occupational socialization. But experienced creatives invariably resent the rejection of their ideas by supervisors since, in their view, administrative authority seems to require lobotomies that excise all memories of the crafts of art direction and writing. Moreover, anyone around for awhile knows that advertising is "a young man's game": younger creatives are thought to be more "in touch," have a "fresh" outlook, and possess in greater abundance the energy and stamina necessary for the grueling marathon work sessions typical of the advertising world. As one gets older, disputes with supervisors about work become fraught with anxieties about occupational mortality.

Eventually, the group head and the creative team decide on which ideas to present to the account people and then to the client. The approval process moves forward through "presentations," which may involve simple conversations with agency colleagues or extraordinarily elaborate "dog and pony shows" for the benefit of clients' top managers. But presentations always mean endless negotiation and revision.

Most creatives see account people as adversaries in the approval process, siding with the client against creatives in order to make a sale. In this view, account people are the client's watchdogs, guardians of the client's sensibilities who bark about "the demands of the advertising strategy" to keep at bay daring ideas that might unsettle their masters. Creatives see such protectiveness undermining opportunities to create "breakthrough" advertising, that is, work with the dramatic flair that could make them into stars. Many creatives develop semiheroic, ironic views of themselves as rebels storming staid bureaucratic battlements under the banner of Creativity, an internal drama that can fuel a centrifugal push toward the use of unusual, sometimes downright bizarre, images.

The hierarchy of the account side, and the organizational protocol that hierarchy always generates, make matters more tangled. Creatives are expected to present their ideas to lower-ranking account people who are supposed to weed out all unsuitable notions before account people of higher status become involved. But account subordinates often veto ideas that creatives consider promising for fear their superiors might dislike them. Sometimes the same process works in reverse. Account subordinates think their superiors will like an idea and ask creatives to work at expanding it; but, when the idea is presented to higher-ups, it is unceremoniously tossed out. For creatives, then, the ideal is to involve top people in decisions as soon as possible. If bosses like an idea, subordinates will not tamper with it; if not, then creatives avoid useless effort. But the protocol of the account-side ladder rarely permits this. This is typical of the modern, segmented workplace; what makes perfect sense for one group creates a senseless situation for another. Moreover, lower-ranking account people have to get their own thumbprints on every ad under their purview; without a change or two, others might think that they are not doing their jobs properly or, perhaps, that their positions are unnecessary. In the business world, everyone has to make their presence known lest others try to arrange their absence. Thus, "creativity" itself, that is, being a font of fresh ideas, is never enough. Creatives must be guerilla fighters for their ideas as well. Writers are especially vulnerable to others dickering with their work because "everybody thinks that they know how to make a sentence better." Even small changes accumulate, often to large effect. But making too prolonged a stand against demands for small or large changes risks gaining a reputation as a troublemaker with powerful account people or with creative supervisors, a label that can imperil one's future. Therefore, one must fight, one can even throw tantrums, but one must also learn when to pull back. Commitment to ideas is actually an occupational disability. Creatives learn how to distance themselves from their ideas so that when a prized "baby" does not survive the approval process or emerges "with its arms and legs cut off," it can be let go without too much regret. In this sense, the market's fickleness becomes a constitutive part of creatives' thinking.

Of course, such organizational give-and-take eats time alive. Creatives see themselves caught in endless rounds of presentations to account people and clients; or doing "cover-your-ass work"; or doing meaningless agency-assigned work, such as extra campaign ideas to beef up presentations for a client, with no expectation of eventual production; or slogging through client-demanded "make-work" designed to keep the agency on its toes. Most creative work is never actually produced, but there is no way to distinguish "real" assignments from those that will go nowhere until an idea emerges from the grinder of the approval process.

The uncertainty about the fate of one's advertising ideas is compounded by other contingencies. One project balloons because the client "loves" a concept; another project just as suddenly disappears because the client cuts his advertising budget to save costs or because new leaders at the client switch advertising agencies to distance themselves from their predecessors. Moreover, the measures of good advertising shift continually, as evaluations of a given campaign fluctuate over time before different audiences, or as new cultural fads make current images seem outdated, or as new research tools claiming to track the effectiveness of ads are promoted. There are no objective standards in the world of advertising, no firm way of gauging the value of creative work. Indeed, the significant arbiters of creative work are always and only

one's creative colleagues whose judgments about one's "creative ability" make or break one's career.

But to reach the broader occupational community of other creatives,
one has to get one's work out of the agency and shown to and approved
by the client. The grinding compromises of the in-house approval process are but a prelude to the main show, that is, convincing a client to
buy the advertising. Client presentations include the use of storyboards
for television commercials and mock-ups for print advertisements to
help clients visualize the actual advertising. These presentations can
be fairly elaborate. If an agency is wooing new business or struggling
to hold a client, presentations might include original music, slide
shows, polished role-playing, or finished work. Most agencies present
several ideas at once even if only one advertisement, if any, will be produced. Clients demand a range of ideas from which to select; and account people hope that clients might be enticed into buying more than
originally planned. In actual practice, of course, it is a great triumph if
only one idea survives a client presentation.

Selling an advertising idea demands selling oneself, that is, fostering
a client's trust in one's talents as a creative. Only writers and art directors who effectively dramatize themselves and their work and, in the
process, project a creative image to clients regularly succeed in presentations. One tries to be witty, relaxed, and enthusiastic at such events,
entertaining clients with stunts, magic tricks, a barbershop quartet, or
whatever will cause clients to bracket the situation and define it as out
of the ordinary. Then one introduces the proposed advertising, ending
with one's favorite idea, always showing how the proposed advertising
fits the firm's overall market strategy, especially when there is little relationship between the two. At this stage, clients expect creatives to
provide them with rational explanations for every detail in the visuals
and scripts they present; the client, of course, needs plausible reasons
to justify the advertisement to his own bosses in his corporation where
rational frameworks must be employed to explain choices, especially
wholly irrational choices. Creatives recognize this need and pander to
it by inventing rational after-the-fact arguments for choices that are
actually intuitive. Thus, a blue dress is selected because it "contributes
a cool tone to the visual image"; Europe is chosen because "Americans
consider Europeans sophisticated"; the word "it" is chosen because its
very lack of specificity allows audiences to conjure up many possibilities. Most clients understand the duplicity at work, even as they welcome inventive rationales. Finally, after all the hoopla and fabrications

of rationality, creatives close advertising deals when they convince the individual representatives of a client that they have the inspiration and the know-how to make the client's product famous and, with that, benefit the careers of the representatives.

But each phase of the approval process, from fights over conceptual frameworks, to the higgle-haggle over details, to the inventions of plausible rationales, to convincing clients of one's ability, takes its toll on creatives' work. Even niggling changes, let alone big ones, alter advertisements, sometimes producing grotesque distortions of original ideas. Many creatives come to despise the final preproduction form of their work after all the approvals are garnered. But there are still further bureaucratic hurdles. Legal departments at the agency, at the client, and, if the commercial is to be national, at each of the major television networks or national cable channels, must all clear an advertisement before it goes into production. The longer this takes, the more nervous creatives get. Whenever the time between approval and production lags, people up and down the ladder begin to have second thoughts. Many done deals become undone at this stage because clients get cold feet. The prototypical story is that of a creative team that flew to a location in California to shoot a breakthrough special effects commercial on a very large budget. But while they were in flight, the client ordered the agency to cancel; the creative team was in California only long enough to be paged with the bad news and catch a return flight back to New York.

The work drama played out in the approval process involves groups with overlapping but ultimately different goals. Clients want advertising that they think will sell their product to consumers, promote their image in the business community, and solidify their own personal positions within their organizations. They value "creativity" in advertising only when it is perceived as a means to such external ends or if it reduces the frequency of being "zapped" by television watchers with remote control devices. Least of all are clients interested in providing writers or art directors with opportunities to express themselves or to build their careers. In fact, some clients suspect creative ideas as ploys by ad makers for self-advancement. Further, some clients, like Procter & Gamble and other companies that produce many lines of packaged goods, have their own rigidly defined standards of what constitutes effective advertising. Any agency that wants their lucrative business will happily leap at ads featuring "Mr. Whipple," or sensitive househusbands lamenting "ring around the collar," or the multitude of spots featuring women in a kitchen chit-chatting about everything from Stove Top stuffing to oven cleaners, even though such "hack" work destroys the reputations of art directors and writers within their occupational community.

Account executives want to keep clients happy, and they want to sell advertising. Therefore, they spend a lot of time figuring out what the client wants, undercutting whatever they think will offend or annoy the client, and maneuvering art directors and writers into creating what they think the client will buy.

Creatives want to produce what other creatives think is good advertising. They want to do interesting, craftsman-like work that will make them well-known and highly regarded among their peers in the world of advertising. If their advertisements are thought to sell a product, so much the better, but only because campaigns fortuitously credited with increasing sales will probably help their own careers by positioning them for good assignments where they can do work that will enhance their creative reputations. And getting good commercials to put on one's "reel" and strong print advertisements to put in one's "book" are absolutely crucial because a strong reel and book are the only aids to salvation in an advertising creative's career. One's reel and book represent the best work that a creative has done. They are the basis on which one is hired, and they are the only fallback when one is fired, a taken-for-granted occurrence in the world of advertising where client accounts come and go without rhyme or reason.

Reels and books are judged on creative merit alone by other creative people. No one really cares about where a print advertisement ran, or how long a commercial was on the air, or whether ads helped sales figures. In fact, if the advertisement that actually gets approved differs significantly from what creatives originally envisioned, they try, while the production crew is gathered together, to shoot and edit a version specifically for their reel or book that shows their initial conception. The reel or book version need never appear in a publicly communicated medium, though such public appearances are important for the annual allocation of prizes by the various creative clubs.[9] But, even if the work is underground, what really matters are the answers that creative peers give to questions about their work, such as: Is an advertisement imaginative, tasteful, craftsman-like, and striking? Does it have an internal logic? Does it turn symbols upside down in an innovative way? Does it make the product the hero in a riveting minidrama that holds people's attention? Only the good opinion of their peers gains creatives the standing in their tight-knit occupational community that ensures survival and that gives them a chance at mobility, big salaries, prestige, good projects, and say-so.

〜〜〜〜〜 The basic structural and experiential features of commercial advocacy work evident in the world of advertising creatives also obtain in the world of public relations. However, in the world of public relations, one can observe another wellspring of the extraordinary proliferation of interpretive expertise in our society.[10]

The thorough specialization and concomitant bureaucratization of every order and sphere of both private and public life in the last century has given enormous impetus to advertising but especially to public relations. Bureaucracies harness the exponential multiplication of ever more refined expertise on which modern society depends. One can scarcely imagine how the modern social order, with its social, scientific, and technological complexities could function for a single day without the knowledge and skills required for areas as diverse as, say, maintenance of heavy industrial equipment, high-steel construction work, actuarial work, computer software programming, chemical engineering, microbiological research, orthopedic surgery, arbitrage on Wall Street, governmental budget negotiations, the prosecution or defense of criminal offenders, or military planning for defense against nuclear attack. Mastery in any of these areas, let alone still more complex undertakings, is daunting indeed. At the same time, the very organizations that coordinate such substantive experts and bring their knowledge and skills to practical fruition, grow more and more intricate. These giant bureaucracies require increasingly complicated administrative expertise, lore that is just as arcane as the most abstruse substantive expertise.

Moreover, expert knowledge of whatever sort makes modern society complex in still other ways. One normally gains expert knowledge or skills only through extensive training. But experts do not remain experts for very long by dispensing such hard-won wisdom and practical skills in an openhanded fashion; instead, experts typically monopolize their expertise unless they can make money by selling it. Still further, professionals in any given arena look, first and foremost, to one another for self-validation. Expertise and the experience and access that it allows generate self-referential social groups scattered perhaps by geographical distance but marked by a kind of cognitive intimacy. The consequence of intensive, specialized training coupled with protective husbanding of knowledge, and of separate, tight-knit occupational communities, is a society that resembles, at the middle levels, a checkerboard with seemingly impassable moats around each square. What really happens in one square is, for the most part, unintelligible and uninteresting to those in other squares.

But, in fact, as substantive and administrative expertise proliferates so too does the demand for interpretive expertise. Coordination of substantive and administrative expertise requires at least a working understanding of both, knowledge that is fashioned by image-making interpretive experts. Moreover, sheer substantive or administrative wizardry in and of itself, like hard work or quality or competence or virtue, rarely brings worldly rewards. Rather, one has to claim expertise and have that claim honored by others. In big organizations, only those substantive and administrative experts who are dexterous with images and symbols, who can articulate their wisdom or managerial prowess to powerful others, get ahead.[11] In the marketplace, only those products positioned to ride the crest of public taste become household words. In the public forum, only those ideas that are acceptably framed and memorably sloganized get heard. And, in big-time public affairs, only those leaders who have risen to the top of their own organizations through the adroit use of interpretive expertise have the chance to step into the overlapping circles of elites from different social worlds where the big games are played.

Public relations practitioners are, first and foremost, interlocutors between worlds apart, wordsmiths with keen analogical and metaphorical acumen who link together people from different arenas of an increasingly segmented and fragmented society. They mediate between different groups of substantive experts whose varying fields of expertise, work experiences, or rank and prestige often impede necessary common efforts. They hammer out the frameworks that allow administrative experts to grasp and make useful the essentials of substantive expertise or to work together themselves despite disparate goals or personal rivalries.

Unlike advertising's appeals to mass audiences, public relations typically targets specific publics on specific issues. Public relations practitioners always work through well-established channels of communication, typically pitching their clients or wares indirectly, in contrast to advertising's direct sell. They create and promulgate various official versions of reality, that is, propaganda of one sort or another, whether directed at capturing the goodwill of the members of an organization through internal communications programs (sometimes accompanied by awards or bonuses), or at shaping public opinion on an issue, or at catching the ear of legislators and regulators, or at inducing the passive acquiescence of mass audiences. They promote institutional goals, products, images, and ideologies or help create a favorable public awareness of an individual or an organization. They manufacture a public persona for a rich, socially ambitious client, complete with fictitious accomplishments, as well as invitations to the whirl of elite social events that crowd Manhattan's fall social calendar. They position consumer products by saturating trade magazines with stories about the research that brought the products to market. They gussy up and pitch the sound but boring fundamentals of undervalued companies to jaded market analysts for big Wall Street brokerage firms. They help corporate managers plan for necessary emergency communications in the event of an anticipated disaster, such as an earthquake in California.[12] Or they develop advance strategies to communicate to multiple interested publics in order to contain the devastation of potential business catastrophes, such as bankruptcy,[13] or to calm and reassure the public during a consumer scare, such as when the media reported that a syringe had been discovered in a can of Diet Pepsi, setting off a frenzy of copycat complaints.[14] They ghostwrite speeches, articles, and sometimes whole books for top officials in both the private and public arenas.

Most important, public relations practitioners craft and package story lines for harried print and broadcast journalists. The practical meaning of the vast expansion in publishing and broadcasting capability in the years after the Second World War is that journalists have more space and time to fill and more deadlines to meet, a boon to public relations practitioners who delight in helping journalists see the world a certain way. Public relations and journalism are joined at the hip. Journalists would be lost without the information and the angles they get from their opposite numbers in public relations; public relations practitioners need the journalistic apparatus to reach their audiences. Both occupations are storytellers engaged in fashioning moral discourse within certain frameworks.

Higher-level public relations practitioners "spin" endless interpretations of events, creating the ambiguity that allows the momentum of exigency to triumph. They provide reporters who smell blood at an industrial, financial, or political catastrophe with plausible explanations for what went wrong; they then craft a restitution program that will help erase the stigma of perceived moral turpitude or business failure. They generate the all-is-right-with-the-world bland euphemisms that allow business as usual in the midst of turmoil as well as the denials of responsibility that keep the wolves at bay. They create the frameworks that make organizations, or particular policies, or mistakes intelligible to the media.

At the highest levels of their trade, public relations practitioners knit together the worlds of art, industry, politics, fashion, commerce, entertainment, and media, sometimes for profit, often for charity or the public weal. Top practitioners are men and women who know and understand people in all of these different worlds and are able to move freely and easily between worlds. They are spokespeople who address particular publics to garner goodwill or acquiescence for individuals and organizations; they recruit for causes, acting as brokers between the big foundations and men and women of substance; they bring people with money and a hunger for immortality together with cultural institutions more than willing to confer prestige for added space. Through underlings, they create and manage the black-tie social affairs that, in every major U.S. city every night of the week, draw together overlapping top circles in the easy give-and-take that seals deals. They are, in short, high-flying men and women who, linked together in their own elite organizations, bridge the separate squares of our society and make the world work.[15]

Public relations practitioners frequently provide the only voices of reason in the wilderness of irrationality that is public life in an unruly democracy. Very often they are the only ones insisting that officials tell the unvarnished truth, no matter how momentarily painful, because they understand better than anybody that hell hath no fury like journalists who discover that they have been fed, and perhaps have swallowed, lies.

And, at the very top of their trade, public relations counselors help men and women of affairs think and plan ahead. They invent better reasons for doing "what has to be done," reasons that give opponents pause, that convince key gatekeepers to open the portals, and, above all, convince men and women of affairs themselves of the wisdom and especially the propriety of their decisions so that they can implement and promote them without moral or psychological ambivalence that might prove fatal.

However, except at the top of the trade, most public relations work today is thoroughly bureaucratized. The public affairs office of any large corporation is as segmented and standardized as any other corporate division, although top-level in-house practitioners might have the ears of CEOs. In public relations agencies, most of which are now owned by big cash-rich advertising firms in order to give their clients double-barreled communications capabilities, partners and senior officials pitch clients and then farm the work out to fresh-out-of-college young men and women organized into account groups headed by senior vice presidents. The account groups are sometimes subdivided into different product lines or into other promotional assignments. Most public relations techniques used by junior practitioners are stock-in-trade: the poll that miraculously shows a rush of public support for one's client (the adage is, "Most people follow anything that moves"); the commissioned report or book that puts one's client at the center of action (the saying is, "If it's printed and between covers, it's gospel to some people"); the third-party endorsement from an authoritative source that herds unformed mass opinion into publics of a sort; and, of course, staged events like bicycle or foot races, tournaments of every sort, parades, marches and demonstrations, ethnic-group celebration days, contests, amusements, attention-grabbing stunts, and the myriad of other crowd-gathering devices that are part and parcel of American public life. Crowd interest in an event becomes a crucial part of the story about it, more fuel for hungry broadcast or print media. In reporting the event, the media inevitably trumpet the event's sponsor, whether it is the Virginia Slims tennis tournament, the New York City marathon with Timex's name at the finish line, DuPont's Solar Challenger flight across the English Channel at the height of widespread chemophobia,[16] AT&T's high-visibility media blitz to cover its divestiture in Hawaii, complete with a Sinatra concert, lei-making contests, and baseball clinic,[17] or the orgiastic self-celebration of the movie industry that is the annual Academy Awards show, all products of the public relations imagination. Prestigious Silver Anvil Awards, known as the "Oscars" of the public relations world, are given annually in different categories by the occupation's largest professional society, the Public Relations Society of America. The awards typically go to firms whose practitioners have displayed the imaginative use of highly standardized techniques in their creation of complete public relations programs.[18]

The paradigm of all public relations techniques, as Carl Byoir pointed out in 1935, is the front. A front is a Potemkin village, a constructed organization, sometimes with real properties, sometimes existing only on paper, that mobilizes public acclaim or acquiescence or opposition on an issue while disguising the driving material or political interests behind it. Thus, in a prototypical marketing front, the International Sleep Products Association sets up the Better Sleep Council that through a media blitz, a sponsored book, newsletters, press kits for radio news shows, quizzes, and the invention of "Better Sleep Month," stresses the keys to peaceful nights: replacing bedding regularly and buying high-quality, preferably king- or queen-size bedding.[19] Rockport shoes, with a view to position its company for a leveraged buyout, creates the Rockport Walking Institute, complete with physical fitness tests based on walking and, of course, a panel of medical experts testifying to the salutary benefits of hoofing it, especially in Rockport Prowalkers. In September 1987, Reebok rewarded the effort by buying Rockport for a premium price per share.[20] With the help of a public relations agency, a large environmental advocacy organization constructs a committee of concerned citizens to mobilize support for one of its causes; its plea for public pressure on legislators, complete with a fundraising letter to support the new committee, goes out on letterhead emblazoned with the names of famous public-cause scientists, well-known men and women of affairs, public figures of various sorts, and save-the-world movie stars eager to be identified with a noble purpose. Or FMC Corporation and Monsanto Chemical Company, two major suppliers of phosphates to the soap and detergent industries, blunt a campaign by environmentalist organizations to ban phosphates in the Susquehanna River, the main inland tributary of the Chesapeake Bay, by putting together a coalition of affected interests, spearheaded by the Pennsylvania Farmers' Association, to propose a constructive alternative to an outright ban.[21] A political faction establishes a "united front" to raise money for the coalition and attract adherents who wish involvement but not entanglement; another political faction establishes a semifictitious organization complete with fax and answering machines, letterhead with glittering names declaring support, and lapel buttons with a slogan proposing a "constructive alternative" to pending legislation; or same-industry big corporations bankroll and coordinate the activities of an association of small suppliers to lobby for favorable regulation. Borrowing such well-established techniques, lawyers well to the left of the political spectrum round up well-known novelists, academics, fashion models and designers, politicians, broadcasters, filmmakers, philosophers, poets, film critics, musicians, and feminists to adopt and champion the cause of Mumia Abu-Jamal, a man convicted in 1982 of killing a police officer in Philadelphia in late 1981. The Free Mumia Coalition argues that Mumia Abu-Jamal, a former Black Panther, "award-winning" journalist, and talk-show host, was "sentenced to death because of his political beliefs."[22] Like bureaucracies that harness into effective action men and women with little or nothing in common, well-constructed fronts mobilize people with dramatically varying degrees of understanding of an issue and with completely different motives for lending their names in support of it. As it happens, they help create a society where shifting institutional identities cloak agency.

〰〰〰〰 Work in advertising and public relations agencies is fraught with anxiety. The external frameworks that shape both worlds are, first of all, extremely volatile. The daily advertising column of the *New York Times,* or *Jack O'Dwyer's Newsletter, PRWeek,* and *Inside PR,* the weekly sentinels of public relations, or *Reputation Management,* a bimonthly journal, are always filled with the latest shifts of client accounts from one agency to another, complete with reports of accompanying personnel cuts in agencies that lose accounts and hirings in agencies that win them. Moreover, accounts often shift for reasons wholly unrelated to agency performance. A client hires a new chief executive officer and, however well her new company has been served by its longtime communications agencies, she decides to "throw the business" to old friends in other agencies with whom she "feels comfortable." A top executive attends a conference with his opposite numbers in other companies and hears scuttlebutt about the newest hot advertising or public relations agency, to which he shifts his communications budget lest he appear out of step with his peers. Advertising and public relations practitioners always suffer when even their best-served clients come to believe the public images handcrafted for them. Once clients internalize the images, they fire the image makers lest they be reminded of the origins of their self-congratulations. Moreover, despite public claims to rational prediction of market directions, practitioners in both disciplines privately shake their heads at the irrationality of popular taste, fads, and opinion in a world where, say, extraordinarily ugly low-cost dolls can suddenly command thousands of dollars in a frenzied market, or where, defying all the rules of reasonable analogical thinking, an isolated incident can be successfully made to symbolize a whole social trend, or where today's scandalous behavior becomes tomorrow's accepted practice, or where, inside their own organizations, a star can become a goat overnight by mistaking a minnow for a whale, or vice versa, or where a lowly greenhorn can suddenly become everybody's bright-eyed girl by hitting upon exactly the image or words that excite rich clients. In such a world, security is elusive ("At any minute, I feel like I could fall off the merry-go-round"), and success often seems arbitrary and capricious.

But the topsy-turvy nature of their world actually makes commercial advocates work all the harder to be attentive to the market, to their clients, and, of course, to each other. One watches every news event, every social trend, the arrival of every new celebrity with an eye to riding whichever wave is cresting and to discerning the successful promotional techniques of their peers. One redoubles one's efforts to please existing clients. This is often a difficult task. Some clients have hoof-and-mouth disease (such as the sugar manufacturer who wanted his public relations practitioners to use the slogan "Eat a little sugar before meals; it will help you lose weight"). Other clients use agency practitioners to wage factional warfare against rivals in their own hierarchies. Other extremely demanding clients become furious when their public relations practitioners are not around to hold their hands and suffer with them; others delight in enforcing their will ("I don't care whether the plane crashed or not; he was supposed to be at that meeting"). And still others, no matter what one says or does, are always disappointed (A client: "Whatever you do, don't let the press come to this party. This is strictly for our guys." And after the affair, which was a resounding success: "If only you had invited the press").

One also scrambles constantly for new clients. In public relations agencies, partners at the top of the always narrow tips of organizational pyramids are always foraging for work and, almost invariably, overpromising clients on their firms' capabilities and on the extent of their own time commitment to projects, even as they pass the work on to lower-paid underlings who bill clients at the partners' rates. Partners thus become hostage to their juniors' capabilities, always on call to man a fire bucket in the event of a conflagration; they respond by standardizing public relations techniques to gain a measure of control over their subordinates. Despite all the promises in the world made to them when they begin their careers, overworked juniors learn quickly that there is no room for them at the top of agencies and, as increased standardization makes integration of other fresh-out-of-college recruits easier, each annual raise in salary only makes them more expendable even as they struggle to cover their bosses' extravagant promises. In overpromising, the relationship of a public relations firm to its employees mirrors its relationships with clients.

The institution of shootouts or gang bangs, mentioned earlier, captures in a paradigmatic way the hunt for clients in advertising and its meaning. The scenario is almost always the same. The powers-that-be at a client with a lucrative account decide that their company needs new advertising ("We've decided that it's time for a change") and that there should be an open competition for its business. They announce the competition, establishing some broad marketing parameters for it. They invite several agencies to jump into the fray, sometimes, but by no means always, including the agency that currently holds the account. The competition takes place at two levels. Each agency commissions research and then divides its creative force into teams that put all other work aside and, with each team usually working in great secrecy, create whole advertising campaigns for the prospective client. The battle inside agencies is invariably fierce since the stakes are high: winners get to present their work directly to the client in the larger interagency competition, where one can step into the spotlight and gain recognition from one's peers. If one gets the client's nod, of course, one can look forward, at least for awhile, to hero status in one's own agency plus all the emoluments of a fat account. But the organizational and psychological costs are also high: work schedules shattered, other clients disgruntled, acrimony and suspicion between work groups, and the abiding perception that clients with big accounts take sadistic pleasure in watching ad makers jump through hoops.

The interagency competition is just as fierce. In the early 1980s, an agency could compete in a shootout by making cardboard mock-ups of commercials, complete with slogans and proposed sequences of ads with creatives as the actors. Then the norm became "ripomatics," commercials spliced together (that is, "ripped off") from bits of finished work, with editing costs running about $500 an hour. But by the late 1980s, successful bids for new business required agencies to produce several highly polished commercials, complete with slogans and music, sometimes at costs of hundreds of thousands of dollars in out-of-pocket agency expenses. The small grants that clients occasionally give competing agencies never approach the real costs that batter the losers in particular.[23]

The volatility of advertising and public relations exacerbates the uncertainty that accompanies the already shifting and ambiguous criteria for judging the quality of work in both worlds. Although bosses' and peers' judgments internally dominate both worlds, clients always have the whip hand ("Clients' wishes are agencies' commands") and become the savior or nemesis of image makers' lives. Today's client's fancy can quickly become tomorrow's new wave, upsetting and rearranging established evaluative frameworks and giving at least temporary ascendancy to the image makers who read clients or the market correctly. In worlds of shifting standards, craftsman-like notions of work are meaningless, despite occasionally expressed longings for such settled frameworks. Instead, one must stay constantly attentive to the way other people want their worlds constructed. One's work, occupational self-image, and indeed one's fate become hostage to others. One sees oneself "standing in a phone booth, waiting for an important call," or one becomes "a hired gun walking down a dark alley, four guys waiting at the end," or one comes to see one's clients as "smiling assassins." Such anxiety breeds the particular habits of mind and the occupational ethics of interpretive experts.

Finally, image makers in both disciplines come to know that the world is made, not given, and that everything depends on getting the right audiences to applaud their productions. This bracing understanding of the world's artifice leads the best practitioners to develop a steely dispassion about their clients and their problems, sometimes taken for cynicism. But the dispassion is less temperamental than practical. Emotional commitment can only blind one to what has to be done to transform a client's weaknesses into strengths. However, one must always be able to summon the requisite emotional energy to convince audiences of one's wholehearted belief in the propositions of the moment.

Image makers are thus always engaged in selling several products to their clients: not only their work, but themselves; not only themselves, but a roseate vision of the future. Clients at the middle levels of corporations, steeped in substantive expertise, cannot grasp the significance of interpretive expertise. Clients at the top often forget its importance and, like a pope at his coronation, need to be reminded that *sic transit gloria mundi* unless one works assiduously at garnering glory.

Therefore, the first rule of thumb for image makers is: mass persuasion depends on relentless self-promotion ("People buy people, not ideas, because they know that ideas are a dime a zillion and that the guy in the next room will have seventeen good ones"). Image makers convince their clients to buy images by inspiring confidence in their own creativity, wisdom, and experience. The second rule of thumb is: clients want to believe that everything is going to be all right. To make their own way in the world, commercial advocates become prophets of good fortune.[24]

5 HABITS OF MIND

Along with the fierce competition and anxiety of bureaucratized work worlds, the exigencies of addressing mass audiences place premiums on the cultivation of particular ways of thinking. Commercial advocates everywhere share certain tools-in-trade. More important, they come to evince characteristic habits of mind.

〰〰〰 Ad makers are the quintessential commercial advocates. They address mass audiences, the anonymous groupings of otherwise unconnected men, women, youth, and children who happen to share certain external demographic characteristics coupled with preferences for particular products, general lifestyles, or sets of opinions. Defining audiences is, of course, a big business in its own right. Scientific market research began with the harnessing of American sociology to the world of affairs in the 1930s. Then, newly developing quantitative social research methods were used first to decipher audiences for advertising firms and subsequently to pioneer early ventures in public opinion polling, now a staple of all electoral politics.[1] Since the financial stakes in market prognostication are enormous, the field regularly goes through great upheavals, as different firms invent and market new measures to make sense of the bewildering variety of values, attitudes, and lifestyles in the United States. Whether they assert the know-how to make focus groups illuminating, or the ability to discern the memorability of tag lines,[2] or, in the late 1980s, the "ethnographic edge" that field-savvy anthropologists can provide, all audience measures claim to provide a rational handle on volatile public tastes and moods, a notion that, however dubious, is comforting to clients who spend millions of dollars trying to reach particular audiences. The need for defensible rationales in internal corporate forums prevents much awareness that mass audiences, so defined, are basically conceptual categories delineating statistically correlated social characteristics and opinions or behavior. Briefly, audiences exist principally in the minds of those who construct and address them. Once an audience is defined and addressed, individual members of that audience may recognize commonalities shared with others in similar social circumstances. In fact, ad makers take as one of their main tasks the fashioning of images and symbols that link individuals in mass audiences to fictive social identities, such as the rugged Marlboro man, the beach-cavorting Pepsi generation, or la femme Victoria.

Television remains the principal medium to reach mass audiences despite the extremely important advances in information technology such as the Internet. Any night of the week, advertisers count on addressing millions of people watching television programs dotted with commercial messages. A sponsor underwrites a program presented to him by a network studio head that, it is argued, appeals to members of the sponsor's defined market. The usual scientific rationales justify the appeal of any program. However, according to one network studio head,[3] the actual decision to proceed with a show is typically extraordinarily casual and determined principally by the studio head's personal relationships with the sponsor and with the producer of a particular show. If a show's market share, as measured by Nielsen Media Research[4] dips below a certain standard, then the sponsor abandons the show, the show collapses, and the process begins anew. The standards for "acceptable" market share have slipped dramatically in recent years, from nearly 30 percent during the heyday of network television to as low as 18 percent today; some network shows get by for awhile with 12 percent. The overall network share of the mass audience has fallen since 1995 from about 70 percent to about 55 percent.

This splintering of the national market is due to the decentralization of home entertainment made possible by video cassette recorder technology and the proliferation of video rental stores as well as by multichannel cable television. The average middle-class family now has access to scores of cable channels with every variety of entertainment and shopping at its fingertips. In addition, according to Nielsen//Net-Ratings, 35 million households (34 percent of all U.S. households) or about 97 million people (36 percent of the total U.S. population), had

Internet access by January 1999. Moreover, each month more and more people are turning to the Internet for news, information, education, shopping, and entertainment. The segmentation of the market is also evident in the explosive growth in the last decade of highly specialized magazines treating virtually every phase of every life cycle, from the anxieties of youth to the frailties of old age, along with special publications catering to every conceivable interest.

As a result of these and related developments, marketers, with an eye to marketing their own craft, have emphasized the necessity of targeting markets more carefully by taking some salient aspect of people's lives and making it the entire organizing focus for appeals. So, for instance, marketers have targeted audiences they call "Wellderlies" (rich widows) and "POSSLQs" (persons of the opposite sex sharing living quarters), also known as "mingles" or "couplets." But, even if one makes the dubious assumption that, say, couplet status definitively shapes one's psychology and spending habits, such targets are still mass audiences, widely scattered and unconnected to one another. Television continues to be the most powerful way of reaching such audiences and linking its members through a constructed identity. Moreover, even if a show garners only 18 percent of a nightly viewing audience, advertisers have a chance to address between 17 and 20 million people. Occasional extravaganzas like the annual professional football championship, the Super Bowl, provide access to mega-audiences of over 100 million people domestically and up to 1 billion people around the world.

But all rational attempts to delineate audiences, however necessary and useful, can only provide the framework for fashioning mass appeals. In fact, advertising creatives privately scoff at social scientific tools to identify target audiences for particular products that go beyond such rudimentary parameters as economic class, age, gender, and color. In shaping their work, they always write or fashion images with specific individuals in mind—a grandmother in Dubuque, a girlfriend on East Eighty-seventh Street, a brother in Atlanta—and not disembodied categories. When they talk about addressing such specific people, creatives echo Bill Bernbach's constantly reiterated axioms about what is persuasive: far more than rational strategies, success in mass image making depends on one's abilities to tap the nonrational, sometimes irrational, emotional wellsprings of human thought, desire, and behavior. Emotion, not reason, sways individuals and mass audiences alike. Empirical facts never suffice. Even formally rational appeals to good sense—for example, that a certain product (a means) provides one with good value for one's money (a desirable end)—lack the "push" to motivate action.[5] Instead, to be successful one must connect a product with raw, sometimes primitive, feelings, such as the fear of social rejection ("Always a bridesmaid, never a bride"); the eagerness for prowess in sexual competition ("If you've got it, flaunt it"); the daydream of becoming a "real" man ("I was a 97-pound weakling"); the quest for individualized personal identity ("It lets you be you"); the desire for validation of personal worth ("L'Oreal: because I deserve it"); the hunger for social revenge ("They laughed when I sat down to play the piano"); the quest for self-improvement ("Be all that you can be"); the desire, whether motivated by longing or guilt, for family-like associations ("Reach out and touch someone"); humor ("If you are over or under 35 . . . you need SNIAGRAB [spell it backwards]"); the fantasy of escape from workaday routine or confining social roles ("The night belongs to Michelob"); or the longing for a simpler, more settled, less fractious society ("I'd like to teach the world to sing in perfect harmony").

One cannot hope to make a complicated, nuanced, rational argument, especially in a few fleeting seconds. But even if longer time blocks were available, the efficacy of reasonable argument is highly problematic. Audiences are besieged by appeals and claims of every variety; one must cut through the "clutter" with sharp-edged sentiments engaging people's hearts rather than their minds. Most people caged in the humdrum routines of modern life are eager for vicarious glimpses of pain, joy, and especially vitality. One tries then to invent "little moments" that allow members of audiences to enter mini-melodramas that are variously funny, clever, inspiring, heartwarming, or downright sentimental. Sometimes the notion of "little moments" is quite specific. Some years ago, Maxwell House was fearful of the declining consumption of coffee among younger consumers because of growing anticaffeine sentiments; their advertising agency created a series of ads, each featuring a "coffee moment," predictably complete with young people mooning over each other while drinking coffee on rainy days at the beach, in sidewalk cafes, and in other locations popularly associated with romance. But the notion of "little moments" also reflects a more pervasive habit of mind, specifically a notion of what is possible in speaking to mass audiences. In a world where even the personal experiences of individuals are fragmented and obscure, the idea of presenting a coherent vision of anything to millions of people seems foolhardy. One settles, then, for fleeting images, done with a broad or impressionistic brushstroke, that appeal to specific people one knows and to oneself and, it is hoped, that will reach across the checkerboard of other people's worlds and elicit some common identification or longing.[6]

One also constructs images of imaginary worlds that, one thinks, specific kinds of people will find inviting. Thus, one has endless soft drink commercials that construct worlds of slim and nubile youth rollicking on the beach, a world of high-spirited innocent fun colored with a hint of sexual promise; perfume advertisements that present a sophisticated, tailored world of mannered elegance; or automobile ads that promise reckless adventure behind the wheel, an escape from routinized boredom and self alike. A classic example of this genre was the late-1980s television advertisement that the network CBS used to promote itself. A young woman comes home from her construction job dressed in overalls. She ignores the panoramic view of Manhattan available from her picture window and flips on the television with her dog at her side. Suddenly, the dog, fascinated by something, leaps into the screen. Like Alice down the rabbit hole, the girl follows him. The advertisement bursts into song: "Come into the world of CBS, you'll be with the friends you love the best." In the course of a whirlwind adventure, the young woman meets all of the stars of CBS's prime-time shows, including a handsome young man who gives her a scarf from his neck. Soon she finds herself outside the television set, back in her room, her dog next to her with the scarf in his mouth. Such advertisements appeal to the millions of viewers for whom the imaginary world of television is both more real and enticing than daily life. A decade later, ABC recycled the same idea with verbal billboard ads, adding tongue-in-cheek irony to its slogans, appealing to the felt importance of the imaginary world of television while acknowledging the widespread psychological ambivalence toward the medium: "8 hours a day, that's all we ask," "It's a beautiful day, what are you doing outside?" "TV is like a muscle, if you don't use it, you lose it," "You can talk to your wife anytime," "Don't just sit there. OK, just sit there," "Don't worry, you've got billions of brain cells," and even "Before TV, two World Wars. After TV, zero."

Political advertisements specialize in images of imaginary worlds. Typically, a candidate's ad makers paint a picture of a world with an appealing moral and social structure, claiming that world as the candidate's own. Ronald Reagan's 1984 presidential campaign contained commercials that are classics of the genre. Along with graceful images of small towns, rolling, dappled hills, and close-knit, friendly groups of people is the story:

> It's morning again in America. Today more men and women will go to work than ever before in our country's history. With interest rates at one half of the record highs of 1980, nearly 2000 families will buy new homes today, more than at any time in the last four years. This afternoon, 6500 young men and women will be married and with inflation at one half of what it was just four years ago, they can look forward with confidence to the future.
>
> It's morning again in America. Under the leadership of President Reagan, America is prouder, stronger, and better. Why would we ever want to return to where we were just four short years ago?

A bleak backdrop, here allusions to the economic vicissitudes of the 1976–1980 Carter presidency, makes imaginary worlds all the more appealing. However illusory, President Reagan's world was one that millions of people decided to join, as measured by the massive Republican victory in the 1984 presidential race.

What is called "negative campaigning" works essentially in reverse. One fashions disturbing, sometimes frightening, images of the world, suggesting what the future might hold if one's opponent wins. In 1964, Doyle Dane Bernbach created the famous commercial urging President Lyndon Johnson's reelection over Senator Barry Goldwater. The ad shows a little girl plucking petals from a flower while counting from one to nine. At the same time, a voice-over counts backwards from ten to zero, when the unmistakable mushroom cloud of an atomic blast fills the screen, obliterating the child's face and suggesting what might happen should Goldwater win the election. The voice-over says: "These are the stakes: to make a world in which all of God's children can live or go into the dark. We must either love each other or we must die. The stakes are too high for you to stay at home." In the late 1980s, in a local campaign in Philadelphia, a church group disturbed by one candidate's advocacy of civil rights for homosexuals ran an ad portraying a world run by black-leather-clad gay activists complete with clenched fists and gleaming silver studs. The coarseness of such images is only an upside-down version of the mawkish sentimentality of most imaginary worlds.

Typically, one flatters audiences to entice them into imaginary worlds. Writers from Plato, Theophrastus, and Plutarch to Castiglione and Joseph Hall have all drawn detailed portraits of the flatterer. The flatterer is endlessly attentive to the person whose favor he wishes to gain, solicitous to a fault, anticipating his every need. The flatterer recognizes that self-love makes everyone his own greatest flatterer. By becoming all things to all men, the flatterer finds a way to rub against the person whom he wishes to entice, seeking every opportunity to praise that person, even if gratuitously, and creating all the while a sense of intimacy, of counsel, of friendship, and of personal caring. The flatterer turns the kindling fire of self-love into a raging flame.[7] Thus, advertising creatives invite men into a world of boisterous horseplay and easy camaraderie by praising and rewarding them for their hard work ("For all you do, this Bud's for you") or by extolling their own purported accomplishments, while picturing athletes in fierce competition ("Bring out your best! You found it in yourself and now you've found it in the beer you drink"). Creatives invite women to smoke and join the company of slim, leggy, avant-garde girls by extolling women's traverse of great social distance marked by a time when female smoking was taboo ("You've come a long way, baby!"). Creatives create a commercial that piggybacks on the powerful social trend toward self-celebration, identifying one's product as a force that will liberate even the recesses of a consumer's soul ("Celebrate your inner beauty"). They insinuate exclusivity by pointedly addressing only those presumably capable of discriminating taste and sensibility in selecting greeting cards ("For those who care enough to send the very best"). They sell a magazine by suggesting that the "success crowd" reads it. They use the MTV-inspired "television within television" gambit in a commercial to josh the self-conscious viewer about watching television. They invite harried families into the maximally safe and predictable world of a fast food chain by noting and rewarding their conquest of the travails of everyday life ("You deserve a break today"). They appropriate (paying appropriate royalties) a jingle or ditty (alternately called "rugs" or "carpets" or "spoonfuls of sugar") turning, say, the Beach Boys' hit "California Girls" into "Herbal Essence Girls" or they create corporate anthems reminiscent of popular hits that everyone who is "with it" recognizes and relates to, manufacturing a kind of instant community of knowing acknowledgment.

Creatives also flatter audiences' sophistication by drawing attention to the artifice used in making advertising images. Creatives acknowledge audiences' disbelief in the contemporary onslaught of media images by placing, as did advertisements for AT&T in the late 1990s, several television screens in a commercial capturing the company's spokeswoman in the midst of her pitch. Other creatives appeal to middle-class irony and sagacity by attributing clodlike Miller Lite ads to a fictive advertising copywriter named "Dick." Other creatives engage in a self-parody of advertising itself by running a Sprite campaign that mocks typical cavorting-on-the-beach ads for a fictive rival soda called "Jooky," proclaiming all the while that "Image Is Nothing."

Caricature, often used by creatives in avant-garde commercials, embodies such self-consciousness to a high degree even as ads utilizing caricature usually praise audiences for other virtues. Only the bright, alert individual finds his way out of the zombie-like regimentation of most white-collar office work into the bright future promised by one Control Data Institute. Only adventurous, courageous computer users joyfully anticipate mankind's liberation from IBM's gray totalitarian Big-Brother-like stranglehold on information technology and vault into the new world with Apple or identify with Bob Dylan, or Miles Davis, or John Lennon in bed with Yoko Ono, all rebels in their own endeavors, whose placards around their career-peak images proclaim: "Think different."

As it happens, within the experience of any particular member of an audience, even the virtues that admit one to imaginary worlds or grant distinction in those worlds might themselves be wholly imaginary or objects of longing. Creatives thus offer advertising blandishments that enable a member of a mass audience both to enjoy the illusion of significant self-alteration and to congratulate oneself at the same time on one's achievement, a plant so hearty that it often astonishes those who sowed the seeds.[8]

〰〰〰 Stories, and only stories, reach individuals in mass audiences. In fact, from the standpoint of commercial interpretive experts, most people in modern society are incapable of sustained, rational, critical, comparative thinking about anything, perhaps especially about their own lives. In this view, most people are trapped within the world of their own personal experiences, through which they see the world and from which they generalize about nearly everything. They organize their lives around little stories, narratives complete with heroes, villains, fools, goats, and moral lessons; whatever consistency any one person's collection of stories might contain remains largely unarticulated. Further, any master narratives that once might have galvanized society and linked people one to another, or aspired to provide overarching frameworks of understanding, are now objects of curiosity or derision, instead of possible enlightenment or inspiration. Half-said notions, false starts, dimly felt sentiments, and unfinished tales mark the lives of most people in modern society. In a time when the unity of experience is shattered, interpretive experts believe that their only hope of communicating clients' messages is to place them within the context of stories that, however briefly, achieve resonance with some aspects of the scattered narratives of audiences' members. This means fashioning stories compelling enough to keep individuals in an audience attentive but open-ended enough to allow them to graft their own meanings onto them.

Both the centrality and the key characteristics of these kinds of stories become clear when one examines the relationship between public relations practitioners and journalists. Public relations practitioners target audiences with greater exactitude than men and women in advertising. Indeed, some of these targeted audiences are well-defined communities, with individuals sharing occupational, professional, friendship, or reputational ties. For instance, one whole public relations specialty does nothing but point out, in endless rounds of breakfast gatherings, newsletters, and personal meetings, the undervalued aspects of particular companies to the normally short-sighted occupational community of Wall Street financial analysts. Other public relations practitioners lobby similarly well-formed groups like the United States Congress, federal energy policymakers, established councils of business leaders, or an association of college presidents, all on behalf of particular clients. Public relations practitioners have always oriented themselves toward "opinion leaders" with the expectation that these leaders will then transmit desired messages through their own networks of communication, thus lending the weight of established institutional authority to facts and views crafted by image makers. But among the many audiences that mediate the work of public relations practitioners to mass audiences, none are more important than journalists.

Journalists are the prototypical storytellers of our epoch. They work under strict deadlines to please their editors and to capture the attention of individuals in mass audiences. Editors guard the reputation, ethos, and tone of their publications principally by insisting on the story form as the vehicle for conveying information and by dictating the kinds of stories they want to publish. Only journalists who can spot and write good stories that interest their editors can survive and flourish in their always competitive world and gain the adulation of their peers. Although one could readily establish a hierarchy of journalistic publications and of broadcast journalism on the criterion of complexity of content, the essential task facing all journalists is exactly parallel to that faced by other interpretive experts: how to fashion accessible tales out of the extraordinarily complex realities that characterize virtually any segment of life in modern society.

In fashioning such stories, journalists perform an important public service. Most individuals in the vastly differentiated mass audiences that constitute the readership of a metropolitan daily paper or especially the viewing audience of television news programs are incapable of grasping the arcane complexities of, say, scientists' worlds. The journalist's task in such a case is to find a way to open up the particular scientific milieu under scrutiny and make it intelligible to the mass audience while at the same time making the journalistic representation resonate with established cultural expectations and vocabularies. As a result, a great deal of scientific journalism consists of stories about "new scientific discoveries" with their implied social benefits or stories that profile working scientists, complete with all their recognizable eccentricities, or if the journalist is enterprising and lucky, stories about fraud, deception, or political squabbles within particular scientific circles. Such narratives almost always highlight the dramatic and personal while downplaying the ambiguous and always provisional character of scientific work. In the process, the journalist helps create a new reality, a world of half-baked pop science, sometimes in collaboration with enterprising scientists themselves. For examples of this genre, one need only read the declarations on virtually any topic made by the social scientists regularly cited in the *New York Times*. One might also follow the vagaries of research on, say, cholesterol (some is good, some is bad) and heart disease, the dangers, innocuousness, or benefits of eating eggs or drinking wine, the wonders or hidden perils of vitamins, or the blessings or potential catastrophes of nuclear fission. One always strives to discover, or invent, a hidden drama even, perhaps especially, out of the grind of empirical work. Of course, the habits of mind required to gain journalists' attention, once adopted by scientists in order to promote their work to wider audiences, find their way back into a scientific community's own allocation of rewards. Put briefly, scientists with their eye on the main chance within their professions find ready allies in journalists who understand modern society's craving for experts willing to make pronouncements that might ease contemporary bewilderment.

Despite the general tendencies of their field toward either attack-dog-aggressive inquisition or hero worship and sentimentality, especially in broadcast journalism, journalists can still open otherwise closed doors for people. They are most successful in doing so when they present unvarnished, first-hand views of unknown, unusual, or difficult-to-access worlds, often at the margins of the social order, or reports from worlds in turmoil such as frontline battle dispatches during wartime, however partial these might be. For instance, Ken Auletta wrote the first widely read, multidimensional account of the underclass in the United States; the most valuable accounts of the Vietnam War came from brave and dedicated men like Bernard B. Fall and R. W. Apple, Jr., both of whom provided graphic, on-the-ground portraits of that savage conflict.

Journalists are least successful in the now ubiquitous "story behind the story," the editorializing sidebar that panders to a media-savvy public's implicit understanding of journalists' role in constructing the very realities they report. Moreover, journalists themselves are often incapable of understanding the intricacies of the worlds on which they report, and they increasingly have trouble finding people who are willing to speak to them openly and honestly for attribution. As a result, in their search for stories, journalists frequently become hostage to both professional and amateur experts in misinformation and disinformation. In New York City, at least, accusations of police brutality or racial bias attacks, when made by appropriately media-certified, minority-group spokesmen, are always big news, whatever the actual merits of particular cases. The same rule applies increasingly to accusations of sexual harassment made against public figures. Journalists are even more dependent on the public relations practitioners who are now key participants in every institutional order. A great many of the latter are themselves journalists who have "crossed the street," who are paid well to dream up and package stories for their former colleagues, and who like nothing better than bright, lazy journalists. According to public relations practitioners, there are plenty of these around. Of course, the joy that public relations practitioners take in manipulating journalists must remain a secret pleasure.

Journalists' images of themselves and of the world emerge directly out of their work and the stances they take toward it. A great many young journalists, especially the ambitious and talented who always provide the clue to understanding the ethos of any occupation, see themselves as moral crusaders, *oculi populi*, ripping away benign public masks to expose rigid bureaucracies, corrupt administrations, and social inequities for everyone to see, while championing the downtrodden. They see their mission, in the old journalistic saw, as a calling to "comfort the afflicted and afflict the comfortable." Their heroes are the reporter played by James Stewart in *Call Northside 777* (1948), who relentlessly pursues the truth about a man convicted of murder whom he believes is innocent, or the crusading editor played by Humphrey Bogart in *Deadline U.S.A.* (1952). Those who long for supersleuth status idolize Carl Bernstein and Bob Woodward, who broke the story on the Watergate break-in and its subsequent cover-up, portrayed on the screen by Dustin Hoffman and Robert Redford in *All the President's Men* (1976), or Sydney Schanberg, the reporter then with the *New York Times* who investigated the secret war in Cambodia, portrayed in *The Killing Fields* (1984) by Sam Waterston. Some journalists never lose their youthful fervor. But, generally speaking, the more successful journalists are in their work, the more they are courted by men and women in power with blandishments that help them see the world in more complex ways. In addition to being wined and dined and transported all over the world, they are given inside dope in return for being, as it were, more responsible. Some who reach this point become pundits, voices of the peculiar, high-minded moralism that emanates from high places. They are aided in this regard by policies now in place in most major newspapers and broadcast journalism shows. "Op ed" pages afford editors a place to allow the expression of sentiments that they do not wish to put on their editorial pages proper and thereby seem to endorse formally.[9] Other journalists, as their access to various social worlds improves, realize that things are often worse than they had imagined early in their careers, though now they find the world colored gray instead of black and white. Most of these settle for simply reporting the always contradictory viewpoints on any issue, appealing to the need for balance and allowing the "marketplace of ideas" to adjudicate the differences. Others seek out sources who provide "quotable" sentiments backing the viewpoint that the journalists and their editors wished to present in the first place. A few journalists transform their early zealotry into a tough-minded skepticism that allows them to assess such contradictions with some judiciousness. Some public relations practitioners undergo a similar transformation in a different direction, from tough-minded, often cynical defenders of the establishment to zealous crusaders for reform.

Journalists' images of the world are shaped by their most distinctive occupational claim, namely, that they are engaged in a search for truth, at least, as their occupational adage goes, the truth as it appears to them at deadline. Moreover, responsible journalists do strive to report ascertainable and corroborated "facts." The search for truth, they argue, sets them apart from the myriad of other storytellers in modern society, especially "PR flaks" and ad makers about whom journalists almost always speak scornfully. But journalists' hunger for stories, coupled with the dramatizing exigencies of the narrative form when directed toward mass audiences, clash with the ambiguities requisite to veracity in such a way that journalists often become indistinguishable from practitioners in the sister occupations that they regularly revile. Editors, of course, play a crucial role here in eliciting narratives with simple, untangled story lines.

Ad makers and public relations practitioners alike find journalists' exalted self-images amusing, although they marvel at the journalistic profession's ability to propagate a high-mindedness that allows for regular self-congratulation. In this view, journalistic stories, just like those produced by men and women in advertising or public relations, or indeed in other arenas of popular culture, are basically forms of pointed entertainment. Among many other possibilities, these stories enthrall audiences through their sheer gripping quality or their bemusing lightheartedness; or they provide vicarious access to otherwise inaccessible social worlds; or they titillate audiences with startling, shocking, or daring themes; or they stimulate outrage at perceived social injustice or official malfeasance. They comfort audiences with stock-in-trade middle-class nostrums jazzed up with appropriate new vocabularies; or they invite there-but-for-the-grace-of-god relief with stories of the quirks and ironies of fickle fortune. Such stories introduce a political slant, a commercial message, or an attempt to mobilize public opinion only in the course of entertaining.

Dramatization with a focus on individuals is the hallmark of this kind of entertaining public narrative. Virtually all advertising strives for it. The Red Cross does not simply appeal for blood; instead, it portrays a little girl and her brother wandering downtown streets forlornly asking passers-by to donate blood for their sick sibling. In seeking volunteers, the Coalition for Literacy does not simply report the staggering number of illiterate or semiliterate people in the United States; instead, it shows an almost illiterate father stumbling through *The Little Engine That Could* with his young daughter, ending with "I knew I could." The United Negro College Fund does not just ask for contributions; instead, it portrays two hard-working parents breaking the bad news to their eighteen-year-old son that college tuition is beyond their means, followed by the young man's little brother offering him a jar of pennies. The Milwaukee AIDS Project does not simply warn young people about the dangers of promiscuous sexual behavior; instead, it presents a tightly packed bar scene with blaring music and young virile and nubile bodies crushed close to one another, with a voice overlay: "Can you find the person who has the HIV virus here?" Then a young woman is seen leaving with a new male acquaintance, obviously heading toward the nearest bed, and the viewer hears: "She did." The Cleveland Scholarship Program does not simply state its annual awards to needy inner-city students; instead, it produces a booklet profiling twenty of its recipients, "using short sentences, tight writing and warm photography to tell [its] story in human terms." [10] The United States Forest Service does not simply warn people about the dangers of forest fires; instead, it shows a lighted match being put to paper-doll figures of a family of four with the reminder that forest fires can burn a lot more than trees.

Most major public relations campaigns also rely increasingly on dramatized stories of one sort or another. When the state of Missouri instituted a lottery to raise monies, it needed to teach both players and ticket agents the rules of the number-picking game in which one tries to pick six out of thirty-nine numbers. The state's public relations practitioners developed a campaign with "fantastic photo opportunities and a participation-oriented theme." Campaign workers launched thirty-nine brightly colored, hot-air balloons, each with a numbered banner, that raced across the central corridor of the state from Kansas City to St. Louis. While the balloons were floating in their mad dash across the state, Missourians were invited to play the "Great Lotto Sky Chase" by filling out play slips predicting which six balloons would win the competition. The race ended with a massive televised photo session at the finish line. [11] When Old Stone Bank in Providence, Rhode Island, desired to burnish its image as an integral part of the community by focusing on children's education, its public relations agency, utilizing the bank's long-term mascot Fred Flintstone, produced a children's book, *Puritans, Pioneers, and Pacesetters: Eight People Who Shaped Rhode Island,* to help youngsters "Leap into Literature." It then developed dramatic performances based on four chapters of the book and produced more than two hundred dramatizations for thousands of children and parents, complete with extensive media coverage and awards from the Library Association. [12] When the Keebler Company wanted to demonstrate its commitment to the youth of the United States, it sponsored its "I believe in me" drug awareness program, complete with a traveling stage show at shopping malls, featuring young performers, puppets, and the dispersal of "self-esteem certificates." [13]

Such dramatized extravaganzas increasingly mark communication in virtually every public arena of our society. Publicists and image makers of every sort vie with each other in fashioning new dramatic ways of commanding audiences' attention. They also try to fashion stories that they know will appeal to members of the mass media who long for what the master publicist Harry Reichenbach called "wish-news," news so compelling that city editors, even as they print it, wish were true.[14] The widely-reported "odyssey" of thirteen-year-old Edwin Daniel Sabillón illustrates just how gripping wish-news can be. Sabillón took New York City, and indeed the world, by storm in late June 1999 with a fantastic saga of the escape/quest variety. Sabillón said that he fled from the devastating Hurricane Mitch in his native Honduras, a disaster that killed his whole family, including his mother and brother. He set off for New York City to find his father, his only surviving next of kin. After hitchhiking through Guatemala and Mexico, he was befriended by immigrant smugglers who sneaked him into the United States free of charge. He hitchhiked, biked, and walked first to Houston and then to Corpus Christi, Galveston, New Orleans, and finally Miami, meeting Good Samaritans all along the way who Godspeeded his journey with money and well-wishes. He arrived in New York City by bus, financed by customers in a Miami restaurant whom he had regaled with his tale, and was aided in his search for his father by a Bronx cabdriver, who alerted the authorities. The boy endeared himself immediately not only to the press, which pounced on the story, but to the offices of the mayor and the police commissioner, to literary agents who know a good story when they see one, and to millions of New Yorkers. As it happens, Sabillón's tale was largely fabricated. Among many other things, his mother turned out to be alive and well while his father died many years ago. One columnist suggested that Sabillón's narrative inventiveness, whether his story was true or not, still made him "a quintessential New York success story." The columnist went on to acknowledge one of the "secrets of media relations in New York: to make it here, sometimes all you have to do is make it up."[15] Today, certain carefully constructed images, even though expressly selling some product, person, or cause, are a kind of wish-news. And sometimes the world presents the media with ready-made wish-news, such as sex-and-politics scandals that everybody can understand, that is so compelling that editors have no choice, in the face of public demand, but to "feed the beast."

The media gravitate to certain images like moths to flame, even when these images are transparently manufactured. Take, for example, the "Tang March Across America for MADD." To bolster lagging sales of its artificially flavored orange drink, Tang, and to launch its new Sugar Free Tang, General Foods sponsored a 4,205 mile, coast-to-coast march across the United States by the Mothers Against Drunk Driving (MADD). General Foods planned a massive Tang coupon drop midway through the march, with a dime of every coupon redeemed going to MADD up to an amount of $100,000 in order to show the corporation's commitment to the safety and well-being of the American family. The public relations program began in April 1985 with notices to the long-lead women's magazines informing them about the march and the coupon drop; there followed the usual New York City press conferences with elected officials, talk show pitches by Cindy Lightner, then MADD's president and spokeswoman, and a gala kickoff in mid-August from the steps of city hall in Los Angeles complete with Hollywood celebrities, orange-colored Tang balloons, and tee shirts with the Tang logo. As the one-hundred-fifteen-day march worked its way through thirty-nine major media markets, two key symbols were highlighted. The "Family Photo Carriage," pushed by the lead marcher in each city, collected snapshots of American families, many of whom had lost children in car accidents involving drunk drivers. A "Declaration of Caring" gave participants and on-lookers alike the opportunity to cast a vote against the abuse. Carefully timed press releases, media alerts, interviews with participating celebrities, and public service announcements on radio and television saturated local media all across the country. Before the march, the master public relations plan had called for finding one mother, a figure with whom mass audiences could personally identify, to provide symbolic continuity by doing the entire walk start to finish. Find her they did, a photogenic young mother with two small children who, with the help of a sponsor, walked the whole route personalizing MADD's cause and providing a continuous "objective" story for the media about an "average citizen's" concern for the problem of drunk driving. Even Cindy Lightner's sudden departure from MADD because of internal squabbles and allegations of misuse of funds did not derail the march. The march culminated in the nation's capital with a candlelight ceremony at the Lincoln Memorial, while similar ceremonies were held simultaneously by MADD chapters around the country. While the hundreds of thousands of photographs of American families were unloaded from the baby carriage and displayed, General Foods officially gave its donation to MADD.[16] The public relations practitioners crafting the whole campaign claim more than 325 million "consumer impressions" in all media during the four-month march, confirmation in their view of the ease of literally creating news provided that one has a sure-fire main image like that of mothers united in a moral crusade to eliminate a social evil afflicting children.

The news industry's propensity to leap at wish-news makes it hostage to those social forces able to concoct and propagate the right dramatic story at the right time. For instance, when Bechtel Corporation was building the Palo Verde Nuclear Generating Station in Arizona in

1983, the company's reputation was suddenly assaulted by the Palo Verde Intervention Fund (PVIF). Based on allegations of former project workers, PVIF charged that Bechtel had buried 1 million dollars worth of new equipment in the project's trash dump, presumably as a way of running up the project's cost and increasing Bechtel's profits. The story, which broke just before a crucial rate-hike hearing, received national exposure through ABC's *20/20* news feature show. Bechtel flatly denied the allegations and produced extensive documentation for the media and regulatory agencies indicating that the interment of tools had not occurred. But its claims of innocence went unheeded and the Arizona Attorney General announced an investigation of the charges. In the meantime, public sentiment against Bechtel and Palo Verde began to rise.

Bechtel's in-house public relations practitioners argued that the company had to fight drama with drama. To undercut the set-piece melodrama of rapacious corporation endangering the environment while gouging the citizenry scripted by Bechtel's accusers, the practitioners convinced top executives to allow a complete and public excavation of Palo Verde's whole seven-acre construction dump under the supervision of criminal investigators from the attorney general's office with, therefore, the possibility of criminal indictments should PVIF's charges prove accurate. "The Big Dig" began in April 1984, complete with a giant D-9 Caterpillar tractor, eight television crews with helicopter, and troops of print reporters. With the former Bechtel workers pointing out presumed sites of tool burials, the Big Dig continued for four weeks discovering nothing except trash. The attorney general issued a final report concluding that the tool burial charges and other related allegations against Bechtel were a fraud. Yet another story on Palo Verde was aired on *20/20*.[17]

The dynamics of this scenario are by now quite familiar to any social observer because the scenario itself is repeated daily in every arena of our society. At least in major metropolitan areas, the news industry's inexhaustible craving for fresh drama makes it easy prey even for amateur image makers. One simply needs to know how to concoct a titillating tale, preferably with a central figure who has a flair for self-dramatization. An astonishing cast of characters regularly appears in the tabloids and on television. Adroit false accusers make sensational charges. Self-professed victims of every stripe make moral claims. Strutting, street-smart impresarios orchestrate disruptive actions on behalf of some constituency. Various self-appointed and sometimes elected leaders righteously voice moral indignation and blame at perceived injustices. Attorneys skilled at grabbing center stage assert fantastic claims for their clients, complete with slogans that reduce complicated legal issues to simplistic visual images. Pompous gurus, self-professed intellectuals, and old-fashioned fire-and-brimstone preachers, all with grandiose conceptual or salvational schemes, stitch together alluring tales, always managing to become the main point of whatever stories they tell. In short, dramatizing and self-dramatizing techniques that command mass attention have migrated far beyond their originating milieux to become the basic idiom of modern public discourse. The widespread dissemination of such techniques, of course, poses new puzzles for professional image makers who, in turn, redouble their efforts both to be and to appear inventive.

〰〰〰 Practitioners in both advertising and public relations place the greatest premium on the kind of radical reinterpretation lionized by Bill Bernbach, turning established perceptions and expectations on their heads by inverting symbols and images. Sometimes simple virtuosity in wordplay accomplishes this goal, such as the transformation of Grey Poupon mustard into a gourmet item ("When you're haute, you're hot") or NYNEX yellow pages' long-running billboard campaign ("If it's out there, it's in here"), complete with funny images of a bull dozing (bulldozer), a stupid table-server (dumbwaiter), or a spotlighted easy chair doing a striptease (furniture stripping). Freshness of approach often requires practitioners to transform perceived drawbacks into virtues. For instance, the famous Doyle Dane Bernbach advertisements for the Volkswagen Beetle made the vehicle's small, squat, and ugly features key selling points. By placing pictures of the miniscule, dumpy "Bug" in a standard car advertising format that usually extols sleek, elegant, and large vehicles, the agency's creatives not only inverted the then accepted image of a status-conferring automobile, but they mocked other car advertisements as well. The advertisements appealed to self-defined middle-class nonconformists, and the vehicle itself quickly became a countercultural symbol during the tumultuous 1960s. Sometimes symbolic inversion means promoting a particular message precisely through an arresting transvaluation of traditional images. Take, for instance, an award-winning advertisement against drinking and driving produced by the Advertising Council. One sees two hand-held wine glasses, each half-filled with rich ruby-colored wine, approaching each other in a traditional toast, only to smash apart on impact splattering wine and glass everywhere, followed by two beer mugs, each filled with foamy brew, repeating the same scene. The voice-over says: "Drinking and driving can kill a friendship." In the last scene, two whiskey-filled tumblers approach each other, with the now expected collision suddenly stopped by another hand reaching in to prevent the disaster, complete with a final warning. The toast, the universal symbol of bonhomie, good will, and friendship, is transformed into a reminder of the menace of mixing alcohol and gasoline. Or symbolic inversion can mean the straight-faced assertion of a fanciful, often humorous, comparison, such as when Adelphi University says in its advertisements that Harvard is the "Adelphi of Massachusetts," making the small (and often troubled) Long Island university the measure of the school with the most exalted reputation in the land.[18] Symbolic inversion can also mean the simple assertion of rational arguments in a tail-wags-the-dog age. Between 1983 and 1985, nine U.S. cities, including New York and Philadelphia, responded to the young vandals destroying subway cars and building walls with graffiti by banning the sale of spray paint to all youngsters and making spray paint relatively inaccessible for everybody else by removing it from retail shelves. The Spray Paint Manufacturers Committee of the National Paint & Coatings Association launched a "Graffiti: It's a Crime" program to remind legislators and the public alike that legitimate spray-paint customers and the industry itself should not be penalized for the depredations of a few youths.[19]

Sometimes symbolic inversion can obfuscate reality entirely. For years, the main imagistic themes in many cigarette advertisements were springtime, vitality, and youth, a nice contrast to the growing public perception of tobacco's relationship to decay and death. Industries that depend to some extent on substance abuse or outright addiction often launch campaigns decrying the evils of both. The lion's share of beer and liquor consumed in the United States is drunk by a tiny percentage of all drinkers. According to creatives working on beer commercials, their target audience is typically those who drink a six-pack of beer at a sitting, a case of beer on a weekend. Whiskey drinking is similarly concentrated. But the liquor industry has long been active in promoting "responsible drinking," in warning against drinking and driving, and in advocating for designated drivers.[20] Similarly, the pharmaceutical industry, which relies to some extent on a core of hypochondriacs, launched a campaign in 1985 against drug abuse.[21] Domestic automobile manufacturers, in whose products about 50,000 people die each year, funded the "National Safety Belt Program" through the organization Traffic Safety Now, urging the enactment of state laws requiring the use of safety belts.[22] Even as the crisis of the lower and underclass African American family had reached the point where some observers spoke of the "zero-parent family," the National Council of Negro Women initiated an annual Black Family Reunion "to call attention to the historic strengths of the black family."[23] Whether motivated by repentance, anticipatory defensiveness, or wishful thinking, such regular assertion of counterfactual images makes already complex realities almost impenetrable.

Stigma removal, one of the main functions of public relations, usually requires symbolic inversion of a singular sort. Sometimes simple linguistic changes can recast tarnished images. In the mid-1980s, processed meat manufacturers found themselves in a grinder of adverse opinion led by upper-middle-class opinion leaders turned health-food faddists. The new converts decried the evils of baloney and salami, causing sales to plummet. Public relations practitioners began to call processed meats "neat" meats or, for the upscale market, "charcuterie"; they worked with magazine food editors to tout the "new" product as nutritious, easy, appealing, and tasty, and the crisis passed.[24] In the modern media era, of course, sensational charges, however illfounded, can damage reputations. A cardinal rule of public relations is that one must respond to charges made against one; to be silent is to consent to the accusations. When false accusations claiming the secret misappropriation of funds were made against the Vietnam Veterans Memorial Fund, the fund's public relations agency responded with an open review of two governmental audits of the fund's books, complete with an offer to a local radio station critical of the fund to conduct its own independent audit. The strategy of openness "removed the stain" of accusations of clandestine skulduggery, and the memorial opened to nearly universal acclaim.[25] Of course, the expectation for prompt public response to charges of any sort, however frivolous, has become so deeply embedded that the reply of "No comment" is often taken as a guilty plea. Officeholders of various sorts thus often find themselves in a quandary when the obligation of confidentiality about administrative secrets requires silence even in the face of abuse. This is particularly true when their silence protects the rights of the very people vilifying them.[26] Sometimes dignified silence can prevail; but when the news media or semifictionalized television dramas start a feeding frenzy on a person or organization, an adroit symbolic inversion of charges is the only hope for salvaging a reputation or at least the credibility that might allow one to fight another day. One attacks the credibility of one's own opponents with the same tactic of symbolic inversion. Among many possibilities, one reinterprets the significance of scientific data;

one points out inconsistencies in public statements and suggests character flaws; or one ridicules the very basis of an opponent's strength through caricature or parody.

Closely akin to symbolic inversion is doublethink, to borrow George Orwell's notion.[27] Doublethink is the highly self-conscious ability to hold in one's mind and be able to voice if necessary totally contradictory versions and images of reality. Sometimes doublethink means displacing reality entirely by asserting words or images that transform or transvalue it. Big success in the world of affairs depends greatly on the ability to doublethink. For instance, men and women who rise to prominent and powerful positions in large organizations face not only the irreconcilable demands of different external audiences as well as the usual intense conflicts within their own bureaucracies but also the disquieting knowledge that whatever choices they do make will inevitably make somebody unhappy and will have unintended outcomes. Only those well equipped to confront the irrationalities of organizations and of the world itself survive and flourish in positions of high organizational authority. Doublethink enables one to grapple with contradictory exigencies, using all the subterfuges and wiles at one's disposal while employing whatever vocabularies ring the right bells with the right groups. Simultaneously, doublethink enables one to project convincingly a sense of belief in whatever version of reality one is espousing at the moment, without a trace of self-betraying ambivalence and without violating one's own personal sense of integrity. Indeed, many men and women of affairs doublethink themselves into enthusiastic belief in their own public performances and become their own best audiences. Interpretive experts, of course, rarely succumb to the artifices they help create. Their role as specialists in helping others learn to doublethink typically dampens easy credulity.

Much advertising embodies a kind of doublethink, usually in imagistic form. In discussing an advertisement featuring a gauzy-lens shot of a woman bathing with a perfume-laden bar of soap, a female advertising creative points out, "You can only charge a woman so much for a bar of soap; but if she thinks she's going to get laid in the bargain, you can charge her anything you want." Here the advertisement transforms a mundane object into the stimulus for a wishful erotic fantasy; in the process, it concretizes the desires and sentiments of some, and perhaps invents them for others. The famous "Fashion Show" advertisement for Wendy's fast food chain suggests some of the multilayered complexities of doublethink. The ad portrays a remarkably unattractive woman modeling on a runway exactly the same outfit with slightly different props to a smoke-filled room of tired Soviet Union Communist Party functionaries, while the weary voice-over intones successively: "day wear, evening wear, swim wear." While implicitly lumping McDonald's and Burger King with America's cold war images of Russia, the advertisement asserts that Wendy's highly standardized, thoroughly processed hamburgers differ from those of its rivals because Wendy's hamburgers are not uniform. The tag line is: "Having a choice is better than none. Wendy's: There's no better choice." In short, standardization equals variety equals choice.

Public relations practitioners utilize a kind of doublethink in framing and reframing issues. They lead various publics to reconsider an issue by asserting a frame of reference that sidetracks, displaces, or turns another framework upside down. Sometimes issues can be transformed simply by invoking widely disseminated off-the-shelf vocabularies like that of "choice." When the Hertz Corporation, for instance, began selling its used rental cars, used car dealers around the nation howled with rage and launched lawsuits and lobbying action for legislation and regulation to stop the "unfair competition" generated by the rent-a-car giant. Hertz responded with a campaign entitled "Protecting consumer choice in car sales" that "redefined the issue as one of vital consumer [not commercial] interest."[28] The campaign then used all the normal tools—media training for executives followed by speeches, placement of op-ed pieces based on the speeches, and rigged support letters to legislators and the media, among other tactics—all beating the drum of consumer choice. In the end, the used car dealers capitulated.

Sometimes interpretive experts invoke high-minded principles to try to transform an issue. For instance, the steady growth of antismoking sentiment since 1980, fueled in particular by successful arguments on the purported dangers of secondary-smoke inhalation, generated municipal and state legislation placing various prohibitions on smoking in public places. By the late 1980s, virtually every state in the union had imposed some strictures on the public use of tobacco. The tobacco industry and its powerful lobbying organization, the Tobacco Institute, vigorously fought both eroding public sentiment and formal curbs on tobacco use. Philip Morris, in particular, took every opportunity to protect its astonishingly profitable Marlboro cigarettes brand, known in the trade as the "Big Red Machine."[29] When New York City passed a smoking restriction law that took effect on 6 April 1988, sharply curbing arenas for open smoking, interpretive experts for Philip Morris launched a campaign for smokers' rights complete with the publication of *The Great American Smoker's Manual*, a play on "The Great American

Smokeout," the annual antismoking bash orchestrated by public relations professionals on the other side of this issue. The following excerpt from the manual's preface captures the thrust of this lengthy brochure:

> There is a new minority in the United States of America. This minority is the victim of legal discrimination every day. Employers can refuse to hire members of this minority. This same minority has to sit in limited areas in the workplace, trains, buses and restaurants. These people have to pay special taxes the majority of Americans don't have to pay. They are also targets of negative stories in local and national newspapers, magazines, television and radio. The U.S. Congress is now considering proposals to make advertising to this minority illegal. Who is this minority? Smokers!

There follow graphic descriptions of how to combat discrimination in public accommodations and transportation, in restaurants, in the workplace, and in the public media, complete with cartoons such as one from the *Daytona Journal Herald* depicting a restaurant door with a sign that reads, "No shirt, no shoes, no service, no old people, no ugly people, no fat people, no poor people, no short people, no singles, no gays, no minorities, no smoking." The brochure also contains calls to arms on the issue of excessive and unfair taxation of tobacco and on the abridgement of First Amendment rights through curbs on cigarette advertising, as well as sample protest letters that readers might send to their congressional representatives, senators, and newspaper editors. Philip Morris also published a shorter brochure called *New York City's Smoking Restriction Law: What Your Business Is . . . and Is Not . . . Required to Do* that spells out the requirements and loopholes in the law. It issued a wallet-sized brochure called *Smokers' Rights in New York City* that delineates succinctly where smokers can puff away. The Tobacco Institute joined the fray with brochures like *Smoking and Young People—Where the Tobacco Industry Stands, Tobacco: Helping Youth Say No,* and *In the Public Interest: Three Decades of Initiatives by a Responsible Cigarette Industry,* all of which argue that, among other things, the tobacco industry, alone among U.S. industries, had taken direct, voluntary actions to steer youngsters away from its product. The Tobacco Institute also published *The Anti-Smoking Campaign: Enough Is Enough,* a sharp broadside attacking the "harassment" that "anti-smoking extremists" were perpetrating on smokers. The Institute also republished and distributed widely "The Hundred-Year War against the Cigarette," a cogent survey of antismoking sentiments beginning with tobacco-phobe James I of England but focusing in particular on the moralistic crusades against the devil's weed that flourished in the United States in the late nineteenth and early twentieth centuries. A classic front organization called the American Smokers Alliance was established. Its public face is that of a grassroots group of wronged and outraged citizens. Its goal is to establish local organizations around the country to lobby for smokers' rights. In a brochure called *Guidelines for Smokers' Rights Groups,* the alliance provides detailed directions for start-up groups on how to organize smokers, raise funds, run meetings, and deal with the media.

Eventually, this vigorous campaign focused on discrimination against smokers in the workplace. The Tobacco Institute published *Smokers' Rights in the Workplace: An Employee Guide* and sponsored a carefully detailed legal memorandum called *An Assessment of the Current Legal Climate concerning Smoking in the Workplace.* It also published another brochure called *Indoor Air Pollution: Is Your Workplace Making You Sick?* that suggests the real culprit in the whole controversy is not secondary smoke but poor ventilation systems. Hitchhiking on then-current vocabularies of the celebration of diversity and the necessity for tolerance, executives warned that the new moral absolutism and puritanical zealotry sweeping the United States, evident in strident attacks on smokers among other offenders of new sensibilities, might eventually be directed to more traditional targets. And, in a pièce de résistance that drew grudging admiration even from their bitterest opponents, interpretive experts for Philip Morris put together a brilliant collection of materials from more than forty archives entitled *No _____ Need Apply: Your Job and Your Privacy.* The exhibition, displayed at Philip Morris headquarters in New York City, surveyed the long and sorry history of job discrimination in the United States around race, religion and national origin, age, disability, and gender. It concluded with a section on the emerging discrimination against smokers. Privately, interpretive experts worried about possible backfires; when one champions others' causes to borrow interest for one's own agenda, one runs the risk of being embarrassed by one's newly chosen bedfellows.[30]

Doublethink also means the ability to switch sides without embarrassment when the tides of fortune change. By the late 1990s, as big tobacco staggered under private lawsuits and criminal investigation followed by a back-breaking lawsuit from the U.S. government, which for years subsidized tobacco farmers and collected fortunes in taxes on tobacco sales, the same advertising agencies that had scrambled for tobacco money enthusiastically sold their creative skills to the National Center for Tobacco-free kids (<www.tobacco-freekids.org>).

Doublespeak, the verbal expression of doublethink, is an essential tool of interpretive experts. Public relations practitioners must become especially adept at doublespeak since, as noted earlier, it is they who invent for men and women of affairs better explanations for "what has to be done," the inevitable hard choices that always leave some individuals and groups unhappy. Doublespeak facilitates action by splitting action from intention, leaving the latter sufficiently ambiguous to bear multiple interpretations. Doublespeak includes the bland euphemistic rhetoric typically used by officials to blunt the sharp edges and possible emotional impact of disturbing policies. Thus, in the corporate world, one almost never hears of mass firings or layoffs, but rather of "restructuring," "the elimination of redundancy," "the release of resources," "involuntary termination," or "downsizing." In academia or government, one never hears of selective hiring on the basis of race, ethnicity, gender, or sexual preference, whether done for reasons of patronage or to achieve the visible diversity now essential for public relations purposes, but rather of the necessity for "multiculturalism" or hiring people with "appropriate backgrounds and sensitivities." Euphemisms cloak the goals, purposes, motives, or ugly consequences of actions. Doublespeak also includes framing an issue in highly technical language, usually to assert a prerogative to act without interference from nonexperts; even the trappings of substantive expertise can often render potential opposition mute, at least until those opposed to an action roll out their own expert. Doublespeak also includes deliberately obscure, abstract, vague, or confusing language that obfuscates rather than clarifies an issue; this is often combined with appeals to primal allegiances of one sort or another. Confusion usually produces inaction, which in the realm of, say, organizational or public politics, is almost as good as assent to action. Finally, doublespeak includes statements that are completely contradictory to fact, including statements that cover one's actual intentions and subsequent actions. Thus, a televangelist preaches family values and the sanctity of marriage to a vast regional audience while sporting with an ex-*Playboy* bunny. Doublespeak keeps possible opponents at bay while allowing one to act expeditiously; doublethink enables men and women of affairs to do "what has to be done" without public embarrassment. It goes without saying that masters of doublethink and doublespeak do not typically betray themselves to their audiences. However, close observation allows one to predict their future behavior with some accuracy since their actions are so frequently the opposite of their avowals. A prerequisite for big success in the world of affairs is a certain adeptness at inconsistency.

This kind of double consciousness underpins the dispassionate detachment and ironic skepticism intrinsic to image-making work. Experts with symbols often talk about their clients as panic-stricken children lost in a dark woods who are out of touch with the world. A public relations practitioner tells about the self-made shoe manufacturer distraught at his company's lagging sales and declining market share who excitedly announces the invention of a brilliant, new, though still secret, marketing strategy that will reverse his firm's fortune. The executive says, "You can't tell a soul about this. Here's the idea. We're going to sell more shoes!" Only detachment enables one to step outside one's immediate predicament, assess one's location, and find a way out of the fastness. In helping their clients learn detachment in order to assess themselves realistically, say, vis-à-vis competitors in a market, interpretive experts become bearers of a kind of instrumental rationality. Of course, detachment and skepticism have their own relentless logic; in teaching others to see themselves objectively, image makers deepen their own self-rationalization, including their willingness to turn even their most intimate experiences into fodder for their work.

This particular aspect of self-rationalization, the affective promiscuity that allows one to make one's private experiences and moral dramas public, frames and paces the widespread "borrowing" of others' work typical of the worlds of mass image making. Borrowing, the commonly used term for appropriation, is endemic to all mass cultural industries. The pace of events and the sheer voraciousness of the mass media, in addition to the media's relentless deadlines, place a great premium on fast turnaround in, say, television programming or in the pulp-fiction market. Indeed, in these fields as well as in others, great initial success often presents the long-term hazard of extravagant popular expectations, along with the promise of lavish rewards. But genuine creativity, that is, the fashioning of material de novo, rarely keeps pace with such external factors. As a result, many popular cultural workers take their material wherever they can find it. Television, movies, and pulp fiction, for instance, regularly borrow wholesale from the daily newspapers, creating thinly disguised docudramas and blurring the line between fiction and reality for large segments of mass audiences. In advertising and public relations, where practitioners typically work under tight deadlines that make sustained original thought an unwarranted luxury, there are always warring pressures. Anxious clients want the tried and true while peers, of course, place a premium on novelty. The result is usually compromised amalgams of familiar formulas with "fresh" angles.

Moreover, at least in advertising, as in moviemaking, there are occupational premiums on borrowing ideas, styles, or specific images from

others' work under certain conditions. First, if one imitates or appropriates aspects of the work of a well-known writer or art director, this
is called "paying homage." Sometimes appropriation of others' work is
nearly complete, such as in J. Walter Thompson's use of Scali, McCabe,
Sloves's Volvo concept ("A civilized car in an uncivilized world") to advertise BMW. This theme also appeared later in advertisements for the
Chevrolet Blazer. Second, if one borrows images or ideas from another
medium, this signals one's sophistication and knowledgeability to one's
peers. Thus, to great acclaim, advertising creatives appropriated the
baby carriage sequence in the 1987 version of *The Untouchables* for a
public service commercial for the Children's Defense Fund. In the film,
a distraught mother watches with horror as her infant's carriage cas-
cades down a train station's marble steps while G-men shoot it out with
desperate mobsters; in the commercial, a momentarily distracted
mother on the steps of some government building releases her grip on
her baby's carriage and turns, with a gasping crowd, to see it hurtling
down the stairs. As it happens, *The Untouchables* borrowed the idea from
Sergei Eisenstein's classic 1925 film *Battleship Potemkin.* Pepsi's famous
commercial "Ropeswing" was a direct appropriation from the scene of
healthy young men rope swinging into a swimming hole in Leni Rie-
fenstahl's 1934 Nazi propaganda classic *Triumph of the Will.*[31] Other films
have also become gold mines for advertising images, including *Modern
Times* (1936), *Brazil* (1985), and the cult classic *Blade Runner* (1982).
Third, an ambiguous and continually contested area is the extent to
which one may claim authorship for typically group-produced advertisements. For instance, in making the rounds of advertising agencies, one frequently sees the same advertisement on the reels of many
creatives, with each person claiming a distinctive contribution to the
creative process, even though others argue that, at best, a claimant may
have passed through a room while ideas were being bandied about. In
this regard, advertising authorship resembles that of multiauthored articles in some academic journals, particularly, though by no means exclusively, in the field of medical science. Finally, it goes without saying
that superiors regularly steal the ideas and images of subordinates with
impunity, a practice widely extant in the world of affairs, whether in
corporations, government, or nonprofit organizations. In appropriating
and claiming others' work as their own, those who borrow wholesale
implicitly acknowledge the value of words and ideas as the coin of the
realm of public discourse, even as they bypass any notions of "intellectual property" or authorship as irrelevant, unless, of course, others
steal their own ideas. Within this framework, ideas are essentially

commodities to be invented, bought, traded, or stolen, cobbled together with other ideas obtained in similar ways, used as necessary to accomplish some practical goal or to further one's own fortunes, and discarded when one is finished.[32]

Once fully institutionalized, this conception of ideas as appropriable and disposable commodities creates the requisite social condition for the "rip-offs," the recombinant "spin-offs," "re-makes," and the other forms of cultural replication that give popular culture its derivative, self-referential, and ever-transitory feel. But cultural workers, although they may be adroit borrowers of the ideas of others, usually feel more ambivalent about the theft or the discarding of their own efforts. Creative teams in advertising, for instance, grumble when a group head or another creative team appropriates one of their own rough ideas, gives it a slight twist, and turns it into something usable. They carefully guard their conversations, their storyboards, and even random materials on their desks; they prefer to meet rival creatives outside their offices to thwart possible prying eyes. At the same time, they recognize the jeopardy in clinging to ideas. So they publicly adopt throwaway stances ("Ideas are like buses. One will be along in another ten minutes"), even while they resent, sometimes bitterly, the hacking and sawing to which the approval process subjects all ideas.

Ghostwriters experience the borrowing of ideas both as thieves and as victims of theft. Typically, in-house public relations staff do the ghostwriting for corporate officials, with detailed work being pushed down the ladder as far as possible. Often, in-house public relations staff farm actual writing out to agencies, many of which have writers who specialize in cranking out speeches, position papers, and annual reports. Agency staff interact almost exclusively with in-house public relations practitioners. The latter frame the problem, define the audience, provide initial materials, usually in the form of old speeches or press releases themselves written by other experts with symbols. Then they take the ghostwriter's efforts, modify them as necessary, and claim credit with their own bosses for a solid piece of writing if all goes well. Agency ghostwriters labor in anonymity. Some take this as license and freely make up facts and stories to expedite their work. Others, longing for a kind of recognition, keep private score of how much of their own prose makes, say, the final cut of an official's speech. Ghostwriters who work at a distance can gain some small measure of satisfaction when advice that they proffer is not taken. For instance, one writer, who tried to leaven the pretentious prose of a real-estate tycoon, had his suggestions for humorous anecdotes based on the executive's occupational jungle rejected. The brawling "Bronx boxer" wanted to sound like a professor and, after the ghostwriter did several painful and ultimately clumsy rewrites, ended up sounding like a bombastic Winston Churchill.

Many powerful corporate and government officials have their own personal ghostwriters. These men and women get to know officials and their ideas firsthand, as well as the rhythm and cadence of their speech patterns. Sometimes special personal bonds, which go beyond customized idea tooling, are said to form between ghostwriters and officials, though, as the unknown and unrecognized subordinates in the relationship, ghostwriters may imagine more than actually exists. Sometimes a ghostwriter comes to think of himself as the alter ego of the official, a view that is rarely reciprocated. In fact, the official most dependent on a ghostwriter is usually the first to deny the writer's existence in some way because the official comes to think of the ghostwriter's ideas and words as her own. Public articulation of ideas, especially when elegantly expressed, brings acclaim, though in American society both in the inner circles of large organizations and in the glare of the spotlight, raw vitality and animal magnetism always matter far more than ideas. But when one combines articulateness with such "personal presence," one becomes very formidable indeed; the origins of one's ideas matter little as long as the sentiments that one expresses find resonance in appropriate audiences.[33]

Ghostwriters simultaneously rejoice in and resent the appropriation of their work. One ghostwriter tells a story that, although surely apocryphal,[34] captures the deeply ambivalent nature of ghostwriter/public figure relationships, complete with a typical dream of vengeance. Jones was a ghostwriter who wrote exclusively for Smith, a top corporate executive very near the apex of his large corporation. As befitted his position, Smith was far removed from practical affairs; it was said, in fact, that he "couldn't find his ass in a rainstorm." Indeed, Smith had no desire to be engrossed in practical details since he saw himself as an industrial statesman. He spent most of his time giving speeches at business forums, like business schools, Conference Board seminars, and various other congresses of business leaders. He delighted in preaching about perennially troubling topics such as the necessity of increasing worker productivity and of making the U.S. economy more competitive in global markets. Moreover, in his talks Smith seemed to keep abreast of the times. For instance, when environmental issues moved to the forefront of the public agenda, he began to give speeches about business's ecological responsibilities. Of course, all of Smith's ideas came from Jones, who had a very fertile mind and who cranked out speech after speech for Smith. Smith was delighted by Jones's enterprising intellectual bent and ability to express his seemingly endless flow of ideas in Smith's diction and idiom. Indeed, after a few years, Smith came to trust Jones's work so completely that he did not even read Jones's speeches in advance. He just went before his audiences, preached from the scripts that Jones provided, and basked in audiences' warm appreciation of the forcefulness of the ideas he articulated. It goes without saying that Smith never acknowledged Jones publicly; the very point of having a "ghost" is to keep him invisible.

For his own part, Jones was initially flattered that such a powerful executive found his ideas interesting enough to appropriate them. Like most men and women who labor their entire lives in obscurity, Jones welcomed the chance to see his own well-articulated ideas voiced by a public figure. Indeed, he felt that he was making some contribution to great affairs. But, at a certain point, Jones began to feel that Smith's appropriation of his ideas implied a denial of his own existence. Specifically, he began to sense that Smith increasingly had come to think of Jones's ideas as his own. Public adulation plays strange tricks on the perceptions and judgments of those who are celebrated, as all public relations practitioners, who orchestrate the flattery, know. Jones plotted his revenge. Smith was due to address a world congress of business leaders on how to reconcile the demands of business efficiency with environmental concerns. Smith took the podium before the expectant audience and began reading the speech Jones had written for him. The first page of the speech was typically brief. "Ladies and Gentlemen, in my talk today, I am going to lay out for you in specific detail exactly how American business can simultaneously improve worker productivity, maximize profits, *and* preserve our environment for future generations." But the second page was even briefer. It read: "Okay, you son of a bitch, now you're on your own."[35]

Whatever the origin of one's ideas, they are meaningless unless one can sell them to one's bosses and to one's clients. Unless one holds enough power in an organization to command acquiescence,[36] selling ideas means selling oneself. One must therefore master the art of presentation and self-presentation. As the great premium on appearances of creativity among advertising art directors and writers illustrates, zany eccentricity convinces many clients of the freshness of ideas. Moreover, the worlds of advertising and public relations are filled with natural salespeople, men and women whose personal presence and bubbly enthusiasm inspire confidence, especially when clients are unsure of

themselves. Increasingly, however, presentational skills are rationalized. Almost all public relations firms have their own "media consultants" whose task is not only to train clients to be effective spokesmen
but to keep other interpretive experts abreast with what is valued in the
public forum. According to one prominent media consultant, whose
advice on how to be a master of the media typifies work of this genre,
a spokesman or spokeswoman of any sort must possess "sparkle and
energy." He or she must use specific action words in order to "create
pictures in people's minds because people think in terms of pictures."
He should come into an interview with "*one* and *only* one idea," supported by "evidence," that is, convincing stories to illustrate the main
point. She must know her audience and have a "*grabber* to get [its]
attention." He must not speak too fast, nor too slowly; he must avoid
long sentences, indefinite pronouns, lack of vocal variety, or fluttery
hands. She must keep her guard up at all times, anticipate queries,
rephrase questions to suit her own purposes, refuse to answer hypo-
thetical questions, and develop "must-say" points that she constantly
reiterates. He must beware of the prototypical enemies of effective
presentation: the "machine-gun interviewer" who riddles his subjects
with rapid-fire queries; the "interrupter" who tries to break one's
train of thought; the "dart-thrower" who characterizes one's arguments with negative labels; and the "paraphraser" who puts words in
one's mouth and tries to steal the interview. Finally, if one is being interviewed for television, one must always wear calf-length socks and
avoid swivel chairs. In a world where "presentation is all," form, technique, and persuasive ability triumph over substance.[37]

The promotion, self-promotion, and self-referentiality of mass persuasion come full circle when image makers are attacked for their legerdemain. In the late 1980s, as part of the advertising industry's ongoing struggle against its detractors, the American Association of
Advertising Agencies sponsored a print campaign of thirteen advertisements called "Advertising: Another Word for Freedom of Choice."
With sharp images and pointed copy, the series challenged stereotypi-
cal but widespread criticisms of advertising. For example, one advertisement, which takes on the standard charge that advertising hurts the
economy by dramatically increasing the market price of consumer
goods, is set against a backdrop of the classified section of a newspaper
and reads: "It's amazing how many people change their views about
advertising the moment they want to sell something." Another confronts persistent speculations about advertising's subliminal seduction
of consumers by putting pictures of female breasts in ice cubes. The

headline: "People have been trying to find the breasts in these ice cubes since 1957." It goes on to point out that, while the breasts were not in the ice cubes, they might very well exist in the eye of the beholder. Another in the series challenges the charge that advertising's influence over people's minds is so far-reaching that it turns consumers into passive automatons. "Is advertising a reflection of society? Or is society a reflection of advertising?" The ad goes on to say: "Some people say that advertising determines America's tastes. Which is another way of saying that advertising determines *your* tastes. Which is, in turn, another way of saying that you don't have a mind of your own." Especially in its virtuoso displays of symbolic inversion that stand all arguments against advertising upside down and in its shameless self-promotion, the series exemplifies the habits of mind that the ethos of mass persuasion shapes in experts with symbols.[38] The trade name for the campaign was "advertising for advertising."

6 ADVOCACY AS A VOCATION

Of commercial advocates, whose work is the seedbed of the ethos of mass persuasion, are indeed prophets of good fortune skilled at celebration, why does the public arena of American society clang with acrimony and strident moralism? Why are mainstay institutions continually under assault? Who is leading the charge against the social order, or against particular institutions, or policies, and why? And who are the new defenders of the established order?

In 1942, Joseph Schumpeter pointed out that industrial capitalism creates hostility to its own social order.[1] In this view, somewhat extended here, capitalism shapes an adversarial, competitive framework that creates incentives and premiums for men and women to work relentlessly and to break traditional bonds in search of new opportunities, new products, new markets, and new experiences. But the very success of capitalism erodes its moral basis. The prosperity generated by the hard work of some men and women comes to be taken for granted by others, subtly devaluing the effort that makes affluence possible (witness the decline in symbolic importance of manufacturing in the United States). Further, the new material comforts make the traditional social frameworks that harness emotional energies to economic exigencies appear quaint (witness the passing of the notions that one's worldly work serves God or that family stability underpins social order). Perhaps most important, the demon of thoroughgoing rationalization that capitalism in its original triumph unleashed on a settled world comes back to gnaw at the system's vitals. Capitalism levels old social rankings by eroding the efficacy of status claims based on tradition, opening the door for a proliferation of other claims; it erases the distinction between sacred and secular, subjecting virtually everything to the impersonal rule of the market; it breeds a critical mentality that, once out of its cage, attacks the legitimacy of capitalist institutions with the same vigor that once brought down kings and lords and with them monarchical and aristocratic institutions. Notions of "common sense" collapse, allowing irrationality and nonrationality to flourish. In short, capitalist rationality inadvertently cuts away the grounds of moral solidarity among citizens and of emotional commitment to its own social order.

The thorough bureaucratization of capitalism in the twentieth century sharpened the double-edged character of capitalist rationality. Schumpeter saw bureaucratization somewhat narrowly, primarily as a deleterious force that sapped the simultaneously creative and destructive entrepreneurial spirit of capitalism. As it happens, despite the reins that external bureaucracies place upon capitalism and the market mechanism, only bureaucratic organization brings capitalist division of labor to full fruition. In corporations, for instance, only the deep refinement of expertise produces the knowledge that leads to technological breakthroughs. But the specializing genius of bureaucracy exacts a price. Specialization induces a kind of myopia, blocking from view the symbolic significance of one's work as it seems to others. Yet, in order to address various external publics, which is a critical part of their own daily work, top organizational officials have greater need of symbols than of arcane substantive expertise. The inevitable reliance of bosses on interpretive experts subtly devalues the very knowledge and skill that make the corporation possible, thus subverting the moral economy of the bureaucratic workplace.

More generally, bureaucracy intensifies capitalism's adversarial framework. In its ceaseless elaboration of new rational procedures, bureaucracy invites legal and moral claims of every sort, offering nearly endless opportunities for dispute and aggrandizement. Those who wish to "work the system" seize organizational resources, or claim exception to general rules, or gain power and change the rules to work in their own favor. Those charged with guarding the system invent new rules and procedures to protect those already in place, inadvertently providing still more angles of possible attack to those who choose to wage a kind of bureaucratic guerrilla warfare. The struggle for power, the adjudication of claims, and the contest over which rules will prevail in any given situation not only pit individuals or groups against one another in an overlay of market competition but also make impersonal organizations, procedures, and rules the mediators and arbiters of social relationships, eroding in some cases even primary social affiliations such as kinship ties.

To make matters still more complicated, the basic assumptions of the free market system of capitalism virtually guarantee that the making and asserting of claims, along with the exploitation of whatever hostility motivates those claims, will become an ongoing enterprise for some people, that is, part of the regular stream of commerce. The notion of the free marketplace of ideas, the necessary corollary of the free enterprise system, guarantees protection even to those who make what seem to be ridiculous claims or who express remarkable hostility to the social order, as long as certain protocols are observed. In this sense, the guardians of the system of bureaucratized capitalism develop a kind of vested interest in hostility to the social order. They cannot thwart such hostility without violating the institutional logic of the system as a whole, at least when the hostility is organized into an enterprise. Moreover, such tamed hostility has its own systemic uses, affording those who guard the system public faces of tolerance and broadmindedness. Of course, hostility to the social order often expresses a quest for personal identity or salvation on the part of individuals, groups, or strata; authority figures become whetting stones for the sharpening of self-images and alternate visions of justice and morality alike. Thus, the systemic absorption of one hostility virtually guarantees the intensification of hostility of other sorts, giving the social order the feel of breaking apart. In such ways, capitalist rationality cultivates irrationality and nonrationality.

Professional advocates, not only men and women in advertising and public relations, but lawyers, lobbyists, consultants of various sorts, as well as men and women of the cloth, are the paradigmatic claim makers. They make claims on behalf of clients, or defend clients against claims made by others, or frame the adjudication of claims, whether in administrative proceedings, in courts, in the realm of public opinion, or as professional carriers of one religious tradition or another. But many men and women who do not see themselves as professional advocates, though they often bring professional skills to their work, also join the public clamor as advocates for one cause or another. One contingent of such advocates on the left of the political spectrum continues a much longer tradition of reformism in the United States, addressing the myriad of social ills that American society generates.[2] They become claim makers for groups whom they perceive to be unable, at least initially, to make effective claims or defenses on their own behalf, champions of the oppressed and downtrodden everywhere, continually inventing new rationales to press a social agenda that revolves around a radical egalitarianism. An opposing contingent of advocates on the right and center of the political spectrum continues an equally long American tradition of conservative protection of the status quo, defenders of what seem to be beleaguered institutions and ideas. Men and women in both camps, though often the beneficiaries of ample funding to support their work, do not see themselves as dispassionate professionals. Instead, they see their advocacy as a vocation, as a quasi sacred calling. Though they often receive financial sustenance from their advocacy and sometimes make whole careers of it, they do not live *off* their advocacy; instead, they live *for* it. Both sides often produce intellectuals who become apostles for certain visions of the whole society. They bring not only acumen to their work, but moral fervor as well, a transvalued, often totally disguised, religious intensity.[3]

〰〰〰 The United States has always thrived on advocacy. More than 150 years ago, Alexis de Tocqueville noted the associational impulse at the core of American society, a tendency that he attributed to the necessity of citizens in a fragmented, democratic society to seek safety and strength in numbers.[4] Most associations in American society either serve as professional lobbyists for groups with carefully delineated material interests or simply link together people with common occupations, experiences, training, lifestyles, or outlooks. But, although all associations are engaged in advocacy of a sort, the very reason for existence of some associations is to advocate for some cause. Indeed, it is these kinds of associations that draw together advocates with a vocation, men and women who want to change the world, that is, reshape social institutions, or shore them up, or redirect the drift of public policy. Even in the 1830s, Tocqueville pointed out the importance of America's "intellectual and moral associations,"[5] a significance affirmed by a moment's reflection on the signal historical role played by groups such as, say, the antislavery abolitionists, advocates of women's suffrage, temperance movements, or patriotic or antiwar societies during periods of war.

Historical periods drawing large numbers of men and women into "intellectual" and "moral" associations for the purposes of advocacy recur in cycles. The flowering of advocacy organizations considered here began in the 1960s. After the Second World War, the U.S. economy started a remarkable period of sustained growth and prosperity that so absorbed national energies that even harsh memories of the Great Depression softened somewhat. Youthful rebellion, though plentiful and vibrant, was largely subterranean and localized, finding its expression in middle-class cultural revolts such as that of the Beat Generation or in working- and lower-class "juvenile delinquency," which for a time became a national obsession. Political dissent on the left was not only marginalized, but internally factionalized, with savage disagreements among socialists, communists, Trotskyists, trade unionists, and liberals, most often revolving around issues of the cold war and the totalitarianism of the Soviet Union and its client states. Apart from some intellectuals in university settings who wanted, in various ways, to redeem American society, advocates with a vocation stood principally on the margins of established institutions. In the Roman Catholic Church, for example, key ecclesiastical authorities construed the role of the clergy to be the traditional preaching of the word of God, comforting the sick, and burying the dead. When younger clergy, inspired by Dorothy Day's Catholic Worker movement or France's worker-priests, began advocating for involvement in various causes to foster "social justice," senior clergy often tried to prohibit their junior charges from engaging in such "nonprofessional social action." And when young Catholic laity sharply questioned the early-1960s advocacy of Church authorities like Francis Cardinal Spellman for increased U.S. military involvement in Vietnam, they found their calls for universal brotherhood with self-immolating Buddhist monks rejected out of hand by prelates whose parochialism tied them to the corrupt, but Roman Catholic, regime of Ngo Dinh Diem.

Conservative dissenters to the accelerating bureaucratization of the American state two-and-a-half decades after the New Deal were found mostly on the margins of the Republican Party or in the editorial pages of journals like *National Review,* until Barry Goldwater's presidential run in 1964. In other institutional sectors, the dominant voices were those that counseled adherence to established constructions of reality. Many of these, in retrospect, seem piecemeal at best and often downright bizarre, such as the paradoxical efforts of key government officials to convince the American people to steel themselves emotionally to the horrors of nuclear war so that, if the worst happened, life could go on as normal, provided that one obeyed the advice of civil defense planners.[6]

The social movements of the 1960s and early 1970s, particularly the civil rights movement, the antipoverty movement, the anti–Vietnam War movement, the student movement in the universities, the countercultural movement, the women's movement, wildcat labor movements among young workers in a few key industrial sectors, and the environmental movement successively mobilized larger and larger sectors of American society into protests against existing institutions, norms, or policies and often into advocacy with a decidedly leftist tilt. The great philanthropic foundations, particularly the Stern, Ford, and Rockefeller foundations, funded many of these movements at one point or another as part of their own mission to improve society. Some of these movements are still flourishing. Indeed, the women's movement has reached the point where it now has its own foundations, such as the Ms. Foundation among several others, to finance its various causes. Other movements seem to have vanished from American society, except in the memories of the participants. Many movements left organizational legacies, often now quite transformed from their original purposes, that still dot the social landscape. Moreover, the federal government bankrolled the antipoverty program and its associated "poor peoples' movements" that enabled the poor and their advocates to demonstrate against the government itself. The government's subsidization of protest left behind a vast tangle of state and federal poverty agencies, welfare advocates, and cohorts of assorted social service bureaucrats.[7]

Despite the great legislative successes of the 1964 Omnibus Civil Rights Act and the 1965 Voting Rights Act, which together undercut the apparatus of unrepentant, visible, institutionalized racism and which paved the way for continuing improvements in the quality of life for African Americans,[8] few government policies of any political stripe have done much since the 1960s to remedy other deep social problems at the core of American political debate and social advocacy. These include unemployment, underemployment, poverty, drugs, crime, the crisis of public education, and the trade-off between the preservation of the environment and the growth of the economy. The underclass, permanently unemployed and perhaps unemployable, with many poor living on the streets, grows each year. In 1992, a full 18 percent of the nation's full-time, low-skill workers earned less than $13,091 annually, the designated poverty level for a family of four, a wage erosion that might, in cyclical economic downturns, precipitate greater future unemployment.[9] By the late 1990s, rising incomes had lifted more Americans out of poverty. Overall unemployment had dropped sharply as a result of a remarkably long-lived bull market, dramatically reducing unemployment rates among groups of workers traditionally the "last to be hired," such as African Americans, Latinos, and teenagers. But the principal beneficiaries of the great market boom were skilled, educated workers whose refined technical capabilities could contribute to an economy increasingly dependent on high-level technology. The economic productivity and concomitant prosperity fueled by the computer revolution has left the underclass, those at the bottom of the American social structure, relatively untouched. Moreover, the United States is by far the world's largest market for contraband drugs, with three million hardcore users and about six million occasional users spending roughly $50 billion a year on substances that bring in their wake devastating personal and social ills.[10] The American public school system in the United States, especially in the great cities, once justifiably the pride of the nation in international circles, has fallen on hard times in the last three decades with sharply diminished student achievement in basic reading and mathematical skills, at least as measured by standardized tests; more often than not, the remedy has been to discount the tests, thus effectively lowering standards. And, despite remarkable declines in violent crimes in all categories across the nation between 1993 and 1999, the United States still has a worldwide reputation as a society where criminal violence is astonishingly high, not least because illegal weapons glut big-city streets.

All the government treasure poured into programs designed to address these and many other related social issues in the last thirty-five years, particularly in the areas of educational and family policies, has failed to solve the problems, though one can reasonably argue that government expenditures may have prevented their worse acceleration. Private foundations have also hurled money at these issues in remarkable amounts with the same results. The principal beneficiaries of this public and private largesse have been the bureaucracies that administer efforts to address the problems and the advocates who support or oppose those efforts. The "poverty industry" (as its insiders call it), the informal consortium of government agencies, private foundations, university academics, as well as various think tanks, policy institutes, publishers, and publications, focuses on the rates, causes, and remedies of poverty or on telling humanizing stories about the poor that prompt identification with their plight. This industry has flourished even as poverty itself, along with its many associated ills, has deepened. The conservative advocates of a return to laissez-faire capitalism, the Saturday-night square-dance partners of liberal reformers, have also benefited. While America's version of bureaucratized capitalism generates intractable problems in its wake, it also ceaselessly produces efforts to solve the problems or, at least, to agonize about them publicly, as well as round condemnations of virtually every proposed reform. Indeed, the inability of the political economy of the United States to solve its many quandaries has institutionalized advocacy and counter-advocacy in virtually every corner of the society and across the political spectrum.

The 1970s, 1980s, and 1990s also brought waves of new leftist social movements. Most of these appealed principally to middle-class constituencies and focused attention on single issues. For example, the drive to make abortion available on demand, initially spearheaded by a small number of feminists and extremely talented lawyers, was a contest won in the courts, not in legislatures or on the streets, although street demonstrations claiming abortion as a right under the feminist movement's slogan, "Our bodies, ourselves," undoubtedly influenced judicial decisions. Other movements worked to protect the environment, to address specific health issues such as the AIDS epidemic or threats caused by different toxins, to extend constitutional rights to animals, to control firearms trafficking, to redirect scientific resources toward "the public interest," or, under the traditional free-speech doctrines and in opposition to rightist religious-based claims, to champion various expressions of cultural freedom. Many movements, such as advocacy for the homeless and for welfare rights, have lower-class people as their primary constituencies, although their key stalwarts and the targets of their appeals are invariably middle-class. Finally, across class lines, movements staking out various identities, complete with associated claims, have proliferated dramatically. The gay, lesbian, bisexual, and transgender movement demands wider public tolerance of open homosexuality and alternative sexual lifestyles. Countless ethnic and racial solidarity movements assert ethnic and cultural "pride" and demand greater inclusiveness, backed by affirmative action policies, themselves the successful product of adroit advocacy extending the civil rights legislative triumphs in legally contested directions. Different movements of "physically challenged" people demand greater access to public facilities. Factions of the Deaf Culture movement assert linguistic-minority-group pride in American Sign Language and even the moral superiority of not hearing. The National Association for Fat Acceptance, with slogans such as "Fat! So?" and "Every Body–Good Body," struggles to gain greater social tolerance for and to extend civil rights protections to "people of size." And the feminist movement has successfully made the savage oppression of some women, even in foreign cultures and worlds apart, the symbol of the station of all women. Finally, there are the transvalued religious quests for personal salvation such as the New Age movement and movements that make into public issues personal rage at misfortune, such as the protests of the AIDS Coalition to Unleash Power (ACT UP) against government AIDS policies. With all of these movements have come thousands of new organizations and front groups, new rhetorics, and new tactics for leftist activists, or at least the refurbishing of old ones for a modern age. Further, the backing of the left in the United States is formidable: at least eighty-five foundations with assets amounting to over \$27 billion annually donate large sums to assorted "progressive" causes and research undertakings. Moreover, an impressive apparatus of publishing houses keep those causes constantly before the public.[11]

Since the 1960s, advocates on the left of the political spectrum have drawn an extraordinarily bleak picture of American society. In this view, reiterated in many college classrooms across the country, the American social order is thoroughly racist to all "people of color," a disproportionate number of whom it imprisons, especially African Americans. It is hostile to women and deeply "homophobic" toward homosexuals. It is abusive of children, sexually repressive of the young, and neglectful of the aged. It is xenophobic and exploitative toward immigrants. It is callous toward the homeless. It is environmentally destructive. It is brutal toward animals because antiquated legal concepts define animals as property and allow inhumane industrialized food production and vivisectionist scientific procedures, amidst other savagery toward beast and fowl. It is mean-spirited toward the poor and wracked by deep social and economic inequalities at home that are the inevitable by-products of capitalism. It is imperialist and exploitative abroad. And it is harsh and intolerant to all viewpoints that do not emanate from white males who are assumed to be a monolithic social group, whence the need for greater representation of all groups in American society and ceaseless advocacy to "counterspin" hegemonic propaganda. In such a view, America is a nation of exploiters and victims. Leftist advocates typically argue that the social pathologies of American society must be remedied by drastic legislative, administrative, or especially, judicial actions.[12]

Virtually every movement on the left has produced reaction and counteradvocacy on the right, typically in very organized form. Conservative think tanks, such as the Heritage Foundation, the Cato Institute, and the Manhattan Institute, have sprung up all across the country, mobilizing intellectuals with rightist leanings to defend the very institutions under assault from the left or to argue against the ideas that underpin liberal policies. Sometimes full-blown movements emerge, such as the anti–affirmative action movements that have successfully mounted referenda to overturn state laws in California and Oregon, or the pro-life movement in response to abortion advocates' triumphs in court, complete, at the movement's edge, with violent, at times fatal, tactics; or sometimes cliques within established organizations have mobilized to reassert traditional doctrines, as in the redoubled efforts of the Roman Catholic Church's hierarchy to condemn homosexual activity in the face of gay and lesbian activism. But, most especially, all over the United States, one sees the formation of grassroots conservative organizations, such as bookstores and book clubs dedicated to conservative ideas, associations for tax reform, citizens' groups to promote conservative curricular perspectives in the public schools, watchdog organizations critiquing what is thought to be the liberal bias of the media, nativist efforts against immigration, centers promoting free enterprise and libertarian ideologies, organizations designed to increase economic privatization and abolish government interference in the economy, patriotic organizations still fighting communism and the cold war, committees to make English the official language of the United States, and various groups dedicated to debunking what are perceived to be the shibboleths of the left. The right also has its own foundations, though these foundations' accumulated assets of about $5.1 billion are dwarfed by the assets of foundations backing the left.[13]

The images of American society from the right and center of the political spectrum both counter and complement the left's bleak pictures of the social order. Conservatives celebrate American society's resilient economy that provides everybody who seizes the opportunity with the chance to succeed, including immigrants who internalize the American ethos of hard work. They tout the nation's vibrant, though flawed, democratic tradition. They salute the bravery of its fighting men and women in war after war in this century. They point out that, when compared with many other countries, American citizens and institutions demonstrate an abiding sense of fairness and, indeed, compassion. But these champions of American society also see dire, possibly fatal, shortcomings afflicting the nation. They excoriate the left's propensity to rely on state administrative solutions to social problems with all the enormous tax burdens such state solutions require, instead of market remedies; they deplore the left's reliance on the judiciary to subvert and contradict the popular will. They lament the left's success in removing religious references and symbols from every sphere of public life. They picture America as a godless country, an indulgent and permissive society without a moral compass. They see America as increasingly balkanized by unchecked immigration, linguistic splintering, an unwarranted celebration of cultural divergence instead of unifying traditional values, and by governmental policies based on ascribed characteristics, such as affirmative action. In particular, they see ever-increasing divorce and illegitimacy rates, successful claims for alternative sexual lifestyles, and government support for abortion on demand as hastening the collapse of the American family, an ominous harbinger of future social disaster. They frequently portray America as a society dominated by cowardly, prevaricating leaders who almost invariably cave in to liberal pressure groups with spurious claims, a society caught in a moral vacuum in which lower-class violence and criminality inevitably increase hand-in-hand with middle- and upper-class licentiousness. And conservatives never tire of claiming that the media in general, the entertainment industry, and the academy are totally in the grip of leftists, liberals, and indeed, radicals bent on propagating an amoral, wholly relativistic set of postmodern worldviews. Some conservatives, such as far-right evangelical Christian groups, and some centrists have made strange alliances with some far leftists, such as Catharine MacKinnon and Andrea Dworkin, and moderates, such as Tipper Gore, to condemn First Amendment shielding of pornography and violent visual and verbal imagery in films and music—principal sources, they argue, of America's purported moral decline.[14]

Thus, throughout contemporary American society, alongside the administrative and technological apparatus that sustains modern civilization, one finds a thicket of parallel advocacy organizations, some anarchic, some thoroughly bureaucratized, some vestigial, others vigorous, some operating at the financial margin, others extremely well-heeled, some well to the political left, others well to the right. Each apparatus produces its own elaborate set of representations of the American social order, complete with ready-made self-images. Advocates on the right usually see themselves defending the besieged fort of "traditional values" against a concerted liberal onslaught. Advocates on the left see themselves as part of a high-minded "public-interest community" and until very recently have been the masters of this kind of advocacy. Throughout American society, one hears the clang and clamor of advocacy. Here, for instance, one finds a group devoted to promoting global dialogue on political and social issues; there, a religious sodality mobilizing public outrage against a museum that exhibits art deemed to desecrate blessed icons; here, a consortium dedicated to reproductive health care and women's rights; there, a think tank dedicated to conservative critiques of liberal policies, pushing, among other programs, charter schools and school vouchers; here, a grassroots leadership program "empowering traditionally disempowered communities"; there, a network of women's colleges training women for public policy careers by providing "mentor" relationships; here, a research organization dedicated to preaching traditional "family values"; there, a fully mobilized parents' association vehemently opposed to a school curriculum designed by a "rainbow coalition"; here, a support center to aid liberal nonprofit organizations in routine business management; there, a youth action program that "seeks to facilitate the involvement of young people . . . in social justice efforts." Everywhere, one finds spontaneous and usually transitory groupings of residents organized to assert common opposition to private interests or public policies, such as tenant associations protesting landlord practices, or a neighborhood or block club opposing a municipality's choice of sites for methadone clinics. This congeries of assorted organizations that their participants variously call associations, agencies, alliances, causes, collectives, cooperatives, collaboratives, councils, coalitions, foundations, forums, funds, leagues, movements, networks, projects, societies, institutes, and, especially, centers constitutes the framework within which those who have a calling to advocacy fulfill their vocations.[15]

〰〰〰 The shock troops of those called to advocacy are usually young men and women, typically college-educated, who become engaged in advocacy work during their undergraduate years. Some advocacy organizations have student-run chapters on large campuses. Others work the speaking circuit or conduct regional workshops, partially as recruiting tactics, though, in general, recruiting is haphazard. Indeed, internship or employment at most advocacy organizations depends almost entirely on volunteers' zeal and initiative. Some organizations sponsor summer-long or semester-long internship programs for college students, offering work experience in a noble cause in return for youthful energy, enthusiasm, and moral passion. The emotional roots of such commitment vary widely, though the intensity of the commitment seems to depend on youths' abilities to identify with the subjects of their advocacy. In any event, the emotional commitment is often all that sustains one. In Washington, D.C., at least, the home of many national advocacy organizations, advocacy work by interning students is rarely remunerated, essentially restricting most advocacy groups to relatively affluent middle-class youth whose parents will subsidize their experiments with social change or their defense of beleaguered values. In some advocacy organizations, promising interns are then invited back for regular staff jobs that are also filled by other young people who bypassed the intern route. Jobs at this level in the advocacy world are invariably difficult. Young advocates are given little socialization or training; one learns the techniques of advocacy by advocating. They are underpaid and often exhibit a very high rate of the occupational fatigue called "burnout," though some young advocates live at the economic margin for years to fight for causes in which they believe. But most "move on" after a period of advocacy work, either going into a new line of work or, in many cases, back to school for graduate or professional studies. There are some opportunities for more advanced advocacy work after further schooling. Some advocacy organizations on the left, in conjunction with universities or congressional offices and even a few law firms, provide grants or fellowships to recent graduates in law or other disciplines for a year's policy work on particular concerns, such as women's rights or environmental issues. On both ends of the political spectrum, institutes offer a few coveted policy analyst jobs on selected issues.

The regular staff of advocacy organizations typically consists of men and women with some professional training or its equivalent in experience. Many come from law; some have backgrounds in journalism, public relations, or other areas of interpretive expertise; policy analysts come from the social sciences, particularly economics and political science, or from public policy schools. On the left, some have been professional lobbyists for the labor union movement, the environmental movement, the educational reform movement, or "progressive" legislators; on the right, some come from business, some as exiles from the academy, but they find their home in advocacy organizations because they approach their work with a religious-like commitment to a calling.

On both sides of the political spectrum, men and women called to advocacy believe in what they do. They deliberately choose to pursue particular lines of advocacy. Often, they make considerable economic sacrifices in the process. It is also the case that some lines of advocacy, say, the burgeoning area of animal rights law dedicated to erasing legal distinctions between persons and animals, not only promise intriguing intellectual work but potentially big money. Expertise and political leanings, in the broadest senses, determine the flexibility and progression of careers among advocates with a vocation. Briefly, on the left side of the political spectrum, one can easily switch from advocacy for children's rights to advocacy for women's rights. One can also switch from one educational issue to another. But the substantive expertise for effective advocacy on, say, environmental issues prevents easy access to that arena. Moreover, one cannot easily convert from a previous advocacy for, say, a conservative plan to alter welfare dramatically to, say, advocacy for the homeless. The political divide between these issues is also a moral chasm. In order to advocate effectively on issues with political import, one must have "impeccable credentials" of the appropriate ideological stripe. However, a shift from the left to the right of the political spectrum, a change that many men and women undergo with age and affluence, is less a bar to effective advocacy than the reverse migration; indeed, former 1960s radicals become effective spokesmen for one or another rightist cause with some frequency.[16] And the whole ethos of the legal profession allows law-and-order prosecutors to "cross the street" to the more liberal defense bar without impediment. Generally speaking, one observes among advocates with a vocation a striking homogeneity of sentiments about a whole skein of issues at any given moment in their development. Those working on a "progressive" cause, for example, are expected to share the moral sentiments and public stances of other advocates on the left working on completely different issues; the same applies to those in the trenches of the conservative movement. Those who waver on questions of doctrine are usually thought to have shaky vocations.

Some advocates have their vocations thrust upon them, as it were, by events. They have no special training in advocacy, nor indeed any larger career aspirations. Instead, they become immersed in an issue entirely out of personal concerns. Thus, the brutal rape/murder of a daughter leads one distraught mother to form a national society for the survivors of homicide victims; the death of a son at the hands of a drunk driver thrusts another mother into the forefront of an organization against drinking and driving; the surviving victim of a gunshot attack, along with his wife, become gun-control advocates; families who have lost a child to street savagery join neighborhood councils demanding greater police control of gang violence. Such men and women become passionate advocates for appropriate reforms, often establishing and leading organizations with the authority and conviction born of deep personal suffering. But theirs is a vocation generally uncluttered by larger ideological commitments. When the pain of their own misfortune eases, they are likely to yield the stage to other advocates with fresh rage and return to normal or seminormal routines. But for some people, such as Larry Kramer, who contracted the HIV virus and was propelled into furious advocacy against governmental policies on AIDS ("a holocaust," according to Kramer), a return to normality is not possible.[17]

Advocacy organizations also offer opportunities for self-expression to men and women who are immersed in their own lives. Many professional interpretive experts in advertising and public relations lend their talents and time to advocacy organizations on a pro bono basis, sometimes as freelancers because of their own convictions on particular issues, sometimes as regular advisers to organizational staff or as members of boards of directors. Some of these professionals stay in their accustomed roles as prophets of good fortune, simply shifting their talents to other arenas as time and opportunity allow. Other professionals, especially account managers in advertising and public relations practitioners, tire of the constant attentiveness to clients that is required of prophets of good fortune or of what many come to feel is the unseemliness of spending one's life on commercial trivialities. They welcome the opportunity to throw off the cloak of self-suppression that modern bureaucratic work requires and become at least part-time prophets of doom, castigating the social structure, or private or public officials, or the culture as a whole for perceived wrongs. Their newfound fervor is rarely appreciated by their colleagues.

Some professors are impelled by the desire to see their intellectual work enacted in public policies. If their work has practical applicability, and if they themselves are sufficiently attuned to the peculiar exigencies of the mass media (that is, they know how to boil complex realities down to bite-sized sentiments), they might be anointed as experts in their areas by key publications such as the *New York Times* or the *Weekly Standard*, or by radio networks such as National Public Radio or the Excellence in Broadcasting System. They then find ready forums for their policy pronouncements or moralistic cavils. Some make the big time and get invited to be one of the regulars trooping across nightly television free-for-alls hosted by Larry King, or Geraldo Rivera, or Ted Koppel. Those less fortunate settle for the eager discipleship of students seeking temporary salvational respite from the anticipated rigors of postgraduation middle-class life. Their classrooms become congregations of a sort where their flocks can prepare for the battle for other souls.

Other intellectuals join the advocacy fray through different kinds of organizational milieux. As always, advocacy journalism and commentary fill the op-ed and editorial pages of the nation's newspapers and journals of opinion, as well as many of the news pages. But the print media have been completely outdistanced by broadcast advocacy. One need only turn on a television or radio in any of the major media markets at any hour of the day or night to hear panels of expert advocates, some self-appointed, promoting one cause or another; or watch media stars, in studios packed with their own fans, hector public figures about unresolved, perhaps unresolvable, social problems; or hear talk show hosts, who command vast audiences, thundering predictions about everything from the failings of current political leadership to the supposedly imminent collapse of American civilization because of the loss of moral fiber.

Those called to advocacy find many rewards in their work. Emotional commitments to causes center many advocates' lives, providing frameworks to integrate learning and action, prisms through which to understand larger social structures, and moral measuring sticks by which to evaluate other individuals and ideologies alike. Advocates' self-images suggest the vibrancy of the internal moral dramas that such centering commitments engender. Some see themselves as guerrillas in the bureaucratic jungles of modern society, fighting to "make the system work." Others see themselves as organizers whose teaching strips the blinders from the eyes of their constituencies and "empowers" them, thus furthering the development of true democracy. Some see themselves as warriors in ideological struggles with great stakes for the nation's future, while other advocates see themselves as compassionate conciliators in a torn social order.

Moreover, advocacy work can provide satisfying concrete results. At times, such advocacy is directed toward engaging people in nongovernmental efforts to improve the world. Two measures of the success of such advocacy are the millions of hours of volunteer charitable work done by Americans each year, as well as the millions of dollars in small donations raised annually for various humanitarian causes.[18] Sometimes such advocacy has the purpose of changing official policies or structures, such as one sees in efforts to obtain formal recognition of a range of nontraditional familial arrangements so, for example, partners may receive the benefits due a spouse, or in the appeals to parents to oppose the institutionalization of school curricula that, it is thought, erode traditional values. When things go wrong, when enemies outflank them, or when bureaucratic systems prove intractable, or when the tide of public opinion runs against them, advocates with a vocation see themselves as Cassandra at the door to Agamemnon's palace, as prophets destined to tell the truth but not be heeded. Even when the singular kind of secular faith that advocates with a vocation have in their work, in other people, and in society's institutions wavers, they maintain their belief in themselves and in their visions for the social order.

But advocacy as a vocation also has its vicissitudes. One must always guard the interests of one's constituency in the public forum even when its claims are weak or perhaps specious, lest one's opponents steal the march in the never-ending battle for resources or public support. When one moves to administrative work in an advocacy organization, far removed from the day-to-day concerns of one's constituency, one must always claim knowledge and experience no longer readily available in order to maintain one's legitimacy as an "authentic" spokesman or spokeswoman for one's constituency.

Moreover, one always confronts the riddles of the unintended consequences of one's advocacy. To take only one example, advocates for the homeless in the early 1980s in New York City portrayed the burgeoning population living on city streets as citizens dispossessed from their residences by hard luck, greedy realtors, heartless city officials, and rapacious capitalism. The entire solution to homelessness, they argued repeatedly, was housing, housing, and more housing. The advocates won a consent decree in court from the City of New York to provide shelter for anyone requesting it. And, eventually, families in shelters were given priority status on the public housing lists, thus creating the widely held perception that the fast road to permanent city-subsidized housing was through the homeless shelters. More "homeless" men and women and families crowded city streets and city shelters than ever before as people abandoned makeshift, difficult, but previously manageable living arrangements to take the city up on its court-brokered pledge and get into the run for city housing. In addition, the core of the homeless population, particularly among single adults, bore no resemblance at all to the this-bad-break-could-happen-to-you-tomorrow image that advocates had pitched to the city's middle class to gain support in their arm-wrestling match with the city. In fact, many core homeless were personally disorganized and disoriented, often mentally ill, and very often substance abusers; some were aimless drifters; many were the products of the post-1960s "deinstitutionalization" of inmates of state mental hospitals, a movement that was itself the product of relentless advocacy.[19] Advocates for the homeless undoubtedly helped some individuals. But, as some advocates themselves later admitted, their insistence on an ideological and, in the end, simpleminded solution to the problem of homelessness postponed necessary social services as well as medical and substance abuse treatment for the core of the homeless, placed crippling strains on city resources, and transferred the burden of individuals' broken lives to the city's public at large. The more effective one's advocacy, the greater is the danger of legacies that are not only unforeseen, but unwanted.

〰〰〰 Today, advocates with a vocation come principally from the new middle classes, the vast, variegated social stratum whose members depend wholly on large bureaucratic organizations for their livelihoods. Most advocates learn with their mothers' milk the fundamentals of claim making in a bureaucratic world. In a world of ever proliferating rules and procedures, one survives and flourishes by learning to make cases, that is, by articulating rational arguments that some authority deems plausible, whether or not the cases have any substantive merit beyond the benefit to the claim maker. The elaborate procedures of our claim-making system keep issues alive long after their graceful natural death might have occurred, producing precisely the ambiguity in which public advocacy can work its magic.

As it happens, contemporary advocacy, no matter how deep the moral convictions behind it, often resembles sleight of hand compared with older forms of persuasion. The very rules of claim making have changed profoundly since the mid-twentieth century in most public forums in American society. For a start, visual images have gained ascendancy over verbal arguments. In the world of advocates with a vocation, this places a premium on "visible" associations and identifications with persons, groups, or symbols that, for whatever reason, are in favor at the moment with one's primary constituencies. A feminist academic acknowledges privately that a male colleague has been falsely accused of sexual harassment by a woman whom she knows and admits to be emotionally unstable and vindictive. But, she argues, she must publicly take his accuser's side and join the chorus of outrage against him in the cause of sisterhood. A minority academic on a national panel to evaluate funding proposals publicly refuses to judge a proposal as excellent because it does not focus on race and the historical exclusion of minorities from mainstream institutions, even when these issues are not germane to the proposal at hand. Here visible solidarity with key reference groups and their interests takes precedence over older rules of evidence, notions of veracity, or principles of fairness. Some leaders of lower-class interest groups have grasped with great accuracy the logic of the middle-class apparatus of bureaucracy, claim making, and passionate advocacy in an epoch of visual mass media. They have become adroit at dramatizing their causes and themselves for the media, exciting their own constituencies, and playing on the self-images of key middle-class groups, not least middle-class advocates with a vocation who cannot afford to be on the wrong side of a "progressive" cause.

Even more to the point, effective advocacy in the public arena today depends entirely on adopting and internalizing the ethos of advocacy. One must keep one's messages simple, emotional, and credible for one's targeted audiences, preferably in the form of a personalized story. One must select and train the right spokespeople because the bearers of a message are as important as the message itself. One carefully releases one's "documented evidence" in support of one's position over a period of time in order to maximize press coverage; one does advance work with key editorial boards, helping them understand the significance of one's research and assisting in framing its interpretation. One writes op-ed pieces for both national and local daily newspapers: if one is on the left, one develops moving story lines that sympathetic media outlets, such as National Public Radio, a gathering place for leftists of all sorts, will find attractive; if one is on the right, one crafts story lines focusing on any of the egregious contradictions of the American social order that will appeal to, say, Sean Hannity's daily nationwide radio brawl. In brief, advocates with a calling must master the techniques of professional advocacy, originally developed by advertising and public relations practitioners, if their work is to have any efficacy within the institutional logic that dominates the public arena. And advocacy as a vocation has begun to manifest the same circular, self-referential logic of commercial, professional advocacy. The Advocacy Institute in Washington, D.C., "studies the art of advocacy." In addition to training current and prospective advocates in the elements of advocacy—on how to tell a story, work the media, build alliances, and gain access to and persuade decision makers—the Advocacy Institute also prides itself on being an "advocate for advocacy."

What exactly is the institutional logic of the apparatus of bureaucracy, claim making, and advocacy in the public arena today? The main framework of advocacy in modern society has official or semiofficial origins and purposes. Generally speaking, pragmatic compromise rules the world of affairs, with hard choices between opposed interests explained with euphemistic language to temper and control emotions and to keep public business on an even keel. The overwhelming percentage of public business is handled in such a routine fashion that the public scarcely notices its accomplishment. But sometimes issues emerge, or are manufactured, that require governmental or corporate authorities to rally public emotions. Here, the vast machinery of official propaganda rolls into action. Political leaders recognize that, say, "keep[ing] the home fires burning" determines their abilities to wage total war.[20] Or, corporate officials use propaganda to appeal to crucial external publics in order to scare their colleagues and opponents alike and work their organizational will. In such cases, issues are cast as melodrama, emotions usually replace reason, images replace argument, and choices dressed as heroes or villains are strutted across the stage. The groundlings acclaim a hero, affirming decisions made by men and women they do not know and have never seen except perhaps in the media. Advertising and public relations practitioners are always big players in such a process, inventing ingenious rationales for "what has to be done" or making heroes out of personalities, ideas, or causes.

Here image makers become "technicians in sentiment," to borrow Robert K. Merton's phrase,[21] discerners and purveyors of key emotional pushes to action. In their unofficial crusades to oppose or reform official systems, or to counter official propaganda, or to mobilize publics for protest, advocates with a vocation are also technicians in sentiment. A great deal of advocacy on a host of causes on, say, the plight of America's neglected children or uncared-for aged, or the unheard cries of its aborted infants, or the erosion of its traditional bases of community, or the suffering of refugees in Rwanda or Kosovo, makes appeals to audiences' sentiments of pity, compassion, generosity, understanding, or longings for peace with one's neighbors. As it happens, sentiments like the longing for reconciliation, or for a bygone world, or for shared common ground, have a short half-life in modern society, where differences between people, institutions, and spheres of life deepen daily and where stories and images of conflict, betrayal, and violence have become a staple of the media.

7 TECHNICIANS IN MORAL OUTRAGE

Some advocates make their claims through confrontation, trafficking in somewhat darker sentiments, those that emphasize the splits between people. They become technicians in moral outrage, men and women who combine the fervor of advocates with a vocation with the studied dispassion of professional advocates necessary for effective mass advocacy.

What tactics, appeals, and habits of mind characterize technicians in moral outrage as a type of advocate? There are hundreds of possible ready-at-hand examples in every corner of the public arena. Some organizations specialize in stirring up moral outrage, at least on certain issues. Thus, the National Rifle Association produces relentless scare propaganda against handgun control. The Massachusetts Department of Public Health leads its anti-tobacco crusade (<www.getoutraged. com>). The National Resources Defense Council (NRDC), in league with the CBS show *60 Minutes,* conducted a concerted, hysterical assault in 1989 against Alar, the plant growth regulator then used to keep ripening apples on the tree, to which the conservative American Council on Science and Health responded with a moralistic counterattack against NRDC and CBS. The Moral Majority and Christian Coalition offer fundamentalist critiques of abortion-rights advocates, and the Family Research Institute works relentlessly to develop social science information to defeat gay-rights ballot initiatives. Some individuals, like the lawyers Johnnie Cochran or Ron Kuby, both specialists in playing the race card in legal cases, or David Duke, former congressman, perennial candidate for electoral office, and advocate for a primitive nativism, become celebrities and even political forces by trading in outrage.

Here are profiles of three individual technicians in moral outrage, two on the political left, one on the right. They are chosen because they are prototypes of the kind of advocacy at issue. They specialize in whipping up maelstroms of moral fervor to serve a cause and in making particular incidents symbols of supposedly general trends. They work across a range of milieux: from the streets, to college campuses, to mass radio broadcasts. They address primary constituencies from different social strata: from lower class, to solid upper–middle class, to new middle class. And their appeals to their respective primary constituencies revolve, sequentially, around issues that dominate public discourse at the start of the new millenium, namely, race, gender, class, and political ideology.

〰〰〰 The history of African Americans in the United States and the social and economic conditions that continue to affect lower- and underclass blacks have produced many African American technicians in moral outrage. African Americans' deeply felt religious worldviews from their countries of origin, coupled with newfound Christian beliefs, sustained them during their years of slavery. Later, the profound symbolic inversion central to Judeo-Christian biblical tradition and rhetoric, one promising that the meek shall inherit the earth, that the weak shall triumph over the strong, provided African American leaders with resonant vocabularies both to awaken their own people with promises and to characterize their struggle for civil rights in heroic, universal moral terms. Many of the most important African American leaders in this century—Marcus Garvey, Martin Luther King, Jr., Elijah Muhammed, Malcolm X, Jesse Jackson—have actually been or are preachers. Moral exhortation or condemnation frame their demands for secular transformation. The public oratory of many African American secular leaders such as the late Shirley Chisolm and Barbara Jordan, as well as Congressman John Lewis, still has the cadence and ring of the preaching style found in black southern churches, a style central to electoral success in black communities. Indeed, the spirit of advocacy, specifically the tone of moral outrage, animates much of the written intellectual work done by African Americans; the fictional works of, say, James Baldwin, Maya Angelou, Alice Walker, Lorraine Hansbury, Toni Morrison, or the more academic preaching of Derrick Bell or especially Cornel West, are notable for the ferocity of their moral visions. Advocacy as a vocation finds deep religious resonance among African Americans.

But, like "subordinate" groups in any social hierarchy, African Americans also have a remarkable tradition of trickster fables, many of them brought with them from Africa,[1] long predating the Brer Rabbit tales collected by Joel Chandler Harris in the late nineteenth century. In the American black version of this universal genre, the trickster constantly dupes, outflanks, pulls the tails of, and outwits his enemies, that is, white folks, whose unwarranted good fortune in real life makes them entirely deserving of fictitious ignominy. Closely related to these trickster myths, and partially legitimated by them, is the institutionalized role of hustler, one who lives by his wits in the interstices of the social order. Indeed, hustlers are tricksters of a certain sort. Like the trickster, they circumvent conventional ways of acting as well as conventional morality, although their striving aims not at a symbolic reversal of the social order but at improving their own immediate fortunes. Hustling of various sorts has often been the only route of upward mobility open to many lower- or underclass African Americans and to other subordinate social groups. Its implicit transgressiveness thus gains sanction from exigency as well as from communal respect for the cunning of the underdog. Moreover, the cultural styles developed by street "players" are regularly appropriated by the popular culture industry and find their way into the mainstream.[2] Finally, African American youth have developed what might be called an oppositional street-culture of defiance, one that celebrates the symbolic inversion of all middle-class virtues, particularly those of the white middle class. In this world, to work hard is to be submissive, to study is to act white, and to act "bad" is to be good; indeed, one of the highest street accolades is to be considered a "baaad nigga."[3] At all times, one must command "respect" from others, an intricate status conception at the core of one's personal and social identities.

Such traditions help explain both the emergence and the considerable popularity, among many African Americans at least, of a technician in moral outrage like the Reverend Alfred Sharpton. Like his early mentor and friend, the late Congressman Adam Clayton Powell, the Reverend Sharpton combines African Americans' preaching tradition (he was a "boy preacher," giving his first sermon when four years old), with the trickster's and hustler's gut sense of how to "get over" in virtually any interaction, that is, how to seize the moment and turn the logic of the system upside down to demand respect and capture one's own advantage. Powell mastered such a strategy well before Sharpton; his extended run in Congress and the committee chairmanships, political power, and control of patronage that came with such longevity were due largely to his constituency's delight at his deliberate nose-thumbing of the establishment, which included evident corruption and personal decadence. Though the Reverend Sharpton has adjusted his style in recent years to fit his ambitions for elected political office, he built his following in the streets, employing flamboyant tactics that more resemble the styles of other important mentors, surrogate fathers and friends, including the "Godfather of Soul" James Brown, Brown's famous promoter, Don King, who is the brawling backer of numerous boxers such as "Iron Mike" Tyson (an alliance shattered in 1998 when Tyson sued King, claiming massive, decade-long fraud), and the Reverend Jesse Jackson, who taught the Reverend Sharpton how to be a civil rights crusader.

The Reverend Sharpton has seized the public megaphone successfully time and again under the rubric of a search for "racial justice" in the United States, always using particular incidents or cases as springboards to command attention and to assert his own ideology. Thus, in the wake of the 1986 death of Michael Griffith, a young African American man killed on a Queens parkway while fleeing a racist white mob in an incident called the Howard Beach case, Sharpton helped organize several community rallies, marches into largely white neighborhoods, and civil disobedience–filled "days of outrage" to protest racial violence, along with endless picketing of police, judicial, and administrative authorities demanding convictions of the twelve white youths indicted. Three of the defendants were convicted of second-degree manslaughter and sentenced to long prison terms; several others were convicted at trial or pleaded guilty to lesser charges; one defendant was acquitted. The case brought a group of black activists who knew one another from previous episodes into a firm coalition that has since frequently acted in concert. The group included lawyers Alton Maddox and C. Vernon Mason; activists Jitu Weusi and Sonny Carson of Brooklyn, Dr. Lenora Fulani of the New Alliance Party, Benjamin Hooks of the NAACP, and the Reverends Calvin Butts, Herbert Daughtry, Timothy Mitchell, Charles Barron, and Sharpton. In later cases, lawyers William Kunstler and Colin Moore, Minister Louis Farrakhan, and sometime NAACP leader Hazel Dukes, among many others, joined that circle.

The case of Tawana Brawley presented the Reverend Sharpton with new challenges and opportunities. On 28 November 1987 in Wappingers Falls, Dutchess County, New York, fifteen-year-old Tawana Brawley was found, presumably unconscious. She was smeared with feces, and "KKK," "nigger," and other slurs had been scrawled on her body. She accused white police officers of abducting, raping, and sodomizing her; one of those accused committed suicide on 1 December. The Brawley family retained Alton Maddox as their lawyer, and immediately the case went into pell-mell overdrive. Hazel Dukes, then head of New York State's NAACP, charged an official coverup. Minister Louis Farrakhan, C. Vernon Mason, Sonny Carson, Sharpton, and others addressed a rally in nearby Newburgh, New York, punctuating their charges with lurid details. The Brawley case received prominent mention in one of the Reverend Sharpton's days of outrage. Acerbic legal skirmishes finally resulted in Governor Mario Cuomo naming Attorney General Robert Abrams as special prosecutor in the case. Abrams convened a grand jury to investigate the matter. The entertainer Bill Cosby and an associate announced a $50,000 reward for information leading to the arrest of Tawana Brawley's assailants. The then world heavyweight champion Mike Tyson—himself later convicted of forcible rape—along with his promoter Don King met with Tawana. Tyson gave the girl a diamond-studded Rolex watch and promised to put up $50,000 for her college tuition. Several marches, organized through WLIB-AM, the African American and Caribbean radio station in New York City, were staged in Poughkeepsie and later in Albany, New York, complete with busloads of appropriately angry demonstrators, many of whom were said to be paid, denouncing the attorney general's handling of the case. Brawley's mother, Glenda, defied a subpoena to appear before the grand jury and disclose her knowledge of Tawana's ordeal. Her lawyer, Alton Maddox, baited and insulted the judge, who sentenced Mrs. Brawley to thirty days in jail. Mrs. Brawley fled to New York City where she was granted sanctuary by Ebenezer Baptist Church in Queens and later by Bethany Baptist Church in Brooklyn.

In the meantime, there were profound disputes even within the ranks of Tawana's supporters about the veracity of her claims, leading to one summary firing from the Reverend Sharpton's entourage and to subsequent court battles about supposed "evidence" that might destroy her case. But in a display of confident unity, Maddox, Mason, Sharpton, and the Brawleys complete with an entourage of supporters, as well as Farrakhan and Fulani, made a joint appearance at the Democratic National Convention in Atlanta, Georgia, in July 1988.

On 6 October 1988, Robert Abrams released the grand jury report charging that Tawana herself was completely responsible, in concert with her mother, for the condition in which she was found. The grand jury found that Tawana and her mother had concocted the entire rape and disfigurement ruse to protect Tawana from the wrath of her stepfather, Ralph King, after the girl had skipped school and been out late once too often without permission. King was a violent man who had been convicted of killing his first wife. He regularly got extremely angry at the then fifteen-year-old's restiveness, sexual precociousness, and growing rebelliousness. Neither Mrs. Brawley nor Tawana, it seems, had any intention of fooling anyone but Mr. King. But when Tawana's friends, instead of her mother, discovered the girl in the pitiful physical condition that she and her mother had arranged and then called the police, the girl and her mother invented the abduction and rape accusations.[4] And the entire state of New York, indeed the entire nation, was plunged into a ritual drama of ancient racial guilt, accusation, and blame.

To this day, the Reverend Sharpton and the coalition of other advocates that championed Tawana Brawley insist that they believe the girl's account that she was in fact raped by white police officers and a local prosecutor, Steven A. Pagones. Tawana herself became and remains something of a celebrity in black circles, and a great many people still claim to believe her version of the story. Some white leftists such as the folk singer Pete Seeger have been jailed for protesting official misconduct in the Brawley investigation. In his 1996 autobiography, the Reverend Sharpton provides an assessment of the readiness of blacks to believe Tawana's accusations:

> I think the majority of the black community always believed Tawana, from the beginning up until now. What I don't think most white people understood was that there is some Tawana in most black people, almost like a collective memory. . . . On the Donahue Show, Phil Donahue said to me, 'How can you possibly believe that these men you've accused could do such a thing?' And I pointed out to the crowd and said, 'How could you ask me that, when you're sitting in a church with five hundred black people and every one of us has a different complexion? Where did that come from? How could I not think it possible that white men might rape black women?'[5]

Here, the specific facts of the individual case at hand, the entire basis of Anglo-Saxon common law, become irrelevant. What matters is "collective memory," itself socially constructed through endless repetition by advocates. Possibility subsumes reality and Tawana, whether her contemporary accusations were true or not, had come to symbolize ancient

wrongs. Sharpton goes on to present a rationale for his own unwaver-
ing defense of Tawana. As it happens, when Sharpton was nine-and-
a-half years old, his father seduced his older half-sister and fathered a
child by her, rupturing Sharpton's family and leaving his hard-working
mother nearly destitute; the family ended up in Brooklyn housing
projects.[6] The Reverend Sharpton became a defender of black women
everywhere.

> And maybe we did bring a lot . . . to the table in the Brawley matter.
> Maybe in my case it also had something to do with what happened
> between my father and sister, all the emotions that were involved.
> Maybe the harder they attacked Tawana, the more I saw a vulnerable
> black woman, like my mother, that no one would fight for. At some
> point it stopped being Tawana, and started being me defending my
> mother and all the black women no one would fight for. I was not
> going to run away from her like my father had run away from my
> mother, like so many other black men had run away. This was going
> to be one time, if I lost it all, that I was going to go all the way down.[7]

Like advertising creatives, the technician in moral outrage feeds off
the rich bottomland of personal experience, here transvaluing the irre-
sponsibility of one's own father and that of some other black men into
a resolve always to be steadfast. Criticism of Tawana's story becomes an
attack on all black women who have ever been betrayed by faithless
black men, prompting among the steadfast a blind, fervent commitment to her cause. Tawana's accusations against white men close the
circle and trigger the rage that enables one to recognize and ignite rage
in others, perhaps similarly grounded.

After he issued his report, Attorney General Abrams initiated disciplinary proceedings against lawyers Maddox and Mason, with a view
to their disbarment. Abrams also began an investigation of the Reverend Sharpton that resulted in a sixty-seven-count indictment for fraud
and grand larceny of various sorts.[8] But the Reverend Sharpton was
acquitted at trial of all of those charges, much to his delight and that of
his followers, and he continues to boast about how he humiliated the
attorney general and, indeed, the entire state of New York. The Brawley
affair, however, came back to haunt the Reverend Sharpton in later
years.

The Bensonhurst case virtually replicated the Howard Beach case,
though on a much larger scale. On 23 August 1989, Yusef Hawkins was
shot to death in Bensonhurst, Brooklyn; he had gone to the neighborhood with two friends to look at a used car. Police made several immediate arrests of local Italian American youths who had assaulted the

trio of black youths. The coalition of black activists led a march of three hundred people into Bensonhurst on 27 August, followed by a 31 August march of ten thousand on the Brooklyn Bridge protesting Hawkins's death as well as the death of Huey P. Newton, founder and former defense minister of the Black Panther Party. On 22 August, Newton's crack-cocaine-addicted body had been found in Oakland, California, with three bullets in his head, a killing that turned out to be drug-related. His killer was arrested on a weapons charge the same day and a few days later admitted the crime to officers from the Oakland Police Department, the organization against which Newton had railed for more than twenty years but which became his final advocate. The organizers of the Brooklyn Bridge demonstration joined Newton's death with that of Yusef Hawkins, attributing both to endemic racism in American society. Other arrests were made in the Bensonhurst case, followed by murder indictments against three people and less serious charges against several others. From September 1989 through early January 1991, the Reverend Sharpton and the by-then well-established coalition of black activists led a series of marches into Bensonhurst, prompting counterdemonstrations, much to the delight of the mass media. As the trials proceeded, scarcely a day passed without courthouse rallies at which the Reverend Sharpton warned that anything less than murder convictions might cause New York to explode in race riots. In the end, Joey Fama was convicted of murder and another participant of riot, unlawful imprisonment, and related charges. Other defendants in the episode were either acquitted or convicted of lesser charges. Sharpton resumed the marches in Bensonhurst where, on 12 January 1991, an assailant, Michael Riccardi, broke through the police lines and stabbed and seriously wounded him. The near-assassination solidified Sharpton's leadership among his followers.

"No justice, no peace!" has been the Reverend Sharpton's signature rallying slogan, and threat, in these and many other cases. His involvement in the New York City trial of the young black men accused of raping and nearly murdering the Central Park jogger, a young white female investment banker, helps clarify the particular definition of justice central to his advocacy. On the night of 19 April 1989 several people jogging or riding bicycles were attacked and beaten in Central Park by roving bands of "wilding" African American and Latino male youths, most of whom lived just north of the park. Around 10:00 P.M., police arrested a group of five youths on charges of assaulting a male jogger who had been severely beaten. The youths were kept through the night in the Twentieth Precinct station house on West 82d Street

between Columbus and Amsterdam avenues. Around 2:00 A.M., uni-
formed police called the station house to report a gruesome discovery.
Two men had discovered the comatose body of a young woman lying
in mud in a culvert off the transverse between the park's east and west
roadways at 102d Street and had alerted police officers canvassing the
park for victims, witnesses, and culprits in the earlier assaults on jog-
gers and cyclists. The woman had been badly beaten, struck on the
head with a blunt instrument, raped repeatedly, and had lost most of
her blood; only the immersion of her nearly naked body in the early-
spring cool mud prevented her from bleeding to death. The only parts
of her body that were not scratched and bruised were the soles of
her feet.

The detectives immediately focused high-gear attention on that attack. They asked one of the youths still in custody how he got the
scratch mark on his face. He claimed that it occurred in a scuffle with
the officer arresting him. The detectives told him that they could easily
call the arresting officer at home to check that story. Then the youngster broke and told the detectives that he had indeed been part of a
band that had attacked the woman. He also gave up the names of other
participants; these included some youths rounded up in the park in
connection with the earlier assaults and later released. Over the following thirty-six hours, several youths were picked up by police and gave
detailed statements, both in writing and on videotape, admitting their
participation in the rape and assault. One young man, named by several others as a participant in the rape, gave no incriminating statements about that crime, although he was videotaped and did sign a
statement admitting to one of the other assaults. Another made a verbal admission to a detective of his participation in the rape, but did not
sign a statement or repeat the admission on videotape.

With DNA tests, the police attempted to match semen found in and
on the woman's body with samples from the youths who had admitted
participation in the assault. But these proved inconclusive for reasons
that are not exactly clear. It may be the case that these particular youths
had not ejaculated during the assault. Or there may have been other
culprits in the assault who had ejaculated and it was their sperm that
was found in the jogger's body. One of the young men who had given
no written or videotaped statements could not legally be compelled to
provide a blood sample for DNA testing, even though several other
admitted assailants had fingered him as an accomplice. One sample
of sperm taken from the jogger's tights was identified as that of her
boyfriend.

Prosecutors separated the case into two trials. The entire case in each trial hinged on the youths' admissions given the night of the attack, admissions that in court the youths claimed had been coerced or tricked from them by police. The charge of police brutality toward African Americans and Latinos has been a constant staple of the Reverend Sharpton's rhetoric, along with his accusations of police corruption and coercion. Here police coercion of the confessions and admissions became a major point of those who supported the accused youths in daily rallies staged in front of the Criminal Courts Building at 100 Centre Street in downtown Manhattan. Moreover, the ambiguity of the DNA tests, coupled with the finding of the jogger's boyfriend's semen on her tights, provided an opportunity for counteraccusation that surprised even grizzled courthouse veterans. A group of supporters of the accused youth, many community people but also many semiprofessional activists who go from trial to trial in New York to protest what they hold to be racial injustice, claimed that the semen in the jogger's body belonged to the jogger's boyfriend, who had, the supporters suggested, either been in the park to do a drug deal or stalked the jogger into the park, attacked her, and raped her. Every day that the prosecutors came into court, and even when the jogger herself appeared, miraculously recovered from near death but still suffering noticeably from her injuries, the supporters chanted: "The boyfriend did it!" Such a version of events was just as plausible as the accusations against the black youths, argued African American newspapers like Brooklyn's *The City Sun* and the *New York Amsterdam News,* which printed the jogger's name in its accounts.

In the midst of the first sensational trial, the Reverend Sharpton, who had become an "adviser" of some of the accused, produced none other than Tawana Brawley for a press conference, saying, "Tawana is here today to see how the criminal justice system responds differently for a white victim than it does for a black victim." Tawana visited the courtroom to observe the trial and then sought out and greeted two of the defendants in the corridor at lunchtime.

In the end, the youths' admissions proved to be barely enough to convict. One alleged participant in the attack pleaded guilty to one count of robbery and avoided trial altogether and the jury in the second trial discounted one youth's confession as coerced by police and convicted him only of sexual abuse instead of rape. Still, all the street demonstrations and courtroom chaos alike could not overcome the defendants' videotaped admissions of the crime. These were replayed constantly on the broadcast media, with one youngster tried in the second trial saying, "This is my first rape." After the first trial, the Reverend Sharpton immediately undertook a fund-raising effort for the convicted defendants' appeals, while the defendants' supporters denounced the verdicts as a "legal lynching" typical of American society when it comes to blacks and of a society where the Central Park jogger would inevitably receive more consideration from the legal system than had Tawana Brawley or where black youths would be convicted while white police officers in Brawley's case were exonerated.[9]

Put briefly, as defined by the Reverend Sharpton and his coterie, justice is what serves African Americans at a given moment. In this view, the racial history of the United States prohibits any possibility of fairness, objectivity, or judicious weighing of evidence. Indeed, from this perspective shared by many, the very notion of truth itself is chimerical, lost forever in the years when the whole apparatus of the state, the courts, and the police did indeed systematically oppress blacks. In such a world, one can only engage in unremitting advocacy for one's own and employ all the techniques at one's disposal for stirring moral outrage. The moral outrage of one's constituents serves many purposes. It emboldens those in its grip, providing the surety of vision needed for decisive action. It puts one's opponents on the defensive; simply being accused of racism today, when picked up by the media, can effectively smear reputations and destroy careers in many circles. It gains support, or at least acquiescence, from those more concerned about the appearance of moral probity than truth. Finally, moral outrage provides a measure of self-respect because it forces one's rage on the social order and its representatives.

As it happens, some African Americans seem to accept such logic with its implied rejection of universalistic criteria, that is, measured, objective standards applicable to all groups. Lower- and underclass blacks delight at the Reverend Sharpton's insouciant tail pulling of the establishment; they see him as a hustler and impressario, a brash trickster who has brought trash talking into big-time political dialogue. Of course, not only accusations against the social order and its most visible representatives, particularly the police, but fantastic ideologies, long a staple of subordinate socioeconomic groups everywhere, regularly find fertile ground in the black underclass. These are often watered, as it happens, by African American leaders and intellectuals who do little to counteract theories such as the notion that whites invented AIDS to wipe out blacks, a sentiment that polls suggest is widely held by lower-class blacks. And many critical-race-theory law professors, such as Patricia J. Williams, equate the felt or stated experience of blacks who claim being wronged with external reality, even when this means blurring the distinction between real and imagined victimization.[10] Such sentiments both reflect and reinforce the sense of special victimhood constantly reiterated by African American leaders as the core of the black experience, a notion that makes universalism seem foolhardy. Such victimology almost inevitably breeds the need to exorcise demons that one observes in the anti-Semitism and other kinds of racism regularly expressed on some black talk-radio stations and in some segments of the African American press, bursting into public view only in celebrated instances.[11]

Even the many voices of reason among middle-class African Americans have been largely mute in the face of the Reverend Sharpton's ascendancy to prominence. Like other technicians in moral outrage, he is an expert in cracking the race whip, always insisting that, no matter what gulfs of class, education, and accomplishment separate blacks one from another, they are all at bottom always and only blacks in a racist society that sooner or later will make them into scapegoats. Many middle-class whites also keep silent about the Reverend Sharpton and his tactics, fearing that if they say anything they might find themselves lumped together with virulently racist whites who openly loathe the Reverend Sharpton. There are also more material reasons for the Reverend Sharpton's black middle-class support. Although he lacks politesse and finesse, his strident and flamboyant assertion of claims provides middle-class African Americans with a streetwise brawler who, in pressing for us-versus-them allocation of resources, serves middle-class interests. Middle-class African Americans as a group always become the principal beneficiaries of remedial governmental policies to improve the lot of blacks as administrators, technicians, consultants, or professionals of the organizational programs designed to provide relief from social problems. Street hustlers of all sorts command great public attention in our society, not only from the media that thrive on drama, however manufactured, but also from intellectuals who from a safe distance celebrate hustlers' "bodaciousness" as part of their own reveries of rebellion.[12]

The Reverend Sharpton has prospered in the electoral arena through his racial politics, gaining a measure of respectability in the process. He received 166,665 votes in the 1992 New York State Democratic primary race for U.S. Senator, almost 14.5 percent of the 1,152,345 votes cast in the election for statewide candidates, an important measure of his appeal beyond the generally nonvoting lower class; he finished third out of a four-person race, beating Elizabeth Holzman, then District

Attorney of Kings County.[13] In 1994, the Reverend Sharpton took on Senator Daniel Patrick Moynihan in the Democratic primary for the U.S. Senate and received 178,000 votes. Then Sharpton led a December 1995 picketing of the 125th Street store of a Jewish merchant, whom Sharpton called a "white interloper," vowing not "[to turn] 125th Street back over to outsiders." A few days later, one of the participants in this demonstration entered the merchant's store and either shot or burned to death seven people as well as himself. Still, the Reverend Sharpton ran against Ruth Messinger and Salvatore Albanese in the fall 1997 Democratic primary for mayor of New York City and received 126,782 votes, 32 percent of the total, forcing, it seemed for a few days, a runoff with Ms. Messinger. The Reverend Jesse Jackson flew in from Chicago to support the Reverend Sharpton and to demand party unity for whoever was the runoff winner from all Democrats against Republican Mayor Rudolph Giuliani. But then the board of elections announced that Ms. Messinger had indeed won enough votes to avoid the runoff. Messinger went on to suffer a severe defeat in the general election. Since Sharpton had done very well in the primary in Brooklyn, former Mayor David Dinkins proposed that he run for Congress there against a Democrat who had supported Giuliani in the mayoral contest.

The Reverend Sharpton exhibits all of the most important characteristics of technicians in moral outrage: a shrewd, calculating understanding of the psychology of his primary constituency, here the victim/rebel cast of mind of lower- and underclass blacks, as well as the romantic appeal of this psychology to many others, here middle-class blacks, whites, and especially mass media practitioners; a sure eye for the event that can be turned into a controversy in which one can play a leading part; a mastery of the rhetorics of accusation, blame, and moral equivalence, as well as of doublespeak, that keep opponents at bay, or at least off guard and confused; and a complete lack of embarrassment bordering on shamelessness about one's actions, words, and relentless self-promotion.

All of these gifts served the Reverend Sharpton well when the Tawana Brawley case reached out of the past in late 1997 and early 1998. Steven A. Pagones, the former Dutchess County prosecutor, had sued the Reverend Sharpton, Alton Maddox, and C. Vernon Mason for slander in accusing him of raping Tawana Brawley, both before and even after Pagones had been specifically exonerated by the grand jury investigating the alleged assault. In his testimony at trial, the Reverend Sharpton cut a well-tailored figure that contrasted sharply with videotaped images of him in the signature powder-blue jogging outfit of his street salad days. He evasively dodged most questions about his past actions and words in his testimony at trial, and with an eye on his political future, he compared himself to Martin Luther King, Jr., and emphasized the burdens and the sacrifice that are the lot of great leaders. Geraldo Rivera made a pilgrimage to Poughkeepsie, New York, the site of the trial, to proclaim the Reverend Sharpton a great civil rights leader. In seemingly endless interviews on local New York television stations during the trial (particularly on New York One, known locally as the "Sharpton Broadcasting Company"), Sharpton projected enormous conviction, even while he answered questions either by sidetracking them or by talking in circles, both kinds of doublespeak, so effectively that interviewers, let alone viewing audiences, could not possibly follow his arguments. All the while he condemned the suit as a politically motivated, racist effort to silence him.

In July 1998, a jury of four whites and two blacks, by a vote of five-to-one, found all three defendants liable for defaming Steven Pagones. The Reverend Sharpton was found liable for making seven defamatory statements. Some of Sharpton's political opponents and some commentators argued that the verdict marked the end of Sharpton's mainstream political ambitions. Indeed, many residents of Sharpton's longtime Bedford-Stuyvesant base saw the verdict entirely in racial-political terms, arguing that the trial's very purpose was to degrade Sharpton and undercut his electoral appeal.[14] But some of Sharpton's supporters, as well as Sharpton himself, argued that the verdict, and the long legal appeals process to follow, would give him still greater media exposure and solidify his hold on black voters. The *New York Amsterdam News* decried the verdict in strident tones saying that "[W]hite men [identified earlier in the editorial as demented racists who used black women as sex toys] arranged the thinking of the masses, through a racist white media, vile public relations organizations and a corrupt criminal justice system, so as to make it impossible for justice to have been served in [the Brawley] case."[15] In such a view, the Reverend Sharpton is yet another martyr in African Americans' long struggle for full equality. When the same jury returned damages only in the amount of $345,000, instead of the more than $300 million that Mr. Pagones had sought, and assessed the Reverend Sharpton only $65,000, even though he had been found liable for six more defamatory statements than either of his codefendants, the Reverend Sharpton declared, in headlines in the *New York Amsterdam News*, "Absolute Victory."[16]

A tragic incident gave the Reverend Sharpton the opportunity to put Tawana Brawley behind him and reestablish his leadership role as

New York City's premier technician in moral outrage. On the night of 4 February 1999, four New York City plainclothes police officers from the Street Crimes Unit were searching the Forty-Third Precinct in the Bronx for a violent predator believed to be responsible for raping or robbing fifty-one women at gunpoint in thirty-nine separate attacks since 1993. The officers confronted a man who, they later said, resembled victims' composite description of the rapist peering suspiciously up and down the street from the front stoop of a building. The police ordered the man to raise his hands. Instead, he retreated into the building's dimly lit vestibule, reached for his pocket, and pulled out an object. The officers thought it was a gun. He was shot nineteen times by the police in a fusillade of forty-one bullets. Police weapons contain sixteen rounds, all of which can be fired in a few seconds. The entire shooting episode consumed approximately eight seconds. The man turned out to be Amadou Diallo, a street peddler from Guinea, West Africa. The "gun" was his wallet.[17]

Within days of the shooting, Sharpton emerged as the leader of a broad coalition that seized upon the tragedy as a symbol of police brutality in New York City, and indeed around the country. The principal task of the Street Crimes Unit is to take illegal guns off city streets. To accomplish that goal, the unit uses aggressive stop-and-frisk practices in high-crime areas of the city that are, as it happens, mostly black and Latino. The zero-tolerance confrontational tactics, authorized by Mayor Rudolph Giuliani when he took office in January 1994, contrasted sharply with the "community policing" advocated by Mayor David N. Dinkins during his mayoralty from 1990 to 1994. Since 1994, despite the Street Crime Unit's unmistakable success in seizing weapons, its tactics have sorely aggravated many thousands of people stopped by the police on "reasonable suspicion." Many of these argue that they were "profiled" because of their color. Indeed, police "profiling" of suspects by race has become a major political issue in several states and in the national political arena.[18] The seething resentment generated among some by aggressive policing, coupled with the distress of relatives of several victims of police shootings over the last several years, even those that were ruled justifiable, and continuing generalized outrage about the case of Abner Louima, a Haitian immigrant sadistically tortured by police officers in Brooklyn in 1997, provided the tinder for the beginnings of a social movement. Amadou Diallo's death provided the spark. And the Reverend Sharpton was there to fan the flames.

In short order, Sharpton became the shepherd in New York City of

Mrs. Kadiadou Diallo and Mr. Saikou Diallo, the parents of Amadou Diallo. He met them at the airport and counseled them not to accept the condolences of Mayor Giuliani that had been extended immediately after the tragedy. Giuliani has been Sharpton's longtime adversary, perhaps the only public official who, for years, has consistently condemned Sharpton's racial politics and has refused to recognize Sharpton as a legitimate spokesman. Sharpton organized a series of protests at police headquarters at One Police Plaza and on Wall Street where he (more than once) and, in the end, more than one thousand people were arrested for nonviolent civil disobedience in carefully orchestrated demonstrations, complete with photo ops of racially diverse arrestees for the dailies. The list of those arrested included former Mayor David N. Dinkins, Congressman Charles Rangel, several members of the New York City Council, State Controller Carl McCall, former Manhattan Borough President Ruth Messinger, and Bronx Borough President Fernando Ferrer, all bitter political enemies of Mayor Giuliani. Actors Ossie Davis, Ruby Dee, and Susan Sarandon were also arrested, as was former congressman and head of the NAACP, Kweisi Mfume, who warned of civil violence unless the police officers who shot Diallo were not only prosecuted but convicted. Every major interest group in the city that opposed one or another of Mayor Giuliani's policies, from welfare reform to zero-tolerance policing, policies credited by many with rescuing New York City from the wilderness of the Dinkins years, also had representatives arrested. Groups on the left such as the Young Communist League, the War Resisters League, and various Free Mumia Abu-Jamal coalitions joined them. The over-the-top rhetoric of the demonstrations, with "Ku Klux Klan" and "Bull Conner" regularly hurled at the police and Giuliani, was matched only by the obsessive, hyperbolic attention that the city's daily newspapers, magazines, and New York One cable TV station lavished on the issue. The *New Yorker*, indeed, ran as a cover a cartoon depicting a laughing policeman drawing a bead on targets of citizens in a shooting gallery.[19]

Sharpton also traveled to Guinea for Diallo's funeral where he pledged to the men of Diallo's village to return after the police officers had "faced justice." Throughout all these events, the Reverend Sharpton, with the help of his associates, shrewdly argued that the number of rounds that the officers had fired demonstrated their criminal intent to assassinate Diallo simply because he was black. And the District Attorney of Bronx County, Robert Johnson, sought and obtained an indictment against the four officers for second-degree murder.

Finally, Kadiadou and Saikou Diallo appointed a Sharpton associate as administrator of Diallo's estate. The estate consists entirely of whatever proceeds Diallo's parents win in their civil suit against the city.[20] Sharpton also arranged for the Diallos to meet the Reverend Jesse Jackson in Chicago and to tour the United States. Mrs. Diallo, a well-spoken, comely woman, became a national spokeswoman against police brutality, elevating her previously unknown son into a martyr, a symbol of "police viciousness" toward minority groups across the land. All of the protests culminated, first, with a march on Washington against police brutality, where the Reverend Sharpton was the universally acknowledged star, and then with a march across the Brooklyn Bridge through lower Manhattan. The Reverend Sharpton wore African robes. The master impresario had, it was reported on radio, taken the name Diallo.

〰〰〰〰 A prototypical feminist technician in moral outrage is Dr. Jean Kilbourne, a Cambridge-based lecturer in the old Chautuaqua Institution style whose subject is the images of women and men in advertisements. Ms. Kilbourne, a 1964 graduate of Wellesley College, where she is occasionally a Visiting Scholar, received her doctorate in education from Boston University in 1980.[21] She travels to colleges and universities throughout the country, giving scores of hour-length talk-and-slide-show presentations each year for a fee of $5000 an evening (in 1998) plus expenses.[22]

In her publicity materials, Dr. Kilbourne claims to have "lectured at over one-third of all the colleges and universities in the United States and at all of the major universities in Canada, as well as scores of private and public schools."[23] Although she has created several videos and slide presentations over the years,[24] her basic talk-and-slide-show presentation for many years has been "The Naked Truth: Advertising's Image of Women." She has produced two films based on the materials used in this presentation, the first entitled *Killing Us Softly* (1979) and its remake, *Still Killing Us Softly* (1987). The framework and most of the content of these two films are identical, although the later edition includes more recent illustrations.

Taking both films together,[25] with the quotations cited taken directly from one or another of them, Dr. Kilbourne develops the following themes in her critique of advertising, which she describes as one of the most powerful educational forces in our society, shaping people's basic attitudes and behavior. Advertising sells values, particularly concepts of normality. It shapes a mythological world that bears little resemblance to actual social life. Still, people do compare their lives to the images they see in advertisements. Nothing is accidental in advertising; "advertisers" [sic] have "enormously sophisticated techniques" and "every detail is planned" out carefully. We know, Kilbourne argues, that advertising is deliberate in its manipulation precisely because it costs so much money—it is a $100 billion a year business—and anything that costs so much must be planned.

In particular, Kilbourne continues, "advertisers" present images of ideal female beauty based on "absolute flawlessness" that become the standard of beauty for all women in American society. In order to achieve this standard, women must transform themselves, every part of their bodies—their faces, their derrières, their hair, and their odor—through the use of products. While seeming to be admiring of women, advertisements actually hack apart and dismember women's bodies, an objectification that leads to "real contempt, loathing, disgust for women's bodies." Women who deviate from the ideal "are viewed with disgust." Overweight women are particularly vulnerable. Kilbourne argues that 20 percent of college-age women in the United States have eating disorders; 80 percent of American women think they are overweight; and 80 percent of fourth-grade girls surveyed said they were on a diet. Advertisements pit women against other women and against themselves. The continual emphasis on slimness and youth leads inevitably to child pornography, "images of . . . adult women being presented as children." The real message here is for women to remain childlike, that is, "passive, powerless, and dependent." Such images of sexualized childhood are pervasive in American society and contribute to the enormous problem of child sexual abuse; "25 percent of all reported rape victims are under eighteen and one in four little girls . . . and at least one in ten little boys . . . [are] sexually molested during . . . childhood."

In fact, Kilbourne asserts, American culture has a pornographic attitude toward sex in general, both "created by and reflected in the advertising and indeed throughout the media." This is true not only because women's bodies are dismembered in advertisements but because sex is used to sell things. Cumulatively, we learn that a woman ". . . is a thing that's for sale." Advertising's objectification of the person implicit in the images of female body parts, unconnected with whole persons, bespeaks a fundamental crisis of values in our society.

Kilbourne charges that advertising "co-opts" deep human needs and thereby trivializes them. Thus, the Virginia Slims cigarette advertisements appropriate the thrust of women's liberation and encourage enslavement to an addictive substance to boot. New stereotypes, such as the notion of "Superwoman, the twenty-four hour woman," imply that women are still responsible for all domestic work in addition to occupational duties. Moreover, our society has a "negative and distorted image of women": "There is certainly contempt for women in our society. There's no question about that. Years of research document this. There's also contempt for all things considered 'feminine,' [such as] . . . compassion, cooperation, nurturance, empathy, intuition, sensitivity, vulnerability." One consequence of such notions is that working women suffer. "A female college graduate today [1987] has the same earning potential as a male high school dropout. . . . Most working women are in dead-end jobs making less than $10,000 a year, and one out of four women working today can expect to be poor in her old age." Moreover, this is a global issue. "Women provide a huge pool of cheap labor all around the world. Multinational corporations depend on this cheap labor and therefore generally fight any movement for equal pay or equal rights for women." Further, professional women are "trivialized and sexualized" in advertisements, images that contribute "to a climate where there is widespread sexual harassment of women in the workplace."

At the same time, men and masculinity are linked with "ruthlessness and brutality," expressed in advertisements [apparently from a gun magazine showing a weapon being holstered with the tag line: "Put your gun into something soft"] that equate penises with guns. One sees such identifications particularly in the growing spate of advertisements with shadowy background figures that, presumably, symbolize romance, but in reality induce fear of male violence in women and reinforce women's restriction. One sees it too in advertisements that portray mock rapes, images that help form attitudes of "aggression and violence" on the part of men. In this context, one must remember that the "*Ms.* campaign project on sexual assault [found that] one-quarter of women in college today have been the victims of rape or attempted rape." Record album covers, music videos, and certain films, like slasher movies, all promote violence against women. Even department store windows have used mannequins to portray female corpses, while casually selling apparel. Most important, "[t]his is not an aberration . . . [but] the inevitable result of everything [presented by Dr. Kilbourne] and of . . . socialization [that] equate[s] masculinity with dominance and brutality and femininity with submission and passivity."

What is the solution? Kilbourne's answer is to rid ourselves of the notion that all problems are personal problems, a notion at the heart of advertising, which pushes products to solve individual problems. The technician in moral outrage urges the recognition that "[r]eal change lies in social and political action regarding our priorities as a nation." Further, immediate action, "not through censorship, but through consumer outrage," is necessary to end these "images [that] are wounding us, all of us, women, men, and children." All of us must "get actively involved in the struggle to bring about change." To such ends, Dr. Kilbourne provides a several-page handout listing various advocacy groups around the country.

Dr. Kilbourne's slide presentations proceed through about one hundred fifty provocative print advertisements through which she races as she talks. Her college audiences are regularly packed, mostly with young women but also with many men; she also gives talks in other forums. Dr. Kilbourne is said to have been a model for a few years before discovering her vocation as a feminist advocate; her wholesome femininity is an important part of her public persona. Moreover, she has an approach to advertising and male/female relationships that many consider funny. A regularly repeated joke in her filmed presentations is, "The effects of advertising are as inescapable as the effects of pollution in the air. One has to breathe. And in America, advertising could really be considered part of the air. It's certainly part of the pollution." Another oft-repeated joke is made against the backdrop of an advertisement pushing weight loss with the tag line, "I probably never would be married now if I hadn't lost 49 pounds"; Kilbourne adds: "one woman said to me that was the best advertisement for fat that she'd ever seen." Both lines draw appreciative laughs from her audiences, complete with knowing glances to neighbors. In both 1988 and 1989, she received the Lecturer of the Year Award from the National Association for Campus Activities. She has appeared as a guest on National Public Radio's *All Things Considered, The Today Show,* ABC's *20/20,* and, of course, the *Oprah Winfrey Show.* Her promotional literature is filled with glowing tributes to the emotional impact of her presentations.[26] According to eyewitnesses, some members of her audiences have been reduced to tears by her talks, some, it seems, from the rage of perceived victimization and others from guilt. The latter include male professors at Ivy League colleges.

Dr. Kilbourne's approach to advertising almost exactly mirrors the industry she critiques. Her claims of advertising's influence echo the pontifications of industry executives who want to sell more advertising, as does her equation of monetary expenditures on advertising with sophisticated, rational planning, claims that are laughable to actual image makers, that is, advertising creatives, or to anyone who has actually studied the making of images. Just like advertising, her selection of images is entirely one-sided and pointed toward very specific goals. The real character of her work is suggested by her marginal-part-for-whole image selection of advertisements from gun magazines or from avant-garde Harvard Square store windows to "demonstrate" links between advertising and violence toward women. She selectively produces "facts" as needed, such as questionable data on the extent of women's eating disorders on college campuses. She cites "studies," such as the extremely dubious, now thoroughly discredited, though not disowned, *Ms.* campus project on sexual assault, to suggest that college women are constant prey to sexually ravenous and predatory male brutes, an image much in favor in some academic feminist circles. Or she bends facts, such as the data on child abuse, ignoring the class and racial distribution of violence. She creates a moral drama of victims (women and girls), honorary victims (men who are also being manipulated), villains ("advertisers"), and heroines (herself and others like her decrying the evil permeating the very air that we breathe). Her argumentation proceeds exactly like most advertisements, that is, through elliptical suggestions, humor, juxtaposition of images that are completely unconnected except through an imposed narrative framework, emotional innuendo, and finally, uplifting appeals,[27] all held together by her own engaging, poised, articulate, and attractive persona.

Such advocacy abounds on college campuses. Left-of-center speakers like Dr. Kilbourne regularly ride the circuit to help groups like women's studies programs, assorted women's support groups, black studies programs, various ethnic studies programs, or gay, lesbian, bisexual, and transgender studies programs stoke the rage that keeps campus fires burning, administrators off-guard, and resources flowing to appropriate programs. The formula is classic. First, define a social evil. Next, identify the members of one's audience as the victims of that evil on the basis of an encompassing status, like race, gender, or sexual orientation that obscures all nuances and social differences among victims. Identify the villains of the piece, showing how they are linked to established systems of "power" and how they are bent on the manipulation of and even the destruction of the victims. Last, offer the victims a path of resistance leading to liberation and salvation from self-submission to oppression. The rage that is generated on campuses by speakers like Ms. Kilbourne is not usually directed against the advertising industry or some other remote oppressor but against enemies closer at hand. On issues of gender, these are administrators, professors, or students who have the temerity to question feminist doctrines or feminist efforts to proselytize students or who question the new doctrine that homosexuality is inborn, not chosen. When speakers like Dr. Kilbourne turn to the issues of race, the enemies become those administrators, faculty, or students who oppose conventional pieties about the wonders of affirmative action or bilingual education, both programs that in many circles are proxies for right-mindedness, or who question the various identity claims of ethnic groups or point out the contradictory rhetoric at the heart of many of their claims. "Political correctness" on American campuses refers primarily to the air of moral censure created by leftist technicians in moral outrage that stifles open debate on such matters or burdens any statements on them with now-necessary layers of disclaimers.[28]

~~~~~~ "Political correctness" created the social and political context within which right-wing talk radio came to flourish. Rush Limbaugh has built a career in talk radio by being a technician in moral outrage on the right. After a series of promotional jobs, most notably with the Kansas City Royals baseball organization, followed by a stint as a disk jockey and then as a talk show host in various provincial outposts, Mr. Limbaugh spent three years as a talk show host at KFBK in Sacramento, California, before moving, in 1988, to WABC, an AM radio station in New York. His deal with the station provides him with a tie-in to the EIB (Excellence in Broadcasting) Network, which he claims to have established; when he started, EIB was a grid with fifty-six stations and a national audience of 250,000 people, half from WABC. By 1994, Mr. Limbaugh's midday radio program was syndicated to 645 stations nationwide, reaching 5.2 million daily listeners per average quarter-hour[29] and about 20 million different people each week. He also had a late-night television program that, for a time, attracted a solid audience, but this was canceled in the mid-1990s.

What accounts for Mr. Limbaugh's appeal? The following appraisal is based on listening for hundreds of hours to his radio show from 1988 to 1999. First, Limbaugh entertains his audience with stock-in-trade, but still effective, radio techniques from his disk jockey days. He fills almost every show with amusing gags and gimmicks. From 1992 to 1994, when the Democrats controlled the White House and both houses of Congress, and again in 1998, when the entire country was besieged by constant news about a sex scandal in President Clinton's White House, every section of Mr. Limbaugh's show was introduced by an echo-chamber announcement declaring a special edition of his program—"America Held Hostage" (to the Clinton administration)—a reference to the Iranian hostage crisis during the Carter administration. After Hillary Clinton said that she had unsuccessfully tried to join the Marines, Limbaugh played the Marine anthem whenever her name was mentioned. For years, he ran his regular "Homelessness Updates," prefaced by Clarence "Frogman" Henry's "Ain't Got No Home," scorching satires on the nation's disastrous lurching on this issue since the early 1980s. He regularly, and effectively, imitates President Clinton's mouth-full-of-blueberry-pie-down-home speaking style, especially when equivocating, and he often has another sound alike to the President singing "All Your Money" (in taxes) or "Whitewater Blues" (telling the sorry tale of what happened to "friends of Bill" in the bewildering Ozark land scheme). Before Mr. Limbaugh went on an Oprah Winfrey–like much-publicized diet, he regularly ate a rare steak for lunch on air with great lip smacking (to offend the vegetarians); he followed this, as he still does, with a good cigar (to offend the antismoking lobby). In his send-ups, Mr. Limbaugh's mock seriousness sometimes fakes out even veteran listeners, always a cause for merriment.

But the real entertainment is his gargantuan ego. Mr. Limbaugh promotes himself shamelessly. He claims knowledge ("Welcome to the Limbaugh Institute for Advanced Conservative Studies") and brilliance (he claims that his talent is "on loan from God" and that he does his show with "half my brain tied behind my back just to make things fair"). And he has an opinion on every imaginable subject, although he sticks almost entirely to current social, cultural, and political affairs. He is never at a loss for words and moves easily from thundering, desk-thumping pronouncements to rueful head-shaking chuckles. Unlike many other talk show hosts, he usually does not insult his callers or engage them in mortal combat.[30] He claims to have instructed his call screeners to put at the head of the queue callers who disagree with him on the issue of the day. If these callers are quick-witted, he debates issues with them vigorously but for the most part cordially, seemingly delighting in the opportunity to match wits with worthy opponents. However, he quickly dismisses callers who seem dull, inarticulate, or unfamiliar with his positions on issues. Generally speaking, his show seems free of planted calls from those favorable to his positions, a practice typical of several other talk shows. If anything, semiorganized call-ins from articulate spokesmen trying to discredit Mr. Limbaugh appear to have been more frequent over the years than ostensible plants of his own seeding.

Second, Mr. Limbaugh's show appeals to mass audiences because it

rides the crest of immediate public interests. As Mr. Limbaugh himself
sees it, Michael Dukakis's loss to George Bush in the 1988 presidential
race—the same year Mr. Limbaugh went national—caused a tremendous proliferation of liberal advocacy groups. From late 1988 until the
presidential election of 1992, Mr. Limbaugh feasted daily on the inconsistencies and absurdities of leftist advocacy groups, delighting his rapidly growing audience with his caricatures of "feminazis," the "gang of
lesbian radicals" centered in NAGS (the National Association for Gals)
that he argued were ascendant in the feminist movement; pro-abortion
activists for whom, he argues, abortion is a matter of casual convenience and who scream "choice" when it comes to abortion but oppose
"choice" when it comes to school vouchers. Other groups Limbaugh
attacked were "environmentalist wackos," tree-huggers whose caring
extends to spotted owls but not to timber company employees whose
jobs are jeopardized by nature lovers; animal rights activists who compare the meat industry with Jeffrey Dahmer's cannibalism; advocates
of condom distribution in schools who become incensed at the notion
of sexual abstinence for young people; members of the anti-tobacco
lobby who also oppose the nation's twilight War on Drugs; and American Civil Liberties Union activists who appear to care more for the
rights of criminals than for those of their victims unless the victim is a
"person of color" abused by the police. His targets were, and still remain, the contradictions and inconsistencies of "knee-jerk liberalism."

Then, according to Mr. Limbaugh, with the election of "President
and Mrs. ('Elect him and you get me, too') Clinton" in 1992, leftist
advocacy groups triumphed, assumed power, and began to implement
into law their deepest aspirations for American society. Since 1992,
Mr. Limbaugh's attack on the logic of liberalism and the behavior of
liberals has concentrated on the follies and policies (in that order) of
the Clinton administration: on Mr. Clinton's rumored, and later con-
firmed, extracurricular sexual activities and the accusations of sexual
harassment made against him; on Mrs. Clinton's astonishing success
in the commodity stock market where, though a self-professed amateur, she increased her stake a hundredfold; on the grab bag of practices called Whitewater that might pass ethical muster in Dogpatch,
but seem sleazy in Washington's hard light; on the Clintons' ill-fated
health-care bill, a prescription, Mr. Limbaugh argued, not only for massive bureaucratization of medical practice, but for a more general de-
railment of the economy; on the Clintons' "politicization" of every
social issue, that is, the First Couple's belief that all social and personal
problems have political solutions if only government officials "care"

enough and if taxpayers can be stiff-armed into footing the bill for bureaucratic remedies; and on the stories of illegal financing by foreigners of President Clinton's successful 1996 reelection campaign.

Third, and most important, Mr. Limbaugh has discovered smoldering coals of resentment in the United States that he effectively fans into a bonfire. The resentment has profound class and status roots and seems reflected in the audience drawn to his show. Mr. Limbaugh's followers proudly identify themselves as "dittoheads," a phrase drawn from the shorthand expressions, "dittos" or "megadittos," used as salutations to Mr. Limbaugh instead of repetitious praise that wastes precious air time. Drawing on data from a number of sources,[31] talk radio shows across the country seem to have the following audience profile. Most listeners are in lower-to-middle to middle-income families ($20,000–$75,000 household income), with listenership skewed to the upper reaches of that range, that is, in the $50,000 and higher category. Moreover, 19 percent of talk radio listeners earn more than $75,000 household income. Listeners are generally well-schooled; 90 percent have a high school education, 35 percent graduated from college, and 9 percent possess a graduate degree. Also, 23 percent of listeners fall into the professional/managerial category of job classification, and 18 percent into that known as technical/clerical/sales, placing a full 41 percent solidly in new-middle-class occupations, that is, occupations entirely dependent on large bureaucratic organizations. Seventy-eight percent of show listeners are between thirty-five and sixty-four years of age, with somewhat more men than women listeners and substantially more men who actually call in to programs. The exact demographic characteristics of Mr. Limbaugh's audience are not available, although they seem to correspond to this general profile of talk show listeners. According to one source, with small percentages not reporting, Limbaugh's audience consists of 70 percent men and 22 percent women, with 8 percent unidentified; 31 percent at least fifty-five years of age, 18 percent forty-five to fifty-four years of age, 26 percent thirty-five to forty-four years of age, with the balance younger; 70 percent married, 18 percent never married, and 12 percent separated or widowed; and 62 percent with children under eighteen years of age living in the household (a mean of 2.1 children per household).[32] However, it seems that a greater proportion of Mr. Limbaugh's audience is better-schooled than that of the average talk radio show: 12 percent completed a postgraduate degree, an additional 9 percent did some postgraduate work, 24 percent graduated from college, while 30 percent have had some college and only 15 percent completed high school or less.

Callers to Mr. Limbaugh's show do not routinely identify their occupations on the air, nor can the callers be taken as completely representative of his listenership. But, on the basis of those who do call and who do identify their occupations, one can make some observations and educated guesses. Callers to the program are mostly men who work in milieux that afford enough independence to allow daytime listening during Mr. Limbaugh's noon-to-three o'clock Eastern air time. Some work in small business enterprises like auto supply shops, electronic parts distributorships, garages, or fish farms. Some drive trucks, both long-distance and local. Many work in the respectable, but lower to lower-to-middle reaches of large organizations, in the nooks and crannies of thoroughly rationalized white-collar work as technicians, managers, or supervisors of one sort or another, catching Mr. Limbaugh's show surreptitiously at work or on their lunch hours. Of these, many listeners seem to become callers because their companies are under assault for some reason, such as when the insurance and the pharmaceutical companies were made whipping boys during the health-care-bill campaign. A good number of listeners are police officers or other law enforcement personnel, riding in their cars or sitting in squad rooms with one ear cocked to Mr. Limbaugh and the other to their squawk boxes. Many listeners work out of their homes, utilizing computers to link them to a variety of markets as consultants, stockbrokers, or salespeople; a good number in this category seem to be casualties of corporate wars. Some listeners are travelling salespeople who tune in to Mr. Limbaugh on their car radios, calling him on their days off or sometimes from cellular phones while on the road. Finally, many listeners are college students in sprawling state universities in the south or southwest where dittoheads have been known to walk out of classes if professors make disparaging remarks about Mr. Limbaugh. From time to time, particularly when complicated legal questions are at issue, articulate lawyers call in and conduct a nationwide seminar on the subtleties of some aspect of the law. Many of the male callers refer, invariably with great pride, to their own background of military service. The women who call the program are often homemakers with children, married to men in occupations like those described; many of these express rage at what they perceive to be upper-middle-class feminist haughtiness toward them and the choices they have made for their lives. But many women who call are also employed outside the home, working in occupations similar to those of male callers; small-business women (one-third of all small businesses are now owned and operated by women) are the most typical female callers. Mr. Limbaugh's audience, like the audience for talk radio nationwide, except for specialized shows, is overwhelmingly white (about 94 percent for Mr. Limbaugh). However, Mr. Limbaugh goes out of his way to praise black conservative intellectuals like Supreme Court Justice Clarence Thomas, a personal friend of Limbaugh's, and Stanford University's Professor Thomas Sowell. When he takes a vacation, Mr. Limbaugh often has George Mason University's Professor Walter Williams act as host in his stead.

The men and women who compose this variegated lower-middle to middle stratum of American society face anxiety-provoking economic and social uncertainties. The failure rate for small businesses remains high (down somewhat in the 1990s from the historical average failure rate of nearly 90 percent), making small proprietors among the most vulnerable groups in the economy. Constant transformations of knowledge make technical expertise obsolete overnight. Corporate upheavals regularly eliminate lower and middle echelons of managers and technicians. Those whose livelihoods depend on riding the stock markets face the possibility of wipeouts every day, despite the 1982-to-late-1990s bull market. And the profound ambivalence, indeed hostility, in American society toward police officers and other law enforcement officials makes their lot a decidedly unhappy one. Status upheavals in the United States, particularly in response to concerted group claims or to administrative or judicial fiat, have begun to turn traditional social hierarchies on their head. Thanks to affirmative action, in a great many professional job situations, for instance, qualified African Americans, Latinos, and women can now write their own tickets and luxuriate as well in a sense of moral superiority that comes with being visibly "diverse." But such changing standards exacerbate economic and social insecurities for those not deemed "diverse." Moreover, traditional beliefs, theodicies, and worldviews that used to offer comforting visions of an ordered world have themselves collapsed. It is clear to anyone who looks that hard work does not necessarily produce success; the meritorious and virtuous do not necessarily triumph; injustice is often victorious and crime frequently pays well; criminals are often celebrated; and governments tap an increasing share of resources from the hard-working middle and lower-middle classes to sustain themselves, pursue illusory goals, and preside over a social system where the best one can hope for is tolerable compromises to bridge irreconcilable differences.

In his radio shows and in his subsidiary publications,[33] Mr. Limbaugh offers his listeners clear targets for the frustration and resentment generated by such structural predicaments among those who cannot buy their way out of such problems. The archetypal villains in Mr. Limbaugh's scenario are liberals of all sorts, advocates and politicians alike, who see government as the savior of society. In Mr. Limbaugh's view, liberals instinctively devise government programs to address entitlement claims and to remedy social problems, invariably escalating the claims and making the problems worse. In the process, government bureaucracies mushroom, never to disappear. Mr. Limbaugh concretizes this critique by proposing a new national symbol to replace the fierce bald eagle, one depicting scores of fat piglets clinging to the withered nipples of a huge, emaciated sow. He rails against the "takers" in American society, with particular animus toward the ominously growing underclass, the permanently unemployed and underemployed welfare class, marked by high rates of teenage pregnancy, out-of-wedlock births, drug use, and violence. Before the Republican congressional triumph of 1994 (after which the echo chamber declared "America, the way it oughta be"), Mr. Limbaugh also pilloried the then Democratic-controlled Congress whenever possible. He did so especially at the time of the House banking scandal when the General Accounting Office discovered that 355 members of Congress had written 20,000 bad checks over a three-year period, overdrawing their House bank accounts without penalty and receiving in effect interest-free loans from taxpayers. After the Republican triumph, he became a champion of "Mr. Newt," Speaker of the House Newt Gingrich, a kindred gargantuan ego, who himself later fell on hard times with the House Ethics Committee.

Since 1996, when not talking about his beloved football team, the Pittsburgh Steelers, Mr. Limbaugh has returned again and again to his favorite targets, President Clinton and especially Mrs. Clinton. He argues that they personify the worst of liberalism, government by a confederacy of upper-middle-class moralistic advocates for the "downtrodden." These advocates are accompanied by left-wing intellectuals who feel that they have superior knowledge about what is good for the country. Together they press their "social agenda" by accusing their critics of lack of care and compassion, even while, Mr. Limbaugh argues, the country has experienced virtually unparalleled economic growth and prosperity due entirely to the workings of the free market. Mr. Limbaugh's animus toward the Clintons reached its apex during 1998 when all the scandals associated with President Clinton's administration came into focus through the prism of the media's frenzied obsession with the president's sexual affair with Monica Lewinsky, at the time a twenty-one-year-old intern at the White House. The media also focused on the possibility that the president might have encouraged the young woman to perjure herself when questioned under oath about their relationship and might have used his office to obstruct justice to conceal the relationship. Initially, Mr. Limbaugh told his audience to keep its eyes on the financial irregularities of Democratic fund-raising, particularly the bed-and-breakfast use of the Lincoln bedroom in the White House and the Democrats' solicitation of political funds from foreign nationals, particularly from the People's Republic of China. Then President Clinton admitted an "inappropriate relationship" with Lewinsky to a federal grand jury and on national television to the American public on 17 August 1998. This was followed by Independent Counsel Kenneth Starr's sensational report to Congress on 9 September 1998, which contained extremely explicit details of President Clinton's sexual encounters with Ms. Lewinsky.[34] With the thinly disguised glee that marked most of the reporting of the debacle, Mr. Limbaugh took the bully pulpit for sermons on the relationship between character and leadership, interspersed with the Clinton-sound-alike singing "Young Girl Get Out of My Life."

What kind of leader is it, Mr. Limbaugh along with other conservative talk show hosts asked, who lies to his subordinates and encourages them to defend him publicly at risk to themselves? What kind of blind loyalty, instead of discerning judgment, led those same subordinates to accept President Clinton's assurances of innocence despite overwhelming circumstantial evidence to the contrary, including exchanges of apparel, logs of thirty-seven Lewinsky-to-Clinton visits, and logs of seventy-five phone calls, some taped, between the pair, not to mention Ms. Lewinsky's utter lack of expertise in any area of public policy that might explain the encounters? The scandal also provided Mr. Limbaugh with an opportunity to ridicule the thundering silence of virtually every major feminist on the fifty-year-old President Clinton's sexual indiscretions in the workplace with a female employee only slightly older than his own daughter after the feminist crusade for rules governing sexual harassment at work between parties of "unequal power."

Limbaugh became the main cheerleader of the House of Representatives' subsequent impeachment of President Clinton, reviewing daily every possible angle of attack on the beleaguered president and even offering tactical advice to Republican members of Congress. Indeed, some members of Congress called Limbaugh's show to give firsthand reports on the proceedings. After the Senate's acquittal of the president, Limbaugh railed against the spectacle of Senate Democrats, and a few Republicans, exculpating President Clinton of perjury despite clear evidence to the contrary. What kind of role model for the nation's children, Limbaugh asked, are these weak-kneed politicians supporting by their willful blindness to wrongdoing in high places? And what kind of people are we Americans, he asked, that we continue to give high job-approval marks to a man whose blemished character embarrasses the United States before the world?

Yet, Mr. Limbaugh does not take on the corporations, whose "take the money and run" ethos from 1945 until 1982 eroded America's competitiveness and productivity. These same corporations exported most of the country's core industries, creating the structural conditions for an economy that can no longer provide honorable, well-paying, disciplined work to absorb physically restless semiskilled men. Nor does he ever challenge the monied interests that still gobble up vast shares of the nation's wealth with little thought about the long-run direction and stability of the social order. Instead, he acts as a front for those interests, deflecting attention and opposition to himself, complete with a mixture of ad hominem attacks, non sequitur arguments, faulty comparisons, absurdist analogies, straw men, and questionable premises.[35] Mr. Limbaugh recognizes that American democracy, with all of its wild contradictions and conflicts, is, after all, the greatest show on earth. And he is the new P. T. Barnum, the ringmaster of a sprawling circus of ideas, conjectures, and opinions, replete with opportunities for self-aggrandizement.

〰〰〰 Technicians in moral outrage become important carriers of the ethos of advocacy, helping to disseminate crucial aspects of that ethos throughout the social structure. First, technicians in moral outrage take commercial advocates' understanding that "logic is not enough" in shaping mass appeals to an extreme conclusion by fanning felt-victimization, hysteria, resentment, and paranoia. They help institute irrationality in what passes for public discourse in American society. Second, in an era where constructed images of reality stand for reality itself, these technicians specialize in transvaluing particular incidents, events, words, or images into symbols of supposedly more general trends in order to scourge their enemies and to champion their own causes. Here they help foster the part-for-whole thinking typical of advertising and public relations that erodes the ability to make even the simple distinctions essential for clear perception of issues. Third, in an era where barely articulated moral sentiments serve as markers for affiliation in a world of highly specialized knowledge, these technicians' constant assertion of moral judgments, grounded in primal affinities like race and gender or semiprimal affinities like class and political ideology, separates the world into starkly opposed factions and fosters a society where shared moral judgments become ever scarcer and ever more difficult. With such a collapse of common evaluative frameworks, moral equivalence increases, making advocacy about the perceived wrongs to one's constituency all the more necessary. This legitimates one's role as a prophet crying in the wilderness.

Finally, technicians in moral outrage recognize that purely personal passions, while always important for some in establishing credibility, do not suffice in larger arenas. Even when one's personal rage is the seedbed for understanding others' indignation, one must project one's feelings onto a larger screen in a resonant and timely way if one hopes to ignite such sentiments and put them to use. The constant work with moral sentiments breeds exactly the same kind of ironic double consciousness that commercial advocates exhibit. The Reverend Al Sharpton has been known to kid police officers, whom he publicly excoriates, by assuming the frisk position against the nearest wall when he encounters them on the street. He has also regaled police officers with rueful tales of the harsh vicissitudes of New York City's tribal politics. More important, in his regularly televised public interviews, the Reverend Sharpton displays a man-of-the-world caginess that bespeaks a shrewd self-consciousness. Dr. Jean Kilbourne usually closes her rousing male-and-patriarchy-skewering presentations with the disclaimer that she seeks no wider polarization between men and women. But one has every reason to be wary of technicians in moral outrage bearing olive branches, since their stock-in-trade is not reconciliation, but discord. Still, Dr. Kilbourne's adroit kind of doublespeak seems to disarm opponents in her audiences. Mr. Limbaugh, like most talk radio hosts, often exhibits an equal degree of ironic self-consciousness about his own role as a technician in moral outrage. On 10 August 1994, while chortling over a bitter complaint about Mr. Limbaugh's attacks that President Clinton had foolishly let slip to the press, Mr. Limbaugh wondered aloud when a sitting president had last attacked a talk show host. One of his staff suggested President Roosevelt's attack on Tokyo Rose during the Second World War. Mr. Limbaugh said: "But Tokyo Rose was a propagandist. We, of course, here are interested in the truth."

Such double consciousness matters little to those members of technicians' constituencies who, caught in the cages of their own emotional responses to a bewildering society, want nothing more than to hear their own deeply felt moral outrage forcefully articulated. But, for the most part, even those championed by technicians in moral outrage, and certainly those attacked by them, recognize in technicians' double consciousness the artifice behind their moral pronouncements. Here technicians in moral outrage help foster a world where moral sentiments become just another rhetoric that contributes to public skepticism and disbelief.

THE DISCERNMENT OF
REPRESENTATIONS

MAKE-BELIEVE
WORLDS

The myriad of advocates in our society, whether commercial or vocational, image makers all, create representations that mask the substantive social and organizational realities undergirding the thorough bureaucratization of every sphere of modern social life. Ironically, it is precisely such bureaucratization, particularly the exponential division and specialization of expertise and the standardization of the external frameworks of social life, that fuels the ascendancy of image making. The more that our world depends on extraordinarily detailed substantive expertise, coordinated by equally arcane administrative expertise, the more knowledge fashioned by image makers becomes necessary to make an increasingly unknowable world navigable even if not wholly intelligible, or to bring worldly rewards to those who do indispensable work. Interpretive experts invent better reasons for "what has to be done" for those charged with the hard choices of our society. When those who command our institutions make grievous mistakes, image makers provide the accounts that permit them to continue to exercise their wizardry, allowing the world's work to proceed without too much interference. At the same time, without the leaven of moral insistence of advocates with a vocation, the bread of social life in a bureaucratized society might be altogether dense and dry. Advocates with a vocation remind us, along with Max Weber, that humankind might not attain the possible unless it continually reaches for the impossible. The more the structural contours of our world become rationalized and bureaucratized, the more men and women seek escape, and perhaps this-worldly salvation, in fancy or in adopted purpose.

The representations that various image makers create displace substantive realities for those with no access to milieux other than their own; indeed, the representations become the realities. Apart from their own everyday milieux, where they possess dense and intimate knowledge through their own personal experience, a great number of men and women live in fictive worlds, or representational frameworks, or dreamworlds assembled by image makers. This occurs even though everyone's very existence depends wholly on realities that are palpable enough, such as the vast bureaucratized apparatus of science, technology, production, administration, distribution, and propaganda that sustains modern civilization. Insofar as it is inaccessible and unintelligible, objective reality collapses.

In a world where images hold center stage, how does one discern between multiple, always competing representations of reality? In such a world, many contemporary intellectuals argue, the old notion of truth as a standard becomes merely quaint or completely irrelevant. By truth, in an epoch that recognizes no transcendent universal verities, one means simply the correspondence of the mind to external reality, or, more exactly, the correspondence between the propositions that one formulates and the realities outside the mind that those propositions describe. One can argue that because one chooses some words rather than others to describe perceived reality, every proposition is also a representation and all representations, including propositions, are invariably partial, sometimes deliberately misleading, sometimes downright false, and, in any event, irreducibly "ideological." In this view, language does not, in fact, refer to external reality at all, but simply to other language; "truth" is just another term in our language, to be used as one wishes. We are caught in a "language game," a game of shifting nuances, fleeting meanings, vague analogies, a world where sentences have as many meanings as contexts, a world that is intrinsically self-referential with no connection to the "real" world. From this perspective, objective reality does not exist because the knowing subject can never apprehend it on its own terms, as it were, but only through the invention of language, which, unfortunately, refers only to other language.

Yet the old notion of truth implies a constant search to achieve correspondence between the mind and the world, if only for one's own satisfaction, let alone to prove something to others. At the least, one can scrutinize propositions for their internal logic: some propositions are verifiable; others falsifiable; all are capable of subjection to rules of evidence and criteria for justified belief. Images, shimmering ephemera that fall away at a touch to reveal still other images, hold no promise of proof or refutation. Images are allusive, beguiling, and seductive; they can convince without argument, lead without explicit direction, and suggest the existence of both realities and meanings that could not withstand scrutiny under the old standard of truth. Of course, some images, like carefully chosen metaphors, accurately reveal the essences of realities.

In a world filled with images, where the notion of truth is irrelevant, what rules do men and women employ for the discernment of representations,[1] for answering the questions: How does one make judgments between multiple and always competing representations of reality? Where, in what, and in whom can one put one's trust? Rules for discerning representations vary dramatically depending on one's social location, education, allegiances, personal leanings and sensibilities, and, for many, on the time of day. Men and women make judgments about the representations of external events, other people, institutions, organizations, and society itself based on many different kinds of criteria. Some automatically believe what people with standard "credentials," that is, wealth, education, occupational prestige, personal appearance, or fame in some arena, encourage them to believe. Those with a skeptical bent always look behind public faces, trying to assess realities themselves, although, without direct access to other worlds, this often produces only encounters with still other images.

For a great many people, the only sure grounds of understanding anything are kith, kin, blood, soil, gender, avowed sexual orientation, race, or neighborhood, while still others find themselves at home only with those who share similar occupational experiences or class backgrounds. For such parochial souls, representations that mirror social worlds other than their own milieux or reflect experiences other than their own experiences are immediately suspect. Such parochialism has its own doublethink and doublespeak. For instance, no contemporary slogan is more widespread than the call for social "diversity" in every institutional sector of our society. In the last thirty years, several social movements, most notably the civil rights, feminist, and gay and lesbian movements, have successfully pressed material claims as well as demands for the recognition of new social identities. Such claims almost always invoke constitutional or legislative provisions for "equitable treatment" under law, that is, demands that our society adhere to universalistic norms in key public arenas. Favorable administrative and judicial rulings have accelerated such claim making, compelling, to take only the most important instance, work organizations to "diversify" and so comply, it is thought, with universal norms. Paradoxically, instead of fostering universalism, this has led to an intensification of particularism of a primitive sort. In a fragmented, specialized world, only "diversity" that is noticeable gets celebrated, indeed only such noticeable diversity "proves" an organization's "inclusiveness," "openmindedness," and conformity both to public expectations and to emerging law. From the perspective of groups designated as "diverse," diversity becomes a focal point for organizing to further group self-interests or a warm cave where one huddles with similarly "diverse" others and howls against the raging winds and darkness, evinced, for instance, by one unintended consequence of affirmative action, the balkanization by race and ethnicity of college and university campuses across the land. From the perspective of organizations, diversity becomes a form of institutional public relations. Organizations get rewarded or avoid penalties not for, say, genuine intellectual diversity or a creative mix of actual skills, but only for "visible" diversity, diversity clearly demarcated by ascribed characteristics such as the current master categories of race, gender, distinctive ethnicity, or, increasingly in some quarters, openly avowed alternative sexual orientation. Thus, organizational brochures and news photo ops alike, whether from corporations, small elite colleges, or the White House, all present make-believe rainbow worlds. The basic premise of such fictive worlds is that experience corresponds with appearance, which in turn, it is further assumed, shapes thinking in a particular way. In the real world of organizations, diversity is as diversity seems. Disguised in a cloak of universalism and a rhetoric of "inclusiveness," powerful organizational premiums fuel the invention and ascendancy of a bureaucratically created and guaranteed particularism, complete with images of moral superiority for its champions.

Still other men and women approach representations guided by a set of standards hard-won by comparative reflection on the puzzles of history, on the lessons of literature, and on firsthand experiences with a range of social worlds. But even such deeply internalized standards often waver in the gale of images. Ways of discerning representations proliferate as rapidly as images themselves.

Public relations practitioners increasingly recognize such profound social and epistemological segmentation and try to turn it to the advantage of their clients. The Public Relations Society of America, with the help of leading academics, men and women of affairs, and the Rockefeller Foundation, constructed in 1999 the *National Credibility Index* that seeks to determine whether one can measure the credibility of specific leaders with specific segmented publics on issues like race, the use of force in foreign policy, and the future of social security.[2] The ultimate goal of the project is to market the assurance of situational trust by providing a way of pinpointing the right spokespeople for the right audiences on the right issues at the right times. The framers of the credibility index understand the elusiveness and fragility of trust in our society, yet, once fully implemented as a tool-in-trade, the index may unintentionally reinforce existing social splits and deepen suspicion between worlds apart. From the standpoint of image makers, there are few other practical choices available. The grand overarching narratives of the past, whether religious or secular theodicies, tales of heroism, or moral fables that capture the ethos of a whole people, no longer weld communities together. Instead, reflecting differentiating processes at work in every institutional sphere of modern society, local narratives, little stories about common people, provide disjointed, partial, usually self-celebratory glimpses of social worlds that, as it happens, are increasingly alien to one another.

The loss of faith in institutions and leaders in American society partly emerges from profound discord about our ways of knowing and discerning the world around us, about the stories we tell about ourselves, and about ways of making the choices that practical affairs pose for us. One's image of our society gets splintered and clouded, as if one were seeing the world through a kaleidoscope darkly.

〜〜〜 Such fragmentation of knowledge and belief presents great challenges to image makers charged with mobilizing mass sentiment that transcends particular milieus. The mechanics of the task remain the same. Experts select or invent an image to stand for a person, organization, or cause, not because of the image's truth-value, but because it is simple to articulate and understand, has emotional resonance with some target audience, an ability to link disparate personal associations, to command belief or the passive assent that follows half-belief, or to elicit the desire for belief. In this sense, emotion replaces reason. The shaping of credibility displaces the search for truth. But are there any grounds for widespread credibility in a fragmented society?

The construction of spokespeople illustrates in a paradigmatic way the attempt to shape credibility that crosses social boundaries. Commercial advocates have traditionally used real-life celebrities to borrow the authority of fame, glamour, excitement, or acclaimed expertise, or to appeal to group allegiances of whatever sort, or to provide reassurance or familiar associations forged elsewhere, or to appeal to personal interest. One links some quality of a celebrity's public persona to one's product or cause. Thus, Susan Lucci, the daytime soap-opera temptress, sells sporty cars at night that promise the likelihood of other sport. In Doyle Dane Bernbach's famous series of commercials for Polaroid, James Garner and Mariette Hartley push cameras for family pictures while elaborating their amusing portrait of the war between the sexes within marriage so well that viewers wish they actually were married. The late Robert Young pitched coffee wearing his Dr. Marcus Welby persona to soothe anxieties about caffeine. Clint Eastwood acts like Dirty Harry, urging people to join him in ostracizing those who litter public parks. Sometimes celebrity directors recreate the central themes of their cinematic ventures to sell products. Thus, David Lynch directs commercials for Calvin Klein's Obsession fragrance with one of his star-crossed couples from his *Twin Peaks* television series ("Between love and madness lies obsession, Calvin Klein's Obsession"), or Spike Lee plays on his own cinematic off-beat self-presentation for his Nike commercials.

But using real-life celebrities presents hazards. Scheduling problems and lack of availability for shoots are common annoyances. Moreover, real-life celebrities die, sometimes provoking unwanted anxieties in audiences that might carry over to particular products. Further, the credibility of real-life celebrities is always fragile. Celebrities commit faux pas, such as when Cybill Shepherd, then the pitchwoman for the National Beef Council, confessed in an interview that she did not eat meat. Also, some celebrities become overexposed. After he retired from the House of Representatives, Tip O'Neill pitched everything from the Trump Shuttle to Commodore computers to Quality Inns, until advertisers began to feel that his commercial promiscuousness smacked of an unseemly buck-hunger. Or, as inevitably happens, a celebrity's popularity begins to wane. Audiences, and even sponsor Smith Barney, eventually tired of the hectoring persona of John Houseman's recreation of his *Paper Chase* role as a Harvard Law School professor. In such cases, one can always opt for an "endorsement virgin," that is, a celebrity who has not yet lent his or her name to any product, a strategy that associates products with fresh faces and is thought to remedy the widespread conviction that every person has his price, a belief not conducive to credulity.

When celebrities suffer reputational crises, moreover, their hard-won credibility can collapse overnight. Leona Helmsley became a celebrity by insisting on starring in all advertisements for the luxury hotel that bears her late husband's name, casting herself as an unrelenting taskmaster in search of quality service. But her trial and conviction for tax evasion not only prematurely closed her thespian career but revealed a portrait of tightwad stinginess toward her employees that led to public cheers at her imprisonment. Michael Jackson's out-of-court settlement of sexual abuse charges against him by a male adolescent ended his relationship with Pepsi, the self-styled drink of young people. And the Hertz Corporation was staggered by the arrest and trial for a sensational double murder of O. J. Simpson, its longtime spokesman, pictured for years running through airports toward his prearranged rental car with the same grace as he once exhibited on the football field. The more successful image makers are in forging deep associations between a celebrity and a product or company, the more the product, company, and the image maker himself become hostage to the celebrity's perceived character. In order to avoid disaster for one's client and particularly for oneself, therefore, one rationalizes the selection of real-life celebrities as much as possible through various indices,[3] although no one has yet developed a measure for latent homicidal rage. Of course, in the contemporary United States even the worst stain on one's reputation might become an asset with proper marketing to the right audience. Latrell Sprewell, a three-time all-star in the National Basketball Association, throttled his coach nearly to unconsciousness. And 1, a basketball-shoe company that sells to fiercely competitive street basketball players, gave him another chance in a commercial set against a strident electric guitar rendition of "The Star Spangled Banner" ("People say I'm America's worst nightmare. I say I'm the American dream"). One can also peddle defiance or repentance to tabloid confessionals, both print and broadcast, even those that may have played a major part in one's original downfall through false accusation, innuendo, the salacious purveying of lurid details, or the moral-fable-like dramatization of one's actual disgrace.

One solution to the tenuousness of celebrities' credibility is to reach back into our national popular cultural subconscious and resurrect clips of fabled Hollywood stars, like Humphrey Bogart or John Wayne, to invoke a mood. But such a strategy assumes that young audiences will recognize the particular icon that one is using and will associate the screen persona with the product one wishes to sell.

The construction of a fictive spokesperson, whether symbolized by a live animal or a wholly imaginary creature or person, enables image makers to avoid such problems for the most part and respond to the exigencies of fast-moving markets. Of course, such a choice deprives one's clients of the opportunity to "starfuck" human celebrities at company gatherings. But one can control the generic character traits in fictive spokespeople, changing them as necessary over time. For 9-Lives cat food, Morris the Cat typified fussy, grumpy, bossy, and aloof felines during most of his long career; but, in the early 1980s, changing notions of desirable qualities in men required a more "sensitive" male cat. Ad makers altered Morris's image from self-centered and disdainful to "cozier." As it happens, cats populate many advertisements, whether to symbolize some aspect of a product through a presumably generic feline trait (looking sophisticated for a classy Volvo, or soundly sleeping for Sominex, or having unknown potentialities for Canon Cat, a combined typewriter and word processor) or simply as props, such as the New York Telephone commercial in which a cat perches on his owner's shoulder staring at a computer screen or in advertisements as varied as those for Empire Blue Cross/Blue Shield, Marine Midland Bank, Swissair, Diet Coke, and Diet Pepsi. Merrill Lynch's use of a restless bull, mimicking Bill Bernbach's identification of Dreyfus with a powerful lion, further illustrates the use of generic animal attributes, as does Budweiser's use of its famous Clydesdale horses whether in drawing a carriage for its annual paean to traditional rural America in its "Christmas Card" commercial or as players in a football game, complete with kicking an extra point over telephone wires, during the gridiron season.

One can also create personalities of a sort for fictive spokespeople. Mavis Beacon (<www.mavisbeacon.com>) sells software kits to teach typing to more than 6 million people, many of whom believe that the image of the beautiful African American woman with the calm soothing voice represents a flesh-and-blood person. Giving names to animal pitchmen provides them with specific identities, such as Spuds MacKenzie, "the original party animal," for Bud Light; or Alex the Mutt for Stroh's beer who sends-up the well-bred Spuds; or Nipper and little Nipper, the dogs who "see clearly now" for RCA; or Austin the Chimpanzee for Bugle Boy clothing who pokes fun at human foibles. With wholly imaginary characters, one can, of course, add further details. In the early 1950s, Muriel Cigar had two stogies that did a song-and-dance routine on stage with the female vamping: "Why don't you pick me up and smoke me sometime?" Bald and brawny Mr. Clean, a ring in his left ear long before males routinely appropriated such feminine gear, perhaps to invoke an image of a genie or pirate, helps busy housewives scour kitchens and bathrooms. The debonnair, fun-loving, dromedary-about-town for R. J. Reynold's Camel cigarettes, Old Joe, gave advice for years to college students on how to be a "smooth character" and woo women. Speedy Alka Seltzer captures the cheerful upbeatness of hotel bellhops from 1940s movies. Charlie the Tuna exuberantly pitches StarKist, which of course, sells Charlie's brethren canned and packed in water or oil. Red Dots leap off 7-Up cans and become daring, mischievous roustabouts clad in sunglasses and sneakers, who, among other adventures, play baseball inside consumers' refrigerators or a game of football with a peanut, disrupting the leisure of live actors. Little Caesars Pizza's gnome, clad in a toga, yells "Pizza, Pizza!" while hapless humans become enmeshed in never-ending strands of mozarella; the California Raisins, caricatures of aging hipsters, dance rhythmically to funky music. The pink Energizer Bunny, complete with shades, relentlessly pitches batteries and even drums his way out of his own commercial into parodies of spots for other products. Ritchie the Recycling Raccoon teaches kids in Lenexa, Kansas, the virtues of environmental responsibility.[4] One can even "borrow interest" from other milieux, one of the principal advantages of real-life celebrities, by employing famous cartoon figures with specific personality attributes to advertise one's wares, such as Metropolitan Life's use of characters from Charles Schultz's "Peanuts" comic strip, complete with lovable, floppy-eared Snoopy as an insurance salesman and shrewish Lucy as the skeptical consumer.

But achieving widespread credibility in mass society means shaping and projecting a relatively complete personality that audiences deem likeable and trustworthy. The construction of McGruff the Crime Dog illustrates the process. In response to the National Crime Prevention Council, a front for business interests working closely with the United States Department of Justice, the Advertising Council decided in the 1970s to undertake a public education campaign to address growing public fears about violent crime. From the start, the strategy focused on alleviating middle-class anxieties about violent street crime by involving people in crime prevention. Thus, the strategy aimed to teach people to look out for their neighbors, to be alert to suspicious circumstances, and to provide teenagers with tips about how to avoid potentially troublesome situations. A citizenry engaged in keeping order can help police remarkably, and it does alleviate some of the frustration and sense of helplessness produced both by crime and the irrationalities of the criminal justice system. The creative team at DFS Dorland Worldwide that had agreed to work on the issue for the Advertising Council toyed with having an older father figure such as Gregory Peck give advice to the audience. But they decided that a fictive pitchman, forever free of mortality and the possibility of scandal, was better suited for a long-term campaign about the morally freighted issues surrounding crime. While traveling in Wyoming, one member of the creative team spoke with a park ranger who commented on the talismanlike importance of the figure of Smokey Bear to forest-fire fighters. Smokey Bear, the central fictive figure of the longest running Advertising Council campaign, stands both as a somber witness to forest fires past and a prophet warning against similar disasters in the future unless people observe safety precautions ("Only *you* can prevent forest fires"). Although it is true that the overwhelming majority of forest fires are caused by people in some way, such fires typically occur in well-traveled or semiurban areas and thus destroy fewer acres of forest each year than lightning-caused fires that ravage whole tracts of wilderness.[5] Smokey helps mobilize public support for fire-fighting work by suggesting human responsibility for all forest fires, including those that are natural disasters.

The DFS Dorland creatives pressed the search for the right anticrime figure by focusing on the slogans that had been circulating within their unit. "Crush Crime" suggested an elephant; "Kick Crime" required a mule. But here the strategy of middle-class people steadfastly chipping or nibbling away at the problem reasserted itself. Eventually, the team hit upon the slogan "Take a Bite Out of Crime," which suggested a dog as the emblematic figure. Snoopy-like figures dressed as Keystone Cops came to mind, but were deemed too cute for such a somber mission. Suggestions about bulldogs who looked like J. Edgar Hoover or golden retriever Wonderdogs also seemed to miss the mark. Finally, the team decided on a prototypical figure in American popular culture, one that evoked the deep-furrowed, world-weary look of Humphrey Bogart as Sam Spade or Peter Falk as Columbo, a figure somewhere in between the private eye and the police detective, one with enough hard-won wisdom to be the commentator in Thornton Wilder's *Our Town*. A bloodhound in a trench coat became the emblematic figure. After the artwork was completed, and initial commercials ran, a naming contest among police officers produced the name McGruff; Jack Keil, the lead creative on the team, provided the gravelly voice that delivers homilies and warnings to adults and children alike about how to keep both property and person safe in a world that is out of middle-class control. In the creatives' view, the appeal and therefore the credibility of McGruff depend entirely on the anomalous but compelling personality they have shaped: a have-seen-it-all father figure who knows the difference between right and wrong yet who remains an approachable moral arbiter. Creatives note that they launched the McGruff campaign by sending out 13,000 dog costumes to police stations all over the country. Children clamored to sit on the laps of police officers dressed as Mc-Gruff, tug on his long ears, and confess to him their own sins and those done against them. When a McGruff walks in Macy's Thanksgiving day parade, onlookers randomly rush to shake his hand, pat him on the head, and thank him for his work.[6]

McGruff's character is always consistent. Audiences know that Mc-Gruff will not engage in doublethink or doublespeak, or lie to them, or confuse them with hair-splitting legal casuistry, or betray them. And they know that McGruff has their safety and other vital interests at heart. Similar figures, such as Crusader Baby, an infant superheroine created by Gaston & Gaston Public Relations for the General Health Care Corporation, provider of the largest cotton diaper service in the United States, stirred identical sentiments among many in her holy war to rid the world of artificial diapers, except, of course, at the headquarters of Procter & Gamble which controls half the artificial diaper market.[7] As it happens, few public figures succeed in constructing their own public faces well enough to enjoy the general affection that characters like McGruff seem to generate. To be sure, the makers of fictive creatures always run the risk of one-upmanship and satiric takeoffs from other image makers or ridicule from some consumer group. And even wholly fictitious images can offend some group or at least provide the opportunity to claim offense. But such discrediting fire is the normal occupational hazard of all in real life who make claims of any sort that infringe on others' claims, ideologies, or established prerogatives. Antismoking advocates accused executives at R. J. Reynolds of using Old Joe to lure children into tobacco use, a claim that eventually prevailed and forced the humpback's early retirement; experts with mass symbols noted that the very fervor of the opposition to Old Joe was a measure of his perceived credibility. This indeed is the main point. Fictive characters invite mass audiences to suspend application of their normal rules for discerning representations and respond to appeals that cross many of the deep social fissures in our society. Here, credibility means the capacity to induce a state of make-believe in a quite literal sense.

In a more figurative sense, inducing a state of make-believe in audiences becomes the goal of all image makers engaged in persuasion. Political consultants, for instance, help candidates and officials alike fashion riveting personalities to "excite" the crucial middle-of-the-road sector of the electorate uncommitted to clear ideological positions. The ideal, of course, is to find a candidate with "charisma," a term no longer reserved to describe supernatural or at least specifically remarkable powers or qualities of an individual personality, attributes that galvanize other people to alter their visions of themselves and of the world.[8] Today, not only in the political sphere but in the whole arena of modern public culture, charisma means a person who has "presence," who is "magnetic," who is "colorful," or who, simply, expresses emotions, exudes sexuality, or voices convictions in public. The term is now applied to men and women in any walk of life, from energetic basketball coaches to aging rock stars, from bombastic college presidents to tub-thumping politicians, from wet-behind-the-ears actors to celebrity chefs. As the rationalization of modern life increases, and with it the necessity for ever more self-rationalization, a properly projected emotional spark gets taken as exceptional. Identification with such personal forcefulness becomes a way of kicking against the desiccation of modern life. Image makers therefore try to construct charisma by harnessing raw vitality in order to fascinate audiences.

Even earnest advocates with a vocation often induce states of make-believe to establish credibility for themselves and their causes. For instance, feminist advocates create a sense of make-believe victimhood for privileged young middle-class college women that invites them to imagine that they already suffer, or inevitably will suffer, terrible indignities solely because of their gender. As it happens, fictive victimhood often exercises a stronger grip on the moral imagination of those recruited to its ranks than actual suffering.

Illusions and myths characterize the psychology of all social orders. In some societies, illusions are so deeply interwoven into the social fabric that disillusionment heralds, perhaps even provokes, a complete unraveling of the social order. By contrast, modern society separates personal illusions, and disillusions, from the main warp of the social order, except for the bureaucratized cultural apparatus that manufactures myths. Modern society allows great personal freedom and diversity of experience in return for conformity to the impersonal bureaucratic rules of key institutions. The workaday world plods on, while sometimes fantastic personal experience and worldviews proliferate in segmented make-believe dreamworlds where alone one's "true self" can flourish ("I dreamed that I . . . in my Maidenform Bra. The Maidenform Woman. You never know where she'll turn up"). Automobiles get sold as, and become, mobile cocoons of personal freedom.[9] Whole Life Expos sell a panoply of devices including liquid crystal flotation platform beds with sound waves and special glasses that wrap one in lights and music and transport one to another world.[10] Theme parks place one in colonial America, or in Tinseltown where ordinary people are treated like celebrities, chased by paparazzi, fawned over by the press, and for an evening, see their name in lights and themselves on the big screen; or for those with darker tastes, in Ulbricht's East Germany, or in the underground maze of the Cu Chi tunnels of Vietnam where one can don black pajamas, pith helmet, and sandals and make believe that one is a Vietcong guerilla.[11] Caribbean fantasy cruises on ships named Fantasy, Ecstasy, and Sensation cater to one's every whim.[12] Television abounds with shows that present make-believe worlds, from professional wrestling, to gladiator shows,[13] to dramas based on pseudo–science fiction, to staged yelling-and-screaming confrontations about subjects ranging from abstruse legal interpretations to intimate sexual encounters. And "virtual reality" technology creates the basis for a solipsistic exploration of a myriad of dreamworlds where one may adopt a wide variety of identities.[14]

Practically everywhere one looks, even among the professional middle classes who, at least from nine to five, epitomize the workaday ethos of our society, let alone among other groups less firmly anchored in mainstream institutions, one finds a carnivalesque mixture of wondrous applications of administrative and technological rationality together with bursts of what, from another perspective, are remarkable irrationalities. These include computer programmers who "channel" ancient spirits or practice witchcraft; upscale suburban housewives who write long letters of advice to characters on television soap operas; major public figures who consult astrologers; a growing antipathy to science among those who have benefited the most from technological advances; a deep resentment against the rationalized forces of order, accompanied by reveries of rebellion and identification with society's underdogs; the wholesale invention of dubious claims to garner resources and of excuses and justifications to evade responsibility; the emergence of new intellectual orthodoxies that eschew empirical work and place speculative mumbo jumbo at the center of inquiry; and, of course, the emergence of the apparatus and ethos of advocacy in which virtually every organized group in the social order utilizes the techniques originally developed by commercial advocates to sell some kind of salvation and broadcast little stories dramatizing one's cause and oneself. In the meantime, the substantive areas of expertise in modern society become ever more arcane, mysterious, and unknowable except obliquely through filters of make-believe.

〰〰〰〰 How do various segments of mass audiences respond to make-believe, taken here as the prototype of the ethos of mass persuasion, and how do image makers assess such responses?

Many men and women find comfort and engagement in particular worlds constructed by image makers. To the extent that representations of a particular world reflect their own predilections, these men and women compulsively affirm both second-hand and momentarily fresh images alike. If they hear echoes of their own sentiments, they accept both bland euphemisms and tall tales from private and public officials, and they take public relations fronts as solid buildings instead of movie-set facades. If scripts tug at their own memory strings, they respond with emotion to the sentimental narratives that ad makers fashion. If leaders, products, organizations, or causes intersect with their own personal agendas, they accept them as heroes for their own lives. In short, they take the highly varnished surfaces of particular areas of the public arena at face value as long as they see their own reflections there. From the perspective of interpretive experts, such representation literally means re-presentation of some audience's self-preoccupation, projected onto a big screen, flattery writ large. The institutional logic at the core of all work with mass images, no matter what make-believe world one wishes to construct, requires mirroring such self-preoccupation. One needs simply to discover which faces to present, which bells to ring, which stories to tell.

To the extent that representations in the mainstream world mirror conventional social arrangements, some groups inevitably feel "unrepresented" or "underrepresented," a claim regularly advanced by advocates. When one must reach one of these groups or placate their champions, one simply applies the institutional logic just described and absorbs the group's self-preoccupation into one's images. Since the early 1900s, for instance, several generations of American middle-class youth, anticipating their own future self-subjection to the rigors of bourgeois life, have rebelled against the cultural consequences of the triumph of industrial capitalism.[15] Ad makers, as well as other experts with symbols in the film, music, and television industries, have consistently and nimbly captured the creative energies of such cultural revolts and harnessed them to commercial ends. Indeed, the process of selection, refraction, and absorption of such cultural unrest has driven popular culture in the twentieth century. Moreover, some groups or their advocates protest against being "misrepresented," a claim typically related to shifting prestige hierarchies. To avoid the charge of being "insensitive," one adjusts the representations at issue in order to flatter the group, although one then runs the risk of being accused by others of pandering. When the previously unrepresented or underrepresented become "visible" or when the misrepresented get "shown in a proper light," they usually join the ranks of those who compulsively affirm the worlds of make-believe as if they were real, at least until their advocates discern new opportunities to exploit. Like mass image makers themselves, of course, advocates for even narrow interests develop a kind of double consciousness, knowing that worlds of representations, as solid as they sometimes seem, are not given but made.

Such double consciousness has become widespread in recent years, not least because media practitioners seem entirely unable to keep themselves out of the picture. Journalists regularly write or shoot documentaries about the "story behind the story." Television apes and promotes its own and Hollywood's films with documentaries about the making of old favorites, complete with profiles of famous media moguls and stars. Television show producers recycle old plots, send up other shows, and even do parodies of their own material. Television legal analysts agonize on the air about the damage excessive media coverage poses for, say, jury selection in celebrated trials, effectively throwing gasoline on already raging fires. And, as noted earlier, both advertising and public relations practitioners take their own peers as their most important audiences, often pirating and parodying others' work. Indeed, in a pinch, on the rare occasions when media practitioners are prohibited from an event, they often interview each other, and the denial of media access becomes the story. Moreover, when critics attack media practitioners for, say, prying into the private affairs of public figures or eliciting emotional statements from people in dire straits, media spokesmen become high-minded defenders of the constitutional privileges extended to the fourth estate. Such institutionalized inability to keep one's thumbprints off one's work causes a growing number of men and women to distrust the entire media apparatus and debunk its creations as artificial, an experience that is heightened when one has direct knowledge of individuals, groups, or events depicted or access to alternate interpretive frameworks. But, even as they excoriate what they see as the bogus world around them, many dissenters remain in petitioners' roles, longing for image makers to provide "authenticity" in representation, that is, a flattering rendition of their own self-images and worldviews.

A great many men and women in modern society find themselves bewildered, ignorant of the bodies of arcane substantive lore that make the world work, befuddled by the bureaucratic intricacies of the society, and psychologically adrift without any clear personal goals, let alone any clear conceptions of or commitments to key institutional frameworks. Some measures of such bewilderment are the astonishing level of adult functional illiteracy in our society and the widespread public ignorance of news events despite endless consumption of news media. Both are often coupled with political apathy.[16] Worlds of make-believe dazzle and confuse people who are bewildered by refracted and contradictory images or, alternately, provide pat answers to life's puzzles but not ways of framing questions that might help people decode the riddles themselves.

Mass bewilderment, of course, has some uses for interpretive experts. Bewilderment facilitates, say, recruitment appeals that help catch drifting men and women in bureaucratic nets. One constructs an ideal image of an organization and then symbolizes it in striking appeals that will resonate with target audiences. Depending on the organizational client, one casts appeals that mesh with audience members' already semiformed self-images or that provide ambiguous representations enabling potential recruits to construct a new self-image as a member of the organization. Recruitment campaigns typically fasten attention on turning points, offering fellowship, challenge, and fulfillment as rewards for the right choices, providing an individual the opportunity to unlock and maximize his or her potential ("Citibank is no gravy train. It's just one fast track"); one does not stress the needs of the organization or institution, but rather how the organization can be an arena for self-expression ("Because you're not like everybody, Stearns-Roger needs you"). Thus, the Benedictine monks run a print advertisement saying: "Sometimes, the best way to change your life is to start a new one." The Neumann Residence in New York recruits young male aspirants to the priesthood for an intensive preseminary residence with an advertisement embellished only with the face of Jesus and the slogan: "If you're thinking of spending the rest of your life with Him, spend several months with us." The United States Army presents difficulties as virtues and offers self-discipline, maturity, and character-building experiences to help recruits "[b]e all that you can be." The United States Marine Corps invokes a medieval tableau complete with armored knight on horseback dubbed by a king-like figure with flashing sword in the corps's search for "a few good men with the mettle to be Marines." The Atlanta Police Department, in an effort to draw mature, educated, and fit twenty-five-year-old men and women to its ranks, designs a billboard campaign featuring an array of actual selected police officers (male and female, black and white) with the slogan "Look at our line-up."[17] Ursuline College, worried about a declining number of applicants, pitches itself to its primary constituency of high-school girls as a serious, but fun-filled, educational arena where they can achieve greater personal and intellectual growth than at a co-ed college.[18] Recruitment appeals often create what Daniel Boorstin calls "extravagant expectations" about organizations and about one's future experience in them.[19] But despite its uses, bewilderment is not felt to be a worthy test of symbolic legerdemain. Image makers prefer to pit themselves against sophisticated audiences that appreciate playful irony, tough-minded skepticism, and self-parody.

At the same time, many men and women become fellow propagandists if only on their own behalf, sometimes with the help of image makers. Consider, for instance, the pervasive self-promotion that marks most professions today. Whole subsidiary industries have burgeoned to school aspiring corporate managers in the arts of adroit self-presentation appropriate to leadership roles. These include workshops on "issue management," that is, how to frame tangled messes rationally so that they seem to be entirely manageable difficulties; seminars on "media management," that is, how to outfox one's opposite numbers in the media; and "public relations counseling" on how to doublethink and doublespeak one's way through the often irreconcilably opposed interests that emerge in practical affairs. Corporations regularly send managers who exhibit exceptional promise in such undertakings to special sessions at Ivy League colleges for further polishing; there one learns how to feign more knowledge than one has, how to tell personal stories that both attract and disarm others, and how to assert one's will subtly, as well as other skills useful for triumph in bureaucratic settings. The corporations have simply formalized a more general process. With proper access to the right circles at the annual meetings of virtually any academic discipline, one can observe professional self-promotion by both individuals and groups in more inchoate form. Such self-promotion includes peddling intellectual wares to publishers, hobnobbing with foundation officers to ensure sympathetic readings of grant proposals, rigging book reviews by cliques determined to highlight or destroy some viewpoint, logrolling and stacking votes for crucial committees or for honors awarded strictly, it is thought, for meritorious work, and arranging for loyal disciples to write hagiographies of iconic figures, especially of those still among the quick who control disciplinary resources. Of course, the self-promotion of managers and academics, which are only instances of a general phenomenon, pales in comparison to the self-flogging of the masters of the art, namely big-time advocates themselves, who see selling an idea inextricably connected to selling themselves.

A growing number of intellectuals, among whom double consciousness about representations is de rigueur, have come to celebrate the make-believe worlds constructed by image makers. They take for granted, of course, the impossibility of achieving "truth," even in the minimalist sense of a correspondence between one's statements and reality outside the mind. One can only know the fleeting verbal and visual images of social life; indeed, even such knowledge is limited by the vocabularies one uses to fix one's experiences with such images. In this view, the notion of "science," for instance, becomes a rationalist delusion, a hopelessly nineteenth-century fallacy that presupposes discernible patterns or structures in the external world that one might discover and illuminate. "Patterns" or "structures" are, in fact, invented by the cognizer. The success of a scientific theory depends not on its accuracy or on its explanatory power, but on the rhetorical skills of the scientist who can first impose order on the world and then impose his or her theory on others. One must not surrender to the ultimately arbitrary authority of science, or to its relentless means/ends rationality, or to its attempt to fix meaning, even in a provisional way. Instead, one should resist the rational "disenchantment of the world," celebrate the differences in reality, and try to subvert arbitrary attempts by authority of any sort to impose order or singular meaning on the world. In intellectual work, one should focus on the peculiar case, rather than search for any norm, in order to find insightful and exciting allegories that will free others' imaginations from the tyranny of rational strictures. Moreover, this struggle must carry over to other arenas. One must constantly "resist" the powerful structural tendencies toward increased bureaucracy and especially the "hegemonic" attempts by some intellectuals or representatives of established institutions to assert frameworks that confine others' creativity or a morality that hems in others' freedom.

One's central intellectual task, in fact, is to deconstruct a wholly constructed world and, by apprehending the way the world has been put together, to vitiate the power of those in authority or those who aspire to it. One celebrates the worlds of make-believe shaped by image makers precisely because they make no claims to certitude; instead, they invite one to revel in the illusions that are the stuff of social life. In this view, everything, after all, including society and human life itself, is a text, encapsulated in and bounded by language, ultimately undecidable, capable of infinite interpretation and reinterpretation without subjection to any empirical limits. "Theory" is indistinguishable from speculation, conjecture, idiosyncratic viewpoint, reflective blather, mere opinion, and ideology. One need not strive to be right, but only to be interesting, inventive, playful, and ironical with one's interpretations, to tease and jest with one's readers or viewers, to employ strategies that will elicit further discussion rather than close debate. How stories are told and by whom they are told are more important than the stories themselves; one must therefore adopt, for instance, a feminine aesthetics of narration, "resisting" masculine illusions of closure, linearity, mastery, and control, and being open to the multiperspectival possibilities of intimate reciprocity.[20] But most important, the point is to be bold, adventurous, and daring. Unless one takes intellectual risks, always reaching for images that might yield fresh perspectives on the world, one can only look forward to the gray-on-gray intellectual conformity of modernity and its hierarchical, authoritarian, antidemocratic, oppressive structures. The worlds of make-believe created by image makers become giant toy chests through which one can rummage for a whole intellectual career, trying on different costumes, wearing different masks, and discovering props for one's fanciful tales. Or one becomes a prophet of doom, a champion of the downtrodden railing against the social inequities suffered by some because of, say, their race, class, gender, or sexual orientation. But in the absence of the possibility of convincing proof about why the world is thus, or, in some cases, even the possibility of knowing or agreeing on facts that might serve as building blocks for one's arguments, everything depends on sustaining the requisite moral fervor to convince others of the correctness of one's position and oneself of one's own moral rectitude. Indignation and its Siamese twin, moral exhortation, become an intellectual style.

Intellectuals who move into high administrative ranks usually end up in a different situation. Since their work requires them to uphold organizational pieties, they become public relations practitioners of a sort subject to all of the vicissitudes of such work. The gravity of their responsibilities usually precludes sardonic or ironic self-appraisals or self-presentations; indeed, their public pronouncements often resemble sound bites or echo well-known slogans—crafted by advocates of one sort or another—that have found their way into popular culture.[21]

Commercial advocates are greatly amused by some intellectuals' preoccupation with and aping of their craft. They work with an identical, though less rarified, epistemological relativism. The considerable crossover into mass symbolic work of intellectuals trained in contemporary literary theory, one important academic seedbed of such now widely scattered ideas, suggests a striking coincidence of habits of mind among different occupational worlds, specifically hermeneutical skills, crucial for spinning the web of endless interpretations of events, and casuistic abilities, essential for the conceptual hairsplitting that underpins doublethink and doublespeak. But intellectuals who migrate from the academy to the world of affairs only highlight the ways of thinking that are deeply embedded in work with mass symbols. These habits of mind in and of themselves generate extreme relativism and concomitant moral equivalence. Creating make-believe worlds in order to make others believe in a product, person, or cause requires abandoning one's own intellectual premises, finding out what triggers an audience's attention, and then constructing the world from that standpoint, all toward the specific end of convincing others. Moreover, both what people will believe and the methods that one can use to induce belief are a constant source of amazement even to hardened image makers. Insofar as they internalize the institutional logic of mass symbolic work in order to be effective, even advocates with a vocation share such epistemological relativism, although the fervent assertion of fixed moral values by those who wish to change the world limits somewhat the emotional promiscuity that usually accompanies relativism.

Audiences' responses to the worlds of make-believe do matter to image makers, but, with the exception of advocates with a vocation, only in so far as they affect how their bosses and peers evaluate their work. For those in commercial work, complacent narcissism, resentment, apathy, bewilderment, or emulation are simply by-products of the exercise of creative persuasive skills or fertile ground to try out new techniques and messages. Commercial advocates take the world as they find it and work with what is at hand. Those who want to save the world, on the other hand, require others' moral fervor to fuel their own inner dramas. And technicians in moral outrage need others' fervor in order to prosper.

〰〰〰 The apparatus and ethos of advocacy have far-reaching consequences for modern society. The mighty media of mass communications, since their initial coordination in the First World War, have become indispensable to modern economy and civilization. Mass communications have also produced a society where public and private are increasingly indistinguishable; where manufactured celebrity, fame, and even notoriety have displaced older conceptions of solid achievement as measures of reputable success; and, especially, where the rush for the new story or shocking representation makes a sense of history seem quaint. Yesterday's secrets are today's front-page headlines; yesterday's hero is today's has-been; yesterday's big news provokes today's uncomprehending stare. Bill Bernbach's codification of his occupation's wisdom has never been more accurate: one must continually try to turn the world upside down just to be heard, let alone understood. It's not just what one says, it's how one says it; presentation is all. In such a world, the tail wags the dog. The norm, precisely because it is normal, gets seen as boring. The premium is on the fresh, the new, and the exciting. The marginal becomes central. As it happens, the fresh becomes quickly stale. The relentless appropriation and recycling of ideas give the public symbolic world a second- or thirdhand feel, making even intimate experience feel borrowed. In such a world, one has little choice but to become an advocate, if only to make one's way in the world or, if one has the calling, to promote one's vision to change the world. Without constant advocacy, one can expect only a Jonah-like existence in the bureaucratic maw of modern times.

The ethos of advocacy has its own relentless logic and consequences. Take, for instance, some of the outcomes of its premises for a social order that is already splintered by the increasing division of labor, refinement of expertise, and a myriad of social and cultural differences. If one cannot attain even simple observational truth, if everything is simply a matter of perspective, if the entire world and all experience is "constructed," if "[t]he event is not what happens . . . [but] that which can be narrated,"[22] if all views are ultimately "political" and therefore self-serving, then all objective standards against which one measures knowledge and experience collapse. Everything becomes advocacy, a war of story against story, of claim against claim, of image against image. Such an epistemological Hobbesianism makes doublethink and doublespeak respectable. It fuels antiscientific sentiment, already a staple of sensationalist pulp journalism for the unlettered, despite modern civilization's complete dependence on science and its technological benefits. It also undercuts the possibility of competing social groups finding common ground through reasonable discussion, reducing "public discourse" to semiorchestrated cacophony, an arena ringing with moral exhortations, from the benign cajolings of the Advertising Council to the strident proclamations of technicians in moral outrage. Moreover, the denial of the possibility of simple observational truth undercuts any notion of responsibility that assumes an accurate attribution of agency to a doer of a particular deed. One can scarcely hold a person responsible for an action if one has no way to ascertain exactly what happened in a given situation, unless one is working with a wholly capricious and arbitrary system of accountability or unless, of course, one gives assent to those images that seem convincing instead of giving assent to justified beliefs based on rational criteria. The contemporary crisis of, for instance, the American criminal justice system, the society's forum for fixing responsibility for grave actions, rests partly on the collapse of common ways of knowing and judging.

One person's make-believe is another person's cause for disbelief. Make-believe worlds that provide solace, delight, and inspiration to some are objects of doubt and even ridicule to others. Some public relations extravaganzas staged in recent years, such as the bicentennial celebration of the founding of the United States that, in New York City, centered on "Our Lady," that is, the Statue of Liberty, were seen by many not as a patriotic occasion to count the blessings of liberty, but as an orgy of uncritical, highly sentimentalized self-congratulation. A series of five anti-cocaine print advertisements for the Partnership for a Drug-Free America, each of which pictured a young person staring at the camera, snub-nosed revolver shoved up one nostril, with the tag line "Cocaine: The Big Lie," stirred enormous public commentary, created a sensation within the advertising industry, and catapulted the career of the creative who thought of the image.[23] Yet scare tactics, which ad makers relish because of their undeniably visceral appeal, are usually tuned out by their intended young audiences,[24] laying the groundwork for future selective deafness, on one hand, and cynicism on the other. Every moralistic crusade's triumph sows the seeds of future sin. Every propaganda success produces doubt and disbelief.

But those who reject one make-believe world often plunge readily into the next. That knowledge frames the work of mass image makers. The task is always to construct inviting worlds that convince even hardened doubters to suspend their disbelief. And the more compelling the make-believe worlds that advocates create to sell products, people, organizations, social policies, or causes, the deeper some audiences will plunge into them seeking like-minded fellowship and flattering glimpses of themselves. Yet the promised companionship of make-believe worlds is always illusory; the celebrations of self are always transitory. The rush into make-believe worlds deepens the social and experiential centrifugality of modern society, the abandonment of the presumption of common ways of seeing, knowing, discerning, and judging, and the lonely retreat into self-contained and self-referential arenas. Such centrifugality poses great obstacles to advocates' own work. So they strive all the harder to create ever more fantastic and convincing fictions.

A Note on Sources

This book is based on years of fieldwork and archival research. Most of the fieldwork came first. In a chapter of *Moral Mazes: The World of Corporate Managers,* published in 1988, Robert Jackall reported fieldwork with public relations practitioners done between 1980 and 1987; it focused on their important role in helping corporate managers frame rationales for "what has to be done." In 1987, Janice M. Hirota's doctoral dissertation at Columbia University reported her fieldwork with "creatives" in more than two dozen New York advertising agencies from 1982 to 1986. From 1987 to 1989, the authors renewed their fieldwork in both advertising and public relations. A particular focus of this round of fieldwork was on the creation of public service advertising, an arena that bridges both image-making worlds. The authors continued fieldwork in a more sporadic way, with both advertising and public relations practitioners, well into the 1990s. Over the years, the authors have interviewed more than 175 advertising practitioners and more than 125 men and women in public relations. Many of these interviews are actually regular, years-long conversations.

Most of the particular research in archives and private libraries is detailed in the endnotes. This overview summarizes this work with some additions not mentioned in the endnotes. We worked in the library of the American Association of Advertising Agencies in 1987–1988, reviewing the history of that organization and its materials relating to the advertising industry's involvement in the two world wars. In July 1988, we collected the materials on the Committee on

Public Information in the National Archives in Washington, D.C. We worked in the Center for Advertising History in the Archives Center of the Smithsonian Institution in Washington, D.C., in July 1988 and July 1994, focusing particularly on the collection's historical materials on advertising campaigns for Pepsi, Alka Seltzer, Marlboro, and Federal Express. We did extensive research during 1987–1989 in the archives of the Advertising Council then located in New York City. We visited the library of the Society of Illustrators in New York in early 1988 to review materials on the Society's founder, Charles Dana Gibson. We worked in the library of the Public Relations Society of America in New York during 1987–1988 and again in the summer of 1993, reviewing the history of that organization and its complete files on the Silver Anvil Awards from 1980 to 1993; later, we also reviewed the award statements of all the Silver Anvil Awards from 1994 to 1998. In the summers of 1991, 1998, and 1999, we worked in the Information Center of DDB Worldwide, Inc., in New York on the extant materials on William Bernbach and the famous agency that once, and now again, bears his name. We visited the Clio Awards, Inc., in New York City in 1990 and worked with the organization's files on the history of the awards; we also reviewed the organization's annual award-announcement publications from 1980 to 1989. We viewed hundreds of award-winning commercials from all over the world in the Museum of Broadcasting's videotape archives in 1990–1991. We visited and did interviews with key staff at the Public Media Center in San Francisco in 1992 and at the Advocacy Institute in Washington, D.C., in 1995. Finally, between 1987 and 1997, we carried on extensive correspondence with advertising and public relations agencies throughout the United States about particular publicity campaigns, receiving and reviewing printed and videotaped materials from more than seventy-five agencies over the years.

NOTES

CHAPTER ONE: ADVERTISING THE GREAT WAR

1. See Frank Presbrey, *The History and Development of Advertising* (Garden City, N.Y.: Doubleday, Doran & Co., 1929) for an illustrated treatment of the ancient origins of advertising and the flowering in England of advertisements in pictorial signboards, shop bills, newspapers, tradesmen's cards, pamphlets, and other kinds of illustrations. Presbrey's book also provides a useful history of advertising in the United States through the 1920s.

2. See Daniel Pope, *The Making of Modern Advertising* (New York: Basic Books, 1983). For a more popular general history of advertising in the United States, see Charles A. Goodrum and Helen Dalrymple, *Advertising in America: The First 200 Years* (New York: Harry N. Abrams, 1990). More specialized treatments include Clarence P. Hornung and Fridolf Johnson, *Two Hundred Years of American Graphic Art: A Retrospective Survey of the Printing Arts and Advertising, Since the Colonial Period* (New York: George Braziller, 1976); Luna Lambert Levinson, "Images That Sell: Color Advertising and the Boston Printmakers, 1850–1900," in *Aspects of American Printmaking, 1800–1950*, edited by James F. O'Gorman (Syracuse: Syracuse University Press, 1988), 83–103; Mary Black, *American Advertising Posters of the Nineteenth Century: From the Bella C. Landauer Collection of the New-York Historical Society* (New York: Dover Publications, 1976); Victor Margolin, Ira Brichta, and Vivian Brichta, *The Promise and the Product: 200 Years of American Advertising Posters* (New York: Macmillan, 1979); and Frederick R. Brandt, Robert Koch, & Philip B. Meggs, *Designed to Sell: Turn-of-the-Century American Posters in the Virginia Museum of Fine Arts* (Richmond: The Museum, 1994). For cultural histories of advertising, see Michael Schudson, *Advertising, The Uneasy Persuasion: Its Dubious Impact on American Society* (New York: Basic Books, 1984); Roland

Marchand, *Advertising the American Dream: Making Way for Modernity, 1920–1940* (Berkeley and Los Angeles: University of California Press, 1985); T. J. Jackson Lears, *Fables of Abundance: A Cultural History of Advertising in America* (New York: Basic Books, 1994); and Thomas Frank, *The Conquest of Cool: Business Culture, Counterculture, and the Rise of Hip Consumerism* (Chicago and London: University of Chicago Press, 1997).

3. The literature on public opinion is vast. For a seminal essay, see Hans Speier, "The Rise of Public Opinion," in *The Truth in Hell and Other Essays on Politics and Culture, 1935–1987* (New York: Oxford University Press, 1989), 143–161. For instance, Speier notes the important, though rarely studied, connection between public finance and public opinion, particularly in eighteenth-century France before the revolution. Fiscal ministers like Jacques Necker contributed greatly to the growing sense of the importance of public opinion by publishing fiscal statements "so that the merits and faults of governmental policy in this field could be appraised in public" (149). For a few years after 1789, of course, respect for public opinion became fear of public opinion.

4. A good example of this is the permanent exhibit at the British Museum on the carefully crafted public image of Augustus Caesar. See Susan Walker and Andrew Burnett, *The Image of Augustus* (London: British Museum, 1981). See also Johann Jakob Bernoulli, *Römische Ikonographie*, 4 vols. (Stuttgart: Union Deutsche Verlagsgesellschaft, 1882–94).

5. See Ray Eldon Hiebert, *Courtier to the Crowd: The Story of Ivy Lee and the Development of Public Relations* (Ames, Iowa: Iowa State University Press, 1966) and Roland Marchand, *Creating the Corporate Soul: The Rise of Public Relations and Corporate Imagery in American Big Business* (Berkeley and Los Angeles: University of California Press, 1998). The best book on the zany world of press agentry remains the incomparable Harry Reichenbach's *Phantom Fame*, as told to David Freedman (New York: Simon and Schuster, Inc., 1931).

6. Commercial radio broadcasting seems to have begun in New York City in August 1922 with station WEAF, owned by Western Electric. The first broadcast commercial, an advertisement for the Queensboro Corporation, a cooperative housing project in Jackson Heights, Queens, was aired on 28 August 1922. See Lincoln Diamant, *Television's Classic Commercials: The Golden Years, 1948–1958* (New York: Hastings House, 1971), 1.

7. See George Creel, *Rebel at Large: Recollections of Fifty Crowded Years* (New York: G. P. Putnam's Sons, 1947), 158. Though not explicit, the reference is to the Sacred Congregation for the Propagation of the Faith *(de propaganda fide)* established by Pope Gregory XV (1621–1623) to train priests for battle against the Protestant Reformation and for the conversion of heathens.

8. In Creel's view, the social divisiveness had many sources. Years later, he wrote:

During the three and a half years of our neutrality the United States had been torn by a thousand divisive prejudices, with public opinion stunned and muddled by the pull and haul of Allied and German propaganda. The sentiment of the West was still isolationist; the Northwest buzzed with talk of a 'rich man's war,' waged to salvage Wall Street loans; men and women of Irish stock were 'neutral,' not caring who whipped England, and in every state demagogues raved against 'warmongers,' although the DuPonts and other so-called 'merchants of death' did not have enough powder on hand to arm squirrel hunters.

See Creel, *Rebel at Large*, 157.

9. "Holding fast the inner lines" was a widespread war slogan. The title of Creel's informal history of the CPI is *How We Advertised America: The First Telling of the Amazing Story of the Committee on Public Information that Carried the Gospel of Americanism to Every Corner of the Globe* (New York and London: Harper and Brothers, 1920).

10. The CPI had an executive division, which housed the organization's top officials and the business management office. The business management office oversaw the work of the division of stenography and mimeographing and the division of production and distribution. The CPI had two main sections, domestic and foreign. In the domestic section were the divisions of news, official bulletins, foreign languages, civic and educational cooperation, reference materials, films, pictures (later merged with the film division), industrial relations, labor publications, pictorial publicity, advertising, the Four Minute Men, speaking, syndicated features, women's war work, and work with the foreign-born. The domestic section also housed the bureaus of war expositions, state fair exhibits, service (information), and cartoons. In addition to its own director's office, the foreign section housed the Russian division, the divisions of wireless and cable service and of foreign films, as well as the foreign press bureau. There were commissioners' offices at Paris, London, Rome, Berne, The Hague, Madrid, Buenos Aires, Santiago, and Lima.

11. *Conquest and Kultur, Aims of the Germans in Their Own Words*, Red, White and Blue Series, no. 5, comp. Wallace Notestein and Elmer E. Stoll (Washington, D.C.: CPI, 1917) and *How the War Came to America*, Red, White and Blue Series, no. 1 (Washington, D.C.: CPI, 1917). Other titles included *The President's Flag Day Address, with Evidence of Germany's Plans*, Red, White and Blue Series, no. 4 (Washington, D.C.: CPI, 1917) and *War Cyclopedia: A Handbook for Ready Reference on the Great War*, Red, White and Blue Series, no. 7, ed. Frederic L. Paxson, Edward S. Corwin, and Samuel B. Harding (Washington, D.C.: CPI, 1918).

12. Joseph Buffington, *Friendly Words to the Foreign Born*, Loyalty Leaflets, no. 1 (New York: n.p., 1918) and Frederic C. Walcott, *The Prussian System*, Loyalty Leaflets, no. 2 (Washington, D.C.: CPI, 1917). See James R. Mock and Cedric Larson, *Words that Won the War: The Story of the Committee on Public Information, 1917–1919* (Princeton: Princeton University Press, 1939), 175.

13. John S. P. Tatlock, *Why America Fights Germany*, War Information Series, no. 15 (Washington, D.C.: CPI, 1918). Tatlock was a professor of English at Stanford University. Samuel B. Harding, *The Study of the Great War: A Topi-*

cal Outline, with Extensive Quotations and Reading References, War Information Series, no. 16 (Washington, D.C.: CPI, 1917). Harding was a professor of European history at Indiana University. Other important titles were *American Loyalty, by Citizens of German Descent,* War Information Series, no. 6 (Washington, D.C: CPI, 1917), *Lieber and Schurz: Two Loyal Americans of German Birth,* War Information Series, no. 19 (Washington, D.C: CPI, 1917), and *The German-Bolshevik Conspiracy,* War Information Series, no. 20 (Washington, D.C.: CPI, 1917).

14. The archives for the Committee on Public Information are located at the National Archives, Judicial and Fiscal Branch, Records of the Committee on Public Information. Immediately after the CPI's dissolution in June 1919, the voluminous files of the organization were put in the custody of the Army Industrial College in a wing of the old Munitions Building of the War Department at Twentieth Street and Constitution Avenue, NW, in Washington, D.C. They were discovered in the summer of 1936 by Cedric Larson, then working for the National Archives. The files were relocated to the National Archives on 6 July 1937. Larson originally thought that the files he had sought and discovered were intact. See Cedric E. A. Larson, "Found: Records of the Committee on Public Information," *Public Information Quarterly* 1 (January 1918), 116–118. Larson teamed up with James R. Mock to mine the records. See Cedric Larson and James R. Mock, "The Lost Files of the Creel Committee of 1917–1919, *Public Opinion Quarterly* (January 1939), 5–30, and James R. Mock and Cedric Larson, *Words That Won the War.* In working through the materials, Mock and Larson discovered that the "Useless Papers Committee" of the army had destroyed all but a quarter of the CPI documents.

The authors are greatly indebted to Mock's and Larson's pioneering work. We have also relied extensively, as did Mock and Larson, on George Creel's informal history of the CPI, *How We Advertised America,* and on Creel's *Complete Report of the Chairman of the Committee on Public Information, 1917: 1918: 1919* (Washington, D.C.: GPO, 1920).

Carl Byoir's CPI papers are voluminous and cover virtually every aspect of the organization. See National Archives, Judicial and Fiscal Branch, Records of the Committee on Public Information, Record Group (RG) 63, files 1-A4, A5, A6, and A7.

The record of Byoir's career before 1917 and his long career as a central figure in public relations after the CPI experience are less well documented. See, however, Robert James Bennett, "Carl Byoir: Public Relations Pioneer" (master's thesis, University of Wisconsin, 1968). In addition to other papers, Bennett had access to Byoir's incomplete, unpublished autobiography, a document that is now missing. Byoir's firm, Carl Byoir and Associates, was absorbed in 1986 by Hill and Knowlton, another large public relations firm. Apparently, most of Byoir's papers, including the autobiography, were lost in the transition, a common occurrence in the corporate world. Fortunately for other scholars, Bennett provides large segments of the autobiography.

One somewhat documented area of Byoir's post-CPI career is his 1933–

1934 representation of German businesses and the German Tourist Information Bureau in the United States after Hitler had been named chancellor of Germany in January 1933. Byoir was excoriated for his business interests by a "Boycott Committee," opposed to any commercial intercourse with the new Hitler regime because of its explicit anti-Semitism. Byoir vigorously defended himself in an undated statement prepared for presentation to the United States House of Representatives, U.S. Congress, Seventy-third Congress, second session, 1934, called to investigate "Nazi Propaganda and Certain Other Propaganda Activities." According to the text of Byoir's statement, which is in the possession of the authors, the "statement was not recorded in official Congressional records but, by implication, it is reflected in the remarks (pertaining to Carl Byoir's personal role in the execution of the subject CB&A [Carl Byoir and Associates] contract) made by Representative Samuel Dickstein of New York on February 27, 1935." See *Congressional Record,* 74th Cong., 1st sess., 1935, 79, pt. 3:2668–2670. There seems to be no official record of Byoir's statement since, as Byoir's statement suggests, it was made to an executive session of the Special House Committee. Later, still other charges were made against Byoir, specifically of being chief of a Nazi spy ring in the United States. Byoir was later vindicated of all charges that might taint his "Americanism" by the Committee on Un-American Activities on 12 September 1940.

15. Some of the most important dissenters were grouped around Max Eastman, editor of *Masses* magazine (later *The Liberator*). Eastman and others were charged with sedition at the height of the pro-war hysteria. See Max Eastman, *Max Eastman's Address to the Jury in the Second* Masses *Trial: In Defense of the Socialist Position and the Right of Free Speech,* Liberator Pamphlet, no. 1 (New York: Liberator Pub. Co., 1918). See also the excoriating attack on fellow intellectuals by dissenter Randolph Bourne in "War and the Intellectuals," *The Seven Arts,* 2 (June 1917), 133–146.

16. In his account, Creel says that the size of the division's staff was twenty-two women, many of them volunteers. See Creel, *How We Advertised America,* 212. In a document called "Personnel of the Women's Division of the Committee on Public Information" attached to the Women's Work Report of 29 May 1918, Committee on Public Information, RG 63, 1-B1, box 42, Clara Sears Taylor names fifteen women, including herself, as comprising the staff of her division with no indication of who was salaried or not. In addition to Taylor, the key figures were Mary Holland Kincaid, a newspaper reporter, feature writer, and editor who made her career in New York City; Mrs. Helen S. Wright, a feature writer and author of six books, from Pittsfield, Massachusetts; Helen Cady Forbes, a librarian from Kennebunk, Maine, who left the New York Public Library to join the division; and Miss Dorothy Kitchen, a newspaper reporter from Kansas City, Missouri.

17. A UNESCO study done at midcentury tried to document comparative rates of illiteracy in several industrial and developing nations. The study found that in the United States 6,180,069 citizens or 10.7 percent of the country's population reported themselves as unable to read or write in

any language in 1900; 5,516,163 or 7.7 percent so reported in 1910; and 4,931,905 so reported in 1920. UNESCO acknowledges that these numbers, which are based only on self-reports from census data without any objective measure, must be considered to be low. See UNESCO, *Progress of Literacy in Various Countries: A Preliminary Statistical Study of Available Census Data since 1900* (Paris: UNESCO, 1953), 150. For a more scholarly historical treatment that reaches broadly similar conclusions, see Lawrence C. Stedman and Carl F. Kaestle, "Literacy and Reading Performance in the United States from 1880 to the Present," in Carl F. Kaestle, Helen Damon-Moore, Lawrence C. Stedman, Katherine Tinsley, and William Vance Trollinger, Jr., *Literacy in the United States* (New Haven: Yale University Press, 1991), 75–128. Semiliteracy is probably at least double that of illiteracy, reported or actual.

18. See Committee on Public Information, RG 63, 1A-A1, B1, B3, C2; 11B-A1, A2, A3, A6, B2, and B3 for the original materials on the Four Minute Men. The most comprehensive and best treatment of this organization is Alfred E. Cornebise, *War as Advertised: The Four Minute Men and America's Crusade, 1917–1918* (Philadelphia: The American Philosophical Society, 1984).

19. Many students of the mass media have argued that the main frequenters of the movies in the early years of the century were working-class immigrants and their offspring. Recent work suggests that the class composition of moviegoers was always very diverse, with middle-class attendance at least equaling that of the working class. See Lary May, *Screening Out the Past: The Birth of Mass Culture and the Motion Picture Industry* (New York: Oxford University Press, 1980). In any event, a lot of people went to the movie houses. A contemporary account estimated that between ten and thirteen million people went to the movies every day in the United States, an astonishing figure considering that the nation's population in 1917 was one hundred million. See "The War Work of the Four-Minute Men: With An Introductory Letter by President Wilson," *The Touchstone,* vol. 3, no. 6 (September 1918).

20. See Theodore Morrison, *Chautauqua: A Center for Education, Religion, and the Arts in America* (Chicago and London: The University of Chicago Press, 1974).

21. See George Creel, *Rebel At Large,* 162. James R. Mock and Cedric Larson tell a different story about Gibson's involvement in *Words That Won the War,* 101. In their account, Creel sent Gibson a telegram while Gibson was involved in a meeting of the Society of Illustrators asking him to arrange a committee of artists to help with the war effort. Gibson later went to Washington to launch the Division of Pictorial Publicity. Creel's more dramatic account is typical of his generally flamboyant self–presentation. In this instance, it served his purpose of emphasizing the spontaneity of the CPI's early growth.

22. There are several collections of First World War posters. See, in particular, Joseph Darracott and Belinda Loftus, *First World War Posters* (London: H. M. Stationery Office, 1972); Joseph Darracott, *The First World War in*

Posters, From the Imperial War Museum, London (New York: Dover Publications, 1974); Philipp P. Fehl and Patricia Fenix, *WWI Propaganda Posters: A Selection from the Bowman Gray Collection of Materials Related to WWI and WWII* (Chapel Hill: Ackland Art Center, 1969); and Maurice Rickards, *Posters of the First World War* (London: Evelyn, Adams & Mackay, 1968). Dartmouth College has an extensive collection of posters from both world wars and from other twentieth-century conflicts. See "On All Fronts: Posters from the World Wars in the Dartmouth Collection," 30 March 1999 to 4 July 1999, Hood Museum of Art, Dartmouth College, Hanover, New Hampshire.

23. See, for instance, the interim "Report of the Work Accomplished by the Division of Pictorial Publicity." The report, signed by Charles Dana Gibson, chairman of the division, documents the division's work from 1 October 1917 to 1 March 1918. Committee on Public Information, RG 63, 1-A5, box 35, folder 12.

24. See Committee on Public Information, RG 63, 1-C5, box 47, for the whole series of the *Bulletin for Cartoonists.* The bulletins cited here appeared on the following dates: no. 1, 7 June 1918; no. 2, 14 June 1918; no. 3, 21 June 1918; no. 4, 29 June 1918; no. 5, 6 July 1918; no. 6, 13 July 1918; no. 7, 20 July 1918; no. 8, 28 July 1918; no. 9, 3 August 1918; no. 10, 10 August 1918; no. 11, 24 August 1918; no. 12, 31 August 1918; no. 13, 7 September 1918; no. 14, 14 September 1918; no. 15, 21 September 1918; no. 19, 19 October 1918; no. 20, 26 October 1918; and no. 23, 16 November 1918. The estimates cited for First World War casualties are from Spencer C. Tucker, *The European Powers in the First World War, An Encyclopedia* (New York: Garland Publishing, 1996), 173.

25. See in particular the Butterfield Syndicate's collection of Macauley's work, "America's Spirit in the War." Committee on Public Information, RG 63, 1-A5, box 33, folder 5. The Butterfield Syndicate, located in New York City, offered five Macauley cartoons a week to newspapers across the country for whatever price the papers wished to pay. In his cover letter to potential subscribers, the president of the syndicate, Henry Butterfield, praised Macauley's "extraordinary ability to picture the moving impulses of national thoughts and deeds, to strip false ideals and show them in their naked hideousness, to glorify the truth and uphold a righteous cause." Ibid., n.d.

26. Bulletin no. 25 appeared on 30 November 1918.

27. See the assessment of the impact of cartoons on public affairs by Isabel Simeral Johnson, "Cartoons," *Public Opinion Quarterly* (July 1937), 21–44. She says in conclusion:

Today is the day of the picture. The public has neither time nor wish for the great editorials which formerly did so much to mould pictorial history. The cartoonist, no longer just a commentator on the passing show, has become an editorial writer who produces a leading article in the form of a picture. At his best, the contemporary cartoonist is an intellectual writer with something of the prophet, the philosopher as well as the humanist, in his make-up. He is quick to gather ideas and to concentrate them into a form immediately transferable to the reader who runs. (44)

28. This section draws largely on George Creel's account in *How We Advertised America*, 117–132, and on James R. Mock and Cedric Larson's treatment in *Words That Won the War*, 131–153.

29. Committee on Public Information, RG 63, 1-A5, box 34, folder 6.

30. George Creel from W. H. Johns, 22 November 1917. G. Creel to W. H. Johns, 21 December 1917, Committee on Public Information, RG 63, 1-A4, box 37, folder 4. In his letter to Johns, Creel says that the CPI had already had offers of help from seven other advertising associations.

31. In a letter to W. C. Freeman, general manager of *Advertising News*, Carl Byoir complained about an editorial attack on George Creel that had appeared in *Freeman's Journal*. Apparently, the editorial had charged Creel with putting himself forward, as usual, at the expense of the advertising profession. After indicating that he had read the editorial "with a feeling closely akin to nausea," Byoir writes that

> If there is one group of men in America in relation to whose work Mr. Creel has demonstrated not alone competence, but a broad visioned comprehension of the possibilities of their profession in helping to win the war, it is the advertising men. If there is one group of men in America who ought to be appreciative of the work of the Committee on Public Information, it is the advertising men. . . . In organizing his Division of Advertising, [Creel] displayed an absolute lack of that desire to thrust himself forward with which your editor charges him, and instead of appointing men toward whom he might have personal leanings, he democratically deferred to the opinion of the advertising profession and appointed men whom they themselves had chosen as their leaders. . . . As an advertising man I do feel very deeply that the editor of a magazine reflecting the thought and opinion of that great profession, has done a very mean and bitter thing in writing such an editorial without one word of acknowledgement of Mr. Creel's unselfish aid to advertising men in war-time.

Committee on Public Information, RG 63, 1-A4, box 30, folder 10. The letter is uncharacteristically sharp for Byoir, whose correspondence is generally marked with a remarkable evenness. The letter is perhaps best read not just as Byoir's defense of Creel, but as Byoir's self-defense vis-à-vis an important occupational reference group.

32. The AAAA had itself just been formed on 4 June 1917. According to Richard Turnbull, a senior vice president of the AAAA, the organization was the final product of at least six efforts to organize the advertising agency business nationally. See Turnbull, "Genesis of the American Association of Advertising Agencies" 1969, located in the library of the AAAA, New York. The national efforts were: the Advertising Agents Convention (1873), the

Association of General Newspaper Agents (1885), the Association of Advertising Agents (1896), the American Advertising Agents Association (1900), the National Association of General Advertising Agents (1912), and the Affiliated Association of Advertising Agents (1916). The last, Turnbull tells us in his introduction, "resulted in a loose amalgamation of regional or local groups, which led directly to [the] creation of the AAAA a year later." The key local group was the Association of New York Advertising Agents, which had its first recorded meeting on 16 March 1911. This group established a committee to work toward a national association, a committee that included among its members Frank Presbrey, who wrote the important book on advertising cited earlier, and W. H. Johns. Only a few weeks after the New York association began, Johns was elected chairman of the organization. Turnbull's account is based on surviving AAAA records. He also utilized the careful work of Roger H. Clapp, "Prelude to the Four A's: The Development of Advertising Agency Associations in the United States 1865–1917" (bachelor's thesis, Amherst College, 1954).

33. Illustrated materials on all of the campaigns cited are in Committee on Public Information, RG 63, 1-A5, box 40, folder 5.

34. Johns made the remark in a report to the executive board of the AAAA, of which, as noted in the text, he was also the president. The remark is cited in an unpublished report by Richard Turnbull, "Marshaling the Forces of Advertising in the National Interest, 1917–1920" 1969. The sentiment seems to have been widely shared among the top echelons of the AAAA. As James O'Shaughnessy, the organization's executive secretary, wrote in a memorandum to all members:

> The advertising agencies are to be put to the test. This is their golden opportunity of proving to the government at Washington and to the people of the United States the value of advertising and the importance of advertising agency service to the government and to the people and particularly at this time of winning the war.

Bulletin 6, 24 December 1917, 2. These materials are in the AAAA Library, New York City.

35. Turnbull, who, as mentioned above, later became a senior vice president of the AAAA and a student of the organization's history, was then the very young assistant treasurer of the Advertising Agencies Corporation. He was present at its demise and undoubtedly heard all extant stories about the Division of Advertising from his senior colleagues. He seems to be the only advertising insider explicitly to link the CPI's advertising efforts in the Great War with parallel developments during the Second World War.

36. See Turnbull, "Marshaling the Forces of Advertising in the National Interest." Turnbull says, "In its purpose and functioning, the Division of Advertising was the World War I counterpart of the War Advertising Council (later renamed the Advertising Council) of the Second World War." James W. Young of J. Walter Thompson, the man usually credited with inventing the idea for the Advertising Council, exchanged letters with Carl Byoir dur-

ing the Great War. Byoir had invited Young to join the CPI, a proposition that greatly interested Young. Byoir wanted him to go to France, but they also discussed the possibility of Young coming to Washington to work for the CPI without severing his business connections. As it happened, Young withdrew owing to business pressures.

37. The early master of placing news was Ivy Lee, whom the Rockefeller family hired away from the troubled Pennsylvania Railroad after the massacre of striking workers and families at Ludlow, Colorado, in 1914. See Hiebert, *Courtier to the Crowd.* Lee knew that public prominence always commands newspaper ink, and he encouraged his clients to be frank and direct. See Ivy L. Lee, *The Problem of International Propaganda, A New Technique Necessary in Developing Understanding between Nations,* Occasional Papers, no. 3 ([New York]: n.p., 1934).

38. Consider, for instance, the uproar that ensued when a visiting Englishman named H. Val Fisher gave an address to the AAAA, later published as a full-page advertisement in the leading newspapers of sixteen cities and circulated in one of the house newsletters of the William H. Rankin Company. Fisher's published talk gave the brief, but frank, appraisal: "No nation stands to gain so much commercially from the war as does America." The executive board of the CPI's Division of Advertising had approved the text of the advertisement. After it was published, Carl Byoir wrote to Rankin, his close professional associate and personal friend, admonishing him for letting the lines get past him. Rankin's response suggests both how taken for granted Fisher's appraisal was among men of affairs and how well Rankin understood the CPI's larger purposes:

> Frankly, the two lines that you quote — 'no nation stands to gain so much commercially from the war as does America' — made no impression on me whatever, and I did not know they were in Mr. Fisher's address. . . . It could have been an easy matter to have cut those two lines out, and, if I had had the same thought regarding those two lines that you have, I would have cut them out. But, frankly, I think those two lines are the truth. . . . [Still] I will take it upon myself to tip Val Fisher off to the fact that it would be a good idea in his future talks not to mention the fact . . . that no nation stands to gain so much commercially from the war as does America. While that is true, yet I agree with you that we do not want to advertise the fact.

William Rankin to Carl Byoir, 21 September 1918. Committee on Public Information, RG 63, 1-A4, box 32, folder 1.

39. Carl Byoir, lecture, 7 October 1935, "Influencing Public Opinion," Army War College Curricular Archives, U.S. Army Military History Institute, Carlisle Barracks, Penn., 3.

40. Committee on Public Information, RG 63, 1-A4, box 32, folder 3.

41. Committee on Public Information, RG 63, 1-A5, box 42, folder 5. The bulletins for the Speaking Division drew on other CPI publications but

framed the issues in the florid language to which the Chautauqua audiences were accustomed. Bulletin no. 2 (January 1918), for instance, suggests some themes for those speaking on the origins of the war:

> All the world is at war with Germany, since Germany makes war on all the world. Germany defies all the world. Germany would master the world. Germany would sack the whole world. Germany so declares. Germany provoked war—We held our peace. Germany invaded Belgium. We held our peace. . . . Germany slew women and children. We held our peace. . . . Germany murdered our citizens. We choked down our wrath . . . . Germany broke solemn promises—We clung to shattered faith. . . . Germany—at length loosed war on us and on all neutrals. Then we saw the only way out was to go through. Beset by war—the United States fights for world peace.

It goes on to suggest similar language for other themes, such as "The Cause at Stake":

> This is the world war; other wars were waged—
>
>> By one prince upon another.
>> By one kingdom upon another.
>> By one coalition upon another.
>> Now Germany setting itself against the world
>> Involves all mankind in the world war.
>> Germany believes with all its strength—
>> In the survival of the fittest.
>> In the conflict of raw forces.
>> In warfare as the supreme test.
>> In Germany's power to prevail.
>
> So Germany challenges all the world.
>
> If Germany is right—
>
>> Other governments must fall.
>> Other civilizations must go under.
>> Other ideas must be cast aside. . . .
>> The people exist for the State.
>> The subject lives by the king's sufferance.
>> Might alone measures right. . . .
>> Frightfulness is sound policy.
>> Mercy is sinful folly.
>> Clemency is silly sentiment.
>> Democracy is an idle dream.
>> The strong shall trample on the weak. . . .
>> All we hold dear is wrong. . . .
>
> It is Germany against civilization.

42. The Four Minute Men, Bulletin no. 22 (28 January 1918). Committee on Public Information, RG 63, 11A-A1, box 131.

43. The Four Minute Men, Bulletin no. 29 (6 April 1918). Committee on Public Information, RG 63, 11A-A1, box 131.

44. Committee on Public Information, RG 63, 1-A5, box 33, folder 5.

45. Matlack Price and Horace Brown, *How to Put in Patriotic Posters the Stuff That Makes People STOP—LOOK—ACT!* (Washington, D.C.: National Committee of Patriotic Societies, 1918). See also Committee on Public Information, RG 63, 1-A5, box 35, folder 12. Matlack Price was the author of another book on posters; Horace Brown was a member of the National Committee of Patriotic Societies.

46. Committee on Public Information, RG 63, 14-A1, box 232. Carl E. Walberg, the Washington representative of the Division of Advertising, wrote the proposal. The proposal is undated, although an internal reference suggests that it was written in early fall 1918 since the proposal anticipates a full-scale drive in late October.

47. See "Plan to Enlist Employers and Employees, Engaged in Essential War Industries, in a 'Victory Army of Workers' by Stimulating and Encouraging Production." Committee on Public Information, RG 63, 1-A4, box 31, folder 31. In the copy in the records, the word "Workers" is crossed out and the word "Industry" written in. The document is undated but accompanied by two sets of handwritten notes to Carl Byoir from a "Hanahan," whose identity is unknown. One of the notes is dated 23 May 1918. The document proposes a scheme to "bring home to the worker himself the direct connection of the work he performs at home with the man on the firing line. . . ." It envisions the cooperation of all the divisions of the CPI to be engaged in the YMCA effort noted in the text, except the Division of News.

48. Advertising and selling plan, "The Liberty War Loan," 3 May 1917, The National Advertising Agency Board, New York.

49. Byoir, "Influencing Public Opinion," 10–11.

50. American Alliance for Labor and Democracy, report, "What Can Your Local Branch Do?" Committee on Public Information, RG 63, 1-A5, box 33, folder 2.

51. American Alliance for Labor and Democracy, "Loyalty Leaflets no. 2," n.d., Committee on Public Information, RG 63, 1-A5, box 33.

52. See, for instance, the correspondence to the CPI from Houstus L. Gaddis, service director of the Great Lakes Engineering Works in Detroit of 31 January 1918, Committee on Public Information, RG 63, 1-A4, box 30, folder 5. See also the article "When the War Will End! A Prediction Based on Incontrovertible Facts" in the *Brooklyn Eagle* of 27 June 1918 by Eugene V. Brewster, the managing editor of the *Motion Picture Magazine* and *Motion Picture Classic,* and the complimentary letter to him from Carl Byoir of 3 July 1918. Committee on Public Information, RG 63, 1-A4, box 30, folder 13. Brewster predicted that the war would end in six years or six months, depending on the extent to which the American public became involved in the war effort.

53. Clarence Howard's letter to Commonwealth Steel Company employ-

ees is in Committee on Public Information, RG 63, 1-A4, box 30, folder 7. Howard's later letter to other companies and the correspondence with Byoir about the responses he received are in RG 63, 1-A4, box 31, folder 11. At one point, H. C. Belville, Howard's assistant president, got into the act as the recipient of replies to Howard's letter. Some of these suggest that the men at Commonwealth did not know quite how to proceed with the flow of ideas from fellow businessmen that their letter had stimulated. The 11 July 1918 correspondence from L. M. Fessenden of Valley Falls, R.I., to Belville illustrates the point. Fessenden asks where is the CPI response to the idea of initiating a Campaign of Education of Employees along Patriotic Lines. RG 63, A4, box 30, folder 7.

54. Mock and Larson, *Words That Won the War,* 187–212.

55. The CPI helped establish loyalty leagues with every group of foreign-born nationals of European extraction. So Swedish Americans formed the John Ericsson League of Patriotic Service; Danish Americans established the Jacob A. Riis League of Patriotic Service; Finnish Americans began the Lincoln Loyalty League; Italian Americans started the Roman Legion; Hungarian Americans had the American-Hungarian Loyalty League, and so on. The most important group was the American Friends of German Democracy, the target of a great deal of controversy, which the CPI backed after extensive investigation. In May 1918, the CPI established the Division of Work Among the Foreign-Born in order to work more directly with these publics. See George Creel's account in *How We Advertised America,* 184–199.

56. For a brief account of Byoir's work with the League of Oppressed Nations, see Robert James Bennett, "Carl Byoir: Public Relations Pioneer," 55–56. Bennett's account is based on an interview with Elsie Sobotka, Byoir's longtime secretary. Robert Jackall heard essentially the same account from George Hammond, Byoir's longtime business associate, in an interview at Mr. Hammond's home in Mystic, Connecticut, on 15 August 1991. Mr. Hammond also provided the original program for the fête at Carnegie Hall held on Sunday, 15 September 1918. Wilson's speech at Mount Vernon is reported in the *New York Times,* 5 July 1918.

57. See letter dated 1 July 1918 from F. Carey of *The Daily States* of New Orleans to George Creel. Byoir responded favorably to Carey on 19 July. Carey had also suggested "organizing a league to be on a lookout for these 'mongers' and report them so they may be sent a personal letter warning them of the harm they are doing." Committee on Public Information, RG 63, 1-A4, box 30, folder 17.

58. Private Harry Rubinstein of the 11th Company, 3d Battalion, Camp Upton, 3 June 1918, Committee on Public Information, RG 63, 1-A4, box 32, folder 3.

59. Charles D. Isaacson, "Giving the National Anthem a New Meaning," *The Globe and Commercial Advertiser,* n.d. This newspaper article was sent to the CPI, along with a letter suggesting national adoption of the idea. Byoir wrote back on 8 April 1918, commending him on the idea. Committee on Public Information, RG 63, 1-A4, box 32.

60. George M. Rittelmeyer of Jackson, Mississippi, to the CPI, Committee on Public Information, RG 63, 1-A4, box 32, folder 3.

61. Letter to George Creel from an official of the United Service Selling Company of Cleveland, Ohio, identity of author unknown, 28 June 1918, Committee on Public Information, RG 63, 1-A4, box 32, folder 6.

62. Jno. S. Tolverson, president of the First National Bank in Fulda, Minnesota, to Charles W. Henke, publicity director of the commission of public safety in St. Paul, Minnesota, 17 April 1918. Henke's organization was apparently one of the many distributors of the CPI's published material; Tolverson wrote to him about getting more copies of pamphlets on German propaganda. Henke sent a copy of the letter to the CPI. Committee on Public Information, RG 63, 1-A4, box 32, folder 7.

63. Letter to the CPI from officials of the Citizens Patriotic League of Covington, Kentucky, 1 April 1918. Committee on Public Information, RG 63, 1-A4, box 30, folder 6.

64. Letter of O. F. Frisbie of Yukon, Oklahoma, to Newton Baker, secretary of war, 18 April 1918. Baker responded with a polite acknowledgement of the suggestion. The correspondence was then sent privately to the CPI, probably because Frisbie's letter to Baker was accompanied by a copy of a letter that Frisbie had written to W. I. Thomas, the well-known sociologist at the University of Chicago, in response to a newspaper article written by Thomas that questioned aspects of the war. Frisbie's letter reads in part:

We have had so far to contend with the dynamiter, the fire-bug, the poisoner—but just now is the beginning *[sic]* to come to light the class of traitor more awful than the worst Pro-German, if you please, the worst Hun, including the Kaiser himself, if such is possible. A miscarriage of nature, in the form of a man, who fails to hold even more sacred, than the honor of his own mother, and his own sister; the sanctity of a soldier's home and the honor of his dependents. . . . To my mind there could only be one punishment sufficient for this crime, and it falls far short of what you have deserved. To take your life in retribution for the wrong you have done, would be entirely inadequate. Every traitor of your class should be by a National Law brought under a surgeon's knife, and in addition your face adequately marked to identify you for all time to every eye that is cast upon you. If you miss this punishment, it will be through a miscarriage of justice.

Such primitive nativism was fairly widespread. Committee on Public Information, RG 63, 1-A4, box 32.

65. The sentiments in Biggers's speech bear some reflection since they suggest in popular form fundamental tensions in American society between the ascetic self-rationalization demanded by the exigencies of ambition or duty and the longing for and sometimes the pursuit of sybarite pleasure. "Young Jimmy Gerson" says to his grandfather the following:

I tell you, we need this war. If we'd stood aside and not got into it, we'd have become the greatest nation of softies that ever sat down to a hearty meal. We were heading that way. Who reads books any way? Nobody—we crowded into movie theaters and dulled our wits with the childish stuff. Who stayed at home and talked things over? No-body—we piled into the car and hit the high spots. Who had time to think about life? Not a soul—we were due for a fox trot at a road house. We were pleasure mad. We'd forgot how to live.

Both the Worchester Chamber of Commerce poster and its accompanying correspondence and the text of Biggers's speech are in Committee on Public Information, RG 63, 1-A4, box 30, folder 18.

66. Committee on Public Information, RG 63, 1-A4, box 30, folder 18.

67. For a general overview of propaganda in Britain during World War I, see Cate Haste, *Keep the Home Fires Burning: Propaganda in the First World War* (London: Allen Lane, 1977). The most important documentary source for British propaganda, commissioned by Lord Asquith in December 1914,was the notorious *Report of the Committee on Alleged German Outrages Appointed by His Majesty's Government and Presided over by the Right Hon. Viscount Bryce* (London: H. M. Stationary Office, 1915). Bryce's report promulgated reports of public rapes, mutilation, and torture. It was based on unsworn, anonymous depositions from about 1,200 Belgian refugees and a few British soldiers; the depositions later disappeared without a trace. Subsequent investigations failed to corroborate any major allegation in the Bryce report. See James Morgan Read, *Atrocity Propaganda, 1914–1919* (New Haven: Yale University Press; London, H. Milford, Oxford University Press, 1941), 200–201. Read is quick to add that actual atrocities did occur, including "extreme ruthless-ness" toward civilians. But the Allies as well as the Germans were guilty of such depredations. Read, 285–286.

68. Byoir, "Influencing Public Opinion," 6.

69. Lewis was assistant superintendent of the documents room at the U.S. House of Representatives. Byoir's letter to him is dated 17 April 1918. Committee on Public Information, RG 63, 1-A4, box 31, folder 31.

70. Byoir wrote to Bliven on other CPI business on 9 July 1918 and en-closed a copy of a speech that he had given to the new Washington Ad-vertising Club. Byoir made the remark cited in the text in reference to that talk.

71. See the correspondence between Byoir and Raymond Ahearn, Eigh-teenth Company, First Officer Regiment, Camp Johnson, Florida, 14 July 1918 and Byoir's subsequent letter to the commanding officer of Camp John-son, Committee on Public Information, RG 63, 1-A4, box 30, folder 4. See also the correspondence between Byoir and John Cavanaugh of Des Moines, Iowa, about one Don Shaw's application for work in the judge advocate's office.

72. William Magill to the CPI, 8 May 1918, Committee on Public Infor-

mation, RG 63, 1-A5, box 32, folder 5. See the letter to Byoir from [P.] L. Atkinson of 6 June 1918. Atkinson was then working at *Cosmopolitan Magazine,* Byoir's former employer. Committee on Public Information, RG 63, 1-A4, box 30, folder 4.

73. The correspondence of H. D. Cullen of Atlanta and George Creel illustrates the point. On 7 April 1918 Cullen wrote asking for a job at expenses, citing his seven years of advertising experience. Byoir wrote back on 3 May 1918 saying that "We have had to make it a rule not to employ any salaried men. . . . [We are] already in a situation where we have dozens of applications on file from those who are in the fortunate position where they can offer their services to the government without remuneration." The story had a happy ending. Cullen wrote back to Byoir on 13 May 1918 telling him that he had just been made state secretary of the Four Minute Men. Committee on Public Information, RG 63, 1-A4, box 30, folder 23.

74. The correspondence between Byoir and Rankin is in Committee on Public Information, RG 63, 1-A4, box 32, folder 1. Rankin was the leading advocate of Chicago advertising. On 20 December 1917, he wired Byoir: "Board as now constituted entirely New York and you know Chicago is advertising center for newspapers of country while New York is magazine center. . . ." On 21 December, he writes:

> However, the one big thing—and I can see that you have it in mind too—is not to have the Chicago men feel that New York men dominate in Washington advertising. As a matter of fact, the Chicago men have led the way in every movement and in nearly every plan where advertising has been used to benefit the Government.

On 23 December in a handwritten note, he submits a request for his appointment: "Have me appointed on the Board—before 31st if you can. Then also have me appointed Special Advisory Counsel, Bureau of Public Information, Chicago—on all subjects—you know that is what I have [wanted] ever since you & I met." On 7 January he writes again suggesting the composition of the board and also urging Byoir to establish a new division, called the Board of Federal Co-operation, with Rankin as chair, to act as liaison between the government and the media. At this point, Rankin's ambitions seem to be focused on both goals. On 8 January Rankin writes to suggest that Cusack might not take a position on the board even if one is offered since Cusack's Washington friends in outdoor advertising were pushing for a separate organization. Rankin also suggests Alfred Mace of the National Biscuit Company as an alternative to Cusack. On 14 February in a handwritten note, Rankin returns to this theme, once again pushing Mace:

> Another thing—Mace, Adv Mgr of the National Biscuit Company is the man for the place—instead of Dobbs of Atlanta. If Mace will not take it, then get a Chicago man. The Chicago Adv. Club feels it is direct[ed] at 'Chicago' by NY men when they do not have an advertiser from Chicago on the Board—It so happens that Johns, Jones, Harn,

Houston are all considered Eastern men [and] that's the way the As-so[ciated] Ad Clubs have been run by Dobbs-Houston-D'Arcy-Harn.

He adds that "I wish you could also take the trouble to write C. H. Burlin-game that I am not *purposely* left off the Board—but you had a bigger job in mind for me which was offered but I could not accept. It will help the Chi-cago *spirit*. . . . "But that week, Jesse Neal's appointment to the board was announced, and Rankin wrote to Byoir on 23 February with evident dis-appointment:

> You know I have been patient and have awaited many Wednesdays and other days, also Thos. Cusack, et al., but when the papers came out this week with Neal's appointment and not mine, I thought, well, after all, is it worth while? I know you will have a good excuse, but it does seem to me that you could have sent my name out first. . . .
>
> Were it not for the fact that some of my friends feel that the New York men have been given preference over Chicago men, who really had the ability and did the work, I would not bother you at all. The Chicago Advertising Club too feels that Chicago has been overlooked.
>
> You know I have made good every promise I have made to you and I want you now to make good on your promises to me. I know you want to make an offer to me that is better than just a member of the Division of Advertising, but let's forget that for the present—that can come later.

But, as it happens, it never did. Despite his disappointment at not getting the job he wanted, Rankin seems to have remained irrepressible. He did a great deal of work to make the war exposition in Chicago the huge success it was, and Byoir wrote him on 12 July 1918 that "I want to thank you for all you have done in connection with the Allied War Exposition. You put me under obligation so often that I do not know how I will ever be able to repay you." Byoir's note may be the main clue to understanding Rankin's character and the reason why the latter was shut out of the inner circle of advertising men in the CPI during the war. He was a man of great energy, drive, and vitality who obligated others to himself with sheer virtuosity and relentlessness. Not everyone appreciates such personal qualities and habits of mind.

75. The whole correspondence between Creel and Cusack, Byoir and Cusack, and various third parties and Creel are located in Committee on Public Information, RG 63, 1-A4, box 30, folder 24. Of particular interest is the incident of the missed meeting between Byoir and Cusack. On 13 Feb-ruary 1918 Creel had wired Cusack to ask him to meet Byoir in New York on the Friday of that week. (Byoir went to New York every Friday, stayed at the Vanderbilt Hotel, and conducted CPI business there.) Cusack wrote back to Creel on 25 February describing what happened:

> I received a wire from you on the 13th of this month, asking if it would be possible for me to meet Mr. Carl Byoir in New York on Friday. I wired you that I would be in New York all week, and afterwards

wired you that you could inform me at what time Mr. Byoir desired to see me.

On receipt of the latter wire, you wired me that Mr. Byoir would be at the Vanderbilt Hotel. As I stop there when in New York, I left my card in Mr. Byoir's box a week ago last Friday. The next day Mr. Byoir left his card in my box. I called up Mr. Byoir's room but he was not in.

I cannot understand this action. I only left the Vanderbilt Hotel last Friday afternoon. I have been there, and at my office at the Flat Iron Building, which has not been visited by Mr. Byoir. I do not know what you wished Mr. Byoir to see me about. On the whole the action is, to my mind, rather odd. . . .

. . . I have been asked by you to serve on the committee on Advertising for the Government, and acquiesced in this after urgent solicitation by Mr. D'Arcy and others.

For some reason the Committee appointment was then immediately held up until Mr. Byoir could interview me. Mr. Byoir evidently thought it was not important enough to interview me about.

Will you be kind enough to explain what this all means. I have not sought the position on this Committee, and acquiesced to it only after urgent solicitation of members of our committee, and by those interested in the Government work.

There followed a flurry of wires and letters until the matter was resolved with Cusack's formal appointment on 22 March 1918.

76. The record of disillusionment in the aftermath of the Great War is vast. To take only a few examples, see Robert Graves, *Goodbye to All That: An Autobiography* (London: Jonathan Cape, 1929), C. E. Montague, *Disenchantment* (London: Chatto & Windus, 1922), and Walter Lippmann, *The Phantom Public* (New York: Harcourt, Brace and Company, 1925). Although it is not entirely accurate to speak of disillusionment in the case of Arthur Ponsonby since he was a dissenter during the war, his *Falsehood in Wartime* (London: G. Allen & Unwin, 1931) was an important document exposing the flimsiness of many wartime distortions. See also Paul Fussell, *The Great War and Modern Memory* (New York: Oxford University Press, 1975). Disillusionment among the Germans was, if anything, even more profound. For only two graphic examples, see the postwar drawings, watercolors, and prints of George Grosz in *The Berlin of George Grosz: Drawings, Watercolours, and Prints, 1912–1930* (London: Royal Academy of Arts, 1997) and George Grosz, *Ecce Homo* (New York: Brussel & Brussel, 1965). See also George Grosz, *Ein kleines Ja und ein grosses Nein*, translated by Arnold J. Pomerans as *The Autobiography of George Grosz: A Small Yes and a Big No* (London and New York: Allison & Busby, 1982).

77. See, for example, Harry Reichenbach, *Phantom Fame*, 240.

78. Creel quotes Wilson as saying, as the two were crossing the Atlantic to the Paris conference:

It is a great thing that you have done, but I am wondering if you have not unconsciously spun a net for me from which there is no escape.

It is to America that the whole world turns today, not only with its wrongs, but with its hopes and grievances. The hungry expect us to feed them, the roofless look to us for shelter, the sick of heart and body depend upon us for cure. All of these expectations have in them the quality of terrible urgency. There must be no delay. It has been so always. People will endure their tyrants for years, but they tear their deliverers to pieces if a millennium is not created immediately. . . . What I seem to see—with all my heart I hope that I am wrong—is a tragedy of disappointment.

Creel, *Rebel at Large,* 206.

79. See, for instance, Edward L. Bernays's book *Propaganda* (New York: H. Liveright, 1928), especially 27–28. Bernays writes:

It was, of course, the astounding success of propaganda during the war that opened the eyes of the intelligent few in all departments of life to the possibilities of regimenting the public mind. . . . [T]he manipulation of patriotic opinion made use of the mental cliches and the emotional habits of the public to produce mass reactions against the alleged atrocities, the terror and the tyranny of the enemy. It was only natural, after the war ended, that intelligent persons should ask themselves whether it was not possible to apply a similar technique to the problems of peace.

CHAPTER TWO: PUBLIC RELATIONS FOR ADVERTISING

1. For this account of the origins of the Advertising Council, we have relied extensively on Harold B. Thomas, "The Background and Beginning of The Advertising Council," (New York: Advertising Council files, 1 April 1952 [retyped February 1983], 42 pages), 1. Thomas's manuscript seems to be the only extant, detailed, firsthand account of the origins of the Advertising Council. According to the council meeting minutes of 19 April 1945, another manuscript on the council's history had been written by one Shelley Thomas (no apparent relation to Harold B. Thomas) who, it seems, submitted the book to the University of Chicago Press, which rejected it. The council's board then toyed with the idea of having Shelley Thomas's book rewritten by a professional writer, but nothing came of this despite much discussion. A survey of some of the same early materials that we utilize in this account, together with accounts of some of the council's early campaigns can be found in Maurice I. Mandell, "A History of The Advertising Council" (Ph.D. diss., Indiana University, 1953). To our knowledge, Mandell's work was also not published.

Harold B. Thomas was a widely experienced businessman and president of the Centaur Company in 1941 when the events that he describes took place. At that time he was also the former chairman of the Advertising Research Foundation and of the Association of National Advertisers. At the formal establishment of the Advertising Council on 4 March 1942, he became the first vice chairman of the organization as a representative of advertisers (that is, the clients of advertising agencies). According to the council's minutes, he very rarely missed the regular (usually weekly, sometimes daily) council meetings in its early months and missed only occasional meetings later in the war years. When the chairman of the council, Chester J. La-Roche, withdrew from his post for health reasons, Thomas, as vice chairman, presided over all the council meetings from 29 October 1943, until the meeting of 26 May 1944, when he was elected chairman, a post that he retained until 9 March 1945, when he stepped down and was replaced by James W. Young. Thomas remained on the board of directors of the organization for more than twenty years after this.

The official archives for The Advertising Council, Inc., the legal name of the organization, are located at the University of Illinois, Urbana-Champaign, in the University of Illinois Archives, Advertising Collections as the Advertising Council Archives (<www.library.uiuc.edu/ahx/adcouncil>). However, between 1987 and 1989, we found all of the primary materials cited in this chapter in the files of The Advertising Council, Inc., 261 Madison Avenue, New York, New York, in the organization's library, in loose-leaf binders containing minutes of meetings arranged chronologically, and in a collection that Advertising Council staff referred to as "archives." By summer 1999, most of the materials that we examined had been transferred to the University of Illinois, with the remainder to follow shortly, organized according to the university's particular system of archival arrangement and description. In our citations, we use the simple notation "Advertising Council files" to refer to materials that we examined in New York City. Our thanks to the staff of the Advertising Council for their patience and assistance during our research. Special thanks to F. Bradley Lynch and Paula Veale for providing us with some hard-to-find materials.

For another account of the Advertising Council's founding, one much less detailed than Thomas's, see Raymond Rubicam, "Advertising," in *While You Were Gone: A Report on Wartime Life in the United States,* edited by Jack Goodman (New York: Simon & Schuster, 1946), 421–446. We have relied on Rubicam's essay for examples of advertising during the Second World War. Special thanks to Donna Vetere of The Young & Rubicam Corporate Library for helping us locate Rubicam's essay.

2. See Thomas, "Background and Beginning," 2. Thomas cites the last names of several authors who attack the business system although he does not include the titles of their books. He also gives the titles of some popular and scholarly works that he feels were important in creating an anti-business and anti-advertising atmosphere. Working from his list, one can piece together the works thought by businessmen and admen to be the most worrisome. Among others, he cites: Arthur Kallet, *Counterfeit—Not Your Money but What It Buys* (New York: The Vanguard Press, 1935); James Rorty, *Our Master's Voice, Advertising* (New York: The John Day Co., 1934); J. B. Matthews and R. E. Shallcross, *Partners in Plunder: The Cost of Business Dictatorship* (New York: Covici, Friede, 1935); and T. Swann Harding, *The Popular Practice of Fraud* (London, New York: Longmans, Green and Co., 1935).

3. Paul West, president of the Association of National Advertisers, wrote a memorandum on 28 August 1941, to members of related associations and to friends in the media, both of which depended on advertising. The memorandum suggests the gravity of the situation as perceived by many in business:

> Grave concern about advertising and what may happen to the business which is largely dependent on it is manifesting itself daily in many quarters. . . .
> There is good reason for this concern. The talk by high officials in government of curbing advertising as a means of controlling inflation and restricting it as a means of controlling production, the recent last-minute incorporation of a tax on radio and outdoor advertising and electric advertising signs and devices in the tax bill now before Congress, the thinly-veiled attacks on trademarks and brands, the push for mandatory standardization and government grade labeling of all consumer goods, the continued charges that advertising is waste, that it fosters a monopoly, that it is simply an added cost to the consumer—all these and more are causing growing alarm that advertising is going to be throttled by whatever method, for whatever purpose, and with whatever motive.

Thomas, "Background and Beginning," 3.

4. J. W. Young, "A Paper Delivered by James Webb Young Senior Consultant, J. Walter Thompson Company, before a joint meeting of the Association of National Advertisers, Inc., and American Association of Advertising Agencies at Hot Springs, Virginia," 14 November 1941 (New York: Association of National Advertisers, Inc.). Advertising Council files, retyped February 1982.

5. Young recounts the following story:

> In a meeting where I was discussing personnel for [a cultural relations project], there was present a certain distinguished former President of a great University. I mentioned the names of certain outstanding advertising men whose services I hoped to secure, and at this point this educator blew up. 'Surely,' he said, 'you recognize that advertising is a *declassé* profession. To put such men in charge of a cultural relations program would kill it at the start.'
> If you think that is an isolated case, I will give you another. Some time ago I was introduced to one of our leading scientists, whose specialty is the physiology of the nervous system and the brain. Having just tried to read one of his books, I said: 'Dr. Blank, perhaps it will surprise you to know that your last book is very helpful to an advertising man.' He looked at me over his glasses, and said: 'I am not only surprised; I am shocked. So far as I can see, there is no connection between brains and advertising.'

See Young, "Paper," 2–3.

6. Young, "Paper," 3–4.

7. Young, "Paper," 7–8.

8. Young, "Paper," 10.

9. Young, "Paper," 13.

10. Young, "Paper," 14–15.

11. Harold B. Thomas, "Background and Beginning," 10.

12. Thomas, "Background and Beginning," 16.

13. Thomas, "Background and Beginning," 19. Thomas's 1952 paper seems to have initiated the emphasis on noncommercial "public service advertising" as the core of the Advertising Council's organizational self-image, instead of a role as business's champion. Thomas quotes James Webb Young's famous 1941 speech faithfully and extensively, but, perhaps in light of how wartime events thrust a public service role on the fledging organization, he reverses Young's original emphases to lend them the weight of prophecy. Young had ended his speech with a call to arms to defend the business system. Thomas highlights instead Young's appeal to admen, given earlier in the speech, to do public service advertising, neglecting to mention that Young proposed the strategy principally as a way of countering charges of advertising's excessive vulgarity.

14. Thomas, "Background and Beginning," 20–26. LaRoche's memorandum reads in part:

> On November 14, at Hot Springs, members of the A.N.A., the A.A.A.A. and representatives of media assembled in the advertising industry's first joint meeting.
>
> At that meeting the need and wisdom became apparent for quickly organizing and putting into operation a representative advertising 'Council.' Definite plans were launched for a Council, which had several purposes and several objectives.
>
> On December 7, 1941, at Pearl Harbor, those purposes and objectives were abruptly changed. All others became completely submerged to the one objective of helping win this war. And the wisdom and need for the Council became more apparent, more vital, more immediate!
>
> Mr. Donald Nelson summed up the picture in an off-the-record talk with several people interested in the formation of a Council on December 15, substantially as follows:
>
> To win the war the total resources of the country must be mobilized into one great national unit. The central and primary purpose must be the production of war goods. Therefore, every industry which can be converted to production of the materials of war, will be. However, the need is recognized for preserving some foundation under the private enterprise structure, else, what are we fighting for?
>
> Mr. Nelson and other government officials recognize that a vitally necessary part of this gigantic job is a corresponding great job of public relations. 'This nation must be converted from peace-time habits and customs (luxuries, spendthrift attitudes, wastefulness, expectations

that anything can be replaced with something just-as-good or better) to an all-out war basis (conserve, scrimp, save and do without).'

The organized machinery of *advertising* is essential in getting this job done and the government has asked our cooperation toward that end.

See Thomas, "Background and Beginning," 21–22.

15. Minutes of meetings of the Advertising Council for 14, 15, and 22 January and 5 February 1942, Advertising Council files. The War Information Board (also known as the Committee of War Information) numbered among its other members John J. McCloy, then assistant secretary of war, and Adlai Stevenson of the navy department.

16. Discussion of all these projects runs through the minutes of all the early meetings of the council. But see in particular the minutes for 5 February 1942 and for 14 February 1942, Advertising Council files. Attached to the latter in the files is an unpublished document, marked "Confidential," entitled "Current Information Objectives and Proposed Programs" produced by the Office of Facts and Figures. The document works from President Roosevelt's famous "Four Freedoms" state of the union speech of 6 January 1942 and is divided into six sections: (1) "The Statement of Our Objectives and the Definition of Our Cause"; (2) "The Nature of the Conspiracy Against Us and Our Way of Life"; (3) "The Counter-Strategy of the United Nations"; (4) "The Production Program to Win the War and Win the Peace"; (5) "The Effect of the Production Program on Civilian Life"; (6) "The Fighting Job and the Task of Our Armed Forces." Each section provides an excerpt of the president's remarks and then shows how his comments must be made operational by the information services.

17. Paul West, secretary of the Advertising Council and president of the Association of National Advertisers (ANA), had a resolution to this effect passed by the board of directors of the ANA on 11 March 1942 and read into the record of the Advertising Council on 21 March 1942. Advertising Council files.

18. See "Words That Work for Victory: The Second Year of the War Advertising Council, March 1, 1943–March 1, 1944," 4. Advertising Council files. For the first eighteen months of its existence, the council went by the name Advertising Council. In May 1943, as explained later in the text, its leaders changed the organization's name to the War Advertising Council. After the war, the council reassumed its original name.

19. Raymond Rubicam, "Advertising," 423–425.

20. "Memorandum on the Work of the Advertising Council 1942–1943," noted "not for publication," 4–5. Advertising Council files.

21. "Ways to Show Your Colors: Tested Advertising Techniques that Help Win the War and Aid Your Product." No date, but mentioned in meeting minutes of 20 July 1944, n.p. Advertising Council files.

22. Ibid.

23. The link was sometimes explicitly stated. See, for instance, the

remarks made to the Advertising Council by Wroe Alderson of the Office of Price Administration on 17 July 1942. Speaking about the economic stabilization program, Alderson said that "The economic stabilization program lies squarely in the middle of today's merchandising picture so that every advertiser should be able to find a way of supporting the program which is at the same time good advertising for himself." "Some Observations Concerning Advertising," attached to minutes of 24 July 1942. Advertising Council files.

24. Supplement to meeting minutes of board of directors, War Advertising Council, 1 October 1943. Advertising Council files.

25. Minutes of War Advertising Council, 29 June 1945, 2. Advertising Council files.

26. See Rubicam, "Advertising," 429.

27. Rubicam, "Advertising," 438–439.

28. Minutes of 14 May 1943. The change of name had been debated for several weeks during the meetings of 9, 23, and 30 April. Advertising Council files.

29. "In the Wake of War: The Fourth Year of the Advertising Council, March 1, 1945 to March 1, 1946," 3. Advertising Council files.

30. The key figures of the early days (before 1950) of the Advertising Council were, among others, William Baker of Benton & Bowles, Frank Braucher of the Magazine Advertising Bureau, Louis Brockway of Young & Rubicam, Thomas D'Arcy Brophy of Kenyon & Eckhardt, Leo Burnett of Leo Burnett, William G. Chandler of Scripps-Howard Supply Company, Evans Clark of the Twentieth Century Fund and later of the *New York Times,* Fairfax Cone of Foote, Cone & Belding, Philip J. Everest of Transportation Displays, Edwin S. Friendly of the *New York World-Telegram and Sun,* Kerwin H. Fulton of Outdoor Advertising, Samuel C. Gale of General Mills, Frederic R. Gamble of the American Association of Advertising Agencies, Philip L. Graham of the *Washington Post* and *Times-Herald,* Arthur W. Kohler of Curtis Publishing, Chester J. LaRoche of C. J. LaRoche Co., Roy E. Larsen of *Time,* Henry G. Little of Campbell-Ewald, George P. Ludlam of the Advertising Council, Howard J. Morgens of Procter & Gamble, Charles G. Mortimer, Jr., of General Foods, Wesley I. Nunn of Standard Oil, Indiana, Stuart Peabody of the Borden Company, W. B. Potter of Eastman Kodak, William Reydel of Cunningham & Walsh, Burr L. Robbins of General Outdoor Advertising, Frank Stanton of Columbia Broadcasting System, John C. Sterling of *United Newspaper* magazine and later publisher of *This Week,* Harold B. Thomas of the Centaur Company among many other associations, Paul B. West of the Association of National Advertisers, Albert E. Winger of Crowell-Collier Publishing, James W. Young of J. Walter Thompson, and Theodore S. Repplier, who became the first president of the council and served the organization for twenty-two years in that capacity. Robert Keim, who succeeded Repplier as president, notes the clublike structure of the early council in an interview with F. Bradley Lynch, then public relations director of the Advertising Council, at Madison, Connecticut, 14 January 1991, 7. Advertising Council files. Also, George Ludlam, in an interview with F. Bradley Lynch on

28 January 1991 notes the clublike conviviality of the Advertising Council's monthly lunches, also in Advertising Council files. Our special thanks to Brad Lynch for providing us with transcripts of both interviews.

The Advertising Council held its widely enjoyed monthly lunches at the Waldorf-Astoria Hotel for most of its early years. Cost concerns prompted a review of matters in mid-1947, from which both the Waldorf, for the time being, and conviviality emerged triumphant. The minutes of 12 June 1947 report:

> Mr. Mortimer said that after comparing the luncheon costs at the Waldorf with those of other hotels, it was found that the Waldorf is not out of line. The only way to reduce the luncheon charges would be to eliminate the cocktails, he said.
>
> It was agreed to continue on the present basis.

Later, the council shifted its meetings to the Hotel Pierre where it met for many years.

31. T. S. Repplier to Harold B. Thomas, 24 July 1944, marked "Confidential." Advertising Council files.

32. See the minutes of the War Advertising Council for 27 July, 3 and 17 August, 29 September, and 6 October 1944. Of particular interest are the minutes for the meeting of 20 October 1944, which contain another memorandum by Repplier entitled "The Council Looks Ahead," discussed at some length in the minutes of the meeting of 27 October 1944. The council also produced a widely read pamphlet entitled "Are We Getting a Little Tired of the War?," mentioned in the minutes of 2 February 1945. Advertising Council files.

33. Minutes of the War Advertising Council for the meeting of 11 May 1945. Advertising Council files.

34. Minutes of the War Advertising Council for the meeting of 8 June 1945. Advertising Council files.

35. The council approved Young's plan by a vote of 22 ayes, 1 nay, and 3 unknown on 27 July 1945. Council staff had drafted the sales plan by the meeting of 10 August.

36. Minutes of War Advertising Council, 28 September 1945. Advertising Council files.

37. Young's speech to the AAAA is quoted in "In the Wake of War," 14. Advertising Council files.

38. War Advertising Council, "From War to Peace: The New Challenge to Business and Advertising," (New York: War Advertising Council, 1945), n.p. Advertising Council files.

39. Minutes of War Advertising Council, 26 October 1945, 3. The use of the council's new name commenced with the meeting of 2 November 1945. Advertising Council files.

40. In an effort to address the "crisis in education," the council became engaged in a campaign to improve the prestige of the teaching profession (explicitly excluding, however, direct advocacy of increased salaries for

teachers), a forerunner of a nearly identical campaign of the late 1980s. Minutes of the Advertising Council, 8 January 1947. Advertising Council files.

41. The Advertising Council, "Annual Report 1946–1947." Advertising Council files.

42. See Francis X. Sutton, Seymour E. Harris, Carl Kaysen, and James Tobin, *The American Business Creed* (New York: Schocken Books, 1962).

43. See the proposal to the Advertising Association of the West from the Advertising Council, late 1949. The proposal states: "Advertising is the only industry which has organized itself to combat the trend toward greater and greater centralization of authority in Washington," 2. Advertising Council files.

44. This consciousness of the plurality of official viewpoints runs through all the minutes of Advertising Council board meetings from the very beginning of the organization. It is articulated most explicitly by its longtime president, Theodore Repplier, in 1963:

> Ever since I first went to Washington in 1942, there have been periodic cries of alarm about Washington and advertising. In fact, I can scarcely recall a time when advertising men were not alarmed over potential threats of one kind or another, either in the form of bills introduced in Congress or actions in the Executive branch.
>
> To put these threats in proper perspective, it seems to me several things must be kept in mind.
>
> *First,* that Washington's view of advertising will pretty much reflect the country's view of advertising. Washington is grass roots gathered under the capitol dome. Washington intellectuals think pretty much like intellectuals in Cambridge, New Haven and Chicago; they will probably change their views at about the same time their peers elsewhere change theirs. And a Congressman from Pocatello reflects Pocatello. Washington is the United States in microcosm. *Second,* government is big, sprawling and unwieldy, with unbelievably bad communication between branches. There is no such thing as 'government opinion.' There is as much difference in the opinion climate of, say, the FBI and HEW as there is between the opinions of an Oklahoma millionaire and a New York social worker. *Third,* executive branch decisions are often made by little pockets of people, scattered here and there throughout a bewildering bureaucracy. While Secretary Hodges is out making a speech praising advertising to the skies, little groups in the Pentagon or Internal Revenue may be whetting their knives for it.
>
> Thus Washington's attitude toward advertising is not a homogeneous thing. It will probably average out at somewhere near what the country at large thinks. Until all segments of the country, particularly the eggheads, come to think advertising is perfect, there will be periodic moves against its alleged imperfections.

"Annual Report," 21 February 1963, 4. Advertising Council files.

45. "Outline of Proposed Business Conference," 4 November 1949. See

also "Report and Recommendations of the Policy Planning Committee," 10 July 1949, a report that seems to have been the substantive basis for the conference. Advertising Council files.

46. The Advisory Committee's first meeting was on 5 June 1946, and it met only a few times a year. According to the minutes of the first meeting, its chairman, Evans Clark, welcomed the members, describing the council's work as "the most powerful private medium for public enlightenment in the United States." Clark went on to stress "the great need for public under-standing of the complex issues that confront the nation" and said that the makeup of the committee was evidence of the council's determination that "no bias or self-interest poison this effort at enlightenment." Advertising Council files.

47. The way the council typically recruited prominent businessmen and -women into their activities is worth recounting. Consider an excerpt from a speech by Frank Abrams, chairman of Standard Oil of New Jersey:

> I want to tell you one thing which I never tire of telling. That is just how I came to 'get the call,' how I was converted to my interest in education. . . . I had an invitation from the head of the Advertising Council in the summer . . . of 1947. Would I come over to a luncheon that they were having at the Waldorf. They were having, all around the country, what they called 'The Crisis in Education' week. Here in New York they were very anxious to get a business man, the head of one of the large corporations, to participate. 'It needn't take much time. Come over for lunch. Only a 15-minute talk.' They would see that an appropriate one was written. . . .
>
> I went over to the luncheon . . . I felt maybe I should have spent a little more time on the speech myself. I got up and read my paper, after some really distinguished individuals had spoken. The meeting broke up and I folded up my speech and I put it back in my inside pocket. As I walked back to the office, I said, 'There, that's that. I hope they liked it and I hope it did some good.' I was through.
>
> . . . It seems to me that it was about 48 hours or less, I think less, when I got telephone calls from college presidents. Then they started to stop by at the office. Then letters and post cards came pouring in. One from a little teacher in Ohio, in the public school system; a let-ter from the president of Princeton; messages from colleges on the Pa-cific coast; requests for reprints of my talk. . . . Well, that's how I got religion.

Quoted in "Year End Report," by T. S. Repplier, 16 December 1954, 3–4. Advertising Council files.

48. The key First World War cases were *Schenck v United States*, 249 US 47, 39 S. Ct. 247, 63 L. Ed. 470 (1919); *Frohwerk v United States*, 249 US 204, 39 S. Ct. 249, 63 L. Ed. 561 (1919); *Debs v United States*, 249 US 211, 39 S. Ct. 252, 63 L. Ed. 561 (1919); and *Abrams v United States*, 250 US 616, 40 S. Ct. 17, 63, L. Ed. 1173 (1919). In these cases the Supreme Court, addressing for

the first time the content of the First Amendment's free speech clause, established that the right to free speech is not absolute but varies according to circumstances. *Schenck* upheld the constitutionality of the 1917 Espionage Act, which prohibited obstruction of military recruitment. The court affirmed the conviction of a Socialist Party official who had circulated a pamphlet encouraging draftees to resist conscription and to lobby the U.S. Congress in opposition to the process. The key cold war case was *Dennis v United States,* 341 US 494, 71 S. Ct. 857, 95 L. Ed. 1137 (1951). *Dennis* affirmed the convictions of eleven Communist Party officials in upholding the constitutionality of the 1940 Smith Act, which in part prohibited advocacy of the violent overthrow of the U.S. government, the organization of groups for that purpose, and knowing membership in such groups. For several years after *Dennis,* federal prosecutors across the country routinely used the Smith Act as a weapon to combat alleged Communist Party activity. See, for example, *Communist Party of the United States v Subversive Activities Control Bd.,* 367 US 1, 81 S. Ct. 1357, 6 L. Ed. 2d 625 (1961) and *Scales v United States,* 367 US 203, 81 S. Ct. 1469, 6 L. Ed. 2d 782 (1961); both cases were settled narrowly (five to four decisions). Our thanks to Duffy Graham for instructing us on these legal issues.

49. See the minutes from the Advertising Council's board of directors, 15 November 1946, when the project was originally proposed by Thomas D'Arcy Brophy, as well as those from the meeting of the Public Advisory Committee of 8 January 1947. Advertising Council files. See also Stuart Jon Little, "The Freedom Train and the Formation of National Political Culture" (master's thesis, University of Kansas, 1989), appendix three. Among the publications produced by the council were *Documents on the Freedom Train,* edited by Frank Monaghan (New York: n.p.), with 2 million copies distributed free, *Our American Heritage: Documents of Freedom* (New York: American Heritage Foundation), with 775,000 copies sold at twenty-five cents each), and *Good Citizen* (New York: American Heritage Foundation), with 1.5 million copies distributed free); see Little, "Freedom Train," 85–116. See also James Gregory Bradshaw, "Taking America's Heritage to the People: The Freedom Train Story," *Prologue* 17 (winter 1985).

50. The Advertising Council, Annual report, "What Helps People Helps Business, March 1947–March 1948," 13. Advertising Council files.

51. Frank Monaghan, *Heritage of Freedom; The History & Significance of the Basic Documents of American Liberty* (Princeton: Princeton University Press, 1947).

52. In early 1956, Theodore Repplier reported that the number of Ground Observer Corps volunteers had increased from 312,000 to 400,000, and the number of observation posts from 7,441 to 15,096. Meeting minutes of board of directors, 19 January 1956. Advertising Council files. Before the Advertising Council's involvement in the Ground Observer Corps, there were reported to be 150,000 volunteers. Of course, volunteers come and go. At least one major participant claims that total recruitment, that is, the number of volunteers who passed through the corps, was over one million

observers due to Advertising Council action. See F. Bradley Lynch, "The Bob Keim Interview," 9. Advertising Council files. However, one should approach all of these numbers with caution, since it seems that several posts reported exactly the same number of volunteers month after month, leading one to suspect that the reported numbers were a function of the corps's paramilitary bureaucratic structure rather than a report of actual recruitment. See John V. McGinnis, "The Advertising Council and the Cold War" (Ph.D. diss., Syracuse University, 1991), 139.

53. See Denys Volan, *The History of the Ground Observer Corps,* Air Defense Command Historical Study, no. 36 (n.p.: Hq. Air Defense Command, 1968), 165. Volan goes on to note that "[i]n 1952, when SKYWATCH began . . . [t]he amount of air traffic in the continental United States, though considerable, did not seem to be beyond the capacity of a motivated and well-manned network of observers. But, with the passage of time, air traffic increased greatly. . . . In fact, the military air defense system, though growing in capability, acknowledged its own incapacity to cope with the congested air traffic over the continental United States by creating more and more 'free areas' inside identification zones, where the calculated risk was taken that aircraft were friendly. This tendency reached its logical conclusion early in 1959 when the entire continental United States land mass was declared an open area," 171–172. See also McGinnis, "Cold War," chapters six and seven, for a briefer treatment.

54. Volan, *The History of the Ground Observer Corps,* 166.

55. Volan, *The History of the Ground Observer Corps,* 99, 111. For a similar campaign, see Guy Oakes, *The Imaginary War* (New York: Oxford University Press, 1994).

56. In early 1956, Major General Norris Harbold wrote to General Earle E. Partridge:

> These men [the Ground Observer Corps] are really selling the Air Force to civilian communities and to a great number of American families. The good public relations and the recruiting value to the Air Force is immense. In fact the returns to the Air Force from this may be greater in the long run than the accomplishment of the assigned mission.

Volan, *The History of the Ground Observer Corps,* 151.

57. Scare tactics permeated the whole campaign, beginning well before the Advertising Council's involvement in 1952. The most dramatic were the air force's drop of leaflets over metropolitan areas, simulating bombing while recruiting volunteers for the corps, and the mock destruction of Buffalo, New York, on 27 September 1952. The rhetoric that pervaded Advertising Council radio and print advertisements focused on the external threat and aggressiveness of the Soviet Union. For a brief description of the Advertising Council's role, see Volan, *The History of the Ground Observer Corps,* 152.

58. Keim began his career in advertising with Compton Advertising, Inc.,

leaving to join the service. While stationed at the Pentagon, he served as aide-de-camp and public relations officer to General Hoyt S. Vandenberg, who was eventually named U.S. Air Force Chief of Staff and who, as commonly happens in large organizations, took Keim along with him. Some years later, Keim told the remarkable story of how the Advertising Council became involved in the Ground Observer Corps campaign:

> At one point, we were in the Korean war (the real fear was the Soviet Union and not necessarily the North Koreans, although we were having a tough enough job with them) and we had practically no air defenses at all, so someone in the Pentagon conceived the idea of a volunteer corps of citizens to serve as sky watchers or ground observers, and it became known as the Ground Observer Corps. People like myself, housewives or kids would volunteer to serve two to four hours sometimes on a daily basis, sometimes once a week, and the need was to recruit them and to get them to stand in towers all over the country. They would work out of tall buildings with binoculars, like bird watching. It sounds a little silly today with all our sophisticated equipment, but we didn't have equipment that could detect Soviet bombers if they were to attack. The fact of the matter is they didn't have the capability anyway but we didn't know that and we had to assume that they had that capability. So I was brought in to handle the public relations and . . . advertising [for] that program.
>
> I was beset with the problem and I had heard of the Advertising Council. So we opened up discussions with Ted Repplier, with George Ludlam, and Allan Wilson, vice president of the Washington office. [N]ow in . . . 1952, [t]he Korean War is raging on and the country is sore beset. . . . Scripps-Howard newspapers called it Truman's war, and they used to run a daily box score on the dead in Truman's war . . . and it was a very controversial period.
>
> The Advertising Council always became important when it was controversial. When it was a time of strife or turmoil, the Council was always at its best. It certainly turned out to be the case in the Ground Observer Corps. We went to the Council, and they were dubious and had to look carefully. I was a young Lieutenant Colonel. We said we will show you what we were talking about and we did. They were wonderful men who were then in their late middle ages, and we flew Ted [Repplier] and Allan [Wilson] out to headquarters, the Air Defense Command, which was then at Colorado Springs. We flew them up to a base (and I will never forget this) with the RCAF [Royal Canadian Air Force] . . . to show that we were working in connection with [Canada], but they didn't have any better radar than we did. Anyway, the supposition was that the plane would come in on the deck under the radar and we would have to scramble fighters by eye. You would have to call in on a very elaborate telephone that was set up and so the Air Force became the number one customer of . . . AT&T.
>
> Then it came to showdown: How do we get this to be approved by

the Board of Directors? I said why don't we have General Vandenberg come up and speak to the Board of Directors of the Ad Council? They were thrilled by the idea. As I said, I was very close to the general, and he had confidence in me and, of course, I was very fond of him and so I said: 'General, you have got to sell this so you've got to come and talk to the Board.' He reluctantly agreed.

He flew to New York and it was a horrible day. The Ad Council in those days always had their board meetings at the Hotel Pierre; very posh, very upscale and it was the third Thursday of every month. It was always the Thursday. It had to be on that day so General Vandenberg adjusted his schedule to that, and it was [in the dead of winter], a miserable day with zero visibility. He flew up, and my immediate boss was a Major General named Smith who was with him on the flight. I had gone up to New York to make the arrangements and I was at the Hotel Pierre. The board meeting would start at eleven o'clock and would go to twelve thirty, and then they would go to lunch. . . .

So the meeting started at eleven o'clock and General Vandenberg was supposed to land and get in and then we had a police escort for him. . . . But they got over New York about 10 o'clock and I still don't know technologically how this happened but suddenly this phone call came in for me and it's my immediate boss, General Smith. 'Bob, I'm with General Vandenberg. We are up here [at] 5000 feet [in] a holding pattern . . . and it is zero visibility and nothing is coming in or out . . . .' So he says I will stay in touch with you but things don't look good. . . . I told [George Ludlam] what General Smith had said. [Ludlam said:] 'Oh my God, he won't get here. You know we have had the biggest turnout we have had in years. He's the Chief of Staff; we are at war. Do something. You have got to do something, get that thing settled.'

I don't know how I did it . . . but this fellow colonel was running the operational side of this Ground Observer Corps and, as I said, he was the biggest customer of AT&T. And I called him in Washington and I said: 'Here is the problem. Somehow they called me and they can't land. Why couldn't we set it up so the General speaks from the plane, put it on a [public address] system and play it to the Board of Directors?' He was always ready for a challenge. He says: 'I'll try. I'll call the President of AT&T.' And he called back in five minutes [and said:] 'They are all squared away. People will be there to set up the linkage from the Hotel Pierre.'

As God is my witness, within 15 minutes there was a crew there. . . . I got the control tower [at LaGuardia Airport] zeroed in and we talked to them and they said that with that kind of communication only one person can talk at a time; so you can't talk simultaneously. . . . [A]s soon as the channel was set up, [General Vandenberg] . . . gave a half-hour speech to the audience sitting at lunch. . . . The board, of course, voted to accept the Ground Observer Corps.

Lynch, "The Bob Keim Interview," 3–9. Advertising Council files.

59. See minutes of Public Policy Committee, 8 January 1947. Advertising Council files.

60. Alton Ketchum, *The Miracle of America: As Discovered by One American Family,* 2d ed. (New York: Advertising Council, 1950). The booklet was largely based on the "Report on the Activities of the Research and Creative Committee to the Twenty-Ninth Annual Convention of the American Association of Advertising Agencies," 17 April 1947, called the "Smock Report" after the committee's chairman, Jack Smock of the Foote, Cone & Belding advertising agency's office in Los Angeles. For an interesting review of the events of this period, see John V. McGinnis, "The Advertising Council and the Cold War," chapters three and four. McGinnis bases his work largely on the papers of Thomas D'Arcy Brophy in the State Historical Society of Wisconsin in Madison, Wisconsin, with some forays into other materials in different archives. We are indebted to McGinnis's work for alerting us to some complexities of this period of the Advertising Council's history.

61. See Lawrence Farrant, "Ad Council Prepares New 'War' Campaign," *Editor and Publisher,* 9 December 1950.

62. The Brookings Institution did an evaluation of *The Miracle of America* in anticipation of a new edition but found the booklet "intemperate" in tone. William H. Whyte, Jr., then an editor at *Fortune,* wrote a scathing analysis of the "great free enterprise campaign" in his *Is Anybody Listening?* (New York: Simon and Schuster, 1952), concluding that businessmen were talking to themselves.

63. See meeting minutes of the Advertising Council, 14 April 1949. Advertising Council files.

64. C. G. Mortimer, Jr., to William Randolph Hearst, Jr., 13 April 1949. T. S. Repplier describes the meeting in the "Report on Columns by Lewis Haney in *New York Journal-American* and other Hearst Newspapers," 18 April 1949. Advertising Council files.

65. Evans Clark to Charles G. Mortimer, Jr., 21 April 1949. Advertising Council files.

66. Some fifteen years later in 1964, the council was again roundly attacked by forces on its right. A widely distributed booklet called *The Enemy Within,* also known as "The Dan Smoot Report," accused the council of being part of an empire of invisible intellectuals who arbitrarily decide what is of public interest and what is not. Specifically, the booklet lambasted the council for its promotion of Law Day, an annual occasion, it argued, to inundate America with "World Peace Through Law" propaganda, a first step in handing American affairs over to the World Court. See T. S. Repplier to Lewis A. Engman of Grand Rapids, Michigan, 30 September 1964. Advertising Council files. Smoot had brought a libel action against Engman's client, the local League of Women Voters, and Engman had written to the Advertising Council for information because of Smoot's attacks on the council.

A year later, Repplier reiterated the council's hold on middle ground. After a nearly vintage cold warrior speech, complete with classical rhetorical stereotypes ("apparatus of troublemaking," "subversion," "political boring-from-within," and so on), Repplier says that:

> Our great dilemma here in today's United States arises . . . from the fact that anti-communism has been carried to such lengths of absurdity and persecution by the lunatic fringe of the right. The wild excesses of the McCarthy era left such a deep wound that conscientious, moderate citizens feel a little self-conscious and even faintly crackpot when they talk seriously about the communist conspiracy. In fact, it almost requires genius to walk the narrow path of concern about communism without straying into the quicksands of communist-stimulated liberalism on the left, or the never-never land of Birchites-with-guns-at-the-ready on the far right.

Report to the board of directors, 20 May 1965. Advertising Council files.

67. "Memorandum on a Public Information Program in Support of Operation Candor," as revised 8 July 1953, marked "Confidential." Advertising Council files.

68. Minutes of meeting of board of directors, 18 February 1954. Advertising Council files.

69. See, for instance, Repplier's year-end report of 16 December 1954. Advertising Council files.

70. Minutes of meeting of the board of directors, 17 November 1955, p. V. His suggestions reflect the conviction that both state and private propaganda were necessary to deflect the communist threat:

> Mr. Repplier then said he feels that thought should be given to the Council's attitude in the matter of participation in overseas propaganda, and asked for expressions of opinion from the Board. He feels this effort cannot be left entirely to official propaganda groups, but inclusion of private organizations in this activity is necessary. He said that USIA has appointed an Advisory Committee of business people in an effort to enlist the cooperation of American business in propaganda. However, communism makes use of people from all walks of life in propaganda activity, and American groups such as Womens Clubs, Veterans Organizations, Kiwanis Clubs, etc. should also be included in our propaganda program. He asked whether the Board felt the Council should participate more actively in this work and perhaps set up a subsidiary group to lead such a program.

Repplier had made similar suggestions repeatedly throughout 1955 after his return from a six-month overseas trip. See meeting minutes for 21 July 1955 and 20 October 1955. Advertising Council files.

71. The call for specifically *moral* impetus and action was in the air. See, for instance, Repplier's year-end report of 16 December 1954, as well as the minutes for the board meetings of 21 July 1955 and 20 October 1955. Advertising Council files.

72. The board appointed the Ad Hoc Committee on Propaganda Policy at the meeting on 15 December 1955. The committee consisted of Marion Harper, who acted as chairman, Harold S. Barnes, Evans Clark, Frederic Gamble, Robert Kintner, and Allan Wilson.

Tangentially related to this whole discussion was the chronic problem of the prestige of advertising, which had once again begun to slip in the public eye. Should the U.S. propaganda efforts abroad be taken over by an advertising man, who, after all, would understand better than anyone else how to sell ideas? Or would the low public image of advertising undercut the propaganda work? In an annual report, Repplier posed this aspect of the problem sharply:

> The U.S. Information Agency gets blamed for all manner of propaganda ineptitudes, most of which are not its fault. For the sake of effectiveness, the American propaganda effort should be headed by an advertising man; yet such is the public image of the advertising man that this would be most unwise. We would be sure to hear again the refrain of 'you can't sell American [sic] like you sell soap,' and USIA's appropriation would probably be cut to an even more inadequate figure.

Minutes of executive committee meeting, 20 February 1958. Advertising Council files.

73. There were two round tables, one in New Haven in November 1956 and the other at the Yale Club in New York in May 1957, with partially overlapping attendance. Some key participants in one or another of the sessions were Dean Liston Pope of Yale Divinity School; Norman Cousins of the *Saturday Review;* Russell Lynes, Jr., managing editor of *Harper's Magazine;* Arthur Goldberg, then counsel for the AFL-CIO; and Edmund Sinnott, dean emeritus of the Yale Graduate School. Several business luminaries associated with the Advertising Council, such as Charles E. Wilson, also attended, along with invited government officials. Professor David Potter, head of American studies at Yale, served as rapporteur for both sessions.

Council leaders enlisted Professor Potter to write a historical article on the notion of People's Capitalism and Dr. David McCord Wright of McGill University to assess the idea from the "moral or social justice standpoint." In addition, they persuaded Dr. Sumner Slichter of Harvard University to rebut an attack on the idea of People's Capitalism by Eugene Varga, a Soviet economist. See "Notes on People's Capitalism Program," [early July 1956; located next to minutes for People's Capitalism Committee meeting of 12 July 1956]. Confirmation of their enlistment appears in the minutes of the board meeting for 18 October 1956. Advertising Council files.

74. The People's Capitalism campaign is reported throughout the board meeting minutes of 1955, 1956, and 1957. But see, in particular, the minutes of the board of directors meetings, 21 July 1955, IV–V; 20 October 1955, V; 17 November 1955, IV; 19 January 1956, III; 16 February 1956, IV–V; 17 May 1956, VI; 19 July 1956, 4; 18 October 1956, 6–7; addendum to

minutes of 16 May 1957; minutes of 20 July 1957, 4; and 21 November 1957. See also the minutes of the People's Capitalism Committee meeting, 12 July 1956. Advertising Council files.

75. The issue of advertising's prestige had come to the forefront once again the year before and Repplier had constituted a special committee to study the problem. When the committee reported back at the executive committee meeting of 20 February 1958, it had few practical suggestions to relieve advertising of its poor public image except a continuation of the work of the Advertising Council. James Webb Young, however, noted that "most of the criticism against advertising has come from the members of the academic profession who . . . [use] advertising as a whipping boy for their own failure to raise the cultural level of the country." Advertising Council files.

76. President's annual report to the board of directors, 15 January 1959. Advertising Council files.

77. Repplier made his argument first in his annual report to the board of directors on 18 February 1960. Advertising Council files.

78. "Recommendation to the Board Concerning American Attitudes," 21 April 1960. Advertising Council files.

79. Minutes of meeting of the board of directors, 21 April 1960. Advertising Council files.

80. On 10–11 April 1961, the council held a round table at Princeton University attended by, among others, Dean Liston Pope, Thurgood Marshall, Eugene McCarthy, Elmo Roper, and William H. Whyte, Jr. Harold Rosenberg prepared the background paper and asked the participants to address two questions: (1) To what extent do our prevalent moral attitudes and will to achievement equip us to advance toward our goals and occupy the position of leadership in the free world? (2) Which among these attitudes need to be, and can be, eliminated or corrected? Minutes of board meeting, 16 March 1961. Advertising Council files.

81. Statement from "Challenge to Americans" in minutes of board meeting, 20 September 1962. Advertising Council files.

82. Annual report to the board of directors, 21 February 1963. Advertising Council files.

83. Annual report to the board of directors, 21 April 1966. Advertising Council files.

84. Echoing sentiments that went back to the council's founding, Keim asked in his first annual report to the board:

> What can advertising do to create a healthy regard for this business of ours, so often maligned, so widely misunderstood, so vulnerable to the snipers, the detractors, the would-be reformers who see—or think they see—our . . . business . . . as the logical and easy target for criticism, curtailment and crucifixion?

Annual report to the board, 16 March 1967. Advertising Council files.

85. *The Advertising Council's First 25 Years: A Report to the American People* (New York: Advertising Council [1967]). The phrase "unfinished business"

seems to have been borrowed from one of President John F. Kennedy's speeches, but it was also the title of a book by longtime board member Helen Hall of the Henry Street Settlement. See Helen Hall, *Unfinished Business: In Neighborhood and Nation* (New York: Macmillan, 1971). Keim later used the same theme in his 21 June 1973 report to the board called "The Unfinished Business of America." Advertising Council files.

86. Annual report to the board of directors, 21 March 1968. Advertising Council files.

87. Ibid.

88. "The 1971 Annual Report of The Advertising Council, Inc." Advertising Council files.

89. See Robert Keim, annual report to the board, "The Roof Raisers," 17 March 1971. On the increasingly religious tone of the Advertising Council's rhetoric, see, in particular, Keim's statements:

> *Our work must be measured above all else by our ability to produce social profit.* . . . The real accounting should be rendered in terms of life or death, sickness or health, filth or beauty, spoilage or conservation of resources. It is the husband and wife who are alive today because they buckled their seat belts and wrote to tell us it was our advertising that prompted them to do so. It is the mother who wrote to tell us that her 8 year old son told her he refused an older kid's urging to sniff glue 'just like the boy in the television commercial did!' It is the college president who wrote to say that we've helped keep his school financially solvent. It is the town of Alliance, Ohio that learned to hate hate rather than each other as a result of our RIAL [Religion in American Life] campaign. . . . (4, 6)
>
> This is my gospel and I'm not a bit embarrassed about preaching it in my Annual Report here today. (15)

Advertising Council files.

90. Annual report to the board, "Quo Vadis, Advertising Council?" 9 March 1972. Advertising Council files.

91. The executive committee of the board of directors was the forum for much of the debate. See, in particular, the minutes for the executive committee meetings for 10 February, 9 and 18 May, 23 June, and 2 November 1972. The entire board joined the discussions in the meetings of 23 June and 16 November 1972.

Throughout the year, the names of potential nominees for the Public Policy Committee were put forward. They included Vernon Jordan, William Vanden Heuvel, Burke Marshall, Bill Moyers, Chet Huntley, Arthur Nielsen, Thomas Hoving, Ada Louise Huxtable, J. Irwin Miller, Laurence Rockefeller, Dr. Carl Kaysen, Leonard Silk, Terry Sanford, Dr. Juanita Kreps, Shirley Temple Black, Daniel Yankelovitch, Louis Harris, Burns Roper, Daniel Patrick Moynihan, Kenneth Clark, Daniel Bell, and Barry Commoner. See, in particular, the minutes of the executive committee meeting of 23 June 1972 and those of the board meeting of 16 November 1972. Advertising Council files.

92. Howard Morgens, who was chairman and chief executive officer of Procter & Gamble, received the council's annual public service award on 18 December 1973. In his acceptance speech, Morgens said:

> Many of us have been speaking out recently about the new public service role of business. We have emphasized the expanding concept of social responsibility for the American corporation. We have expressed our willing acceptance of these new dimensions to the job of management for they clearly represent one more way that private enterprise can promote the *public* interest and contribute to a better society.
>
> However, the expanding social responsibilities of business, as important as they are, should not obscure the *fundamental* way in which business advances the public interest. . . . I'm referring to the 'profit motive.' It is a competitive system. It is a free market pricing system. It is an incentive system. . . .
>
> Increasingly . . . we businessmen try to justify our companies by referring mainly to their 'good works'—in aiding education, in helping to solve social problems of all kinds, and in serving our communities in a great variety of ways. . . . However, one cannot organize the economic activity of the nation based solely on altruism, good works, or volunteer public service. Too often . . . we shy away from talking about how the dynamic force of the profit motive works to build a better society. I'm told there are some members of the Advertising Council itself who might be reluctant to support a campaign explaining how our private enterprise system operates because they feel it would be too controversial or self-serving. We practice capitalism, yet are reluctant to preach it.

Morgens goes on to dismiss several standard criticisms of business, ending with a pointed message for the council itself:

> The Advertising Council, other public service organizations, business itself, and we as individuals should do whatever we can to make sure that this miraculous business system of ours is not gradually crippled by a public and a Congress who do not understand it. We can do this only by educating the public about how this system works. This means that we must deepen the public's understanding of how well profits and the profit motive serve the public interest.

Advertising Council files.

93. The campaign on productivity is first mentioned in the minutes of the board meeting, 18 January 1973, and was introduced in the fall of 1973. Talk about productivity was in the air. Around the same time, the United States Steel Corporation launched a spirited campaign on productivity, complete with business-magazine thought pieces, eleven one-minute television

commercials, a film for two hundred thousand United States Steel employees, and productivity kits containing decals, buttons, and banners with the slogan "Anything We Can Do, We Can Do Better." See meeting minutes of the board, 14 March 1974. Advertising Council files.

94. On 30 September 1974, the council had received a request from the White House to prepare an "inflation fighter kit." The council and its volunteer advertising agency, Benton and Bowles, quickly developed the "Whip Inflation Now" (WIN) idea and sent President Ford two WIN buttons. President Ford wore a WIN button during his Congressional address of 8 October 1974, referring to it during his speech. The council promptly received hundreds of phone calls requesting WIN buttons. Robert Keim was appointed to the Citizens Action Committee to Fight Inflation, an organization that quickly gained widespread business support, complete with sponsored advertising in newspapers all over the country. On 27 November 1974 Keim received a letter from Democratic Congressman Benjamin Rosenthal from the Eighth District in New York condemning the Advertising Council for "serving as a propaganda vehicle for a partisan scheme." The letter went on to criticize the council for "serv[ing] increasingly as the federal government's free advertising agency . . . paper[ing] over ineffective governmental action in dealing with root social problems." The letter, which was also sent to the press, was co-signed by twenty-nine other members of the House and Senate. Keim drafted a bland reply that was debated at a board meeting before it was sent, and the matter ended. But the council had been put on notice that, in a time of soaring energy costs and high inflation, it entered the arena of economic advocacy at its peril. See the minutes of the board for 23 October and 12 December 1974. Congressman Rosenthal's letter of 27 November is attached to the latter. Advertising Council files.

95. Paul Moroz, senior vice president of the research department, presented Compton's findings at the Advertising Council's board meeting of 26 February 1975. The report itself, entitled "National Survey on the U.S. Economic System: A Study of Public Understanding and Attitudes" was presented to the council in April 1975. The study consisted of open-ended interviews with three thousand respondents, one thousand of whom were targeted special publics. The Advertising Council distributed its own summary of the research findings to the board in a document called "Preliminary Statement on Major Public Service Mass Communications Program by the Advertising Council, Inc. To Help Create a Better Understanding of the American Economic System," April 1975. The results of the survey were announced at a news conference on 31 July 1975, and were offered to the public for ten dollars. Apparently, demand was brisk, especially from corporations and college groups. Minutes of meeting of the board for 9 September and 13 November 1975. Advertising Council files.

96. Minutes of the board, 21 January 1976. Advertising Council files.

97. See meeting minutes of the board for 10 June 1976. One can get a feel for most of the events of the bicentennial from the sketch for a television special entitled "Celebration America" planned by the council as a "birthday

gift to America." The sketch calls for "an enormously ambitious, big scale, grand and glorious TV Special produced by the Advertising Council. . . . A spectacular, compelling, fun show. And through it all a strong underlying call to action. The viewer is artfully excited and motivated to get involved in America. To help make America better." The event was to be "Academy Awards style," a black-tie gala with an audience of government, business, and social leaders, along with show business personalities. The format might be based on "Laugh-In," or "Sesame Street," a "free form kind of thing. Variety. Loose. Swinging. . . . Short and fast-paced. Singers, comedians, film clips. Very upbeat. Heavy with music. Geographic variety." The choice of hosts ran from Bill Beutel to Mary Tyler Moore to Orson Welles or Grace Kelly. Panel guests might include Margaret Mead, Julian Bond, Thomas Pynchon, Joseph Heller, and Ralph Nader. Music would range from The Who to the American Ballet Theater, from the Grateful Dead to the New York Philharmonic, and from the Rolling Stones to a group called The Young Americans. The show was to be broken into sections, covering such topics as the environment, people, national health, education. But most of all, it was to be a "fast-paced gutsy show. Solid entertainment. . . . Quick tape cuts of Americans saying what they'd like to see better in America." There is no record of what became of this particular show. However, the memorandum aptly captures the spirit of many shows that were produced. It also contains in compact form advertising's approach to almost everything. See meeting minutes of the board for 26 February 1975, to which the proposal is attached. Advertising Council files.

98. Memorandum entitled "Advertising Council Propaganda," 9 June 1976. President Keim sent Ferguson's memorandum to the executive committee noting Ferguson's strategy of "rounding up" statements against the council, closing with "And he accuses us of propaganda!" Memorandum of 24 June 1976. Advertising Council files.

99. Congressman Rosenthal's press release of 27 July 1976, cites the respected economists James Tobin of Yale University and Lester Thurow of the Massachusetts Institute of Technology. Rosenthal's press release went out on the letterhead of the Committee on Commerce, Consumer & Monetary Affairs, which he chaired. On 30 July 1976, Congressman Garry Brown, the ranking minority member of Rosenthal's committee, issued a press release publicizing a letter that he had sent to Rosenthal criticizing Rosenthal's use of committee stationery, with Brown's name, when "expressing an individual opinion." Advertising Council files.

100. Annual report to the board, 9 September 1976. The controversy over the American Economic System campaign dragged on for two more years. The council initiated a second phase of its advertising campaign, with a copy theme of "E.Q." (Economic Quotient). Compton Advertising conducted a "benchmark" study, a nationwide telephone survey with 2,006 people, duplicated a year later and for several years after that, on people's awareness of the AES campaign. On the basis of the first two studies, Compton researchers "projected" the findings of the survey, arguing that 46 mil-

lion adults were familiar with the Ad Council's campaign; 18 million adults remember specifics of the campaign; and 4 million people received the accompanying booklet, with one and a half million claiming to have read it. Whenever Keim or other council officials discussed the AES campaign, they used the projected figures as if they were actual. See minutes of the board meeting of 15 September 1977, as well as Robert Keim's annual report, called "A Taste of Honey," of the same date. Keim says that the "drumfire" from opponents to the AES campaign had abated somewhat by that point. But he nonetheless spends a good portion of his report justifying the campaign, comparing it to a "potential Vietnam" that the council had survived. See also the minutes of the board meeting of 13 June 1978 for a later extended report on the campaign. By this point, the campaign was utilizing the whole panoply of media blitz devices, including speakers, planted editorials and feature articles, bumper stickers, lapel buttons, and a cartoon series.

Beginning in the mid-1980s, the AES campaign turned toward the problem of America's declining productivity growth rate (that is, a decline in the rate of increase of productivity). The campaign focused in particular on America's slipping international competitiveness, and the imagery selected echoed several contemporary popular cultural themes:

> Uncle Sam is in a boxing ring, being knocked down while an announcer's voice-over tells the viewer about the problem of low productivity growth. Then Uncle Sam gets up, with a determined look in his eyes, while the announcer talks about the problem. Uncle Sam delivers the final blow in the film . . . while the announcer says, 'It won't be easy. America, we've got a job to do. Every one of us.'
>
> A second film . . . show[s] each of the three target audiences [top level managers, supervisors, and workers] blaming the productivity problem on somebody else . . . [until] Uncle Sam becomes determined to change things.
>
> A third . . . was entitled 'Jobless Babies' featur[ing] Uncle Sam in a maternity ward, with the line 'These Americans just lost their jobs' . . . explain[ing] how declining productivity *now* affects jobs in the future.

See the minutes of board meetings for 12 June and 12 November 1980, and particularly for 3 December 1981. Advertising Council files.

101. See the annual report for each of the years 1982–1983 and 1986–1987. Advertising Council files.

102. By mid-1999, the Advertising Council had jumped into eighth place in the ranks of most visible advertisers on the Internet. In June 1999 alone, banner advertisements for some two dozen nonprofit clients appeared 133 million times on the Internet, reaching more than 16 percent of those who surf the Web from home. At that point the Internet universe in the United States was estimated to be over 100 million people. The council was and continues to be the beneficiary of the vast amount of unused (well over half) advertising space on even heavily trafficked Web sites. Instead of letting that space go empty, Web sites often "plug in" public service advertisements that

they can obtain by visiting <www.adcouncil.org>. Web sites thus avoid saturating their visitors with self-promotional advertisements and benefit from associating themselves with a public cause. See Nielsen//NetRatings, "June [1999] Internet Ratings from Nielsen//NetRatings," <www.nielsen-netratings.com>.

103. This is the title of Robert Keim's annual report to the board of 18 September 1986. Advertising Council files.

104. Public service advertising conducted through the Advertising Council constitutes only a tiny fraction of that done every year. Virtually every advertising agency in the United States contributes pro bono efforts to local and national charities and causes. For instance, in the aftermath of some bitter racial confrontations in New York City in the early 1990s, the advertising agency Smith/Greenland, New York, formed an organization called Citizens for Racial Harmony that plastered the city with messages like: "You're drowning. You begin to panic. A hand reaches in to save you. It's black. Is that a problem?" and "Your son needs a kidney. In 18 hours they found a donor. He's white. Is that a problem?"

CHAPTER THREE: TURNING THE WORLD UPSIDE DOWN

1. See Frederic Wakeman, *The Hucksters* (New York: Rinehart & Co., 1946), a fictional caricature of admen that was turned into a movie the following year with Clark Gable fighting for his integrity in a world of yes-men. The most influential attack on advertising in the years following the Second World War was, of course, Vance Packard, *The Hidden Persuaders* (New York: David McKay Company, 1957), a popular book that has since had many academic emulators. For attacks on public relations, see William H. Whyte, *Is Anybody Listening?* (New York: Simon and Schuster, 1952), a widely read lampoon of public relations men. Whyte followed this with *The Organization Man* (Garden City, N.Y.: Doubleday, 1955), a popular critique of the bureaucratization of corporations replete with broadsides against public relations. Sloan Wilson, *The Man in the Gray Flannel Suit* (New York: Simon and Schuster, 1955) was another extremely influential fictional portrait of public relations; the novel was made into a 1956 movie starring Gregory Peck as the struggling young man trying to make his way in a slick world. Another important attack on public relations was Irwin Ross, *The Image Merchants* (Garden City, N.Y.: Doubleday, 1959).

2. On advertising, see, for instance, Giancarlo Buzzi, *La tigre domestica* (Florence: Vallecchi, 1964), translated by B. David Garmize as *Advertising: Its Cultural and Political Effects* (Minneapolis: University of Minnesota Press, 1968); Stuart Ewen, *Captains of Consciousness* (New York: McGraw Hill, 1976); Judith Williamson, *Decoding Advertisements: Ideology and Meaning in Advertising* (London and Boston: Boyars, 1978); Stuart Ewen and Elizabeth Ewen, *Channels of Desire: Mass Images and the Shaping of American Consciousness* (New York: McGraw Hill, 1982); Eric Clark, *The Want Makers: The World of Advertising: How They Make You Buy* (New York: Viking, 1989); Priscilla Agnew, *Sex, Death, and Advertising,* videocassette of presentation at Chapman University, Orange,

California, 1991; James B. Twitchell, *Adcult: The Triumph of Advertising in American Culture* (New York: Columbia University Press, 1995); Anthony B. Pratkanis and Elliot Aronson, *The Age of Propaganda: The Everyday Use and Abuse of Persuasion* (New York: W. H. Freeman, 1992); and Robert Goldman and Stephen Papson, *Sign Wars: The Cluttered Landscape of Advertising* (New York: Guilford, 1996). On public relations, see, for instance, Sidney Blumenthal, *The Permanent Campaign: Inside the World of Elite Political Operatives* (Boston: Beacon Press, 1980); Stuart Ewen, *PR!: A Social History of Spin* (New York: Basic Books, 1996); and Larry Tye, *The Father of Spin: Edward L. Bernays & the Birth of Public Relations* (New York: Crown Publishers, 1998). On both fields, see Daniel J. Boorstin, *The Image; or, What Happened to the American Dream* (New York: Atheneum, 1962).

3. We base the following account on three sets of sources. First, Janice M. Hirota, sometimes accompanied by Robert Jackall, interviewed more than ten Doyle Dane Bernbach employees before the agency's demise in 1986. In the course of a much larger field project on advertising, she also interviewed more than two dozen other former DDB employees scattered in various agencies. Although these interviews focused on the structure of work in advertising rather than on the history of DDB, they are filled with anecdotes and portraits of the agency.

Second, we did a complete survey of the materials on Doyle Dane Bernbach in the DDB Needham Worldwide, Inc., Information Center at 437 Madison Avenue, New York. As mentioned later in the text, the corporation changed its name on 1 June 1999 to DDB Worldwide Communications Group. The information center is now known as the DDB Worldwide Inc. Information Center and we use this name in all following references. The materials that we surveyed at the information center include most of the editions of the internal agency newsletter going back to DDB's inception; the newsletter was published sporadically during certain periods and under different names. There is also a collection of 206 news articles from various journals about the agency or some of its principal actors, beginning with the newspaper notice of the agency's founding in 1949 all the way until October 1984. There are several interviews with Bill Bernbach with various reporters from both mainstream and trade presses. And there is also a collection of twenty speeches and papers given by Bill Bernbach over the years, most in manuscript form, a few complete with his own marginal delivery notes. Finally, there are a few collections of aphorisms and quotes attributed to Bernbach by his followers as well as several self-celebratory publications issued by the agency on important anniversaries. Taken together, these materials constitute the official public image of the organization. As often happens with archival materials in corporations, many other DDB materials were apparently destroyed when Doyle Dane Bernbach merged with Needham Harper in 1986. Our special thanks to Ms. Alice Bromley, Director of the Information Center, and to her assistant, Ms. Carmela Cangialosi, for their generous help to us during the summers of 1991, 1998, and 1999.

The third set of sources consists of targeted interviews conducted by the authors. Robert Jackall interviewed a former, well-placed DDB insider twice, once in August 1993 and again in January 1994. This source, who wishes to remain anonymous, contributed perspectives on the inner workings of the agency and on Bernbach himself. Robert Jackall and Janice M. Hirota also interviewed James Heekin in Williamstown, Massachusetts, during the summer of 1988, and Robert Jackall interviewed Mr. Heekin again on 9 September 1998, in Williamstown. Mr. Heekin provided many important insights into the struggle for power at DDB discussed here and the vicissitudes of the agency vis-à-vis its clients in its later years. Finally, Robert Jackall interviewed Charles Piccirillo, executive vice president and creative director of the New York office on 1 July 1998. Except for two brief sojourns outside the agency, Mr. Piccirillo has been with Doyle Dane Bernbach and the successor firm for thirty-eight years and provided us with rich historical insights.

4. Bernbach attended NYU from September 1929 until August 1932 when he completed his requirements for graduation. However, he did not graduate until June 1933 since the graduation ceremony was held only once a year. Letter to the authors from George T. Gilmore, Jr., Registrar, New York University, 4 August 1998.

5. See, for instance, the entry on Bernbach in *Current Biography* 28: 3 (March 1967), 6–9, which draws on a half dozen articles in journals like *Time,* the *Saturday Evening Post,* and the *New York Herald Tribune* magazine. See also Bernbach's obituary by Robert D. McFadden in the *New York Times,* 3 October 1982.

6. See the interview with Bernbach in Barton A. Cummings, *The Benevolent Dictators: Interviews with Advertising Greats* (Chicago: Crain Books, 1984), 39–48. The reference to Mr. Greenlee is on page 40. Seventy-three audiotapes of Cummings's interviews with advertising greats are at the University of Illinois at Urbana-Champaign. See interviews for the book *The Benevolent Dictators,* Communications Library, University of Illinois, Urbana-Champaign; the interview with Bernbach is volume 5. The 18 January 1982 taped interview with Bernbach differs somewhat from the version that Cummings eventually published first in *Advertising Age* on 8 November 1982, immediately after Bernbach's death, and later in his book. Bart Cummings was chief executive officer of Compton Advertising, Inc. (later Saatchi & Saatchi Compton Worldwide) for more than fifteen years. During his long career in advertising, among many other positions, he served as chairman of the American Association of Advertising Agencies in 1969–70 and chairman of the Advertising Council in 1979–81. In addition to his conversation with Bernbach, Cummings's book contains interviews with Emerson Foote, Charles H. Brower, Marion Harper, Jack Tinker, Edward M. Thiele, David Ogilvy, Robert E. Healy, Edward L. Bond, Jr., Paul Foley, Arthur C. Fatt, Arthur W. Schultz, Neal Gilliatt, William A. Marsteller, Raymond O. Mithun, Alfred J. Seaman, Neal W. O'Connor, and Brown Bolté.

7. Grover Whalen's account of the fair is in his autobiography, *Mr. New York: The Autobiography of Grover A. Whalen* (New York: G. P. Putnam's Sons, 1955), 173–221.

8. Interview with Bernbach in Cummings, *The Benevolent Dictators*, 41.

9. Interview with Bernbach in Cummings, *The Benevolent Dictators*, 40. Frank Monaghan's original pamphlet is: *The New York World's Fair 1939: The Fairs of the Past and the Fair of Tomorrow* (Chicago, New York, and London: Encyclopaedia Britannica, 1938), 48 pp. The revised edition is *The New York World's Fair 1939: The Fairs of the Past and the Fair of Tomorrow* (Chicago: Encyclopaedia Britannica, 1939), 52 pp. Sometimes Bernbach claimed even greater credit for writing work during his years at the New York World's Fair. See the interview with Bernbach in *Communication Arts Magazine* 13, no. 1 (1971), 13ff. In response to a query about how he got into advertising, Bernbach says: "I was a writer, and I was also interested in art. I'd been a ghostwriter for a lot of famous politicians. I wrote Grover Whalen's speeches for many years running. He was the head of the New York World's Fair, the old one in 1939. I worked there, and finally headed the literary department—we called it the research department. We wrote articles for various publications, speeches, books, a history of fairs for the Encyclopaedia Britannica and so forth" (13).

10. See the entry on Monaghan in *The National Cyclopedia of American Biography*, vol. 56 (New York: J. T. White, 1975), 201. About the fair, Monaghan said, "By summer [1940], it was evident that the creative aspects of the Fair had vanished. There were only the operational aspects—the most dull and painfully unprofitable." *Current Biography*, vol. 4 (New York: H. W. Wilson Company, 1943), 536.

11. Interview with Bernbach in Cummings, *The Benevolent Dictators*, 41–42.

12. See Paul Rand, *Thoughts on Design* (New York: Wittenborn, Schultz, 1951), v. Rand's other books are *Paul Rand: A Designer's Art* (New Haven: Yale University Press, 1985), *Design, Form, and Chaos* (New Haven: Yale University Press, 1993), and *From Lascaux to Brooklyn* (New Haven: Yale University Press, 1996).

13. "The creatives" is a term used formally and informally throughout the world of advertising. As with all social labels, "the creatives" circumscribes the group to which it refers, defining art directors and copywriters as a cohesive occupational group found across agencies. At the same time, it distinguishes the group from other groups in agencies, such as account people and researchers, and from clients who buy advertising. The use of the term here reflects this general social usage in the industry and does not, of course, imply any evaluation of talent, aesthetic taste, heightened sensibility, or imaginativeness.

14. At the time, the chief advocate of this view was Rosser Reeves, former chairman of the Ted Bates agency. See Rosser Reeves, *Reality in Advertising* (New York: Knopf, 1961).

15. William Bernbach, speech at Polaroid-DDB 25th anniversary, Boston, Mass., 2 July 1979, DDB Worldwide Inc. Information Center, New York. See also William Bernbach, speech presented at American Management

Association/ESOMAR conference, Paris-Hilton, Paris, France, 31 March 1981, DDB Worldwide Inc. Information Center, New York.

16. William Bernbach, speech delivered at Chicago Advertising Executives' Club, 13 October 1959, DDB Worldwide Inc. Information Center, New York.

17. See, for instance, William Bernbach, speech at Monitor Environmental Conference, Americana Hotel, New York City, 30–31 October 1975, DDB Worldwide Inc. Information Center, New York.

18. Collected aphorisms of William Bernbach, "Bernbach Quotes . . . ," n.d., DDB Worldwide Inc. Information Center, New York.

19. These are constant themes in Bernbach's speeches. See, for instance, "Speech at Advertising Seminar: New York University," 1 November 1955; speech from AAAA regional convention, New York, "How To Do It Different," 1956; speech delivered at Chicago Advertising Executives' Club, 13 October 1959; speech from AAAA annual meeting, New York, "Advertising's Greatest Tool," 1961; speech from western regional annual AAAA meeting, Pebble Beach, Calif., "Some Things Can't Be Planned," 3 November 1965; and speech from annual AAAA meeting, White Sulphur Springs, W. Va., "Facts Are Not Enough," 14–17 May 1980. All of these speeches are located at the DDB Worldwide Inc. Information Center, New York.

20. William Bernbach, speech presented at American National Advertisers annual meeting, Scottsdale, Ariz., "Your Side . . . My Side . . . And the Truth," 27 November 1978, DDB Worldwide Inc. Information Center, New York.

21. William Bernbach, speech presented at Polaroid-DDB 25th anniversary.

22. Collected aphorisms of William Bernbach, "William Bernbach Quotes," n.d., DDB Worldwide Inc. Information Center. There exists also a third collection of Bernbach's sayings, "Quotations from William Bernbach," n.d., DDB Worldwide Inc. Information Center, New York. Many of Bernbach's aphorisms that found their way into these unpublished efforts, culled by various people at various times, can now be found in print in *Bill Bernbach Said* . . . (New York: DDB Worldwide Communications Group, n.d. [compiled 1982–1986, reissued on 1 June 1999]).

23. See Carolyn Pfaff, "Bernbach Comments Ruffle Researchers," *Advertising Age,* 13 April 1981.

24. See Doris Willens, "The Bernbach Image," *Advertising Age,* 22 April 1991, 24.

25. Ibid.

26. Ibid.

27. Interview with Bernbach in Cummings, *The Benevolent Dictators.* The interview was conducted on 18 January 1982, the last year of Bernbach's life. In it, in addition to claiming coauthorship of Frank Monaghan's work on world fairs and assistance to Paul Rand in his books as noted earlier, Bernbach claims that a "General Somebody" in Washington, "the guy who ran

public relations," found out, a day too late, that Bernbach was stationed in Fort Eustis and sent for him (42). He also claims that right after he, Doyle, and Dane opened their new agency, he was offered $100,000 by a "famed headhunter" for a job that he turned down because "I had this wonderful opportunity to do what I felt was right, to initiate things, to innovate" (43).

28. Interview with Bernbach in *DDB News*, 25th anniversary issue, June 1974. Bernbach told his interviewer that he was having lunch that very day with his publisher to finalize the agreement for the book that publishers had sought for years. See also Doris Willens, "Bill Bernbach: In Search of the Man Behind the Legend," *Advertising Age*, 4 March 1991, 20ff.

29. See, for instance, Bob Donath, "Bernbach Busy, Memoirs Still Wait," *New York Daily News*, 5 July 1978.

30. Charles Piccirillo, interview by Robert Jackall, 1 July 1998, DDB Needham Worldwide, Inc., New York.

31. Bob Levenson, *Bill Bernbach's Book* (New York: Villard Books, 1987), x.

32. Bob Levenson's tribute to Bernbach, United Nations Chapel, 5 October 1982, *DDB News*, 21, issue 4 (December 1982), 11. Levenson is referring to the citation by the Salk Institute when it awarded Bernbach its Partner in Science Award, one of the many awards for public service that Bernbach received.

33. When competing for a new client, big law firms go through an equivalent process called a "beauty contest."

34. Claude Hopkins, *My Life in Advertising* (New York and London: Harper & Bros., 1927).

35. See, for instance, Rosser Reeves, *Reality in Advertising;* Fairfax M. Cone, *The Blue Streak: Some Observations, Mostly About Advertising* (Chicago: Crain Communications, Inc., 1973); Leo Burnett, *Communications of an Advertising Man: Selections from the Speeches, Articles, Memoranda, and Miscellaneous Writings of Leo Burnett* (Chicago: privately printed, 1961); John E. O'Toole, *The Trouble with Advertising* (New York: Chelsea House Publishers, Inc., 1985); and even David Ogilvy, *Confessions of an Advertising Man* (New York: Atheneum, 1963).

36. Levenson, *Bill Bernbach's Book*, 45.

37. Piccirillo, interview.

38. See the special tribute to Ogilvy & Mather in *Advertising Age*, 17 September 1998.

39. See Doris Willens, "William and Mary," *Advertising Age*, 17 June 1991, 20ff. and "DDB Deal That Failed," *Advertising Age*, 24 June 1991, 30ff.

40. Joe Daly was a central figure at DDB on the account side of the agency almost from the beginning. Many observers credit Daly and Daly alone with keeping big clients like Polaroid at DDB for long periods. But not everybody shared such a benign view of Daly. Some observers argued that Daly owed his position entirely to Ned Doyle, a kind of Irish legacy. By his own account, Daly seemed to favor old-time advertising methods of retaining clients, that is, wining and dining them and creating opportunities where

they could mingle with celebrities and movie stars, like Sophia Loren. See Joseph R. Daly, *Luck is My Lady* (New York: Vantage Press, 1989).

41. See "Heekin Quits with Blast at DDB's Execs," *Advertising Age,* 2 September 1974 for Heekin's description of the circumstances leading to his dismissal by Daly. Heekin elaborated on this account in the interviews with the authors in Williamstown, Massachusetts, during the summers of 1988 and 1998.

42. See Willens, "William and Mary."

43. See Cone, *Blue Streak.* Cone was one of the founders of Foote, Cone & Belding (FCB). The book is an edited collection of memos or bits of memos that Cone sent to FCB's Chicago staff over a period of twenty-two years, from 1948 to 1969. See also O'Toole, *The Trouble with Advertising.* O'Toole headed FCB during the merger talks with Doyle Dane Bernbach.

44. "Trying to Pull Doyle Dane Out of the Doldrums," *Business Week,* 5 November 1984.

45. For an overdrawn, humorous, but still revealing discussion of the pervasive fear and uncertainty in advertising, see Jerry Della Femina, *From the Wonderful Folks Who Gave You Pearl Harbor: Front-Line Dispatches from the Advertising World,* edited by Charles Sopkin (New York: Simon and Schuster, 1970). See especially chapter 3, "Fear, Son of Fear, and Fear Meets Abbott and Costello." See also the novel by Jack Dillon, *The Advertising Man* (Greenwich, Conn.: Fawcett Publications, 1972). Dillon, who was a copywriter and creative vice president at DDB, presents a scathing portrait of the ongoing occupational struggle between the forces of communications creativity and the forces of business rationality. Sounding very much like Bill Bernbach, Dillon presents advertising creatives' daunting task: how to break through to an increasingly skeptical, cynical, fed-up, disillusioned, and disbelieving public in the face of unrelenting pressure from clients, and, in Dillon's fictional agency, from account executives, both of whom have placed their faith in scientific measures of advertising efficacy that lead inevitably to predictable, dull ads that, in the end, deepen public scorn for and disbelief of advertising.

46. Willens, "Bill Bernbach: In Search of the Man behind the Legend."

47. According to a count done by DDB's own people, more individuals at DDB won more major advertising awards than any other agency for the years 1976–83. DDB had ninety individual awards and its closest rival, Young and Rubicam, had seventy-nine. For the same period, DDB claimed a total of 141 advertising awards, counting both individual and firm awards; its closest rival in the overall count, Ally & Gargano, had 135 total awards.

48. See Dick Stevenson, "Special Report: Up and Down with Doyle Dane Bernbach," *Ad Forum,* October 1984, 10ff.

CHAPTER FOUR: ADVOCACY AS A PROFESSION

1. In addition to the main groups treated in the text, various other occupational groups, both inside and outside the agency, also participate in advertising production. We can only briefly mention some of these here. For

example, an agency research department, and sometimes one at the client, might be involved in a project from its inception through the appearance of the advertising, particularly in the case of television commercials. Research aims to rationalize the effectiveness of advertising by systematically determining the target audience and how best to reach it. The size and influence of research departments vary among agencies, yet creatives generally have skeptical views on the meaning and influence of research on the advertising they fashion.

Agency media researchers and buyers also participate in advertising projects from the beginning. These men and women make up media plans that most effectively utilize a client's budget in purchasing, for example, television and radio time and space in magazines and on buses. These plans consider such factors as the target audience profile, desirable media mix, and budgets. After the time and space have been purchased and the advertising produced, media people, with the assistance of outside companies, monitor the media to make sure advertisements and commercials run smoothly and as scheduled.

Once a client approves an advertisement for production, various other groups of workers get involved. Generally speaking, for a print advertisement, these include a photographer, with whom the creatives, especially the art director, deal directly; the photographer's assistant(s); models, if necessary; graphics artists in some cases, both those who work with pencils and the new breed of computer graphics experts; and technicians at the printer. In the case of a television commercial, other workers include an agency producer who acts as the liaison between an agency and a production house, the organizational base for the director. In addition to the director who actually shoots the film footage, people in a production house generally look for appropriate sites for on-location shoots; help find necessary props; and arrange for technicians to operate sound equipment, lights, and perhaps some special effects. Moreover, directors sometimes help creatives and agency casting departments or independent casting consultants find "the talent," that is, the actors or models, for a commercial. Sometimes after directors shoot the film footage, they make the "first cut"; that is, they retain the right to do an initial rough edit of the film before turning it over to the creatives. Most of the time, however, directors simply deliver the raw footage. In either case, their connection to the project ends upon delivery of the film. Then, technicians at an editing and mixing house work on the footage with the creatives, the agency producer, and often the client. Together, they select frames for the "final cut," and using highly sophisticated equipment, edit the footage, splice it together with microsecond accuracy, and match the sound track to the visual images. Art directors and writers usually remain involved in the "production end" of projects until clients accept the final advertisements.

2. Creatives use the term "client" all the time; they almost never use the term "advertiser" in conversation. But whenever the term is used, it always refers to the client. A quick way to spot someone who knows nothing about the advertising world is to see how they use the word "advertiser." If the

term is used to refer to people at an agency, whether account people or creatives, one can be reasonably sure that the person has never set foot inside an agency.

3. "Advertising" and "advertisements" are generic terms that refer to both print and electronic advertising. Advertising that appears in print is generally specified as "print advertisement" or "print ad." The term "commercial" always refers to broadcast advertising and, when used alone, always means advertising that appears on television; a radio commercial is always so specified.

4. Trade advertising is generally print ads that appear only in trade publications, as distinct from, say, national advertising appearing in the mass media. Corporate advertising, which is actually a form of public relations, presents a desired corporate image rather than a sales pitch for a particular product or service. The oil companies have specialized in corporate advertising. Years ago, Texaco ran a campaign emphasizing the company's efforts to find new sources of oil and thus decrease America's dependence on Middle Eastern sources of oil. Mobil's regular think pieces on the op-ed page of the *New York Times* try to position the company as a thoughtful contributor to public discourse on a wide range of issues. Doyle Dane Bernbach did Mobil's earliest work in this area beginning in 1965. One campaign, calling for uniform national driving standards and greater driver education, consisted of a series of print advertisements showing, variously, a boy killed in a game of chicken, a young couple necking while driving, and a car wrapped around a tree after a horrific crash. There was also a commercial showing a car dropped off a ten-story building to simulate a crash at sixty miles per hour. The tag line for the series was, "We want you to live," that is, "our business here at Mobil is to sell you gasoline and oil, and we want you to be around to try them."

5. A few creative departments are not organized into creative groups headed by group heads. Instead, creative directors simply select the creatives they want to work on particular projects. This permits considerable flexibility in pairing teammates and therefore in bringing together people thought to be best suited for a particular project.

6. This is generally true for creatives of both junior and senior status, although one finds variations on this work arrangement. For instance, some groups have assistant group heads; these creatives have some supervisory authority over particular accounts or over other, more junior creatives. Such supervisory relationships may be perceived by both the senior and junior creatives involved as tinged with mentor-apprentice overtones. Theoretically at least, partners may shift constantly just as creatives on a particular account may be continually changed. Creative supervisors who have long-term affiliations with accounts provide stability and continuity in such situations.

7. The Museum of Broadcasting, "The Advertising of Chiat/Day: Examining the New Creativity," 18 September–15 December 1990.

8. Stuart Elliott, "Campaigns Are Making Mistakes on Purpose in the Quest to Stand Out from the Crowd," *New York Times,* 20 January 1998, D5.

9. The most important advertising awards over the years have been, arguably, those given out by the One Club for Art and Copy and the Clio Awards, Ltd. For an historical treatment of the Clio Awards, see Deborah Kauffroth Morrison, "Approaches to Clio: 1964–1980, A Study of Social Communication in Clio Award-Winning Television Advertising From Three Interdisciplinary Perspectives: Communication, Culture, and Creativity" (Ph.D. diss., University of Texas at Austin, 1988). However, the Clio Awards collapsed in June 1991; after a disastrously inept presentation by Clio's spokesman that briefly featured the event's food caterer as an emcee, advertising creatives stormed the awards table to steal Clio statues. For a lively description of the event, see Richard Morgan and Sherrie Shamoon, "Clio Free For All," *Adweek* 32, no. 25, 17 June 1991, Eastern edition. The debacle was followed by bankruptcy, a lawsuit to block an attempt at "New Clios," and the temporary flourishing of new award-granting organizations. Only in 1997 did the Clio Awards reestablish itself under new ownership/leadership as a premier arbiter of creative advertising. Lesser awards are the Andys, given by the New York Advertising Club; the Effies, given by the American Marketing Association (these are known as the account people's and clients' awards, respectively); the International Film and TV Festival of New York, which honors the best television commercials; the New York Art Directors' Club; the International Advertising Film Festival in Cannes; and the Addy Award given by the American Advertising Federation.

10. In what follows, we are indebted to Max Weber's many writings on bureaucracy and to the seminal article by Israel Gerver and Joseph Bensman, "Towards a Sociology of Expertness," *Social Forces* 32 (March 1954).

11. For a thorough treatment of this theme, see Robert Jackall, *Moral Mazes: The World of Corporate Managers* (New York: Oxford University Press, 1988).

12. With the help of public relations practitioners, Pacific Gas & Electric did thorough planning that prepared the company well for the 17 October 1989 earthquake in San Francisco. When the quake occurred, employees reported within minutes for duty and worked continuously to restore service. Through continuous press releases, advertisements, management leadership tours, and newsletters, PG&E was able successfully and quickly to address the media, shareholders, employees, political figures, customers, the investment community, and the public at large. See Public Relations Society of America (PRSA), *Silver Anvil Winners, 1990* (New York: Public Relations Society of America, 1990), 59–60. The Silver Anvil Award reports may be obtained by writing to the Public Relations Society of America at 33 Irving Place, New York, New York 10003-2376.

13. For instance, when REVCO declared bankruptcy in 1988, making it the biggest leveraged buyout failure in business history to that point, it had to cope with a number of disasters: hostile takeover challenges; closing 100 of its stores; accusations of insider trading; necessary layoffs of employees at 712 of its stores. Its public relations practitioners had to develop multiple messages to suit its different constituencies: employees ("Don't leave;

together we can beat this"); product vendors ("Ship products to us; you'll get paid"); customers ("Shop at REVCO; it's business as usual"); and the media ("Trust us; we'll level with you"). The company survived and, with it, so did thousands of jobs. See PRSA, *Silver Anvil Winners, 1990*, 69–70.

14. PRSA, *Silver Anvil Winners, 1994* (New York: Public Relations Society of America, 1994), 79–80.

15. One of the most important and elite groups in the public relations world is Public Relations Seminar, which has about one hundred top public relations people, called "Seminarians," from major corporations as well as a few agencies, especially Burston-Marsteller and Hill and Knowlton. The group holds annual several-day meetings at plush resorts in the United States and Europe, complete with high-powered speakers from key institutional arenas. Another key elite group, thought by many observers to be the most powerful in the occupation, is the Wise Men, a group of seventy senior men and women that meets monthly for dinner at the Harvard Club in New York, addressed by high-status speakers. Two other groups also command great prestige. The Evanston Group, composed of top public relations people from major U.S. banks, meets biannually, and the PR Society, composed of about fifty top corporate public relations practitioners, meets monthly in New York. See "PR's Top Private Club Opens Its Door a Crack," in *O'Dwyer's PR Services Report*, August 1988 and "PR Field Has Its Own 'High Society'," in *O'Dwyer's PR Services Report*, February 1989.

16. PRSA, *Silver Anvil Winners, 1982* (New York: Public Relations Society of America, 1982), 13–14.

17. PRSA, *Silver Anvil Winners, 1987* (New York: Public Relations Society of America, 1987), 51–52

18. The Silver Anvil Awards were first handed out in 1946 by the American Public Relations Association, an organization founded in 1944. The Public Relations Society of America was born in 1948 out of the merger of the northeast National Association of Public Relations Counsel, previously called the National Association of Publicity Directors founded in 1936, and the West Coast American Council on Public Relations founded in 1939. In 1961, the American Public Relations Association merged with the PRSA. The PRSA became the official sponsor of the Silver Anvil Awards. See Rea W. Smith, "The PR Chronicle," in *Public Relations Journal* (October 1970), 124–125. Since 1948, the PRSA has also annually honored an individual practitioner with a Gold Anvil Award for major contributions to public relations. And, since 1969, it has given Bronze Anvil Awards for outstanding public relations tactics that are components of larger campaigns.

19. PRSA, *Silver Anvil Winners, 1988* (New York: Public Relations Society of America, 1988), 21–22.

20. PRSA, *Silver Anvil Winners, 1987*, 59–60.

21. PRSA, *Silver Anvil Winners, 1988*, 69–70.

22. See the op-ed piece by E. L. Doctorow in the *New York Times*, 14 July 1995, complete with a petition signed by more than one hundred people, including such luminaries as Paul Auster, Naomi Campbell, Jacques Derrida,

David Dinkins, Eileen Fisher, Henry Louis Gates, Nadine Gordimer, bell hooks, Casey Kasem, Tony Kushner, Maya Lin, Norman Mailer, Paul Newman, Joyce Carol Oates, Salman Rushdie, Gloria Steinem, Sting, Oliver Stone, Alice Walker, Cornel West, and Peter Yarrow. The Mumia case is paradigmatic for a study of political advocacy. See the vast amount of literature from the Committee to Save Mumia Abu-Jamal, such as Leonard Weinglass, *Race for Justice: Mumia Abu-Jamal's Fight against the Death Penalty* (Monroe, Maine: Common Courage Press, 1995). See also Mumia Abu-Jamal, *Live from Death Row* (Reading, Mass.: Addison-Wesley, 1995). Voluminous materials on Abu-Jamal are also available on the World Wide Web at <www.freemumia.org>. Abu-Jamal's claims are countered by extensive materials from the group Justice for Police Officer Daniel Faulkner (the man that Mumia Abu-Jamal, then Wesley Cook, was convicted of killing). See <www.danielfaulkner.com>.

23. For instance, in 1986, BBDO New York spent over $500,000 to win the account of Apple Computer and, in 1987, Chiat/Day spent $1 million for the Nissan account. According to the American Association of Advertising Agencies, agencies that bill more than $100 million annually spend about 1 percent of their gross revenues on speculative work, but some agencies spend considerably more. See Randall Rothenberg, "For Ad Agencies, a Costly Hard Sell," *New York Times,* 4 February 1991, D1.

24. The phrase is Max Weber's. See *Ancient Judaism,* translated and edited by H. H. Gerth and Don Martindale (Glencoe, Ill.: The Free Press, 1952), 325. The reference is to prophets in royal courtly circles who consistently upheld images of hopeful futures or who interpreted current disasters favorably.

CHAPTER FIVE: HABITS OF MIND

1. For an account of some of the key institutional developments in the application of sociology to marketing, see Paul F. Lazarsfeld, "An Episode in the History of Social Research: A Memoir," in *The Intellectual Migration: Europe and America, 1930–1960,* edited by Donald Fleming and Bernard Bailyn (Cambridge, Mass.: Belknap Press of Harvard University Press, 1969), 270–337. Three years after Lazarsfeld emigrated from Vienna in 1933, he became the first director of the Newark Research Center. In 1938, he became the director of the Office of Radio Research and Policies at Princeton University, which was transferred to Columbia University a year later. This became Columbia University's Bureau of Applied Social Research. For parallel developments, see Roper Public Opinion Research Center, *The Roper Center: University of Connecticut; Williams College; Yale University* (Storrs, Conn.: The Roper Center, 1978), which provides a brief history of the Roper Center since its 1946 founding, and Arthur Charles Nielsen, *Greater Prosperity Through Marketing Research: The First 40 Years of A. C. Nielsen* (New York: Newcomen Society in North America, 1964).

2. To take only one example, see Yankelovich Clancy Shulman's newsletter, *Yankelovich Monitor* (New York: Yankelovich, Skelly & White, Inc.), which provides vast amounts of demographic information with guesses about

their implications. Research departments in advertising agencies regularly skim materials for audience profiles right out of such publications. There are also any number of books providing taxonomies of American lifestyles with instructions on how to recognize and market to each one. See, for example, Arnold Mitchell, *The Nine American Lifestyles: Who We Are and Where We're Going* (New York: Warner Books, 1983).

One of the basic tools of marketing research is focus group studies. These studies, often run by independent consultants, take place in representative cities considered key for the particular strategy and project at hand. They entail creatives and others watching through one-way mirrors and listening to groups of consumers talk about, say, frozen dinners in general, or a particular brand of frozen dinners, or their images of the kinds of people who eat frozen meals—single people, busy people, people who do not like to cook—or their reactions to advertising approaches stressing convenience, or fast meals, or different choices for a family of finicky eaters. Practices such as focus groups are meant to help creatives root their advertising in "real life," in the stated concerns and interests of "real people." However, very frequently, what creatives hear in focus groups are recycled advertising slogans from previous campaigns.

Both slogans and commercials are usually pretested. In addition, while work is in progress on an advertisement, a research department sometimes helps test concepts under consideration by, for example, asking shoppers in a supermarket parking lot to respond to specific proposed advertising tag lines or, again, to a cardboard mock-up or some other less-than-full-production version of a commercial. Even full-production commercials are at times televised in selected test markets pending national release; after regular release, too, researchers gauge viewers' responses in attempts to determine a commercial's effectiveness.

But, from creatives' standpoint, research does not help get commercials made and shown. In one instance, a client was trying to alter the image of a food product suffering from declining sales, especially among young adults. Market research attributed the decline in large part to a growing concern with chemical additives and a concomitant growing valuation of natural ingredients. The trend especially alarmed the client since it could mean that as older consumers died, sales would continually shrink. The client, therefore, placed great importance on the advertising. Before beginning work on developing the advertising, a research group composed of the creatives, account people, the client, and research people went to four cities, one each in western, southern, eastern, and middle United States, to research the issue. The methodology included a telephone campaign to interview young adults; in addition, each member of the group conducted a series of "one-on-one" interviews of young people in three of the four research cities. Upon concluding their work, the team wrote a report distilling and interpreting the gathered data from the perspective of marketing strategy; based on this, the creatives developed two different concepts for commercials. In the end, the client authorized the agency to make full-production commercials ready to air on television, from both of the campaigns. When the commercials were ready, the client and agency tested them in focus groups composed of young adults, and learned that target group members not only preferred one of the commercials over the other, but were generally enthusiastic about it. The client then asked for more commercials in the preferred style, which the creatives produced. However, rather than put the campaign on national television as originally planned, the client decided to test the preferred advertising further, now to see whether it would actually change attitudes and promote sales. Thus, the commercials began to air in a test urban area; preliminary research reported both more positive attitudes toward the product among target audience members and increased sales. But even after two years on the air in the test market, the agency was still unable to convince the client to release the campaign for national distribution, a reluctance that the creatives found extremely frustrating. To make matters even worse, another agency produced a campaign with a similar advertising concept for a different product, one that appeared on national television and won advertising awards. The art director was convinced that her team's concept was plagiarized by someone who saw the commercials running—as they continued to run for months—in the test market. For creatives, a concern with and reliance on test results and research data are often traps that freeze decision making, rather than guides that aid the process. The fear of making a mistake and the concomitant paralysis of action are at times reinforced by the availability of seemingly sophisticated and revealing research tools; clients avoid clear-cut decisions while calling for more and more test results and research data.

Research departments sometimes use recall tests to measure the effectiveness of commercials. Such tests entail calling people the day after a commercial runs for the first time and trying to establish whether or not viewers who were watching the commercial, remember it. Sometimes researchers make follow-up calls, say, a week later, to see whether the impact of a commercial lasts over time. Creatives argue that such tests do not measure effectiveness and, further, that the memorability of a commercial is better measured after several airings in any case. Moreover, some claim that such research produces useless results that frustrate rather than help creatives fashion integrated, intelligible pieces; the discovery that a foghorn blast at the beginning of a commercial effectively grabs the attention of viewers, for instance, had some clients demanding foghorns whether or not they made sense in particular commercials.

The size and influence of research departments vary among agencies, yet creatives from agencies across the entire spectrum from the most creative to the most conservative have skeptical views on the meaning and influence of research on the advertising they fashion. Despite claims from at least some researchers that "We give creatives the ideas for their ads," creatives deny that they need surveys and statistics to tell them what is happening. They argue further that other research tools, such as recall tests, have no meaning and that research is used most effectively to bolster and legitimate decisions already made on other grounds. Research departments and the research data they generate do touch in some way all advertisements, but this does not mean that research results directly and inevitably influence the shape and content of advertising. Rather, research gets used in different ways and to different ends by the main actors involved in advertising production.

3. In July 1997, Robert Jackall interviewed a studio head at a major network in New York City about the selection of television programs. This studio head wishes to remain anonymous.

4. Although the numbers fluctuate from year to year depending on demographic changes, each national ratings point, as measured by Nielsen Media Research, represents about 980,000 homes. National figures trail an event by about a week. Overnight, preliminary ratings are only from the top 28 cities in the country and each point represents about 463,000 homes.

5. The distinctions between rational, nonrational, and irrational deserve some elaboration. The kind of rationality most predominant in our epoch is what Max Weber termed "instrumental rationality *(Zweckrationalität),*" that is, the selection of the proper means to achieve some assigned goal, whatever that goal might be. In Weber's view, the Western world is characterized by the pervasiveness of this rationality of calculable action. Ideally speaking, bureaucracies are the organizational embodiment of instrumental rationality, with elaborate hierarchies and procedures designed to attain already determined goals in a measured, orderly fashion. Of course, the instrumental rationality of many, if not most, bureaucracies gets subverted in amazing ways so that large organizations often seem to be wonderlands of nonrationality or irrationality. "Value rationality *(Wertrationalität)*" means rationality from the standpoint of some particular substantive end, value, or belief. What is substantively rational from one standpoint may be considered nonrational or irrational from another perspective. One exercises value rationality, as contrasted with instrumental rationality, when one calls taken-for-granted goals into question and carefully articulates the rationales either for the old goals or for new ones. There is always a tension between instrumental and value rationality. "Nonrationality" refers to the emotional, subconscious, or unconscious impulsive wellsprings of human action. One of the paradoxes of value rationality is that, ultimately, all substantive choices of values, ends, or beliefs are at bottom nonrational, although, once chosen, people may order their lives in an instrumentally rational manner in order to achieve them. "Irrationality" means, variously, the perversion of fixed goals by the deliberate choice of wholly inappropriate means to reach them, the adoption of goals that are wholly inappropriate to circumstances or abilities, or the triumph of nonrationality in a situation to such an extent that it altogether crowds out all rational thinking. Weber's thinking on the problem of rationality runs throughout his work. The best place to begin is with his essays "Politics as a Vocation," "Science as a Vocation," "Bureaucracy," "The Social Psychology of the World Religions," and, especially, "Religious Rejections of the World and Their Directions." All of these are in *From Max Weber: Essays in Sociology,* translated, edited, and with an introduction by H. H. Gerth

and C. Wright Mills (New York: Oxford University Press, 1946), 77–128, 129–156, 196–244, 267–301, and 323–359.

In the real world, the difference between what is rational and what is not gets still more complicated. In the late 1980s, for instance, there was an alarming increase of fatal motorcycle accidents involving young men who refused to wear helmets. Wearing helmets was seen to contradict the ethos of motorcycle culture, an ethos in which the mistrust of authority and the celebration of individual freedom and deliberate risk taking are paramount. The Motorcycle Safety Foundation had made no headway at all with rational appeals to avoid death or severe injury by wearing helmets. Indeed, the foundation came to believe that the only way to reach the young men in this culture was through nonrational, highly emotional identificatory appeals that linked motorcyclists with sports personalities in other bruising undertakings, such as football, coupled with a nonauthoritarian pitch. In effect, the foundation had to use what it saw as a nonrational tool (the imagistic, emotional appeals) in order to be rational (save young men's lives). If rational appeals are met with irrational rejection, is it any longer "rational" to stay with such appeals? See PRSA, *Silver Anvil Winners, 1988* (New York, Public Relations Society of America, 1988), 29.

6. This habit of mind is a microcosmic paradigm of a larger intellectual retreat in modern society away from cohesive explanatory schema of any sort. The trend is most evident in the growth of antiscientific sentiment in intellectual circles but also in fields like the new social history, which rejects any attempt to construct a grand narrative to explain the drift of events in favor of voicing the views of marginal groups who have been "silenced" in official histories. Feminists in particular have embraced this approach not only in history but in all the social sciences. Journalists have always purveyed human-interest stories as one essential part of their stock-in-trade. But broadcast and print journalism has, it seems, increasingly made human-interest stories the norm in the entire field. The self-description of Anna Quindlen, formerly a regular op-ed page writer for the *New York Times,* now freelance writer and novelist, suggests the style of this sea change:

> I am a working mother, a feminist and a reporter whose enduring interest has been in the small moments of the lives of unsung people, the kind of people who only ride in limos when someone in the family dies.

New York Times, 4 November 1992, A31. Ms. Quindlen was awarded the Pulitzer Prize for her work in 1991.

7. Plato treats flattery cursorily in the *Letters,* the *Sophist,* the *Republic,* and the *Laws.* His most extensive treatment is in the *Gorgias* (463b, ff.) in which he discusses several kinds of flattery, always arguing that flattery is that which aims at the pleasant instead of the good. See *The Collected Dialogues of Plato, including the Letters,* edited by Edith Hamilton and Huntington Cairns, Bollingen Series, no. 71 (New York: Pantheon Books, 1961), 245ff. For Theophrastus, see *The Characters of Theophrastus,* an English translation with

introduction and notes by R. C. Jebb, 1870; new edition by J. E. Sandys (London: Macmillan and Co., 1909), "The Flatterer," 38–43. See also, *Theophrastus: The Character Sketches,* translated with notes and introductory essays by Warren Anderson (Kent, Ohio: Kent State University Press, 1970), "The Flatterer," 10–13. Plutarch has an extended essay on flattery, "How to Tell a Flatterer from a Friend," in *Plutarch's Moralia* (London: William Heinemann, 1922), translated by Frank Cole Babbit, vol. 1, 263–295; Plutarch also frequently treats flattery in his biographies of famous Greeks and Romans. Joseph Hall, *Characters of Vertves and Vices* was originally published in London in 1608. It was republished with some of Hall's other work as *Heaven vpon Earth and Characters of Vertves and Vices,* edited with an introduction and notes by Rudolf Kirk (New Brunswick: Rutgers University Press, 1948), which includes the portrait "Of the Flatterer" (181–182). And see Baldassare Castiglione, *The Book of the Courtier,* translated from the Italian by Sir Thomas Hoby, 1561, with an introduction by Walter Raleigh (London: David Nutt, 1900), 85–86, 123–124, and 298–299.

8. Castiglione sharply describes flatterers' astonishment at the credulity of those they flatter.

> Because we are of nature al the sort of us much gredy of praise then is requisite, and better to our eares love the melody of wordes sounding to our praise, than any other song or soune that is most sweete. And therfore manye tymes, lyke the voices of Meremadens, they are the cause of drownyng him that doeth not well stoppe his eares at such deceitfull harmonie. This daunger being perceived, there hath bene among the auncient wise men that hath written bookes, howe a manne should know a true friend from a flatterer. But what availeth it? If there be many of them (or rather infinit) that manifestly perceive thate are flatterers, and yet love hym that flattereth them, and hate him that telleth them the trothe, and often times (standinge in opinion that he that praiseth them is to scace in his woordes) they themselves helpe him forward, and utter such matters of themselves, that the most impudent flatterer of all is ashamed of.

Castiglione, 85–86.

9. Thus, Bob Herbert in the *New York Times* writes columns regularly excoriating the New York City Police Department with a vociferousness unseemly for the front page, and Anthony Lewis regularly expresses sentiments on Middle East policy or even on weighty domestic issues that seem quite in line with the sentiments of the *Times's* editors. See Lewis's attempt, beginning with his article in the *New York Times* on 27 January 1998 and extending throughout President Clinton's impeachment and trial, to discredit Independent Prosecutor Kenneth Starr.

10. PRSA, *Silver Anvil Winners, 1989* (New York: Public Relations Society of America, 1989), 57–58.

11. PRSA, *Silver Anvil Winners, 1987* (New York: Public Relations Society of America, 1987), 21–22.

12. PRSA, *Silver Anvil Winners, 1987,* 3–4.

13. PRSA, *Silver Anvil Winners, 1987,* 33–34.

14. Harry Reichenbach, *Phantom Fame,* as told to David Freedman (New York: Simon and Schuster, Inc., 1931), 123.

15. See John Tierney, "Hard Hearts Were Softened by a Boy's Tale," *New York Times,* 1 July 1999. For some initial reports on the story, see Susan Sachs and Jayson Blair, "Seeking Father, Boy Makes a 3,200-Mile Odyssey," *New York Times,* 28 June 1999 and Michele McPhee et al., "An Incredible Journey: Boy, 13, Travels 4,500 Miles by Bus & Foot to Find Dad," *New York Daily News,* 29 June 1999.

16. PRSA, *Silver Anvil Winners, 1986* (New York: Public Relations Society of America, 1986), 21–22. Also, Richard Weiner, Inc., "The Tang March Across America: A Transcontinental Relay To Benefit Mothers Against Drunk Driving," presented to General Foods on 19 March 1985.

17. PRSA, *Silver Anvil Winners, 1985* (New York: Public Relations Society of America, 1985), 53–54.

18. *New York Times,* 6 September 1990, D28. The advertisement reads in part:

> Harvard. The Adelphi of Massachusetts. Believe it or not. Harvard actually lives up to this reputation.
>
> Its academic mission is every bit as lofty as Adelphi's: to develop the whole man and the whole woman; to expose students to liberal learning, the 2500-year tradition of Western Civilization; to prepare you for life, not just to occupy your mind for the years between high school and post-pubescence.
>
> Its location in Cambridge, just across the river from Boston, may not promise the Museum of Modern Art, Lincoln Center, Broadway, or the United Nations. But it holds its own against Adelphi's campus, which is less than an hour from New York City.

19. PRSA, *Silver Anvil Winners, 1989,* 43–44.

20. See, for example, The House of Seagram, "Responsible Drinking: The Story of a Point of View" (New York: The House of Seagram, n.d.). The pamphlet contains advertisements dating back to October 1934 advocating moderation in drinking as well as cautions against driving while drinking.

21. PRSA, *Silver Anvil Winners, 1985,* 17–18. The program was entitled "Pharmacists against Drug Abuse."

22. PRSA, *Silver Anvil Winners, 1988,* 37–38. The program claims great effectiveness. It began in 1984 when no states had such laws; by 1987, thirty-one states and the District of Columbia had passed legislation requiring safety belts. Traffic Safety Now claimed saving 2,200 lives during 1984–1987 through its legislative advocacy.

23. Derk Arend Wilcox, editor, *The Left Guide: A Guide to Left-of-Center Organizations* (Ann Arbor, Mich.: Economics America, Inc.), 271.

24. PRSA, *Silver Anvil Winners, 1985,* 35–36.

25. PRSA, *Silver Anvil Winners, 1985,* 41–42.

26. To take only one example, heads of university departments sometimes become subject to vilification during difficult tenure decisions where confidentiality is crucial to protect the rights of candidates for tenure. In the academy, character assassination is generally more muted than in, say, the political arena.

27. George Orwell, *Nineteen eighty-four* (San Diego: Harcourt Brace Jovanovich, 1977). Orwell's book was originally published in 1949.

28. PRSA, *Silver Anvil Winners, 1988,* 31.

29. Marlboro earns millions of dollars each year for Philip Morris, a great deal of it pure profit. Cigarette smoking has declined precipitously in the United States since 1964 when approximately 44 percent of the adult population smoked cigarettes. In 1994, according to the Office on Smoking and Health of the Centers for Disease Control and Prevention, between 26 and 28 percent of the adult population, or more than 50 million people, still smoked cigarettes despite all the scientific evidence of the habit's injuries to health. Although the figures are closely guarded, the best estimate is that about 20 percent of all cigarette smokers smoke Marlboro. Only a few pennies of each pack of Marlboros go into the cigarettes themselves; about double the cost of the material goes to packaging and marketing. All the rest goes to profit and taxes. The mounting legal and settlement costs incurred by Philip Morris and the rest of the tobacco industry in the 1990s seem to be covered by price increases.

30. The brochures cited in the text are: Philip Morris U.S.A., *The Great American Smoker's Manual* (New York: Philip Morris, Corporate Affairs Department, n.d.); Philip Morris U.S.A., *New York City's Smoking Restriction Law: What Your Business Is . . . and Is Not . . . Required to Do* (New York: Philip Morris, n.d.); Philip Morris U.S.A., *Smokers' Rights in New York City* (New York: Philip Morris, n.d.); Tobacco Institute, *Smoking and Young People—Where the Tobacco Industry Stands* (Washington, D.C.: Tobacco Institute, n.d.); Tobacco Institute, *Tobacco: Helping Youth Say No* (Washington, D.C.: Tobacco Institute, n.d.); Tobacco Institute, *In the Public Interest: Three Decades of Initiatives by a Responsible Cigarette Industry* (Washington, D.C.: Tobacco Institute, n.d.); Tobacco Institute, *The Anti-Smoking Campaign: Enough Is Enough* (Washington, D.C.: Tobacco Institute, n.d.); American Smokers Alliance, *Guidelines for Smokers' Rights Groups* (Nashville, Tenn.: American Smokers' Alliance, n.d.); Tobacco Institute, *Smokers' Rights in the Workplace* (Washington, D.C.: Tobacco Institute, n.d.); Covington & Burling, P.C., *An Assessment of the Current Legal Climate concerning Smoking in the Workplace* (Washington, D.C.: Tobacco Institute, 1988); and Tobacco Institute, *Indoor Air Pollution: Is Your Workplace Making You Sick?* (Washington, D.C.: Tobacco Institute, n.d.). Philip Morris's exhibition *No _____ Need Apply: Your Job and Your Privacy* was also accompanied by a brochure by the same name. Its cover had a facsimile of a help-wanted advertisement indicating that applicants were not to apply if they were black, Chinese, Hispanic, Japanese, Jewish, Catholic, over 45 years old, disabled, overweight, female, or a smoker. For the paradigmatic speech on discrimination against smokers, see Hugh Cullman, *A Plea for Tolerance* (New

York: Philip Morris Viewpoints, 1985). The brochure contains remarks made by Mr. Cullman, then vice chairman of Philip Morris, on his receipt of the 1984 Human Relations Award from the American Jewish Committee's Tobacco and Allied Industries Division, New York City, 11 December 1984. All of these documents are what might be called corporate ephemera, sophisticated descendants of the broadsides and chapbooks that disseminated information and propaganda in early modern Europe. These pieces may or may not be collected in company libraries or in special collections. The authors obtained all the publications cited from either Philip Morris or the Tobacco Institute. See also the piece by Gordon L. Dillow, "The Hundred-Year War Against the Cigarette," *American Heritage*, February/March 1981, republished by the Tobacco Institute in the late 1980s.

31. "Ropeswing," along with other famous Pepsi commercials, is part of the Pepsi Generation Advertising Oral History Collection, 1946–1987, in the Center for Advertising History, Archives Center, National Museum of American History, Smithsonian Institution, Washington, D.C. Our thanks to John Fleckner and Mimi Minnick for their assistance during our work there in July 1988 and 1994.

32. One form of appropriation in virtually every bureaucratized occupation is so common that it is rarely noticed, that is, the recycling of "boiler-plate" prose. Even boilerplate was originally written by someone or, more likely, by some group. But along with phrases from Shakespeare, well-crafted book titles, or advertising slogans, it is thought to be available for common usage without acknowledgement.

33. The case of Martin Luther King, Jr.'s, plagiarism is apposite here. The case came to light through an article by Frank Johnson in London's *Sunday Telegraph*, 3 December 1989. Mr. Johnson, relying on information from Ralph Luker of Emory University, an associate editor of the King papers project coordinated by Clayborne Carson at Stanford University, revealed that King had plagiarized large sections of his doctoral dissertation, done at Boston University in 1955, from one Jack Boozer, another graduate student. Nine months after the *Telegraph* article, *Chronicles*, a self-styled "paleolithic conservative" journal, denounced King's plagiarism in a September 1990 editorial. Then the *Wall Street Journal* featured the story on its front page on 9 November 1990, followed by similar reportage by the *New York Times* on 10 November 1990. *Chronicles* then published an extensive analysis of King's plagiarism by Theodore Pappas in January 1991. Pappas's article was entitled "A Doctor in spite of Himself: The Strange Career of Martin Luther King's Dissertation." The reports forced an acknowledgment from the repositors of King's papers and the guardians of his reputation that they had known about his "unacknowledged textual appropriations." The case caused an uproar but was squelched when intellectuals, African American and white, rallied around King's memory, proffering various justifications, including an appeal to what was said to be the African American southern religious tradition of "voice merging," that is, freely borrowing material from others, even when it was revealed that King had plagiarized not just his dissertation but much

of his most famous speeches and essays. On "voice merging," see, for instance, Keith D. Miller, *Voice of Deliverance: The Language of Martin Luther King, Jr., and Its Sources* (New York: Free Press, 1992). But King's public reputation, especially among blacks, seems unaffected by the revelations. The visually recorded memories of King's powerful personal presence and, even more importantly, the untimeliness of his death in the midst of a timely moral crusade, obliterate his personal faults. Public officials who had renamed countless streets after King and fought for a national holiday to honor his memory ducked the issue as best they could. See the collection of materials on the subject in Theodore Pappas, editor, *The Martin Luther King, Jr., Plagiarism Story* (Rockford, Ill.: The Rockford Institute, 1994).

34. The same story appears in a shorter and somewhat different form in Roger Ailes with Jon Kraushar, *You Are the Message* (New York: Doubleday, 1988), 64–65. All occupational communities and subcommunities have collections of such stories that make the rounds, changing shape with each new telling. The stories usually come complete with barbed humor. For many years, the incessant travel of U.S. businesspeople prompted the rapid migration of such tales. While travel is still important, it is rapidly being displaced by electronic mail and facsimile as vehicles for disseminating such humor.

35. It is worth noting that, despite the academic world's self-image as a guardian of the integrity of ideas, appropriation of ideas is widely practiced there. "Research assistance" for students is thoroughly industrialized in every large university town. Students can now purchase off-the-shelf or tailor-made papers on the most banal or esoteric of subjects. Many students who do their own "research papers" often just cobble together others' work, sometimes with and sometimes without attribution. One must see student idea borrowing, of course, within the context of many faculty practices. For instance, the "managed texts," now common at least in the social sciences and in business schools, borrow wholesale from others' work, often simply paraphrasing and thereby popularizing original texts. More to the point, many faculty adopt predator-like stances toward student ideas, appropriating any fresh insights at will in much the same way that bosses in the world of affairs treat their subordinates. For instance, a prominent sociologist sitting on the faculty committee for a student's dissertation refused to approve the student's work, but then published chapters of it intact under his own name. Some well-known and well-published senior faculty are known to their junior colleagues to be such adroit pickpockets and rapid packagers of ideas that one speaks of ongoing projects in front of them only at one's peril.

Moreover, there is in the academy the perennial question of who "owns" data collected in a bureaucratized research endeavor, the person who collects it or the person whose grant money funds the work. For instance, working with the help of a large grant, a young anthropology professor hired a group of assistants to do field interviewing for her in an industrial community. The students became totally absorbed in the work. One of them, wanting to use some of the interview material that she had personally collected for her own dissertation, approached the professor and was shocked to be forbidden to broach the subject again. All materials collected and any work done on the project by the assistants were, the student was told, the property of the professor. Appeals to intellectual ideals and even to feminist solidarity fell on deaf ears. The student persisted, citing compelling interest in problems that the interviews had raised. At that point, she was told by the chairman of the department, who had entered the fray on the junior professor's behalf, that the student could expect to fail her qualifying examinations, thereby ending her graduate career at that university. And fail she did.

In short, when it comes to the appropriation of ideas, there seems to be little difference between the standards of segments of the academy and those of the world of affairs, except, of course, for the academy's loftier public moral standards and concomitant self-image.

36. Every bureaucratic organization has leaders who fashion cognitive frameworks for their subordinates sheerly by the authority of office, sometimes enhanced by personal magnetism. Sometimes leaders insist on a univocal organizational stance on certain issues. What outsiders perceive as harmony, insiders usually see as the product of an intricate system of patronage that keeps lieutenants who enforce desired frameworks in line and of outright bribery that buys assent or at least silence from possible defectors who might influence others to see the organization differently.

37. All of the quotes and examples in the text are drawn from Joyce Newman Communications, *Power Speaking and More,* 3d ed. (New York: Joyce Newman Communications, 1988). Ms. Newman's clients include executives at many major corporations and nonprofit organizations, as well as several best-selling authors. Robert Jackall interviewed Ms. Newman in late 1988.

38. See *Advertising—Another Word for Freedom of Choice* (New York: American Association of Advertising Agencies, n.d.). Our thanks to Bernard Ryan, formerly AAAA senior vice president for public affairs, for providing us with copies of the advertisements.

CHAPTER SIX: ADVOCACY AS A VOCATION

1. Joseph Schumpeter, *Capitalism, Socialism, and Democracy,* 3d ed. (New York: Harper & Brothers Publishers, 1950), 143–155.

2. See in particular, Richard Hofstadter, *The Age of Reform: From Bryan to F. D. R.* (New York: Knopf, 1954) and Christopher Lasch, *The New Radicalism in America, 1889–1963* (New York: Vintage, 1965).

3. In the United States, the well-known reformist impulse emerging out of Protestantism is by far the most important. Those imbued with the Protestant spirit try to remake the world in God's image, urging men and women to change their ways and their social structures and establish a secular version of God's kingdom here on earth. The this-worldly orientation of Protestantism has been one of the great catalysts of modern institutions. See Max Weber, *The Protestant Ethic and the Spirit of Capitalism* (New York: Charles Scribner's Sons, 1958).

4. See Alexis de Tocqueville, *Democracy in America* (New York: Alfred A. Knopf, 1948), vol. 2, 106ff. By the early 1990s, more than 23,000 national associations, let alone at least 100,000 local or regional societies, addressed every conceivable need and desire of the citizenry, whether cultural, commercial, charitable, recreational, religious, or salvational in a more secular way. For a profile of the scope and reach of associations in the contemporary United States, see *Association Fact Book,* revised ed. (Washington, D.C.: American Society of Association Executives, 1993).

5. Tocqueville, *Democracy,* 110.

6. To cite only one example, see Guy Oakes, *The Imaginary War: Civil Defense and American Cold-War Culture* (New York: Oxford University Press, 1994).

7. For an invaluable look at the inside workings of a local "poverty organization," see Joseph Bensman, *Dollars and Sense* (New York: Schocken Books, 1983), 102–121.

8. Some African Americans made striking occupational and educational strides in American society between 1940 and 1990, with the lion's share of gains coming before 1970. For instance, in 1940, only 5.2 percent of employed black men and 6.4 percent of employed black women were in white-collar occupations (professionals, proprietors/managers/officials, clerical, and sales). By 1970, 21.7 percent of employed black men and 36.1 percent of employed black women were so engaged; by 1990, 32 percent of men, and 58.9 percent of women were in the white-collar sector. Again, in 1940, 4.1 percent of all those enrolled in college were African American; by 1970, 7 percent of total enrollments were of blacks; by 1980, 9.9 percent; and by 1994, 10.7 percent. Income figures are less reliable indices of the gains that some blacks have made because the dismal incomes of African Americans at the bottom of the social and economic ladder sharply lower aggregate income figures for blacks as a whole, obscuring the rise of the black middle class. For the figures cited, see Stephan Thernstrom and Abigail Thernstrom, *America in Black and White: One Nation Indivisible* (New York: Simon & Schuster, 1997), 185 and 187 on occupation; 389 on education. There are other indications of a growing African American middle class. By 1998, African Americans very nearly reached parity with whites in high school graduation rates. Birth rates of single African American women dropped to a forty-year low. Less than 30 percent of African American households were below the official poverty level for the first time, and African American unemployment and underemployment were down. African American home ownership was up despite evidence of continuing discrimination against African Americans (and Hispanics) in certain regional mortgage markets. And investment firms have targeted blacks, who historically have favored real estate for investment, as a yet-untapped pool of possible investors in stocks, bonds, and mutual funds.

9. See Bureau of the Census, *The Earnings Ladder,* (SB/94–3) (Washington, D.C., 1994). The brief notes that "About 18 percent of the nation's 81 million year-round full-time workers earned less than $13,091 per year in

1992—a 50 percent increase over the 12 percent who had low earnings in 1979." Calculations were expressed in 1992 dollars, adjusted for inflation. Although workers earning such low wages, about $6.50 per hour, may not themselves be classified as in a poor household because they are living with other earners, the figures alarmed officials because they measure a single worker's ability to lift a family of four out of poverty.

10. See the study by ABT Associates Inc., *What America's Users Spend on Illegal Drugs, 1988–1993* (Washington, D.C.: Office of National Drug Control Policy, 1995). The report estimates that, over the six years covered by the study, $347.1 billion was spent on all illegal substances (an average of $57.8 billion per year), with the lion's share going for cocaine and heroin in that order.

11. For a comprehensive listing of leftist organizations in the United States, see Derk Arend Wilcox, editor, *The Left Guide: A Guide to Left-of-Center Organizations* (Ann Arbor, Mich.: Economics America, Inc., 1996). The figure in the text for assets of philanthropic organizations that typically back leftist causes are totals from 1993 or 1994 public-record amounts culled by *The Left Guide* from annual reports.

12. Wilcox's *The Left Guide* is an excellent resource to begin exploring the vast and continually expanding number of works from leftist advocates. Almost all of the organizations listed in *The Left Guide* regularly issue newsletters, bulletins, broadsides, or calls to action. Many publish books and annual or special reports. Many provide recommended reading lists of other cognate resources. And most have their own World Wide Web sites. On the issues cited in the text, see the Southern Poverty Law Center in Montgomery, Alabama (<www.splcenter.org>) and the National Council of La Raza (<www.nclr.org>) and the Sentencing Project (<www.sentencingproject. org>), both in Washington, D.C.; the Feminist Majority Foundation in Los Angeles, California (<www.feminist.org>) and the National Organization for Women in New York City (<www.now.org>); Lambda Legal Defense and Education Fund in New York City (<www.lambda.org>); Children's Defense Fund in Washington, D.C. (<www.childrensdefensefund.org>); North American Man-Boy Love Association in New York City (<www.nambla. org>); Grey Panthers Project Fund in Washington, D.C.; the Center for Immigrants Rights in New York City; National Coalition for the Homeless in Washington, D.C. (<nch.ari.net>); the National Resources Defense Council in New York City (<www.nrdc.org>) and Greenpeace in Washington, D.C. (<www.greenpeace.org>); People for the Ethical Treatment of Animals in Washington, D.C. (<www.peta-online.org>) and the Animal Legal Defense Fund in Petaluma, California (<www.aldf.org>); the Center for Popular Economics in Amherst, Massachusetts (<www.ctrpoec.org>) and the Institute for Labor and Mental Health in Oakland, California; the Institute for Policy Studies in Washington, D.C.; and Fenton Communications in New York City (<www.fenton.com>), Common Courage Press in Monroe, Maine (<www.commoncouragepress.com>), *Tikkun* magazine in San Francisco (<www.Tikkun.org>), and the Association for Progressive Communications,

an association of Internet service providers joined together "to support the people and organizations working together worldwide for social, environmental and economic justice" (<www.apc.org>).

13. For a comprehensive listing of conservative organizations in the United States, see Derk Arend Wilcox, editor, *The Right Guide: A Guide to Conservative and Right-of-Center Organizations,* 3d ed. (Ann Arbor, Mich.: Economics America, Inc., 1997). The figure in the text for assets of philanthropic organizations that typically back rightist causes are totals from 1994 or 1995 public-record amounts culled by *The Right Guide* from annual reports. According to these figures, the foundations backing the left have about four-and-a-half times as much assets as those backing the right. However, the editor of *The Right Guide* points out that of the $5.1 billion in assets for foundations supporting rightist causes, a full $2.8 billion comes from the Lilly Endowment. Moreover, only 3 percent of Lilly's grants go to conservative organizations. If one removes the Lilly Endowment from consideration, the ratio of assets of "left" as opposed to "right" foundations is twelve to one.

14. Derk Arend Wilcox's *The Right Guide* is the best place to begin exploring the remarkably varied world of conservative organizations and the worldviews that they espouse. As with organizations on the left, most conservative advocacy groups issue a variety of their own publications and point those interested to a host of other resources. On the issues mentioned in the text, see the Center for the Defense of Free Enterprise in Bellevue, Washington (<www.CDFE.org>) and the Competitive Enterprise Institute in Washington, D.C. (<www.cei.org>); the Cato Institute (<www.cato.org>) and the American Enterprise Institute for Public Policy Research (<www.aei.org>), both in Washington, D.C.; the American Studies Center/Radio America in Washington, D.C.; the Citizens Against Government Waste in Washington, D.C. (<www.GOVT-WASTE.org>); the Center for Individual Rights in Washington, D.C.; the American Center for Law and Justice in Virginia Beach, Virginia; the Ethics and Public Policy Center in Washington, D.C., the Institute on Religion and Public Life/*First Things* in New York City (<www.firstthings.com>), and Rockford Institute/*Chronicles* in Rockford, Illinois; the American Immigration Control Foundation in Monterey, Virginia, the American Nationalist Union in Allison Park, Pennsylvania (<www.anu.org>) and the Federation for American Immigration Reform (<www.fairus.org>) and the United States English Foundation, both in Washington, D.C., and the National Association of Scholars in Princeton, New Jersey (<www.nas.org>); the Family Research Council in Washington, D.C. (<www.frc.org>); the Law Enforcement Alliance of America in Falls Church, Virginia; and the Center for Education Reform in Washington, D.C., *Culture Wars* in South Bend, Indiana, the Media Research Center in Alexandria, Virginia (<www.mediaresearch.org>), Accuracy in Media and Accuracy in Academia, both in Washington, D.C., and the Center for the Study of Popular Culture/*Heterodoxy* in Los Angeles, California (<www.cspc.org>). On alliances in the crusade against pornography, see Morality in Media in New York City and the following publications: Catharine A. MacKinnon and

Andrea Dworkin, editors, *In Harm's Way: The Pornography Civil Rights Hearings* (Cambridge, Mass.: Harvard University Press, 1997); Andrea Dworkin, *Pornography: Men Possessing Women* (New York: Plume, 1989); and Catharine A. MacKinnon, *Only Words* (Cambridge, Mass.: Harvard University Press, 1993).

15. See the publication *Change for the Better: Building New Dimensions in Public Interest Leadership* (Washington, D.C.: Advocacy Institute, 1991), 47–58, for a directory of some of the organizations across the country engaged in advocacy. All quotes in the text are taken from descriptions of organizations provided in this directory.

16. See, for instance, Peter Collier and David Horowitz, former leftist radicals and authors of *Destructive Generation: Second Thoughts about the Sixties* (New York: Summit Books, 1989) and the editors of *Second Thoughts: Former Radicals Look Back at the Sixties* (Lanham, Md: Madison Books, 1989). Horowitz also wrote *Radical Son: A Journey through Our Times* (New York: Free Press, 1997). Collier and Horowitz edit the journal *Heterodoxy,* a reincarnation in different guise of the old leftist journal *Ramparts,* issued by the Center for the Study of Popular Culture. They also head up the Committee on Media Integrity.

17. Larry Kramer, *Reports from the Holocaust: The Making of an AIDS Activist* (New York: St. Martin's Press, 1989).

18. Sample data indicate that in 1995, 45.1 percent of males and 52.2 percent of females over 18 years of age did 4.2 hours of volunteer work each week in fields ranging from the arts, to education, to health and human services, to churches, to more informal kinds of service. Treasury Department, Bureau of Statistics, *Statistical Abstract of the United States, 1997* (Washington, D.C.: Government Printing Office, 1997), table no. 813, "Percent of Adult Population Doing Volunteer Work: 1995," 391. Data also indicate that, in 1995, 68.5 percent (down from the 73.4 percent in 1993) of all U.S. households contributed something to many different charities in varying amounts. Bureau of Statistics, *Statistical Abstract,* table no. 815, "Charity Contributions—Percent of Households Contributing by Dollar Amount, 1991 to 1995, and Type of Charity, 1995," 391. See also Independent Sector, *Giving and Volunteering in the United States: 1996 Edition* (Washington, D. C.: Independent Sector, 1996), 4. Although the percentage of households contributing to charity slipped between 1993 and 1995, the average dollar amount per household rose from $880 to $1,017. Also, the percentage of population volunteering rose from 47.7 percent (89.2 million people) to 48.8 percent (90 million people).

19. Janice M. Hirota, *Life and Work in City Shelters: Homeless Residents and Organizational Dynamics at the Borden Avenue Veterans Residence* (New York: Human Resources Administration, Office of Policy and Program Development, 1991). The homeless male veterans whom Hirota studied exhibited a pervasive social psychological "drift": a basic lack of self-direction, an aimlessness in daily activities, accompanied by expressions of extremely vague or unrealistic goals; a willingness simply to leave threatening or difficult situations; and a reliance on the push of external events to dictate courses of action.

20. See Cate Haste, *Keep the Home Fires Burning: Propaganda in the First World War* (London: Allen Lane, 1977).

21. Robert K. Merton, *Mass Persuasion: The Social Psychology of a War Bond Drive* (New York and London: Harper and Brothers, 1946).

CHAPTER SEVEN: TECHNICIANS IN MORAL OUTRAGE

1. For a sense of the African cultural origins of black trickster figures in the United States, see Robert Pelton, *The Trickster in West Africa: A Study of Mythic Irony and Sacred Delight* (Berkeley and Los Angeles: University of California Press, 1980), and Oyekan Owomoyela, *Yoruba Trickster Tales* (Lincoln and London: University of Nebraska Press, 1997).

2. On hustling, see Bettylou Valentine, *Hustling and Other Hard Work* (New York: Free Press, 1978). See also the folkloric collection of "toasts," probably the street antecedents to the rap music industry: Dennis Wepman, Ronald B. Newman, and Murray B. Binderman, *The Life: The Lore and Folk Poetry of the Black Hustler* (Philadelphia: University of Pennsylvania Press, 1976).

3. See the important treatment of the cultural transvaluation at issue by John Roberts in *From Trickster to Badman: The Black Folk Hero in Slavery and Freedom* (Philadelphia: University of Pennsylvania Press, 1989).

4. See *Report of the Grand Jury and Related Documents Concerning the Tawana Brawley Investigation,* State of New York, County of Dutchess issued pursuant to criminal procedure law section 190.85 subdivision (1)(b), New York State Attorney General's Office. See also the account in Robert D. McFadden, Ralph Blumenthal, M. A. Farber, E. R. Shipp, Charles Strum, and Craig Wolff, *Outrage: The Story Behind the Tawana Brawley Hoax* (New York: Bantam Books, 1990).

5. The Reverend Al Sharpton & Anthony Walton, *Go and Tell Pharaoh: The Autobiography of The Reverend Al Sharpton* (New York: Doubleday, 1996), 136.

6. Sharpton & Walton, *Go and Tell Pharaoh,* 27–28.

7. Sharpton & Walton, *Go and Tell Pharaoh,* 136.

8. Mr. Maddox was suspended from the bar in 1990 for his conduct in the Tawana Brawley affair. On 2 August 1994 a five-judge panel of Brooklyn's Appellate Division barred Mr. Maddox for a period of five more years for his refusal to cooperate with an ethics panel investigating his involvement in the Brawley matter. C. Vernon Mason commented: "Alton H. Maddox has been handed a nine-year sentence for standing up as an African man." *New York Times,* 3 August 1994, B4.

9. Our thanks to Assistant District Attorney Elizabeth Lederer of the office of the District Attorney of New York for briefing us on this case. ADA Lederer was the lead prosecutor for both of the Central Park jogger trials.

10. See Patricia J. Williams, *The Alchemy of Race and Rights: The Diary of a Law Professor* (Cambridge, Mass.: Harvard University Press, 1991).

11. The most infamous recent instance was the speech given by Khallid Abdul Muhammad, a spokesman for the Nation of Islam, at Kean College in New Jersey on 29 November 1993. The full text of his speech is available

from the Anti-Defamation League of B'nai B'rith in New York City. In the media firestorm that followed his anti-Semitic and antiwhite diatribe, Mr. Muhammad was chastised, somewhat gently, by Minister Louis Farrakhan and his speaking tour was somewhat curtailed. He did, however, continue to give speeches and, at one of them, he was shot and wounded by another member of the Nation of Islam. But even this assault did not deter Mr. Muhammad. See his speech at San Francisco State University of 21 May 1997, also available from the Anti-Defamation League. Our thanks to Alan Schwartz for making these materials available to us.

Mr. Muhammad made a return to controversy in early September 1998 in a dispute with New York City Mayor Giuliani's administration. Mr. Muhammad wanted to hold a Million Youth March on Malcolm X Boulevard in Harlem to dramatize the problems of black youth, complete with gang members from around the country. He named as an alternative site Crown Heights so that black youth could "confront the Jews." Mayor Giuliani predictably refused permission for the march at the places desired, offering instead relatively remote alternative sites, such as Randall's Island, laying the groundwork for the kind of confrontation that Mr. Muhammed relishes. Mr. Muhammad won a federal court order allowing the march to take place in Harlem. But the court sharply restricted the streets available to marchers and mandated that the march could take place only between 12:00 P.M. and 4:00 P.M. Only about seven thousand marchers turned out. Mr. Muhammad began another fiery speech near the appointed end of the march, encouraging the crowd to disarm police who tried to interfere with their right to free assembly and to turn their weapons against them. On orders from the Giuliani administration, the police moved in with force just after 4:00 P.M., causing a melee. This led to outraged denunciations of Giuliani's "police state" tactics from normally sensible Harlem politicians, surely the exact outcome that Mr. Muhammad desired. Exactly the same scenario was repeated in September 1999 except that numerous Harlem residents and politicians objected to the march. Under close scrutiny from the federal court, both Mr. Muhammad and the police exercised greater restraint. For more everyday material, one might listen to several of the radio talk shows on WLIB-AM in New York City.

12. See, for instance, Houston Baker, *Black Studies, Rap, and the Academy* (Chicago and London: University of Chicago Press, 1993). Baker is a distinguished professor of English and human relations at the University of Pennsylvania and director of that institution's Center for the Study of Black Literature and Culture. In his book, Professor Baker argues that black studies create a "moral panic" in the academy because of the conflict between black "urbanity" and white Anglo-Saxon Protestant conventionality. He goes on to give "readings" of the Central Park jogger case and the trial of the rap group 2 Live Crew, both of which provoked, he argues, different kinds of moral panics. He ends with the beating of Rodney King, which he calls "the image of the late-twentieth-century," in which "[r]ich, cynical white citizens

and their henchmen are everywhere pounding the hell out of the 'rest of us' average Americans" (102). Professor Baker's choice of "the image" fits his own purposes well, since it casts "state authority" against normal, average citizens, although many people, whatever the depredations of the police in this instance, might object to being made bedfellows with Rodney King, a convicted robber and substance-affected driver who led police on a 100-mile-per-hour chase and who was unfazed by two, normally completely stunning, laser shots. King's two comrades were detained without incident. In the end, Professor Baker looks to rap music for "ethical reinforcement" and to black studies as the academy's salvation.

13. In 1992, Elizabeth Holzman garnered 144,026 votes; Geraldine Ferraro, 415,650; and Robert Abrams, 426,004. Senator Alfonse D'Amato then defeated Abrams in the general election.

14. See Jim Yardley, "Rage a Decade Ago, But Now, Alienation," *New York Times,* 15 July 1998, B1ff.

15. Wilbert A. Tatum, chairman of the board of the *New York Amsterdam News,* "Editorial: No Justice for Mason, Maddox or Sharpton? No Peace for Anybody Else!" *New York Amsterdam News,* 16 July–22 July 1998, 12.

16. *New York Amsterdam News,* 30 July–5 August 1998, 1.

17. The sequence of events later pieced together by police investigators and reporters is prototypical of the confusion, chance, and mischance of street policing. The police, passing by in an unmarked police vehicle, spotted a man who resembled the suspected rapist peering up and down the street. They interpreted this as suspicious behavior. Officers Sean Carroll and Edward McMellon got out of the car and approached the man with guns drawn. Identifying themselves as police, they asked the man to raise his hands. The man did not respond. Instead he went inside the vestibule of the building. The two policemen repeated their orders. The man reached for his rear pocket and pulled out an object. Carroll yelled, "Gun." McMellon, believing his partner's perception and fearing for his life, fired his nine-millimeter handgun at the man. McMellon mistook, it seems, his own bullets' ricochets as hostile fire and stepped and then fell backward. The fall fractured his tailbone. Carroll also opened fire. The other two officers leapt out of the police car. Apparently mistaking their partners' pistol-burst reflections in the building's glass or their partners' own bullets' ricochets as hostile fire, or attributing McMellon's backward fall to a gunshot injury, they began firing their own nine-millimeter guns at the man in the vestibule. As mentioned in the text, the four officers fired forty-one times, hitting the man nineteen times and killing him. What the officers had seen as a gun turned out to be the man's wallet.

Although working as a peddler selling bootleg videotapes, Diallo hailed from a well-educated and prosperous family in Guinea, West Africa. His legitimate visa was due to expire in April 1999. Wishing to stay in the United States, he filed for political asylum with the Immigration and Naturalization Service (INS), a request that was denied. In a sworn deposition, Diallo fabricated a sure-shot story before a judge at the Executive Office for Immigration Review. He claimed that he was from Mauritania, an "Arab Republic" where light-skinned Moors dominate and sometimes enslave blacks. Mauritanian soldiers had, Diallo claimed, murdered his parents and tortured his uncle to death. Diallo claimed that he had been beaten and carted off at gunpoint to a military camp and later to Senegal, from which he escaped to the United States. The judge granted Diallo asylum, though the INS had that decision under appeal when Diallo died. See *New York Times,* 17 March 1999, B3 and 9 April 1999, B1. Obviously, the officers confronting Diallo knew nothing whatsoever about his difficulties with the immigration authorities. But, the officers' lawyers later argued, Diallo's awareness of his illegal status may have prompted nervous behavior on his own part that the police interpreted as suspicious behavior.

18. Mayor Dinkins presided over the worst street-violence years in New York City history with homicides soaring well over 2,000 each year of the early 1990s. See, for example, Robert Jackall, *Wild Cowboys: Urban Marauders & the Forces of Order* (Cambridge: Harvard University Press, 1997) for a detailed treatment of drug-related violence in Washington Heights in upper Manhattan, one of the bloodiest precincts in the city, state, and nation during this period. Between 1994 and 1999, homicides dropped 70 percent in New York City. This was partially due to a nationwide drop in crime rates. But nowhere did the crime rate drop as sharply as it did in New York. The aggressive policing permitted under Mayor Giuliani was certainly one major reason for the city's declining rate of violent crime. In particular, the seizure of illegal weapons through stop-and-frisk practices helped reduce street violence. First, the actual weapons seized were permanently put out of circulation. Second, according to police debriefings of informants, the threat of seizure caused many criminals not to pack weapons in their street ventures. This reduced dramatically incidents of deadly violence spurred by spontaneous disputes about honor. The Street Crime Unit reported 45,000 stop-and-frisks in 1997–1998, with 9,500 arrests or one arrest for every 4.7 stops. Of these, 2,500 arrests were for illegal guns or one gun for every 18 stops. There are undoubtedly more stop-and-frisks than reported.

The seizure of illegal weapons, police argue, saves many lives and injuries. Moreover, since the high-violent-crime areas of New York City are almost exclusively black and Latino, police argue that the principal beneficiaries of aggressive policing are blacks and Latinos. The assailants, as reported by victims in, say, robberies—the bellweather violent crime where guns are employed—are overwhelmingly black or Latino. The victims of violent crime are largely black and Latino, often the old, the lame, and the halt; blacks and Latinos are four times more likely to be the victims of violent crime than whites. In this regard, police argue, blacks and Latinos have far more to fear from criminals in their own communities than they do from police, a perception that is widely held in the most vulnerable communities, but almost never reported.

19. See Heather Mac Donald, "Diallo Truth, Diallo Falsehood," *City Jour-*

nal (summer 1999), 12–28, for an excellent analysis of the New York media during the Diallo episode.

20. Kadiadou and Saikou Diallo initially appointed Sharpton associate Wyatt T. Walker as administrator of their son's estate. Walker selected Johnnie L. Cochran, Jr., and his famed "Dream Team" of five other lawyers to represent the Diallos in their wrongful death suit against the city. However, in mid-August 1999, Kadiadou Diallo, who is divorced from Saikou Diallo and reportedly at odds with him on this issue, hired another lawyer in an attempt to replace the estate's administrator, a prerequisite to hiring new lawyers to do the litigation. See Andy Newman, "Mrs. Diallo Seeks to Replace Legal 'Dream Team'," *New York Times,* 13 August 1999.

21. Dr. Kilbourne's doctoral dissertation is "The Changing Images of Females and Males in Television Commercials: Plus Ça Change, Plus C'est Le Même Chose," (Ph.D. diss., Boston University School of Education, Division of Humanistic, Developmental, and Organizational Studies, 1980).

22. Figures obtained on 21 July 1998, from Mr. Kevin R. MacRae at Dr. Kilbourne's speaking agency, Lordly & Dame, Inc., Boston, Massachusetts. Dr. Kilbourne's fees have risen over the last few years. On 29 April 1994, her fee was $3,500 according to a conversation with Mr. MacRae on that date.

23. The publicity materials are available from Lordly & Dame, Inc., as well as from Dr. Kilbourne's Web site (<www.jeankilbourne.com/index.html>).

24. These include *Under the Influence: The Pushing of Alcohol via Advertising; You've Come the Wrong Way, Baby: Women and Smoking; Slim Hopes: Advertising and the Obsession with Thinness; Marketing Misery: Selling Addictions to Women;* and *Deadly Persuasion: Advertising and Addiction.* Dr. Kilbourne has recently completed two new videos entitled *Pack of Lies: The Advertising of Tobacco* and *Calling the Shots: Advertising Alcohol.*

25. The remarks that follow are based on several viewings of both films in May 1994, together with a detailed analysis of transcripts of their audio portions. Our thanks to Bruce Wheat of the audio-visual department at Williams College for audio-taping these films and to Ms. Peggy Weyers of the faculty secretarial office at Williams College for transcribing the materials.

26. To take only two examples, Jennifer Gibson, outreach coordinator of the University of Montana Women's Center, wrote to Dr. Kilbourne on 28 April 1993:

I feel that your presentation had a profound effect on the audience . . . [It] came at a crucial time on the University of Montana campus. We are in the midst of numerous campus-wide discussions on the topic of gender issues involving administration, faculty and students. We have a Women's Studies program that is just beginning to get rolling and a recent survey done by a sexual assault task force demonstrated the extent to which violence and sexism affects every woman on this campus. . . . Also, your talk was so popular that it gave the Women's Center both visibility and credibility on campus, and has been helpful in allowing us to negotiate for more funds.

Robert Brink, executive director of the Flaschner Judicial Institute in Boston wrote to Dr. Kilbourne on 5 June 1992:

I feel compelled to let you know that your narrated slide presentation at last month's 'All Court Conference on Gender Issues' left many of the 300 Massachusetts judges in the audience speechless. Accustomed as they are to parse and analyze written and oral arguments, judges were defenseless when confronted with the scores of visuals flashed before them. Pictures *do* speak louder than a thousand words. The images (coupled with your instructive, funny and fast-paced comments) made a strong case about the demeaning sexual stereotypes that pervade American society. Drawn as they were from everyday advertising, it is beyond reasonable doubt that these images affect us all.

Even Charles Jackson of *Adweek* magazine, who went to one of Dr. Kilbourne's presentations, likened Dr. Kilbourne to a "prophet calling out in the wilderness for fundamental change in the way we communicate publicly with one another." And George Gerbner, Dean Emeritus, The Annenberg School, University of Pennsylvania, with whom Dr. Kilbourne recently completed a video entitled *The Killing Screens: Media and the Culture of Violence,* said that Dr. Kilbourne's "slide presentation is a form of mass vaccination with a symbolic antidote of a most powerful kind." All these quotes are taken from publicity packets for Dr. Jean Kilbourne, Lordly & Dame, Inc., 1994 and 1998.

27. Dr. Kilbourne leans toward rousing endings. Her dissertation ends:

We must challenge this ideology, this mythology. We must not allow the advertisers *[sic]* to define us. We must insist upon *our* truths, *our* realities, and defy their myths, myths that shackle us. We must believe that women and men together can create a new future, one that includes authentic liberation for all of us.

Kilbourne, "Changing Images of Females and Males," 217. The earlier version of her talk ends on a similar note:

[W]e really need more than ever human beings who share human qualities. Women and men who can be both strong and gentle, logical and intuitive, powerful and nurturant, all of these—the full range of human qualities within each of us. The results of this would be positive for all of us.

28. For a scholarly treatment of disclaimers, see John P. Hewitt and Randall Stokes, "Disclaimers," *American Sociological Review* 4, no. 1 (February 1975), 1–11.

29. Donna Petrozzello, "Talk, Talk, Talk: Formula For Success," *Broadcasting & Cable*, 13 June 1994, 36.

30. The classic example of the genre of talk radio that confronts callers is the *Bob Grant Show*. In 1999, Grant, the acknowledged "king of talk radio," celebrated fifty years on the air. He broadcast daily for many years on WABC (770 AM) to the tristate area of New York, New Jersey, and Connecticut. But in the midst of a firestorm of accusations of racism against him, precipitated by an acerbic and tasteless remark that Grant made at the time of the accidental death of Ronald Brown, President Clinton's secretary of commerce, WABC fired him. However, WOR (710 AM) picked up the daily show and even hooked Grant into a nationwide broadcast. Grant is the antithesis to Limbaugh in style and tone, even though they share, for the most part, the same political ideology. Briefly, Limbaugh ridicules his opposition as he calls for a restoration of "common sense" and a wresting of control of the nation's institutions from the clutches of liberals, but his approach is essentially optimistic and expansive. Grant argues continually that the nation's moral fiber has deteriorated so far that there is no hope for the future ("It's sick out there and getting sicker"). Grant's audience, as judged by his callers, seems considerably less educated than that of Limbaugh. Grant regularly insults his callers, excoriating them for their boorishness and the lack of originality of their complaints. He abides no opposition and regularly hangs up on callers who voice opinions contrary to his, calling them "scum," "jerks," "swine," "crumbs," "pusillanimous pipsqueaks," and "vermin." His authoritarianism toward his audience is matched by his obsequiousness toward many in authority who appear on his show. Grant is credited in many circles with ending the gubernatorial reigns of Mario Cuomo in New York and James Florio in New Jersey through his constant vituperative attacks on them. In early 1999, Mr. Grant began considering on the air a run for the United States Senate from his home state of New Jersey. Callers from that state, but also from across the country, beseeched Grant to make the run in order to bring plain talk back into public life.

31. Data are from *Simmons Study of Media and Markets* electronic database from 1993. Also, Carol Bowman, editor, *The Vocal Minority in American Politics* (Washington, D.C.: Times Mirror Center for the People and the Press, 1993).

32. Horizon Media, Inc., "Demographics of Rush Limbaugh Listeners," facsimile communication to the authors on 18 August 1994. Horizon Media, Inc., is in New York City.

33. The monthly *Limbaugh Newsletter* has a subscription list of more than 450,000 people. Mr. Limbaugh's two books *The Way Things Ought To Be* (New York: Simon and Schuster, 1992) and *See, I Told You So* (New York: Simon and Schuster, 1993) have sold well over 1 million copies each. For some counterattacks, see Steve Randall, *The Way Things Aren't: Rush Limbaugh's Reign of Error* (New York: New Press, distributed by Norton, 1995) and Leonie Halmson, *The Way Things Really Are: Debunking Rush Limbaugh on the Environment* (New York: Environmental Defense Fund, 1995). Mr. Limbaugh has issued position papers rebutting these critiques.

34. See Referral to the United States House of Representatives pursuant to Title 28, United States Code, Section 595(c), submitted by Kenneth W. Starr, Independent Counsel, 9 September 1998.

35. See Ray Perkins, Jr., *Logic and Mr. Limbaugh: A Dittohead's Guide to Fallacious Reasoning* (Chicago: Open Court, 1995).

CHAPTER EIGHT: MAKE-BELIEVE WORLDS

1. We borrow the idea of "discernment" from Ignatius of Loyola, "Regulae ad Spiritus Dignoscendos" (Rules for the discernment of spirits) from his "Exercitia Spiritualia" in *Thesaurus Spiritualis Societatis Jesu* (Rome: Typis Polyglottis Vaticanis, 1948), 221–236. One can find a good translation of the Latin version of the rules in George E. Ganss, S.J., editor, *Ignatius of Loyola: The Spiritual Exercises and Selected Works* (New York: Paulist Press, 1991), 201–207. See also the interesting commentary on the rules on pages 423–428. As Ganss points out, the rules were originally entitled "aliquot regulae ad discernendos varios spiritus animam agitantes" (some rules for discerning various spirits agitating the soul) in the first Latin version of the *Exercises* published before 1534. The notion of "discernment" (from the Latin *discernere*, meaning to separate, divide, set apart, to distinguish, to separate one thing from another, to decide, to settle) means accuracy in reading character or motives.

2. Ronald H. Hinckley, Robert Shapiro, Mariana Servin-Gonzalez, and Serban Iorga, *The National Credibility Index* (Sterling, Va.: Research/Strategy/Management, Inc., 1999).

3. One of the most commonly used measurements of celebrity status is the "Q Ratings" done by Marketing Evaluations, Inc., of Port Washington, New York.

4. PRSA, *Silver Anvil Winners, 1990* (New York: Public Relations Society of America, 1990), 3–4.

5. Conversation with Andrea Wojtasek, United States Department of Agriculture Forest Service, 2 December 1994. For instance, between 1984 and 1990, over 80 percent of all forest fires were caused by humans, caused by electrical mishaps, construction or traffic accidents, railroad-related incidents, arson, smoking, or other events. But, during the same period, over 65 percent of the forest acreage lost was lost to fires caused by lightning. Calculations providing comparative damage assessments of the loss of man-made real estate versus the loss of wilderness are not available.

The Advertising Council did help stop certain kinds of man-made forest fires. On 28 January 1991, F. Bradley Lynch, then the public relations director of the Advertising Council, interviewed George Ludlum, former vice president of the council, who told the following story about a special council campaign for the United States Forest Service:

> [I]n certain parts of the backwoods south there were some of the Southern Crackers who liked forest fires because when the woods would burn down, the second growth came along [with] a lot of berry

bushes and these people made their living on growing and picking berries. So [the Forest Fire Prevention people] knew that some of these people were deliberately setting forest fires so that these berries could grow better and one of the things that the Advertising Council did was to make radio commercials with local musical groups that appealed to these backwoods people (kind of a jazz band singing slogans about how bad it was to have forest fires and making the point of 'Nobody but a damn Yankee would start a forest fire').

Advertising Council files. For a history of the USDA Forest Service fire prevention program and its advertising symbol, Smokey Bear, see Ellen Earnhardt Morrison, *Guardian of the Forest: A History of Smokey Bear and the Cooperative Forest Fire Prevention Program,* 3d ed. (Alexandria, Va.: Morielle Press, 1994).

6. The National Crime Prevention Council (NCPC) in Washington, D.C., issues an extensive catalog of its books, kits, reports, posters, and booklets. It also issues a catalog of McGruff licensed products, including license plates, wall clocks, wastebaskets, welcome mats, frisbees, hand puppets, and complete character costumes as well as a series of papers entitled "Topics in Crime Prevention." In conjunction with NCPC, the United States Department of Justice also produces a series of booklets featuring McGruff with titles such as: "How Not to Get Conned," "Got a Minute? You Could Stop a Crime," "How to Protect Children," "Youth and Crime Prevention: Youth Can Make a Difference," "How to Crimeproof Your Business," "How to Crimeproof Your Home," and "How to Be 'Streetwise' and Safe."

7. Crusader Baby received wide press coverage as well as letters from individuals all across the country asking her how they could help in her crusade. Gaston & Gaston Public Relations, in Flemington, New Jersey, put the campaign together. See also PRSA, *Silver Anvil Winners, 1989* (New York: Public Relations Society of America, 1989), 51–52.

8. Consider for a moment a classical example of personal charisma, that of Maximilien Robespierre. He was by most accounts an arid, puritanical, moralistic, thoroughly unlikable man, with very little personal charm or magnetism. But his piercing and unrelenting articulation of the logic of events became crucial to the temporary triumph of the Jacobin cause in the French Revolution that more than any other modern revolution depended precisely on one's persuasiveness in open assembly. The last two centuries have eroded the possibilities for the kind of charisma that Robespierre exercised, at least that which changes the course of nations. To have any kind of major impact today, the charismatic leader must be able to reach not just a small band of devoted disciples, or an open assembly of representatives who listen closely to argument, but vast segmented masses. To address the latter, one must subject oneself to the logic of the mass media. As it happens, the intellectual, analytical, and oratorical gifts possessed by Robespierre do not mesh well with the personality attributes that the media desire. See J. M. Thompson, *Robespierre,* 2 vols. (1935; reprint, New York: Howard Fer-

tig, 1968) for a thorough analysis of Robespierre's character and intellectual gifts.

9. See Andrew H. Malcolm, "On the Road Again with a Passion," *New York Times*, 10 October 1988. Mr. Malcolm quotes David Davis, editor and publisher of *Automobile Magazine:* "Our national passion for autos is really more a passion for the personal freedom that comes with ownership of a car that can take anyone anywhere anytime. There are a lot of unpleasant aspects to modern American life. But you can get in that sucker, lock it up, turn on the radio and control the climate and it takes you where you want in an enjoyable way."

10. See Trish Hall, "As New Age Ages, Practicality Wins Out," *New York Times*, 28 October 1990.

11. See Neil Strauss, "The Price of Fame Includes Dinner; At Tinseltown You're a Star and the Employees Merely Players," *New York Times*, 13 January 1999, and Seth Mydans, "Cu Chi Journal: Visit the Vietcong's World: Americans Welcome," *New York Times*, 7 July 1999.

12. Joseph B. Treaster, "Cruises Find a Demand for Fantasy," *New York Times*, 13 June 1988.

13. Trish Hall, " . . . And in This Corner, All Kinds of 'Gladiators'," *New York Times*, 23 January 1991.

14. Trish Hall, "'Virtual Reality' Takes Its Place in the Real World," *New York Times*, 8 July 1990.

15. See Duffy Graham, *Stuck Inside America with the Middle-Class Blues Again*, forthcoming.

16. On adult illiteracy, see Leonard Lund, *Literacy in the Work Force*, conference report 947 (New York: The Conference Board, 1990), which argues that about 30 percent of Americans are functionally illiterate and "ill-prepared for modern workplace assignments"; on widespread public unawareness of news events, see David S. Kellermann, editor, *The American Media: Who Reads, Who Watches, Who Listens, Who Cares,* (Washington, D.C.: Times Mirror Center, 1990); and on political apathy, see the findings of the Markle Commission on the Media and the Electorate in Bruce Buchanan, *Electing a President: The Markle Commission Research on Campaign '88* (Austin: University of Texas Press, 1991) and *Renewing Presidential Politics: Campaigns, Media, and the Public Interest* (Lanham, Md.: Rowman and Littlefield Publishers, 1996).

17. PRSA, *Silver Anvil Winners, 1990,* 47-48.

18. PRSA, *Silver Anvil Winners, 1990,* 51-52.

19. To our knowledge, no one has yet explored how the idealized images of organizations and concomitant extravagant expectations of recruits affect the actual experiences of those who enter organizations.

20. See the growing body of feminist scholarship on the "narratives" of soap operas, for example, Tania Modelski, *Loving with a Vengeance: Mass-Produced Fantasies for Women* (Hamden, Conn.: Archon Books, 1982); Martha Nochimson, *No End to Her: Soap Opera and the Female Subject* (Berkeley and Los Angeles: University of California Press, 1992); and Suzanne Frentz, edi-

tor, *Staying Tuned: Contemporary Soap Opera Criticism* (Bowling Green, Ohio: Bowling Green State University Popular Press, 1992).

21. A classic example of this was given in a commencement address at Williams College on 4 June 1989, by a president of a liberal arts college who was the recipient of an honorary degree. Her remarks included the following statements:

> I hope that the lesson you have learned is that women and men need bread, but women and men also need roses.
>
> And I trust you now know as a Native American saying puts it, 'Women hold up at least half the sky.'
>
> But unless we as a nation can discover not only the will but the means to positively intervene into the lives of millions of black youngsters, they will be wasted. And a human mind—like a body and a soul—is a terrible thing to waste.
>
> Quite simply because, in the words of Martin Luther King, Jr., until all of us are free, not a single one of us is truly free.
>
> As men and especially as women—remember that your place is in the House—and in the Senate too.
>
> I believe that Mary McLeod Bethune was not only speaking to women who look like me, but all women when she said, 'Black women have got to stop playing bridge and start building bridges.'
>
> I believe that the slogan of the Negro Women's Club Movement is as good today as it was in an earlier era, and it is as imperative for men as for women, for white Americans as for black Americans, for various Hispanic Americans, for various Asian American communities and for the first Americans, American Indians. The slogan was simply and most powerfully this: 'Lifting as we climb.'
>
> Today, as you graduate from Williams College, may you make a silent pledge to reach out and touch someone.

Our thanks to the Williams College News Office for providing a complete transcript of the honorary-degree recipient's remarks.

22. This quote appears in Allen Feldman, "On Cultural Anesthesia: From Desert Storm to Rodney King," in *American Ethnologist* 21, no. 2 (August 1994), 414. Feldman is citing his own previous work. Feldman's article provides an apt example of virtually all the habits of mind that mark what one might call the postmodern sensibility, combined with self-righteous moralism. The article is short on facts, long on interpretation, weaving together events that proceed from wholly different circumstances and institutional settings into a mosaic, laced throughout with Feldman's indignation against presumed authoritative abuses.

23. Interview by Janice Hirota with a creative from DDB Needham Worldwide, 26 January 1988. His comments on the advertisement itself and how he came to make it bring together several themes developed earlier. He said:

You know, when you look at that ad, there's a power behind the ad. It's like there's something else there. And, you know what it is? It's that man, and he's looking right at you and you know what he's saying? His eyes are looking right at you and he's saying, 'You stupid schmuck.' That's what he saying, 'You stupid schmuck.' He's confronting you with his eyes and he's saying, 'Listen, you asshole, you stupid schmuck.' That's what gives the ad its power—not the gun, not anything like that. It's the eyes looking right at you. 'If you use cocaine, you are a stupid schmuck.' And you know, that has nothing to do with the research I did, nothing. It doesn't come out of research. We're talking abut a human emotion here. It's a basic human emotion. It's magical; it's beyond logic. 'You schmuck.' That's not research, that's emotion.

I presented the idea to the client, the National Institute on Drug Abuse, and they rejected it. They didn't like it. But I couldn't get the idea out of my mind. So after I got back from the client meeting, over the weekend, I got a friend to pose for me and I took a Polaroid of him. And, I dunno, I just had the thing in my office—I didn't have it on the wall or anything. I think I just had it tossed on my desk somewhere. I don't really know why exactly, except I couldn't get it out of my mind. And then, it was amazing, like people starting coming into my office and they'd see the Polaroid and they'd go crazy over it and said it was unbelievable, it was so powerful.

[Why did the client reject it?] Oh, I don't know, they said things like they were worried about the gun control issue. And they had to think about things like teenage suicide. Typical client reaction taking the thing so literally, as if somebody's going to go put a gun up their nose because they saw the ad. And the thing is, it's not the gun at all; it's the eyes. People were just having a visceral reaction to it, it's so emotional. And it's saying 'You are a schmuck.' It's pure emotion.

People in the agency who saw it said, 'You can't just sit on this. It's so strong, it's so powerful.' And it started to have a life of its own. It was like a volcano about to explode. They said, 'We have to produce this.' And they took it to the Partnership for a Drug-Free America and the [Partnership] said, 'This is unbelievable. We're doing it.' And the agency paid for all the production costs. And it got in the papers.

I've produced good advertising before, and I've known when I've done good work, but never something like this. It's incredible. [Did you know when you were creating it, that it was incredible?] No. [When did you begin to sense it?] When I had the Polaroid and people kept coming into my office to look at it. Then I knew the power of it. I mean, they took the ad to the chairman of the board of my agency, and he looked at it and said, 'We have to produce this.' The chairman of the board. And you know what he said? He said, 'We just have to do this, and not just because it's a social issue. I mean, it's an important social issue and all and everyone knows that. But [here his voice becomes even more animated] because the agency will get awards and fame for it. It'll bring in at least $20 million in new business.'

[An expert in drug addiction] didn't like the ad. She knows about addiction, but this goes beyond logic. It stirs an emotion and when you have that emotion, you can translate it into anything, into buying toilet paper. Some of my work before has been great, I've won big gold medals, but never anything like this. This is like an instant classic. And it's totally by the eyes and the angle that the eyes look at the reader. If I had posed the model just a little differently so that the eyes didn't look straight into you, it wouldn't have worked. But, as it is, it has a power. It's like the Vietnam Memorial—the guys carving the letters in one by one didn't know they were making something incredible, but the thing takes on a power all its own. The campaign isn't just *this*, although it's the only ad you've seen. There are five ads in the campaign. Besides the guy, there's one with a black kid, another with a Spanish girl. The black kid is looking right at the reader and he's saying, 'You are a fucking asshole.' At first we had some cute line about putting powder up your nose, but then we knew it didn't need any line.

24. Dr. Jay A. Winsten and Dr. William DeJong, "Recommendations for Future Mass Media Campaigns to Prevent Preteen and Adolescent Substance Abuse," *Health Policy* (summer 1990).

INDEX

AAAA. *See* American Association of Advertising Agencies

ABC, 124

abortion, 159, 161, 195

Abrams, Frank, 257n.47

Abrams, Robert, 176–77, 178

Abu-Jamal, Mumia, cause of, 115, 187, 281n.22

academia: balkanization by race and ethnicity, 210; borrowing in, 291n.35; double consciousness among intellectuals, 224–26; "political correctness" in, 193; professors as public policy experts, 166; tenure decisions, 289n.26

Academy Awards show, 114

account executives: "account" versus "creative" agencies, 82–85; in advertising agency organization, 72, 91, 92; in approval process, 104–10; award for, 280n.9; as buffers between clients and creatives, 93; business rationality represented by, 93; corporate uniform worn by, 96; creatives on, 93, 105; at Doyle Dane Bernbach, 73, 86, 87; in packaged-goods work, 82; "servicing" the client, 82, 92–93; on tantrums by creatives, 96; volunteer advocacy work

by, 166

account groups, in public relations agency organization, 114

ACT UP (AIDS Coalition to Unleash Power), 160

Adams, Samuel Hopkins, 15

Ad Council. *See* Advertising Council

Addy Award, 280n.9

Adelphi University, 138, 288n.18

Ad Hoc Committee on Propaganda Policy (Advertising Council), 53, 264n.72

advertising: of advertising, 151; as advocacy profession, 90–110; ancient roots of, 11; anxiety in, 116–19; authorship in, 146; awards for, 109, 280n.9; borrowing in, 146; and Committee on Public Information, 13; CPI Division of Advertising, 21–24, 26, 30–31, 33–34, 239n.36; creative revolution of the 1960s, 68, 81; criticism of, 37–39, 67, 90, 150, 251n.3, 271n.1; cultural revolt exploited by, 220; doublethink in, 140; dramatization in, 132–33; existing sentiment molded by, 32; as fear-driven business, 87, 277n.45; first broadcast commercial, 232n.6; of First World War, 11–35; in the Great